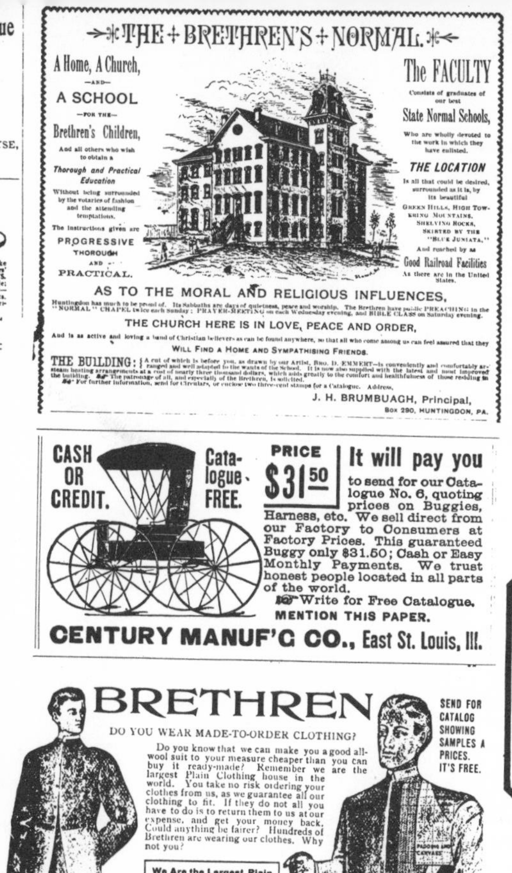

THE BRETHREN'S NORMAL.

A Home, A Church, —AND— A SCHOOL —FOR THE— Brethren's Children, And all others who wish to obtain a *Thorough and Practical Education* Without being surrounded by the votaries of fashion and the attending temptations.

The instructions given are PROGRESSIVE THOROUGH AND PRACTICAL.

The FACULTY Consists of graduates of our best State Normal Schools, Who are wholly devoted to the work in which they have enlisted.

THE LOCATION Is all that could be desired, surrounded as it is, by its beautiful GREEN HILLS, HIGH TOWERING MOUNTAINS, SHELVING ROCKS, SKIRTED BY THE "BLUE JUNIATA," And reached by as Good Railroad Facilities As there are in the United States.

AS TO THE MORAL AND RELIGIOUS INFLUENCES,

Huntingdon has much to be proud of. Its Sabbaths are days of quietness, peace and worship. The Brethren have public PREACHING in the "NORMAL" CHAPEL twice each Sunday; PRAYER-MEETING on each Wednesday evening, and BIBLE CLASS on Saturday evening.

THE CHURCH HERE IS IN LOVE, PEACE AND ORDER,

And is as active and loving a band of Christian believers as can be found anywhere, so that all who come among us can feel assured that they WILL FIND A HOME AND SYMPATHISING FRIENDS.

THE BUILDING: A cut of which is before you, as drawn by our Artist, Bro. D. EMMERT—is conveniently and comfortably arranged and well adapted to the wants of the School. It is now also supplied with the latest and most improved steam heating arrangements at a cost of nearly three thousand dollars, which adds greatly to the comfort and healthfulness of those residing in the building. The patronage of all, and especially of the Brethren, is solicited. For further information, send for Circulars, or enclose two three-cent stamps for a Catalogue. Address,

J. H. BRUMBUAGH, Principal,
Box 290, HUNTINGDON, PA.

CASH OR CREDIT. Catalogue FREE. PRICE $31.50

It will pay you to send for our Catalogue No. 6, quoting prices on Buggies, Harness, etc. We sell direct from our Factory to Consumers at Factory Prices. This guaranteed Buggy only $31.50; Cash or Easy Monthly Payments. We trust honest people located in all parts of the world.

Write for Free Catalogue. MENTION THIS PAPER.

CENTURY MANUF'G CO., East St. Louis, Ill.

BRETHREN

DO YOU WEAR MADE-TO-ORDER CLOTHING?

Do you know that we can make you a good all-wool suit to your measure cheaper than you can buy it ready-made? Remember we are the largest Plain Clothing house in the world. You take no risk ordering your clothes from us, as we guarantee all our clothing to fit. If they do not all you have to do is to return them to us at our expense, and get your money back. Could anything be fairer? Hundreds of Brethren are wearing our clothes. Why not you?

SEND FOR CATALOG SHOWING SAMPLES & PRICES. IT'S FREE.

We Are the Largest Plain Clothing Makers in the World.

Our materials are the finest, our tailors the best and our prices the lowest. If you expect to purchase a Fall or Winter all-wool suit, overcoat or ulster don't buy until you get our special Clothing Catalogue, showing our 50 different patterns of goods and prices marked in plain figures. Write to-day for catalog, order blank and how to take your own measure. Get the habit of wearing **Albaugh Bros., Dover & Co.'s made-to-order clothing.** Address:

ALBAUGH BROS., DOVER & CO., CHICAGO, ILL.

P. S.—About March 1 our new Catalogue showing samples of Spring and Summer goods will be ready to mail. Better make a memorandum and send for one of them.

For Plain Clothes We Lead.

Mention the Brethren Almanac.

White Wyandottes ... in special shipping ... Send for circular and price list of this popular breed. J. H. BASINGER, East Lewistown, Ohio. Mention the INGLENOOK when writing.

The Great Family Medicine! ... VICTOR REMEDIES CO., Frederick, Md. Mention the INGLENOOK when writing.

ECLIPSE ENGINES, VIBRATING GRAIN THRESHERS, SEPARATORS, SAW-MILLS, ETC.

"ECLIPSE" PATENT TRACTION ENGINE.

BUILT ON WHEELS FROM 3 TO 30 H. P. ON SILLS FORM 3 TO 40 H. P.

IMPROVED PLAIN FARM ENGINE.

"ECLIPSE" SAW-MILL.

Persons who contemplate buying ENGINES, THRESHERS, SEPARATORS, COTTON GINS, SAW-MILLS, OR STEAM-BOILERS, should correspond with us for Catalogue Prices, &c.

FRICK & CO., Waynesboro, Franklin Co., Pa.

UNION PACIFIC THE OVERLAND ROUTE

SUGAR-BEET INDUSTRY IN NEBRASKA AND COLORADO is attracting the attention of capitalists and farmers along the

UNION PACIFIC

From beets averaging 15 to 25 tons to the acre, the factory can extract 14 per cent. granulated sugar, or 280 pounds to the ton of beets.

For full information about the Famous Platte Valley, Its entire length traversed by the Union Pacific.

ADDRESS E. L. LOMAX, G. P. & T. A, Omaha, Neb.

WHY PAY RENT? Better Own a FARM. Start NOW!

Thousands of Acres of fertile lands, capable of raising the finest quality of farm products in luxurious abundance Are FOR SALE, Upon Reasonable Terms In Wisconsin, Minnesota, South Dakota, Iowa, Nebraska and Wyoming. Reference to reliable statistics will demonstrate the fact that the pursuits of agriculture, stock-raising, and dairying in these States are attended with profitable results.

CHICAGO & NORTH-WESTERN RAILWAY Affords EASY Access to Unfailing Markets

Correspondence solicited from intending settlers. Send for free copy of *The North-Western Home Seeker.*

H. R. McCULLOUGH, 3rd Vice-Pres't. W. B. KNISKERN, Gen'l Pass'r and Ticket Agt. CHICAGO.

Save the Babies.

By Using SENG... SOVERE... BA... BA... POWD...

It relieves them of all stomach and b... trouble. It aids digestion; tones, stren... ens and invigorates the stomach and ... els; acts as a gentle laxative if give... small doses, or a physic if given in la... doses.

Green discharges are always an in... tion that baby's food is not properly di... ed and such condition may result in ... rhœa or cholera infantum. The Pow... will put the child's stomach in a ... healthy condition, so that it can prop... digest and assimilate its food. Much o... vomiting and wind colic common with ... fants is prevented by its use. Send f... bottle. Price, 25 cents. Six bottles, $...

Address: D. B. SENGER & CO., Box 400. Franklin Grove, ...

...EBAKER Is the Greatest Wagon of the Century.

...CONSTRUCTION...

AXLES, Indiana Black Hickory, straight grained.
SKEINS, Cast or Steel, take in more axle wood than others.
SPOKES, Slope Shouldered, Indiana White Oak.
HUBS, Patent, Oil Mountain Black Birch, are check proof.
TIRES, Patent Round Edge, Welded on.
GEARS, Soaked in Boiling Oil, Moisture Proof.
PAINTING, only Best Oils, handsome finish.

Hitch to a "Studebaker" and SAVE YOUR TEAM, REPAIRS, TIME, MONEY, PATIENCE.

Every Wagon guaranteed. Every promise made good. If not on sale in your town, write direct to

Studebaker Bros. Mfg. Co., South Bend, Indiana.

FREE LANDS

IMPROVED FA... Crop Pa...

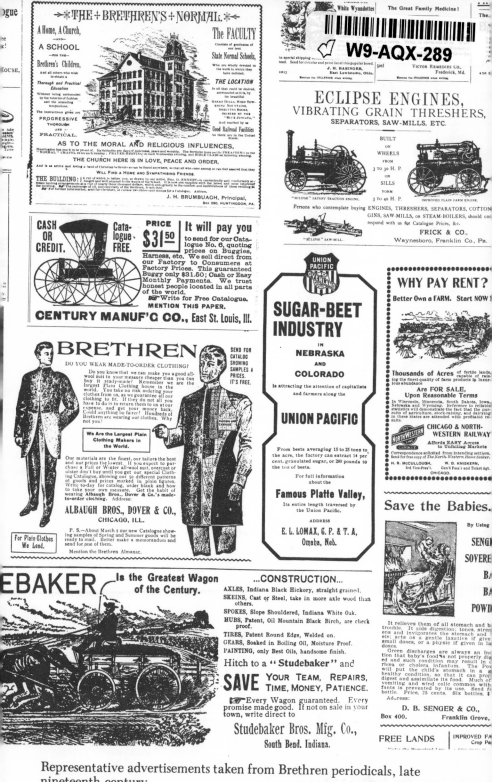

Representative advertisements taken from Brethren periodicals, late nineteenth century.

THE BRETHREN IN INDUSTRIAL AMERICA

THE BRETHREN IN INDUSTRIAL AMERICA

A Source Book on the Development of the Church of the Brethren, 1865–1915

Compiled and edited with an Introduction by
ROGER E. SAPPINGTON

BRETHREN PRESS
Elgin, Illinois

THE BRETHREN IN INDUSTRIAL AMERICA
A Source Book on the Development
of the Church of the Brethren,
1865-1915

BRETHREN PRESS, 1451 Dundee Avenue, Elgin, IL 60120
Edited by Kenneth I. Morse
Design by Kathy Kline

Library of Congress Cataloging in Publication Data

Main entry under title:

The Brethren in industrial America.

Includes bibliographies and index.
1. Church of the Brethren—History—19th century—Sources. 2. Church of the Brethren—History—20th century—Sources. 3. United States—Church history—19th century—Sources. 4. United States—Church history—20th century—Sources.
I. Sappington, Roger Edwin, 1929-
II. Title.
BX7816.B73 1985 286'.5 85-4698
ISBN 0-87178-111-5
Printed in the United States of America

CONTENTS

LIST OF ILLUSTRATIONS

Unless otherwise noted, all illustrations are from the Brethren Encyclopedia, Inc. (BE) collection or the Brethren Historical Library and Archives (BHLA). Used with Permission.

INTRODUCTION

During the years from 1865 to 1915, the half century covered in this volume of source materials related to the growth and development of the Church of the Brethren, the United States of America witnessed remarkable growth. Part of the reason for this growth was that the government was quite stable and maintained a period of peace and tranquility in foreign affairs. The only exception was a brief war in 1898 called the Spanish American War, which did not last long enough to have any impact on the Brethren. Consequently, when the government took action with regard to the people, it was related to economic concerns. Such laws as the Interstate Commerce Act of 1887 and the Sherman Anti-trust Act of 1890 represented attempts by the United States government to regulate the economic activities of the American people.

Another reason for remarkable growth in the United States during this period, which is sometimes identified as the Industrial Revolution, was the abundance of such natural resources as coal, iron, and oil, essential to the development of an industrial economy. Perhaps the most important reason, however, was the availability of an abundance of human resources to provide the immense quantities of human labor needed in the coal and steel industries, and also in such essential activities as agriculture. Much of the human labor was provided by native-born Americans, particularly young men and women who left the farm to move to the cities to find jobs in industry and related occupations. Members of the Studebaker family, who became very prominent in South Bend, Indiana, had strong Brethren roots in agriculture. In addition, another source of human resources was from foreign immigration. Millions of immigrants came to the United States in this half century. Although he had arrived in the United States before 1865, Andrew Carnegie is certainly one of the most noted examples of a successful immigrant. Most immigrants, however, were poverty-stricken workers in the cities and the mines. If an immigrant had any training or skill or financial resources, that person might find a more highly developed type of work. Such an immigrant was a Dane, named Christian Hope, who settled in the Mississippi River valley where he encountered the Brethren. Eventually he became a leader in the foreign mission movement in the church.

As the result of political peace and tranquility, economic growth and expansion, and human increase from large native families and from immigration, the United States became one of the world's leading nations during these years. Geographically the United States added Alaska and Hawaii, later to become states. More importantly, the people settled the area between the Mississippi River and the Rocky Mountains, so that by 1890 the federal census taker reported that no longer could he find any unsettled frontier. At about the same time, in the 1890s, the United States had surpassed all other nations in economic production and had become the world leader in business and economics. At least for many people, the United States was a daring and challenging place to live.

Brethren reacted in various ways to the challenges presented by these changes taking place in the United States. They were much involved in the geographical expansion, and large numbers of Brethren settled in agricultural lands in the states west of the Mississippi River such as Kansas. Some of the changes taking place were rejected by a group of several thousand Brethren who became known in the 1880s as the Old German Baptist Brethren. However, the large majority of Brethren, who changed their name in 1908 from German Baptist Brethren to the Church of the Brethren, were prepared to accept—if slowly—many of the changes. Their ancestors in Germany in the early 1700s had separated from the state churches because they wanted to make changes. Also, they left Germany to come to America because they were dissatisfied with political and economic conditions in Europe. In America they had scattered and settled first in the colonies from Pennsylvania on south, primarily seeking better economic opportunities. So for Brethren to accept the challenge of seeking similar opportunities in the last one-third of the nineteenth century and first decades of the twentieth century was nothing new in the life of the church. In fact, the evidence seems to indicate that the Brethren changed more in these fifty years than in any comparable period in Brethren history.

In proposing the importance of economic changes on the life and history of the Brethren, let me say personally that I am probably more deeply indebted than I have realized to Floyd E. Mallott, my mentor and teacher of Brethren history at Bethany Theological Seminary. He encouraged and pushed me along, when I was a young student much interested in Brethren history some thirty years ago. I believed then, and still do, that he had been overly influenced by economic determinism, which he had probably learned at the University of Chicago. I am not now, and never have been, a believer in economic determinism as the interpretation of history. I am certainly willing to accept the importance of economic change on society, but ultimately history is made up of the ways in which leaders and their followers bring about economic changes. From my perspective, the greater emphasis is on the leaders.

As in other periods of their history, Brethren during these years were led by outstanding men, such as Henry R. Holsinger, certainly the most controversial figure of his day, D. L. Miller, Enoch Eby, and Galen B. Royer. For whatever reasons, it is certainly true that the Brethren expanded geographically and grew significantly in numbers. Geographically, the newly developing railroads played a major role in making it possible for Brethren to cover long distances rapidly and inexpensively. Thus they settled in new areas such as the Dakotas. In numbers Brethren grew both by having large families, in which more children lived to adulthood as the result of significant improvements in medical care, and by a vital program of evangelization, in which large numbers of new people were brought into the church, including Civil War veterans. According to the best statistics available, the Brethren increased from an estimated 10,000 in 1850 to 57,749 in 1882. By 1910, membership in the Church of the Brethren had reached 82,215, and in 1920 it was 96,076. Certainly the membership in the Church of the Brethren had increased significantly in the years since the major divisions in the early 1880s.

Since no bibliography is included in this volume, let me make a few comments at this point. First of all an overwhelming amount of material is available regarding the Brethren during these years. The most difficult problem in compiling this volume was the selection of material to be included. Certainly much valuable material was not included (which I am sure will be noted by any reviewers). In that context definite limitations on the length of this volume were set forth by the publishers. Second, I have turned almost completely to printed sources, including minutes, tracts and pamphlets, and journals. Only a few scattered references are included from unpublished minutes or letters. In most places the quoted material has been reproduced as it appeared in the original source. Third, virtually all of the material in this volume may be found in two libraries—the Brethren Historical Library and Archives at Elgin, Illinois, and the Library of Bethany Theological Seminary at Oak Brook, Illinois. Several years ago, in a rewarding two weeks in those two libraries, I had photocopied more than 1800 pages of material. Obviously, only a small part of it is included in this volume. Fourth, I trust that the footnotes at the end of this volume will be adequate to identify my sources without a separate bibliography.

Since it may not be obvious, let me make it quite clear that I am deeply indebted to the staffs of the Brethren Historical Library and Archives at Elgin and the Library at Bethany Theological Seminary. In addition, I have many friends and associates at Elgin and at Bethany. All of these individuals have contributed to making possible the publication of this volume. They have met my needs in countless ways. In particular I am appreciative of the work of Kenneth I. Morse, Fred W. Swartz, and David Eller, the book editors of the Brethren Press, with whom I have worked closely in the preparation and publishing of this volume. Finally, I am always and most deeply indebted to my family, especially my understanding and patient wife, LeVerle, and our four children, who have in many ways sacrificed in terms of time and effort, while I was busily engaged in completing this study. I can only hope that their sacrifice (and mine) will be worthwhile for all of those interested in this material.

Roger E. Sappington
Bridgewater, Virginia

I

GEOGRAPHICAL EXPANSION

INTRODUCTION

By 1865 Brethren were claiming farm land as far west as the Pacific coast in Oregon. In the years following 1865 they settled in much of the territory between the Mississippi River and the Pacific, e.g., in the Dakotas, often in "colonies." Since the first transcontinental railroad was completed in 1869 and other transcontinentals followed over the next quarter of a century, Brethren were able to utilize the railroads in moving into newly opened agricultural land. They helped to bring civilization to an area reaching from Texas to Canada and from the Mississippi River to the Rocky Mountains.

A second major area of geographical expansion was the rapidly growing cities of the United States. A significant number of Brethren were leaving the farms, especially in the eastern United States, to find work in the cities. At least in a few of these cities, particularly those that were close to strong rural congregations, Brethren were able to establish urban congregations by 1915. This activity, however, proved to be very difficult.

EXPANSION IN RURAL AREAS

The Brethren churches on the west side of the Mississippi River were generally prospering in these years. Especially was that true of states such as Iowa which had been in the free, or non-slave, territory preceding the Civil War. By 1882, when Howard Miller compiled a census of the Brethren, he identified 38 congregations and 3,056 members in Iowa. That population was greater than the number of Brethren in any other state west of the Mississippi.[1] *Kansas was next to Iowa in the number of Brethren at this time. It had about the same number of congregations, but only 2,358 Brethren.*[2]

Farther south along the Mississippi valley was Arkansas, a state of the former southern Confederacy which had been of very little interest to the Brethren. According to Miller's information, "Arkansas is estimated as having, at most . . . 20."[3] *However, the Civil War ended slavery in Arkansas and Missouri and these states were now open to Brethren activity. In 1895 the General Missionary and Tract Committee reported that Brethren were at work in Arkansas.*

Arkansas.—Bro. D. L. Forney entered this field last summer, to assist those located in this extensive mission territory. With their co-operation a large number of meetings were held, and as an immediate result 30 were received by baptism and 4 by letter. The members at the different places are much encouraged. It is to be regretted that Eld. James R. Gish, the founder and moving spirit of these missions for the past years, must, on account of advanced years, quit the field. Another will be placed in his stead as soon as possible.[4]

Like Arkansas, Minnesota was another state which had not witnessed any large Brethren migration. Samuel Murray, a Brethren minister who did much traveling, described his experiences in Minnesota.

Finely the time came I had to go to Minnesota all alone into parts I never had been, and where none of our members lived, and our church entirely unknown. My brother John and wife took me to the city. He expressed a regret to see me go alone as old as I was. I felt lonely but I was sure the Lord could, and felt He would care for me, and he did. I stopped in Green Co. I do not remember the name of the town. I had wrote to the woman that Basher had said wanted to be baptized, to have some one to meet me. When I stepped off of the train, I was asked by a buss-man whether I would go to a hotel. I expected to be met by a country man who would take me out. I told him the man's name, he said he did not know him. He pointed to another buss-man and said he could tell me. I went to him. He pointed to a man saying you see that man on that wagon? I said yes, he said that is the man. I stepped out said, is your name Lindersmith? he said, yes sir. I asked him if he came after some one, he said, yes sir. I said I guess I am the man. He said jump in and ride. I have a trunk that must go with me; he said I cant leave my team, his team stood very quiet. He and his big daughter sitting quiet on the spring seat. I thought the introduction was cool. I stepped on the platform, spoke to a young man, for his help with the trunk, yes sir he said we carried it out put it on the wagon the old gentleman again said jump in he had a narrow strip of a board hid across the bed for me to sit on; off we went. Not much talk on the way, only three miles to go. We soon got to his home. I said did you get my card? he said she did. That is the way it goes here. I never know anything. She handed me the card last evening. I thought I would go in and see who it was; I said then there is no appointment for preaching; he said preaching no use talking about preaching and every body haying and nearly all belong to church, except my family, and a few others and we are the best people in the country. . . .

At the dinner table I spoke about meeting again, but he again said yes we have a school house we ought to have some meetings then he said if you will go with me I will hitch to the spanker (we call it the spring wagon here) and we will go and see some of the neighbors, so we went; the first one we seen was running his mower cutting down grass as they have no fences in that country he drove close up to the man, jump off of the spanker, walked up to the him and said this man is a preacher he wants to preach. I told him no use to talk about preaching every body haying; the man said O! yes we must have preaching we can quit work earlier. My old friend said alright. We went to the next house close to the road, he called, the man and wife came out to the road. He again said this man is a preacher he wants to preach, I told him no use to talk about preaching every body buisy haying. They both said yes we must have preaching. He said well all right. I then said to these people, make it as public as you can that tomorrow evening there will be preaching at your school house. We went to one more place; they wanted meeting, then he said it seems they all want meeting. So we had two meetings at their school house; Friday and Saturday evening, for Sunday evening it was moved some three miles to a little town where they had a good sized house, which was well filled, and good attention to the preaching. As the people knew nothing about our church, the second evening I read what we call the Commission. I told them how we baptized. Read from John 13 and told them how we washed feet and ate a full meal for supper in connection with the communion, (the bread and wine;) also read several verses treating on the Salutation of the kiss. Told them how we practiced it, many of them nodded their heads to sanction what was read; some of the men put their heads down low. . . .

Brother Ohlinger came on Sunday afternoon: on Monday when my trunk was brought down stairs the mother and daughter said I should leave my trunk and come back and preach some more. I prefer taking it with me. I do honestly believe that right at that place a good brother could have done much good. I know that their are thousand of such places in our United States where churches could be planted and cultivated if we had the right men to send out willing to make self-sacrifice.

On Monday Bro. Ohlinger took me over the country from Steel county to his home in Rice county. It was a very pleasant enjoyable days travel, a very fine clear day. The grain, all over the beautiful prairie country was just turning to golden yellow. Wheat, rye, oats, and barley, all ripen about the same time. It was grand to look over the golden yellow country with occasional green spot of corn or a small field of pasture. I now made my home at Brother Ohlinger's for nearly two weeks, as every body was busy harvesting, and there was much of it to do. At the close of two weeks on Tuesday the mother and son-in-law and wife took me a cross the country to Seble county to where they had a daughter living, also a few families of members; a very hard days drive. At this place I preached twice on Sunday in a brothers new house, in a good sized room not yet occupied by the family. I did some visiting and private preaching throught the week; I preached twice at two different places in Lakure [Le Sueur] county, where two of Bro. Ohlingers sons lived; as many farmers were not done harvesting, our congregations were small; people were no respector of days: worked and went to city trading hauling reapers out on Sunday the same as on week days. So we were not not very far from the great cities: St. Paul and Minneapolis.

After our visit in Seble and Lasure Co., and the cities of St. Paul and Minnespolis we went to Rice Co., had preaching twice on Sunday. On Monday Brother Ohlinger took me to the train. Where I took the train for Lewiston, Vincent Co., where I was met by brother Werts who took me to his home and his wife and two sons, made the family a very good place for me to make my home. On Saturday evening we commenced meetings, preaching every evening over two Sundays; in all eleven sermons. The Brethren and Sisters begged for me to stay, and Sister Werts said you ought to stay, old and young wants you to stay. I confess I did wrong, I ought to of have stayed.[5]

Perhaps if Murray had stayed in Minnesota, there would have been more Brethren in that state in the twentieth century. Certainly he was only one of many Brethren ministers who traveled extensively in the western United States. Another interesting account published in one of the church's periodicals has particular importance because it represented the beginning of Brethren work in Idaho. David Brower visited a number of Brethren and organized a congregation.

I left my family and residence on the 6th of Nov. [1878], enroute for Washington and Idaho Territories, on a mission of love. Traveled most of the way by steamboat, some by railroad, some by stage, sometimes on a wagon, some on horseback and some on foot. Arrived at brother Moses Hunts, Columbia Co., W. T. on the 11th of November. . . .

On the 17th, in company with brother Flory, we started to brother Abraham Steward's. Arrived there the same evening. This is in Nezperce county, Idaho Territory. We found nine members of the church residing in this neighborhood. Here we held a series of meetings; had ten public meetings and one council meeting, at which time we organized a church, calling it the Palouse Valley church. There were seventeen members present, and all agreed to carry out the general order of the church. We then held a choice for a minister and deacon; the lot fell on brother Thomas Steward for minister and brother Nathan West for deacon. May the Lord enable them to be useful and faithful in their calling. They had one deacon before we organized the church, viz, brother William R. King. The address of all these official brethren is Moscow, Nezperce Co., Idaho Territory. During these meetings there was one accession by baptism. These were the first meetings ever held by the Brethren in that county.

On the 28th of Nov., in company with brethren Thomas Steward and Nathan West, we started for the Pataha church, Columbia Co. W. T. Arrived at brother A. E. Troyer's on the 29th. Remained here one week; had seven meetings and one council meeting. Found things in a pitiful condition with most of the members—so much so that it was necessary to disorganize this church. . . .

I arrived [home] on the 31st of Dec.

Distance travelled on the above journey is between eight and nine hundred miles.

Now after taking the above long and tedi[o]us trip, being absent from home eight weeks, and having labored hard for the cause of our Divine Master, I wish to say to the Brethren in the Atlantic States, that we need help here on the coast very much indeed. We have a scope of country all of 500 miles in length, with only one ordained elder to preside over these scattered brethren and churches. Eastern Oregon, Washington Territory and Idaho Territory, as it stands now only have one organized church, with only one young minister and three deacons who reside at Moscow, Idaho Territory, near the line between W. T. and I. T.[6]

As both Murray and Brower indicated, much of their travel was by railroad. This means of travel revolutionized life in the United States. Brethren took advantage of this new means of travel in many ways, one of which was by migrating to the northwestern part of the United States. An excellent account of such a migration has been written in connection with the earliest Brethren settlement in North Dakota in 1894.

The first settlement of Dunkers in North Dakota owes its existence primarily to the activity of the Great Northern railroad, which, in the last two decades of the nineteenth century, spent much money and employed many men in finding settlers for the vacant government land lying within the territory of its newly built lines in the northwest.

At the head of the immigration activity of the railroad from 1892 to 1909 was Max Bass, a man to whose remarkable energy and personal enthusiasm for his work is due, in very large measure, the rapid settlement and consequent development of the northern half of our state. North Dakota owes much to Max Bass, for it was his vital interest in the settlers themselves, his sympathetic concern for their welfare, born of a larger impulse than that of merely earning his salary, which made him so important a factor in laying the foundations of the commonwealth. . . .

The plan of establishing a colony of people who were bound together by religious ties suggested to F. L. Thompson the idea of securing a Dunker colony for North Dakota. This was very natural since he had lived as a boy near such a community at Girard, Illinois, and had had many dealings with them while in the mercantile business at that place. He had had ample opportunity to become acquainted with them, and was confident that they would make good settlers and desirable citizens. Particularly was he impressed with the fact that in the matter of religion they practiced what they preached. Accordingly he communicated his ideas to Max Bass and suggested that he visit the Girard community with a view to organizing an emigration from that district. Following this suggestion Bass visited the Illinois community, and endeavored to interest its members in North Dakota lands. He found them, however, unwilling to move. This was due and very naturally, to the fact that they were enjoying very prosperous conditions and had no reason to be dissatisfied. Although this visit did not yield any direct results in the matter of immigration, it served to bring him into touch with the Dunkers, and to impress him with their desirability as settlers. His next move was to visit the annual conference of Dunkers at Muncie, Indiana, in June, 1893. In answer to his inquiries he obtained the information that Rev. A. B. Peters, of Walkertown, Indiana, and T. Judson Beckwith, of Teegarden, Indiana would probably be glad to change their locations and move to North Dakota.

The visit of Max Bass to the conference resulted in some correspondence between him and Rev. Peters, and ultimately in a visit on the part of Bass to Rev. Peters' home. The possibilities and advantages of the northwest were presented to the latter, free transportation was offered him for a trip of investigation and prospecting.

Rev. Peters was much interested in the prospects held forth, and asked permission to take a number of friends with him. This request was readily granted by Bass, and a committee of Brethren was immediately organized for the trip of investigation. They were T. Judson Beckwith of Teegarden, William Baughman of Walkertown, William Holland of Tyner City, Rev. J. R. Miller and Samuel W. Burkhart of Nappanee, Indiana.

It was with much hesitation that this group of men consented to take the trip, for they knew that if they sold their homes in Indiana and cast their lot with the p[i]oneers of North Dakota there could be no going back; they would be obliged by reason of their slender finances, to remain where they settled. The price of land in Indiana was so high that once they sold, they could not re-establish themselves there. The prospect of free government lands, however, was sufficiently alluring to induce these men to make the initial trip of investigation.

This committee of Brethren, accompanied by Max Bass, left Chicago, August 2, 1893, for North Dakota. They arrived at Mayville,

August 4, where they made their first stop. The appearance of the country and its apparent possibilities highly pleased the visitors. They found the prospects, however, unsuited to their financial condition for the government land had been taken up and improved, and could be had only by outright purchase, or on the crop-payment plan. By the crop-payment plan is meant that system whereby the purchaser of land pays a certain amount at the time of purchase and agrees to give the original owner a certain per cent of each crop raised on land, usually one-half, until the whole amount agreed upon is paid. This plan is subject to much variation, however, depending upon the individual agreements between buyer and seller. This fact decided them to go further west, where government land was still open for filing.

Leaving Mayville, they continued their trip west. A stop was made at Lakota, August 6, but the conditions upon which they could acquire title to land were the same as at Mayville. On August 7 they arrived at Cando. Here they were hospitably received and entertained by the citizens of the town. Several days were spent in looking over the country. U. S. Land Commissioner F. L. Thompson, C. J. Lord of the Towner County Bank (now the First National), and E. J. Hanson assisted the visitors in the matter of transportation, and, being familiar with the quality and physiography of the land still open for settlement, were of much assistance in helping the Brethren to find a suitable location.

The first day was spent east of town. Thompson and Hanson conducted the party, and took them as far east as the present town of Newville. None of the Brethren, however, was sufficiently satisfied with the country to file. Burkhart, who had lived in Kansas from 1885 to 1888, years when Kansas suffered from severe drought, thought this compared unfavorably with Kansas land, especially that it was less level.

That evening as the party gathered in Thompson's office, a remark was made, which, though unimportant in itself, is yet remembered by all the Brethren, and is still told by them with much interest. Rev. Peters had said, "We're ready to locate, but have not yet seen the spot."

"I'll show the spot tomorrow," replied Thompson, indicating a certain quarter-section on the plat-book.

The following day, August 10, the party having been joined by C. J. Lord, spent the day west of Cando. Having covered a large amount of territory, the party returned towards town and arrived at the quarter mentioned by Thompson the night before. This quarter is comparatively level, with a well-rounded hill at its approximate centre, and is admirably situated for a building site. Rev. Peters liked the land but could not make up his mind to file. He consulted Burkhart, and, after agreeing to stand by each other through thick and thin, both decided to take land.

Rev. Peters filed on the quarter mentioned above, and Burkhart contracted for another quarter on the crop-payment plan. Beckwith, too, decided to file at this time, and selected the quarter adjoining that of Rev. Peters on the south. The homesteads of these three men marked the central point around which the future colonies settled. The people of Cando were given an opportunity to become acquainted with the Brethren, both in public and in private. Rev. Peters, who was an elder in the church, preached to the general public during the visit of the committee. His friends take great pride in the fact that this was the first sermon preached in North Dakota by a minister of the Brethren Church.

The committee returned to Indiana. All of its members were convinced that North Dakota's opportunities were well worth seizing. They were enthusiastic about it and began to communicate their enthusiasm to their friends and neighbors. The Great Northern railway now employed Rev. Peters to act as immigration agent, particularly among his own brethren. As a result of this activity a second party of twenty-nine homeseekers was organized. With Max Bass and Rev. Peters this party came to North Dakota early in September, 1893. This party was especially impressed with the prospects offered to the poor man. Of the twenty-nine, twenty-two filed on homesteads. They returned at once to their homes and began to make preparations for moving in the following spring.

Still a third party was organized the same fall and came to North Dakota about the middle of October. This party numbered thirteen and resulted in several more filings.

The movement had now assumed large proportions and a colony of Brethren in North Dakota was definitely assured. Rev. Peters started an active campaign in Indiana. He endeavored to interest the members of his church, as well as others outside the church, in North Dakota. He did not restrict his operations to his own locality, but covered an extensive range of territory in north central Indiana, even going across the border into Ohio to gain recruits. The method pursued by Rev. Peters in securing immigrants was largely that of personal solicitation among his personal friends and the members of his church. He traveled from community to community, telling the poor man of the wonderful opportunities which awaited him in the northwest. He visited the homes of those he thought he could interest, took a meal with them, or perhaps stayed over night. His work took the form of a personal canvass, and, because he himself was a poor man, and was venturing his all in a new country, the people whom he approached placed especial confidence in him.

In the work of securing immigrants for North Dakota Rev. Peters was aided at every opportunity by Max Bass. The far-sighted judgment of the latter in selecting a man of the type of Rev. Peters for the particular work for which he did is only another instance of his thorough knowledge of men. One plan which proved exceptionally satisfactory was that of calling public meetings in the smaller towns for the purpose of coming in touch with a large number of people and advertising North Dakota. Bass spoke at most of these meetings and explained the conditions which awaited the prospective settler. Other officials of the Great Northern were present at some of the meetings and in every instance pamphlets and circulars descriptive of North Dakota were distributed. Those who had definitely decided to emigrate were usually requested to sign a paper to that effect.

In a letter written December 18, 1893, to F. L. Thompson, Bass said: "I take pleasure in advising you that the prospects for a large emigration to your country are growing brighter and brighter every day. I am making new converts right along and receive the heartiest co-operation of all the parties who filed on land this fall." In another letter of January 20, 1894, he urged Thompson to see that accommodations were made for a large number of colonists in the spring. He suggested also that the Cando papers take the matter up and that the citizens of the town perfect an organization for the purpose of assimilating the new settlers when they should arrive. This organization would operate a central bureau where a list of rentable lands would be kept on file; also the names of those who wished to hire help. Bass felt that he was undertaking a great responsibility in bringing such a large number of people to North Dakota, and wished to assure himself that they would be well taken care of.

That his predictions for a large colony were well founded was shown by the gathering of emigrants at Walkertown, Indiana, the last week in March, 1894. They came from all parts of the north central portion of Indiana. A majority came from farms, a few from small towns of Marshal and Elkhart counties. They brought their families with them and they brought their household goods, their live stock, farm machinery, in fact everything which could possibly be moved. Those who owned land either sold it or offered it for sale. They had prepared to sever all connections with their old homes and establish themselves permanently in new ones.

A special train was made up for the emigrants at Walkertown which was to make a through trip to Cando. The date set for departure was March 27. For several days previous to this date Walkertown was the scene of unusual activity. Everybody was busy loading household goods and live stock into freight cars. The excitement caused by their leaving for a new country was accelerated for the emigrants by the leave-taking of friends and relatives. Rumors of the terrible hardships to be met in North Dakota, the rigor of its winters, were on every tongue. News of the Bomburger murder had just reached Indiana, and friends of the colonists freely predicted for them a similar fate. Stories of starving and freezing were heard on every hand. But the colonists were not deterred in the least. They continued their preparations for leaving, and found that comradeship in a new and uncertain venture made strong friends, so that their sorrow at leaving some friends was not wholly without recompense. The gathering of such a large number of people and their effects naturally caused some delay, and it was not until two o'clock on the morning of March 28 that the long train was ready to start. When finally assembled the train consisted of over thirty emigrant, or freight cars, and eight or nine passenger cars; the number of passengers was about 350.

The experiences of the emigrants on this trip were many and varied. Each passenger car was provided with a stove which could be used for cooking so far as its limited capacity allowed. This stove was used chiefly for coffee-making. The colonists took ample lunches with them from their homes, and were enabled by frequent stops along the route to buy such provisions as bread and fruit.

An experience most vividly remembered by the members of this first colony was the water famine. The water supply gave out, there was no water to drink, neither was there any for washing. Only those who have the privilege of eating and sleeping in an emigrant coach can fully appreciate the significance of this latter statement.

The sleeping accommodations, too, were limited. There were beds only for the women and children, the men generally were obliged to content themselves with the chair cars. There were no porters on board, every one was his own porter. At St. Paul a free lunch, consisting of coffee and buns, was furnished during the wait at the Union depot by the Great Northern. Max Bass had a photograph of the train and colonists taken during the wait in the yards. This he afterwards used for advertising purposes, as well as for personal remembrances to those who had taken the trip.

Bass accompanied the colony throughout the entire trip. To advertise the trip and arouse "Dakota fever," he so arranged the train's schedule as to travel through Indiana, Illinois, and Wisconsin during the day time. The outside of the cars was covered with large banners upon which the opportunities of North Dakota were set forth in conspicuous letters. One, for example, bore the following statement: "From Indiana, to the rich Free Government Lands in North Dakota, via the Famous Red River Valley, the Bread Basket of America! For information about them apply to F. I. Whitney, Gen'l Pass. Agt., St. Paul, Minn., or Max Bass, Immigration Agt." The route from Walkertown to Chicago was by the Baltimore and Ohio; from Chicago to St. Paul, the Chicago and Great Western, and from St. Paul to Cando the Great Northern. From St. Paul the train ran in two sections.

On March 31, 1894, the two sections of the emigrant train arrived at Cando. The citizens had made extensive preparations for the reception of the colonists. The town hall was thrown open to afford sleeping accommodations, and private residences were generously placed at their disposal until they could find permanent locations. In a few instances small temporary shacks were erected.

Three boarding cars were sidetracked by the Great Northern for temporary use and a number of tents were provided from the railroad's construction crews to be used in case of necessity. The livery barns and some private barns were opened for the reception of live stock and household goods as they were unloaded.

All the immigrants wished to rent land the first summer, pending improvements upon their homesteads. Bass endeavored to discourage renting as much as possible, for he realized that the settlers should be homesteaders rather than renters. All but one, however, lived on rented land the first summer.

Those living on rented land, after putting out their crops, immediately began to improve their homesteads. The Homestead laws at that time provided that, in order to make his claim good, a homesteader must establish a residence upon the land filed on within six

Fig. 1. *Chartered Great Northern train with Brethren settlers on the way to North Dakota, St. Paul, MN, March 29, 1894. (BE)*

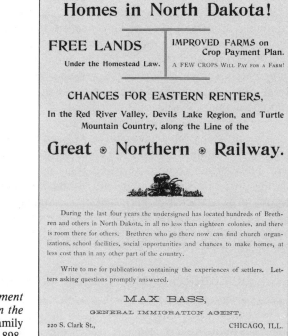

Homes in North Dakota!

FREE LANDS Under the Homestead Law.	IMPROVED FARMS on Crop Payment Plan. A FEW CROPS WILL PAY FOR A FARM!

CHANCES FOR EASTERN RENTERS,

In the Red River Valley, Devils Lake Region, and Turtle Mountain Country, along the Line of the

Great ⊛ Northern ⊛ Railway.

During the last four years the undersigned has located hundreds of Brethren and others in North Dakota, in all no less than eighteen colonies, and there is room there for others. Brethren who go there now can find church organizations, school facilities, social opportunities and chances to make homes, at less cost than in any other part of the country.

Write to me for publications containing the experiences of settlers. Letters asking questions promptly answered.

MAX BASS,

GENERAL IMMIGRATION AGENT,

220 S. Clark St., CHICAGO, ILL.

Fig. 2. *Advertisement appearing in the* Brethren's Family Almanac, 1898.

months of the date of filing. By the following spring they were living on their own homesteads. With hardly an exception, the colony of 1894 was made up of farmers. Some followed the carpenter trade, but only as a sideline.

Nearly every colonist was his own carpenter, blacksmith, mechanic. In fact, each family was, to a remarkable degree, self-sufficing. This characteristic is traceable back to the German ancestry of the Brethren, and to a time when division of labor among those specially trained in certain trades was either unknown or not generally practiced.

The homesteads filed on by this group of Brethren were, for the most part, situated in Township 158, Range 68, around the homesteads of Elders Peters and Beckwith and Mr. Burkhart. A few filed in Township 158, Range 67 to the east and 159, 68 to the north. But the greatest number, nine-tenths at least, settled in 156–68, and later additions to this colony have made the township predominantly Brethren.

Such is the history of the first Brethren Colony. As is shown by the report of Max Bass to the Great Northern for the year 1902, there were other colonies and immigrations in ever increasing numbers every year thereafter for six years. But as the number of immigrants continued to increase they no longer settled together in one community but spread out over the state to different localities.

Then, too, after the year 1894 the total number of immigrants did not come in a single body; neither were they predominantly Brethren. In all these respects the first colony of Brethren was unique. It was composed almost wholly of Brethren; all of its members settled in one community, and all came at the same time.

For these reasons I have confined myself to this one colony, leaving the interesting story of other colonies for later treatment. I shall add, however, an account of the religious activities of these Brethren during their first summer and fall. Although no church was built, a church organization was perfected and a Sunday School organized. Such an account belongs properly to the story of the first colony, and may be considered part of the first chapter of the history of the Brethren in North Dakota.

RELIGIOUS ACTIVITIES AND FIRST CHURCH

As every one who is familiar with the Brethren or Dunkers knows, they give religion first place in their various activities. Religious duties hold precedence over all others. It was to be expected, therefore, that, after the colony of 1894 had attended to their most urgent material wants, its members would look to their spiritual welfare.

A real zeal for religious work manifested itself in this colony from the first. The immigrants no sooner satisfied their immediate needs for food and shelter than they began to look for a place in which to worship. The Methodist Church was placed at their disposal for this purpose, and it was there that they held their first public meeting. Rev. Peters preached the sermon on this occasion. Later, after the immigrants had found homes upon farms and until a church was built, the county court house and the public school building at Cando were used as meeting places. Regular services were also held in a country school house twelve miles northwest of Cando near their settlement. A Sunday School was organized within six weeks after the arrival of the colony.

The first definite church organization was effected August 4, 1894 four months after the colony's arrival. This was done at the J. W. McVey farm seven miles southwest of Cando, where a meeting was called for the purpose. The local Brethren were assisted in perfecting the church organization by Elders W. R. Deeter of Milford, Indiana, and Daniel Whitmore of South Bend, Indiana. Elder Deeter acted as moderator of the meeting; George C. Long was chosen secretary; Judson Beckwith, treasurer; Samuel W. Burkhart, clerk.

Burkhart estimates the number of bona fide church members present at one hundred. Of these, eighty-four were admitted to membership in the new church by presenting certificates of membership from their home churches. Some of those present were not supplied with such certificates and some who were so supplied did not wish to present them. At the same time there were admitted four ministers and four deacons. The four ministers were G. W. Strong, A. B. Peters, Levi E. Miller, and S. N. Eversole.

The four deacons were Wm. Kesler, senior member, T. Judson Beckwith, Samuel W. Burkhart, and Wm. Baughman. After the meeting the ordinances of Foot-washing, the Love Feast, and the Salutation were observed, after which the Communion was administered. This church organization is noteworthy because it was the first of its kind in North Dakota. With the account of this organization the history of the Dunkers' first year in North Dakota is complete.[7]

These Brethren in North Dakota were settling on government land which was made available under the terms of the Homestead Act of 1862, which provided 160 acres of land for any settler who remained there five years. An illustration of such a homestead grant of land secured by a Brethren settler in North Dakota included the following provisions.

THE UNITED STATES OF AMERICA

Homestead Certificate No. 5626
APPLICATION 8350

To all to whom these presents shall come, Greeting: Whereas There has been deposited in the GENERAL LAND OFFICE of the United States a CERTIFICATE OF THE REGISTER of the Land Office at Devils Lake North Dakota, whereby it appears that, pursuant to the Act of Congress approved 20th May, 1862, "To secure Homesteads to Actual Settlers on the Public Domain," and the acts supplemental thereto, the claim of Emeline Hoff has been established and duly consummated, in conformity to law, for the South West quarter of Section twenty-one in Township one hundred and sixty-one North of Range sixty-six West of the Fifth Principal Meridian in North Dakota, containing one hundred and sixty acres. according to the OFFICIAL PLAT of the Survey of the said Land, returned to the GENERAL LAND OFFICE by the SURVEYOR GENERAL:

Now know ye, That there is, therefore, granted by the United States unto the said Emeline Hoff the tract of Land above described: To have and to hold the said tract of Land, with the appurtenances thereof, unto the said Emeline Hoff and to her heirs and assigns forever; subject to any vested and accrued water rights for mining, agricultural, manufacturing, or other purposes, and rights to ditches and reservoirs used in connection with such water rights, as may be recognized and acknowledged by the local customs, laws, and decisions of courts, and also subject to the right of the proprietor of a vein or lode to extract and remove his ore therefrom, should the same be found to penetrate or intersect the premises hereby granted, as provided by law.

In testimony whereof I, Theodore Roosevelt, PRESIDENT OF THE UNITED STATES OF AMERICA, have caused these letters to be made Patent, and the seal of the GENERAL LAND OFFICE to be hereunto affixed. GIVEN under my hand, at the CITY OF WASHINGTON, the fifteenth day of May, in the year of our Lord one thousand nine hundred and three, and of the Independence of the United States the one hundred and twenty-seventh.

BY THE PRESIDENT: Theodore Roosevelt

By Fidle McKean, Secretary,

Recorded N. Dakota, Vol. 150, Page 98

C. Brush, Recorder of the

General Land Office.[8]

In addition to homesteading on United States government lands, Brethren also found some excellent farm land across the border in Canada. Evidently, Brethren settled in a number of different areas. In 1890 the **Gospel Messenger** *reported that it had received a letter from George Hossack of Leask Dale, Ontario, Canada, who urged the Brethren to engage in missionary work in Canada. The editor observed:*

The General Missionary Committee has decided to locate a brother in Canada as soon as it is possible to find the right man for the place, who is willing to go and labor in that field, not for a few weeks or months, but for years, as did Paul at Ephesus. A brother, able to defend the Truth, faithful to the cause of Christ, ready to go and stay, will find in Canada an ample field to labor in.[9]

Ontario is located in the eastern part of Canada. Somewhat earlier, the Foreign and Domestic Mission Board had reported to the Annual Meeting of 1882 that John Wise had been employed in 1881 to engage in evangelistic work in various areas. Included in his work were forty days and forty appointments spent in Canada.[10] *Unfortunately, no indication is given about the exact location of this work. By the time of the First World War, the major Brethren activity in Canada had moved farther west into the prairie provinces of Alberta and Saskatchewan where Brethren eventually organized several congrega-*

tions to serve the needs of more than three hundred members. Something of the importance of the Canadian Brethren was indicated by the decision to hold the Annual Conference of 1923 at Calgary, which was located in the new District of Western Canada. It was the first Annual Conference to be held outside the United States.[11]

EXPANSION IN URBAN AREAS

Although the Brethren in America had usually made their living as farmers, the Industrial Revolution, which became an increasingly important part of the life of people in the United States in the years following the Civil War, also made an impact on Brethren. As new and improved farm machinery made it possible for fewer farmers to produce more food for industrial workers, Brethren farm boys and girls were forced off the family farm to find other types of employment. They moved to the cities; consequently a demand developed for the establishment of Brethren congregations in cities. The generally accepted policy of the church was that city churches would be the responsibility of the district in which the city was located. That such an arrangement was not satisfactory in every situation was evinced in a decision of the Annual Meeting of 1886.

XVI. Whereas, the work developing in some of our cities is proving too burdensome to the Districts in whose care they fall, will not Annual Meeting relieve those Districts, by placing all work in the cities under the care of the General Mission Board, except those cities that fall properly in the limits of a congregation?

Answer: Inasmuch as our city missions are being cared for by the Districts in which they fall, we see no cause for action in the matter at present.[12]

Obviously this decision was a repetition of accepted policy. It did not answer the basic problem of financing the establishment of urban congregations in those districts which had numerous cities but no large and prosperous rural congregations to support the city congregations. It should not be surprising, therefore, that the matter was returned to the consideration of the Annual Meeting, which responded with a more satisfactory response in 1895.

2. We ask Annual Meeting to appoint a committee to report to next Annual Meeting a plan for more efficiently carrying on city mission work, and properly guarding the same.

Annual Meeting referred it to the General Missionary and Tract Committee. Report of this special committee appointed by the Missionary Committee is as follows:

1. City missions should be placed in charge of exemplary ministers, who are able and willing to teach and maintain the doctrines and practices of the church.

2. They must be men who understand the character and wants of city missions, and can adapt themselves to that class of work.

3. In order that they may give the work their entire time and attention it is necessary that they receive a reasonable support.

4. State Mission Boards are hereby authorized and urged to establish missions in cities where there are favorable openings, and sustain them in accordance with the above provisions.

5. State Boards that cannot raise, or devise ways for raising what is needed to maintain such missions, may apply to the General Missionary and Tract Committee for assistance.

6. City missions thus established and maintained must sustain the same relation to the respective State Districts as other congregations, and should be urged to become self-supporting as soon as practicable.

Passed by Annual Meeting.[13]

One of the very significant cities in the United States, where, in contrast to the general situation, the Brethren had a well established congregation which did not need outside financial assistance, was Philadelphia. Early in the nineteenth century, the Brethren there had built a meetinghouse on Crown Street. However, the years following the Civil War brought to a climax new problems for these urban Brethren.

This meeting was held June 24, 1869, resulting in unanimous accord to sell and build in a more suitable place. The principal reasons on which the vote was taken were:

1. Better facilities for general Church and Sunday School work—the present location being no longer considered a good one, being surrounded by lager beer saloons and other annoyances;
2. To procure a place further up town that will be more central for the scattered members, many of whom have moved away from the vicinity of Crown St.

The last meeting at Crown Street:

"Meeting was held for the last time in the old meeting house in Crown Street, on Sunday the 22nd of September, 1872. Services morning and evening. The Brethren and Sisters having tried to worship the Lord our God in accordance with the teachings of the New Testament in that house for 55 years feel sorry to leave the dear loved spot. But believing it to be for the best to promote the cause of Christ, and the salvation of precious never-dying souls, have consented, and are willing to make sacrifices, and thereby assist in the building of a new house, wherein to continue by the blessing and assistance of our good God, our worship in a more convenient place."[14]

The Crown Street property was sold for $13,000, which was considered a profit. A new property was secured on Marshall Street, and after an interim of more than a year of meeting in a hall, the Brethren moved into new quarters in July, 1873.

"Dedication of School Room Church of the Brethren, Through the Blessing of Divine Providence, we were permitted on Sunday, July 13th, 1873, to Dedicate to the Worship of God, The Sunday School Room of our new Church of the Brethren on Marshall Street below Girard Avenue. Sunday School was held at 9 o'clock A.M. At ½ past 10 o'clock the morning service was opened with the reading of the 1st Psalm by our aged Elder John Fox, now nearly 87 years old. After singing a hymn, prayer was offered by Elder Jacob K. Reiner, and the reading of the 5th Chapter of Matthew by Brother John Goodyear, after which Brother Reiner preached from the words of David, recorded in the 27th Psalm, & 4th verse, 'One thing have I desired of the Lord, that will I seek after; that I may dwell in the house of the Lord all the days of my life, to behold the beauty of the Lord, and to enquire in his temple.'

"At 3 P.M. the teachers and scholars of the Sunday School, with many others, met, and after singing and prayer, were very appropriately addressed by Brother Isaac Price, from the words found recorded in the 4th Chapter of Philippians and 8th verse.

"In the evening Brother Isaac Price preached choosing for a text part of Soloman's prayer at the dedication of the temple, recorded in the 1st Kings, 8th Chapter, 27, 28, 29 and 30 verses.

"The meetings were good, the subjects ably defended, with a good attendance, and very good attention by all."[15]

The church part of the building was completed in the summer of 1873 and dedicated in September with Isaac Price preaching. This church met the needs of the Philadelphia Brethren for some fifteen years, but a changing urban population created a new crisis for the Brethren; the resulting decline in membership also brought a financial crisis. The conclusion was a decision to sell the property.

October 15, 1888, at a special meeting of council, the following report was received from the trustees, duly approved, and the committee empowered to sell:

"1. As a reason for selling—the very poor location, and the surrounding material on which the church is compelled principally to depend for its success;
2. The present financial condition of the church and its members, compared with what it was three years ago; . . . Now the mortgages . . . and the interest must be paid, together with the accumulating unpaid taxes whilst our membership is only about one-third with an outlook of increased debt and reduced membership;
3. The advantages of selling this property must be apparent to all, and are as follows: The reduction of expenses with the great relief and satisfaction of knowing that there will be no further probability of its going into the sheriff's hands, whilst we will have from the proceeds of the sale sufficient funds to buy a lot and build a suitable place of worship in a more desirable location."

The sale was finally made March 11, 1890, to Frederick Taylor Post, G.A.R. [Grand Army of the Republic], for $13,500.00—a material loss, as contrasted with the sale at Crown Street which represented a substantial profit.

The Post held it for twenty years when it was acquired by Hebrew interests, and again converted into a place of worship, this time as a synagogue, serving as such today. What a change in the environs from fifty odd years ago! Both sides of the street in the vicinity of the old church is alive with small-powered Hebrew merchants displaying their babbling tongues among the never ceasing streams of humanity moving in both directions.

Jacob T. Myers preached the farewell sermon at the last service held at the Marshall Street Church, April 13, 1890.[16]

How ironic indeed for the meetinghouse to be sold to a group of Civil War veterans! But the Brethren needed "a more desirable location."

The Philadelphia congregation then purchased for $8,900 ap-

proximately 7,750 square feet on the corner of Carlisle and Dauphin Streets. Since that was less than a quarter acre, it should not come as a surprise that Brethren farmers found it difficult to understand how expensive it was to build Brethren churches in the city. The completion of the church was facilitated by the donation of carpet and stained glass and memorial windows, the total expenditure for the building and fixtures was only $11,000. The new church was dedicated in May, 1891.[17]

T. T. Myers preached his first sermon in Philadelphia, April 26, 1891, in Columbia Hall, No. 2215 Columbia Avenue, where services were held pending the construction of the new church building on Dauphin Street.

His subjects were: Morning "The need of Christian Earnestness," Hebrews 2: 1–3. Evening: "What is Man?" Psalm 8:4.

These were the last services held at the Hall, for which the church paid $204.00 rent in 1890 and $84.00 in 1891, plus $6.00 rent of an organ.

May 3, 1891, the new church was dedicated. W. J. Swigart preached both morning and evening. His subjects were: "Dedication of the Temple," 2nd Chron. 6th chapter; and "Dwelling Place of the Righteous," Psalm 90:1.

The church approved the board's recommendation of April 13, 1892, for the erection of a Sunday School building to the rear of the main structure "providing sufficient money is subscribed to justify the building committee to proceed with the work"! It was completed and dedicated in the fall of that year at an approximate contract cost of $5,000.00 and presented in its entirety to the church by Mary S. Geiger. Elder Jacob T. Myers preached the sermon at the dedication.[18]

Tobias T. Myers has been considered the "first full-time regularly salaried pastor" in the Church of the Brethren. He was paid $60 per month by Mary S. Geiger.[19] *Later in his life Myers recalled his years in Philadelphia.*

In the winter of 1891 the Philadelphia Church was looking for a pastor, and at different times they asked my brother if he knew of some one they might get. He said he believed he did, and in course of time suggested me. He told them I was young—a mere boy—but had pretty good success in the work at Mt. Morris and in the evangelistic field in the summer. It was that winter that I had a protracted meeting in the chapel at Mt. Morris and baptized a large number of students. Bro. D. L. Miller wrote it up for the Messenger, and his reference to me, along with other reports that appeared concerning my evangelistic work, appealed to Sister Geiger. She told me after I came that she had been earnestly praying that they might be directed to a man who would fit into the place, and that in her prayers I always came into her mind (appeared before her, although she had never seen me). So Brother James A. Harley was instructed to write me. They thought I would want to spend my vacation somewhere and it might be nice to spend it in Philadelphia and learn something about the city.

I agreed to come. I arrived the last Saturday in April; was met at the Baltimore & Ohio Station by N. R. Baker, E. J. Zern, and others. They were to take me to Sister Krupp's, but misunderstood and took me to Sister Geiger's on 13th St. she gave me a most hearty welcome and at once said that I should just stay with her as long as I wanted. She knew I was a country boy unaccustomed to city ways, and when she showed me my room for the night she explained about the gas—about turning it out. A little later after she had left me, she came back and rapped at the door and said she was just a little worried and wanted to make sure that I understood how to operate the gas.

The next morning (Sunday) she went with me to 22d and Columbia Ave. where the meetings were held and where I preached the last sermons preached in that hall.

The following week I went to Sister Krupp's on 8th Street where they had selected that I should board.

The next Sunday, the first Sunday in May, was the dedication of the new church. Brother Swigart preached the dedicatory sermon at 10:30 in the morning. I preached in the afternoon, and he preached again in the evening.

During the week before the dedication we had a prayer meeting at Brother Hunsberger's. For a year or more they held their prayer meetings at the homes of the members during the time they had no church.

On Monday evening following the dedication we held a meeting to provide for the re-starting of the Sunday School, and we decided to make a house to house canvas in the neighborhood and see what we could do towards gathering in children. On Sunday, the 10th of May, 1891, we started Sunday School. Brother W. S. Price was the first Superintendent.

Two of the most active members of the church were Brother

Chas. C. Hartmann and Brother Samuel B. Croft. Their hearts were evidently in the work. They were earnest, understood each other, and worked well together. Bro. Hartmann's life was wrapped up in the church. He would a good deal rather miss a meal than miss a meeting, and he was one of the best receivers of strangers at the door that I ever knew.

We all felt the need of getting hold of the young people. They of course had scattered, and the dedication of the new church naturally was a means of drawing them together at least temporarily. The point was to try to hold them—get them permanently interested. I conceived the idea of occasional social literary evenings. We met at homes like Sister Geiger's, Brother Hartmann's, Sister Krupp's, and others. We had literary programs, and social times, and after they were over we served ice-cream, cake, etc.

There is something a little sad I must mention. I had learned to know Grant Hunsberger, Isaac Hunsberger's son. He was a dentist. He was not a member of the church. He attended the dedicatory service and some how he was taken with me—I do not know how. He told his parents when he went home that he believed that things were going to go, that he thought we had the right man. He was interested, and a few weeks after that he suddenly took sick and died. I had been to see him a couple times. His death had a most wonderful influence over the people. I remember in preaching his funeral sermon I had for my text "The Master is come and called for thee," and his sister May Hunsberger, now Sister Bowman, took it right to heart and others likewise, and in the fall we had a short series of meetings and baptized quite a number of young people in whom we had been especially interested.

I had merely been called to spend the summer with the church, because they did not know me and I did not know them, but it was not very long until at a church meeting they decided that I should stay permanently if I would do so.

I agreed to stay, and it was in that connection that Brother Isaiah G. Harley referred to the pool with come embarrassment and feeling. He was not sure that I was quite in sympathy with it, and explained that it was difficult to baptize in the river, and had been so for some time. So they put a pool in the church for such to be baptized as were to be saved, and he hoped that we might have occasion very many times to trouble the waters there. I assured him that I had no objection to the pool and hoped that we might baptize many.

Our Sunday School soon filled our little church and we felt the need of more room. Brother Harley in one of the church meetings said he realized that we had already outgrown our quarters but he did not know how we could enlarge as we did not have the money unless, said he, Sister Geiger will take pity on us.

A little later it was decided to build a Sunday School addition, sister Geiger having given expression that she would help. When the Sunday School building was completed it became known that she was paying it all herself.

In that same fall we decided to start a Christian Endeavor Society and for that purpose I called in Horace Geiger who was doing that kind of work, and we organized a Christian Endeavor Society in the fall of 1892.

Of course the literary society was then taken from the homes to the church, and we enjoyed those social occasions there, frequently with treats in connection with them.

When I came east to assume the pastorate of the church there was a Committee from Annual Meeting that had been appointed the year previous who were to visit these eastern churches, having them in charge, to get them more in love with the Brotherhood. Elder J. G. Royer was the Chairman of that Committee, and when the church called me I was at Mt. Morris to consult with Brother Royer. He encouraged my coming. He felt the work was worthy, and assured me that it was needed. He personally and privately gave me to understand that we need have no fear of any crisis to be brought on; that we should go along and do the best we could, and the Committee would not cause us any anxiety.

There was a good deal of trouble in various parts of the Brotherhood, notably in Virginia. Brother Royer was somewhat concerned that it might affect our work, that is: the hearing of those troubles, and he took occasion to send special word that I should not allow my fears to be aroused by what was going on around us; that we should just move quietly on.

At that time Elder Daniel Vaniman, one of the most prominent Elders, visited the church, and he was wonderfully pleased with the outlook; especially was he pleased with our Sunday School. Walking down Broad Street on Sunday afternoon he said: "Brother Myers, you are doing a good work; keep right on; if in any way you or your work should come up at the Annual Meeting, there will be—just a whole lot of Brethren who will stand right up for you."

The work went along nicely and the neighborhood was sympathetic. It took an interest, and we baptized a great many people right around the church.

In the course of events, strong sentiments were formed to start a mission somewhere. Expressions were given various times to this feeling, Sister Geiger taking the lead in making the way possible. Brother J. W. Cline had been with us and had manifested a good deal of interest in the work of the church. He was then in Europe. I immediately wrote him to return to Philadelphia, that we had decided to start a mission and wanted him to take charge of it. When he came back to Philadelphia, he and I looked around in various parts of the city—south Philadelphia, and Kensington. Finally we decided on 26th St. and Lehigh Avenue as a suitable section. We rented a house at No. 2610 West Lehigh Avenue, and started a Sunday School, and the work prospered.[20]

The history of the Philadelphia Church of the Brethren, which has been voluminously described, abundantly illustrated the many problems Brethren faced in attempting to organize congregations and build churches in urban America. One type of urban development which was not too difficult for Brethren and in which they were quite successful was the assembling of congregations in cities surrounded by strong rural congregations. A good example is the city of Roanoke, Virginia. As early as 1892 Brethren were conducting worship services in rented halls in the city. In September, 1893 more than thirty Brethren organized a new congregation, First Church, under the leadership of Jonas Graybill, T. C. Denton, I. N. H. Beahm, and D. Newton Eller, all from the Botetourt congregation. Many Brethren were moving into Roanoke seeking work; within the first fifteen years, some three hundred members were received into this congregation by transfer of letter from other congregations. The first building was constructed in 1894 at a cost of $2,000; in 1906 and again in 1915 it was enlarged to meet the needs of a congregation of five hundred members.[21] *Obviously the Brethren were prospering in Roanoke.*

Another city where Brethren were able to establish a congregation with a relative minimum of difficulty was Hagerstown, Maryland. Three congregations—Manor, Beaver Creek, and Welsh Run—surrounded Hagerstown and contributed members to the city. The first public worship service was held in the fall of 1883, and by the end of 1884 the Brethren were dedicating their own church, built at a cost of less than $2,000. That the congregation was increasing in membership was demonstrated in an item in the **Gospel Messenger** *in 1890.*

In Hagerstown, Maryland, we have an example of what may be accomplished in our towns and cities. Thirty years ago we remember that the question of holding meetings in Hagerstown was discussed among the Brethren, and it was held by many that it was not best to do so. Later an effort was made, and the result is, that there are now about seventy-five members living in the city. They have a comfortable house of worship, which, at times, is crowded, and does not accommodate all who desire to gain admittance. Faithful, consecrated effort in the Lord's work will succeed in the end. Let those, who are struggling to establish churches in towns and cities, not be discouraged.[22]

A final step for a group of Brethren like those in Hagerstown was to declare their independence and organize as a separate congregation. This action was carried out in 1893.

The committee appointed to prepare and present this petition, for themselves and for the other members, say: They reluctantly ask to be separated from the congregations in which they live. They are loath to undertake the responsibilities of a separate organization, and make this petition for reasons given below.

FIRST,—They realize the necessity of an organization. There are about one hundred members living in town. The number is constantly increasing and the probabilities are that there will be a steady gain. For a number of years they have regularly held Meetings, Sunday-school, and Prayer Meetings. The expenses incurred have been almost entirely borne by themselves.

SECOND,—This work has been mainly carried on by the members in town. They have been compelled, although without authority, to assume the duties and responsibilities of an organized church. The ministers have had the work of ordained elders; the lay members much of that of deacons.

THIRD,—Much of the work can be most conveniently done by those living in town. It is impossible for the officers of the churches living a long distance away to be thoroughly acquainted with the needs of the members in the city. Members moving into town from other churches could hand in their certificates at once and be known and recognized as members. The members would be more closely bound together is belonging to one congregation, than they are by being divided among the three congregations. . . .[23]

The Hagerstown group thus became an independent congregation. It continued to grow in membership both by evangelism within the city and by the movement of Brethren into the city, reaching a membership of more than 1600 in the twentieth century.

In contrast to such cities as Roanoke and Hagerstown, where there were strong Brethren congregations in the rural areas adjoining the cities, numerous cities in the United States did not have such an advantage in establishing new Brethren urban congregations. Chicago in the late 1880s was typical of the cities into which the Brethren had moved, but no Brethren congregation had been organized for them to attend. These isolated Brethren sometimes were interested enough to contact other members or the church's periodicals. The **Gospel Messenger** *of 1890 included at least four different references to Brethren in Chicago. On April 22:*

There are now about fifty members of the Brethren church living in the City of Chicago. Of this number forty-five have handed in their letters. Members, living in the City or those contemplating moving there, should take letters with them and identify themselves at once with the church. The place of meeting is on Oakley Avenue, a few doors north of Harrison Street. Those, desiring to correspond in relation to the church, may address W. R. Miller, 420–22 West Van Buren St. We give this information by request.[24]

On July 8:

The Missionary Committee, of Northern Illinois, met at this place on the 30th ult. They found, upon looking over the money subscribed for the meeting-houses in Chicago and Sterling, that something over $2,000 had been raised,—about $900 for Sterling and over $1,100 for Chicago. Several of the churches in the District failed to report their quota. If all had done so, there would have been $2,000 reported for Chicago and $1,000 for Sterling. The Committee decided to urge the churches, that have not done so, to raise the amount so that the meeting-houses may be built. They made a call on the General Missionary Committee for help to build the Chicago house, but deferred the matter until their next meeting, when it is hoped that all the churches in the District may be ready to report their quota in full. The churches in Northern Illinois are doing well in the matter of giving to work of this kind and the Lord is blessing them. Brethren and sisters, let us now grow weary in well-doing, for we shall reap in due season if we faint not. The Lord's work demands our means. Let us give willingly and with a cheerful heart, knowing this that "he that soweth liberally shall also reap liberally."[25]

On August 5:

Bro. W. R. Miller,—to whom we referred to our former communication,—is the minister in charge of the Chicago church, and though he was only called to the ministry in the last year or so, he seems to realize the responsibility of the position to which he has been called by the church and manifests a disposition to take hold of the work and do the best he can. This is certainly a commendable spirit in Bro. Miller, and we trust he may experience God's blessing in the effort to do what he can to promote primitive Christianity in the great city of Chicago.

Bro. Miller is a comparatively young man yet, and, with proper application and dependence upon the grace of God for help, may become an efficient minister in our church. One thing, however, will militate considerably against Bro. Miller's usefulness to the church, for which he has been called to minister, and that is, he is enabled to give only his spare time to the church, owing to the fact that he has an extensive and growing business to look after, and to make both a success is hardly to be expected, unless Bro. Miller is a second Wanamaker. The men are rare, indeed, who can manage to run two things at the same time and make both a success. Bro. Miller is aware of this fact, and seems to be quite anxious that the Chicago church should have a good man to take general charge of the work and give his whole time and labor to the cause.

We could not help but think that this would be the better way to do, as we are convinced of the fact that our church, in the large towns and cities, ought to have ministers who can look after the interests and needs of the church in the pastoral and all other respects.[26]

On October 28:

A committee has been appointed to secure a suitable lot for building a house of worship in the City of Chicago. There are now fifty-five members living in the city, and we are glad to know that there is a fair prospect that a church will be built. Money enough has been raised to purchase a lot, and we believe the amount necessary to put up the house will be forthcoming. The members in the city have done well in raising money, but they are not able to build without help, and the help will come. Hard work and implicit trust in God will accomplish great things.[27]

The Brethren poured human and financial resources into the attempt to get a congregation established in the city of Chicago. As indicated in the July report in the **Gospel Messenger,** *the District of Northern Illinois was organizing the work in Chicago. However, the project was too significant and too demanding for one district to handle, and in 1894 the work was taken over by the national organization of the church. The General Missionary and Tract Committee included in its 1895 report to the Annual Meeting:*

Chicago.—This mission came under the care of the Committee one year ago, and since that time the Committee has been studying more closely the needs of the work here. To think of one mile square of the city, teeming with eternity bound souls, and not having one church, one Sunday school, or one mission within its limits, is appalling. The mission has been doing the best it could. Regular services were held throughout the year in the meetinghouse at 183 Hastings St., and a series of meetings in the winter; 7 accepted Christ and were baptized. During the year 4 were received by letter. W. R. Miller, the missionary, has now closed his business and will give his entire time to the work.[28]

W. R. Miller was considered the minister in charge of the Chicago work and was probably financially supported by the General Missionary and Tract Committee. Also, many volunteers spent time in Chicago contributing to the total effort. Much of their time was devoted to the children of the city, who were being encouraged to attend the Sunday schools established by the Brethren. The 1895 Annual Meeting Minutes included a report of the Sunday school work.

The mission conducts two Sunday schools each Lord's Day. The one is at 183 Hastings St., in the church, in the morning. This had an enrollment in October last of 65 and closed the year May 30 with 75. The average attendance is 62, and the collection, $31.82. The other Sunday school is in the afternoon, held in a hall at 180 Henry St. This school began with an enrollment of 35 and closed the year with 40. The average attendance was 36, and the collection, 75 cents.

Fig. 3. *Sod home in North Dakota, late 19th century. (BE)*

Fig. 4. *Hastings Street mission in Chicago, ca 1909. (BE)*

Besides the Sunday school work the two missionaries, sisters Alice J. Boone and Lizzie B. Howe, held 138 industrial meetings and 132 religious meetings during the week days, in which the life of Christ and other lessons from the Bible were taught. At the industrial meetings the children are taught how to sew, and at the same time instructed in general work. The missionaries also visited 800 different families, made 1,200 visits and distributed 1,500 tracts. The missionaries work among all classes and nationalities of children, and many are the touching scenes revealing misery, want and ignorance of a better life. The work especially commends itself to every one who wishes to help raise fallen humanity to a higher life, and now, that the General Committee has taken the work under its care, it is hoped that its needs will never go unsupplied.[29]

Several Brethren who were interested in Christian education in general and in Chicago in particular combined their efforts to produce a book in 1904 entitled ***The Chicago Sunday School Extension.*** *Grant Mahan prepared the Introduction.*

The great problem before the church is the evangelization of the world. And in order to reach a right solution of it the method of procedure must be carefully and prayerfully considered. How shall the church work, and where shall she begin? Those who live in the country think that the place to begin, and for those in the cities it is where they are. One fact is clear: The urban population is very great and the percentage is constantly increasing. This makes it evident that the cities must not be neglected; for if they are not Christian the country cannot be.

This belief has led our workers in Chicago to devise plans for winning souls from sin to righteousness. And they have begun at the right place-with the children, the boys and girls who in a short time will be the men and women of the city. Seeing on every hand the influences that drag down to ruin, they have sought to set in motion an influence which will lead up, build up, save. Being interested themselves, they have succeeded in interesting a large number of boys and girls throughout the country in the work. Contributions have been sent in, and new Sunday schools have been started. Only a beginning has been made; yet if the leaders in it accomplish the task which they have set themselves, a great host of boys and girls will be drawn from the vice of the streets to the house of God, there to be taught the truths which will make them wise unto salvation. It means much to the church, everything to these boys and girls; for the church will need them as workers, and they need a knowledge of the truth. They must not be left exposed to all the temptations which assail them on every hand. Stop on some corner and watch them, and then think what your feelings would be if your boy and girl were among them and the Christian people put forth no greater effort to save them from that which must bring death to both body and soul.

Millard R. Myers wrote the final chapter which included a section on the city.

THE CITY

We now come to the most important field for study, the great city. In another chapter of this book Brother Miller tells you about the great need for every kind of rescue work in Chicago. This great city of the West may be worse than any other in the land. Yet in every city there is great need for new Sunday schools.

There are many plans for making the city better, but most of them are intended for men and women rather than for children. Yet it pleases me to see how much attention the boys and girls are receiving the last five years. Wise men have learned that the best time to save a life is in its beginning. Someone has said, "Save a man and you save a soul; save a child, and you save a multiplication table." In other words, the soul of a man may be saved later in his life, but if the boy is saved, he has a whole lifetime in which to work for the cause of his Master.

In the cities we have schools of reform, prisons, and many rules, regulations and institutions which are good. They have a work to do. Our cities cannot be run without them. Yet of all the forces at work, the greatest to my mind in behalf of children is the Sunday school. The Sunday school takes the child through its Cradle Roll right from the mother's arms. When properly run, it keeps the child in its classes and leads him tenderly and carefully and naturally into the church. By and by, when the days of real work are over, and sickness or age keeps men and women at home, the home department carries the lesson there. So all through life the Sunday school works for the welfare of everyone.

But we praise the Sunday school most because of what it does for the boys and girls rather than for men and women. Could I have my way, I would start a Sunday school in every wicked block in every city. I would secure the names of boys and girls as soon as they were born, gather them into classes as soon as they were able to walk, and keep them in classes, though but half a dozen in a class, until they were too old and feeble to come.

THE SUNDAY SCHOOL PLAN IS THE BEST because it gets the children before they go wrong. A life may be reclaimed after falling into sin, but where one is saved thousands go on to ruin. On every hand, at every turn, in our cities, a hundred temptations stand ready to lure one on and on to destruction. Against these temptations the modern Sunday school rings out its cheerful song. Its kind teachers draw the pupils from the neglected homes of rich and poor alike. From the ranks of the Sunday school the children are stepping every day by hundreds and by thousands over into the church.

No one will ever know the great good that is being done by the faithful missionaries, teachers and superintendents who are going down the dark lanes and into the dismal homes in Chicago and other great cities to tell the old story of Jesus and his love. Only the angels in heaven can count the good that will be done through this great work.

Praise God for the boys and girls out in the country who are helping to make this work possible in Chicago, these children who have taken upon their hearts and into their hands the work of opening new Sunday schools here. For the benefit of those who do not know what has been done, I will give a brief history of the Sunday-school extension work in our city.

On Christmas, 1901, our main Sunday school in Chicago, numbering about 125 members, gave the children pocketbooks for presents. A bright nickel was placed in each pocketbook. The children were told that the pocketbook was for them to keep, but the nickel was not. They were asked to invest the nickel in anything they could and see how much money they could earn by Easter for the Master's work. How hard these little ones worked! They were not all little children either, for some of the larger ones took an interest. They ran errands, sold newspapers, washed dishes, and did ever so many things. One little girl sold potato peelings. By Easter time they brought into the treasury for extension purposes $25. This was called the Sunday School Extension Fund and was to be used for opening new Sunday schools where they were needed. The sum being small, it was thought best to make it larger before beginning any work. So a letter was written to the superintendents out in the country, explaining what had been done by the boys and girls in Chicago, and asking that the children in the country be given a chance to help on the free purse plan. In response to the letter several hundred purses were asked for by boys and girls in all parts of the United States. The country army went to work in real earnest and God greatly blessed them. Within one year from the time that the first bright nickel was given in the Chicago mission, several hundred dollars were in the Lord's treasury for the purpose of opening new schools.

Then our church in council decided that one new school should be opened. After a careful canvass of the city by districts a hall was selected on the South Side of the city, about nine miles from our mission at 183 Hastings Street. It was thought that the students who were attending the University of Chicago would help to carry on this school. This was proven true, and over seventy-five children have been enrolled in the new school in less than one year. The majority of these children would not have been in Sunday school anywhere had our new school not been started.

THE SECOND YEAR

Many purses were asked for the first year which were to be sent out the second year. So the second summer more purses were sent out than the first, and again during the long, hot days the little ones were toiling for the good of the boys and girls in the city, and when the returns came in the committee felt that Extension Sunday School No. 2 could be opened. This school was opened in a storeroom at 466 Van Buren street, a distance of one mile from the home mission. This school now enrolls nearly one hundred members. Through the efforts of our great work there are now enrolled in the Sunday schools of Chicago nearly four hundred children.

THE THIRD YEAR

Under the blessings of a kind Heavenly Father the Chicago Sunday School Extension Book was published and sent out along with the purses the third year. Some of the children took purses and many of them took Extension Books, and through their efforts large returns were received. These were fully reported in the April number of the *Missionary Visitor* of 1905. In answer to prayer God sent to the work three consecrated sisters, two of whom have worked faithfully in Extension No. 1, and one of them devoting all her time to Extension No. 2. Both of the schools have prospered and increased in attendance and zeal. Two manly boys have been baptized as a result of the work in Extension No. 1. The fourth year begins full of hope and promise.

In addition to the Sunday school we now have preaching and much other work in each of these places. Only our Father in heaven knows how many hundreds and thousands in the years to come will hear the Word of God through this work started by the boys and girls who believe in Sunday-School Extension—the basis of church extension in *every* city and EVERY LAND.[30]

Another major city in the United States where Brethren were attempting to establish a congregation was Washington, D.C. A report to the Annual Meeting of 1894 noted that a minister had located in the city and was holding meetings.

Washington, D.C.—The work of which this is a report began last June. Since that date Bro. Lyon held 74 meetings, having an average attendance of 27. Four were received by baptism. The total membership in the city is 24. The work is much retarded because the church does not own its own house of worship. People in the city have an aversion for worshiping in halls. To meet in Bro. Lyon's home does not give the impression of permanency of the work; hence the Committee has decided to make a special effort to raise funds to build a plain house of worship. This is greatly needed, and it is hoped that the brethren and sisters will respond liberally.[31]

The report of the following year indicated that the work was continuing, although the need for a meetinghouse was a major problem.

Washington, D.C.—Considerable interest has been awakened for this mission through the special call for donations to build a much needed meetinghouse; to date, however, sufficient funds have not been raised to justify the Committee to arrange for the house. Though the year has been a trying one in the city, yet the results have been encouraging on the whole. Bro. Lyon, the missionary, held 114 regular meetings, 15 special meetings, with an average attendance of about 40. One love feast and 2 council-meetings were also held; 4 were received by letter and 1 by baptism.[32]

The activity of the Brethren in Washington, D.C. illustrated the new interest in ministering to the needs of Brethren who were moving into the cities in the United States. This activity was an important part of the total geographical expansion in which the Brethren were engaged in the years following the Civil War. Another part was the development of new congregations in rural areas such as the Dakotas and across the international border in Canada. Clearly, the Brethren were growing in terms of geographical areas involved, in the number of congregations, and in total membership.

II
RELATION TO SOCIETY

Introduction

During the half century from 1865 to 1915 the relation of Brethren to the society in which they lived changed significantly and in many ways. The Brethren were in the process of shedding their sectarian garments and taking on the clothing of a secular world. Decisions regarding the garb of the Brethren provided specific evidence of this change. Another major aspect of change was the attitude toward government; Brethren became much more active in politics, including voting and office holding. A variety of changes are examined in this chapter.

Political Activity

One of the most basic political activities of any citizen in a democracy is to claim the right and utilize the responsibility of voting. However, Brethren had taken the position that voting might bring about the election of officials who would violate some of their basic beliefs with regard to military service. Therefore, it would be best if the Brethren did not vote at all. This policy was reiterated at the end of the Civil War.

Article 1. A number of questions being presented upon the subject of voting, and some asking for a repeal of former minutes, the following resolution, as an answer to those questions, was adopted.

RESOLVED, That we think it most expedient not to repeal any minutes touching voting; that this Annual Meeting recommends to the members of the church to refrain from voting, fearing that by voting we may compromise our non-resistant principles; but we recommend forbearance toward those who vote, not making voting a test of fellowship, hoping that in time they will see with the body of the brethren upon this subject.[1]

This policy of toleration was challenged on several occasions, as in 1869, but the policy remained unchanged throughout this period.

Art. 12. Shall we not determine, at this Annual Meeting, to make voting a test of fellowship? If not, then shall we not leave the whole matter to the decision of the brethren to do as they individually will, with all the discord and confusion we now have throughout the brotherhood?

Answer: We conclude to readopt the decision of the Annual Meeting of 1866, Art. 1.[2]

If some Brethren did choose to vote, since it was not a "test of fellowship," then the next question was whether or not Brethren could accept or campaign for political office. This question came to the Annual Meeting of 1866, as had the voting issue, and again at numerous later Meetings.

Art. 38. Can a man be received into the church, and hold his office as assessor?

We think we can not consistently with the gospel. John 18:36; Matt. 6:24.[3]

This answer seemed to suggest that a political official could not be accepted into the church, but it did not answer all of the questions regarding accepting political assignments, such as serving on a jury.

Art. 45. We ask this Annual Meeting to reconsider Art. 6, of 1864, and, if not changed, to give a more scriptural reason why brethren should not serve as jurors.

Answer: We advise our brethren not to serve as jurors when they can avoid it.[4]

The basic issue, however, was whether or not Brethren could campaign for an office, and if elected, serve in a legislative role. On this issue, the Annual Meeting refused to change the policy established before the Civil War, as in this decision in 1872.

Art. 22. We desire the Annual Meeting to reconsider Art. 3, of the minutes of 1844, and if the present answer may be adopted, then what shall be done with a brother who violates the decision? The query above alluded to, with the answer, are as follows: "Whether a brother may go to the legislative assembly, as a representative of the people, aggreable with the gospel?

"Considered, that though we look upon the higher powers of the world as being of God, for the protection of the pious, etc., and desire to be thankful to God for the benefit we enjoy under our government, and feel it our duty to pray fervently and daily for the same, we can not see how a follower of the meek and lowly Savior can seek and accept an office of this kind consistently with the gospel which he professeth. (See Matt. 20:25–28; Mark 10:42–46; Luke 22:25; John 17:16, etc.)" The query was reconsidered, and the following answer given by this meeting: Answer: We readopt the answer to the minutes alluded to, and consider that any brother who suffers himself to be elected to such office as that named, and to serve in it, can not be retained as a member of the church.[5]

One of the few politically-oriented positions the Brethren could accept was that of a postmaster, according to this decision of 1875.

Art. 9. Is it right for a brother to hold office of postmaster?
Answer: We know of no reason why he should not.[6]

The Brethren in Pennsylvania reasoned that a position related to the schools should be acceptable. The leaders of the Annual Meeting of 1876 had other ideas regarding such a position.

Art. 3. Is it agreeable to the gospel and faith, and order of the brethren, to hold the office of school director under the present laws of Pennsylvania?

Answer: We think it best for brethren not to serve in such capacity, where a school director, according to the laws of the state, may have to collect school-tax, and imprison a person if he does not pay his tax.[7]

Any use of force or of violence related to a political position was evidently what the Brethren opposed. The Annual Meeting of 1891 compromised the issue to some extent by placing the responsibility in the hands of the local congregation to decide what positions were acceptable by "Gospel principles."

22. Is it right, according to Gospel principles and decision of Annual Meeting of 1857, Article 30, for a Brother to hold the office of township trustee? If not right, what should be done with a local Church allowing the same?

Answer: We decide that Brethren should not ask or electioneer for civil office, or attend nomination conventions, but if they are elected without such efforts and the office is imposed upon them, they may, with the consent of their respective churches, serve, when so doing will not compromise any Gospel principles; and, further, we strongly advise Brethren to keep out of politics altogether.[8]

How this decision was applied in actual practice in the congregations was suggested in a letter from a leader of the Brethren in North Dakota to Galen B. Royer, a member of the national staff of the church.

"In behalf of the master's cause I write you. Here in the Pleasant Valley Congregation, N. D., we have a problem that is a little hard to adjust, especially unless there be advise from others too.

This is why my entering of the second year to try to lead this flock. The members have for as long as 8 yrs. successively held township office, such as treasurer, secretary and road supervisor and etc. etc., but have never been called into advise. Preachers deacons and laity holding of these offices. Now one of the deacons is on the run for the primary for County auditor. He has been from the Methodist faith and his former teaching has not been to astrange himself to office seeking, and has even held township office for 8 yrs in the midst of the brethren, and acted in full capacity of his office, but now since he is on the race for the county office it appears to some to now draw in the annual meeting ruling, but he is not inclined to give up the race. He intends to work the field but not illegally, as the manner of some is.

It has appeared that the rulings of annual meeting will soon throw us into anarchy worse than we have ever been before, unless there be some way provided that will turn the tide. Some things are therein stated that we may say every one is not heeding, and then on certain things be strict and cant give one bit is too inconsistent to be different from a pharisee.—It has appealed in my own mind to do the best things is not to stand in that brother's way, for he is trying to get on a better footing that he may move nearer the church. He cannot sell out where he is to any advantage and if he can get the office he intends to move where he may have church privileges. He is not able financially to leave his farm at present, and if we stand in his way we will lose him entirely, and he is a talented brother and can be of much use to us or any congregation where he may move.[9]

Royer's prompt response indicated his interpretation of the policies of the Church of the Brethren regarding holding political offices.

There are many inconsistencies and much looseness in the church. Tactfulness is what is needed. I can readily see what would happen if you would shut down on the deacon brother running for auditor when so many others have run for office, and filled the positions. I of course am puzzled how any of these offices could have been filled properly and not violated the rules of the church, or I should say the principles of the Bible. But they have served. I take it for granted that they were loyal to the truth and did not violate gospel teaching. These same ones should accord to the brother running for auditor the same privilege they have had. Suppose he is elected, the church will have to wait until he violates the Bible before they can find fault with him,—unless, however, and always all those who have served in office of every kind against the rulings of the church will voluntarily get up and make sincere apology for running and serving as such officer and ask the church's pardon for their own violation. If every member is agreed to do this, then perhaps you can begin closing down on the brother now.

How will you stop? The church can agree that after this brother has served his term that as far as that congregation is concerned she shall go on record as not allowing the holding office contrary to Annual Meeting decision. This perhaps can be brot about after proper teaching. When such a resolution passes the church strongly, then you can discipline the member who violates it. My opinion is I would have a talk with the brother, guard him against violation of church and gospel principles and get a promise from him that he will remain loyal

Fig. 5. *Fourth of July Sunday school picnic, 1914, Arcadia, NE. (BHLA)*

Fig. 6. *Governor M. G. Brumbaugh, Brethren minister and educator, at the executive mansion, Harrisburg, PA, April 6, 1915. (BE)*

to the Christ and his church, and then let him move on. He may strike breakers that he himself may not like. If he does not and he violates gospel principle in administering oath or enforcing against our non-resisting principles without the consent of the church, then you have something tangible to act upon.[10]

In addition to problems related to voting and office holding by Brethren, another problem of this type was the use of the courts by Brethren. In most cases, especially where there was strife or litigation, the use of the courts was forbidden. A decision of the Annual Meeting of 1867 set forth "the established usage of the church."

Art. 24. What is the established usage of the church in the use of the civil law in collecting debts, etc.? Is it altogether forbidden? If not, what is the extent of the privilege? If it is, can it be allowed for members, and especially ministers, to advise persons to sue, and publish a notice to their creditors that if their bonds are not paid when due they will be coerced by law?

Answer: We consider it is contrary to the gospel, as understood by the brethren, to use the civil law in collecting debts, or in any other case where it would involve strife or litigation. Friendly suits are admitted, when the case is decided to be such by the council of the church. But to advise others to sue, or to publish that we will sue, is inconsistent with our principles, and would subject a brother to the judgment of the church, according to the gospel. (See Matt. 5:40; Luke 6:29.)[11]

A similar issue came to the Annual Meeting of 1869, and again the basic objection to using the legal system was that Brethren could not use the courts "to compel men to do any thing."

Art. 7. Can a brother, consistently with the gospel, take the benefit of the law by getting up a petition to locate a ditch according to law, and thus compel others to ditch?

Answer: We consider it most in accordance with the gospel, and the general principles of the brotherhood, not to use the law to compel men to do any thing.[12]

Another form of compelling someone to take action by the use of the courts was the foreclosing of a mortgage. In 1871 the Meeting objected to such action.

Art. 21. Inasmuch as the Annual Meeting has decided that it is not proper to secure a debt by mortgage (See Minutes of the Annual Meeting of 1825, Art. 2), would it be proper for a brother to close such mortgage when the debt is not paid according to contract?

Answer: We have no objections for brethren to secure money by mortgage, but we can not advise brethren to close a mortgage by a process of law.[13]

Finally, in 1891 at the same time that the Annual Meeting was turning other types of political action over to the local congregations, it decided that Brethren could take whatever action received the consent of the church.

23. Is it according to the Gospel and the practice of the Church for a brother to go to law with unbelievers, in any case, to compel the payment of money, and how far may a Brother go in that direction? Is it right according to 1 Cor. 6:1–7 for Brothers to go to law with unbelievers, in any case, before a worldly judgment seat? If not right, what shall we do with members who will do so?

Answer: No member is allowed to go to law without first consulting and obtaining the consent of the Church.[14]

One final area of importance in the relation of Brethren to the government was traditional Brethren pacifism, known as nonresistance, which included rejection of military service. This belief had been tested thoroughly during the Civil War which had just ended in 1865. During the next fifty years, however, the United States was involved in no major wars. A minor conflict, the Spanish American War of 1898, lasted less than six months and was not long enough to have any significant impact on the Brethren. Consequently, not much emphasis was placed on pacifism by the Brethren during these years. On several occasions, the Annual Meeting did consider issues that were related to this subject. In 1874 the Meeting reaffirmed the Brethren position on peace.

Art. 2. Inasmuch as the public mind is awakened on the subject of peace, both among nations and societies, should not the church at large take notice of "the signs of the times," and teach more earnestly at this time this cardinal doctrine of Christ and the church?

Answer: We think the church should do so.[15]

The following year the Meeting refused to cooperate with other peace organizations but agreed that Brethren as individuals were authorized to support peace programs.

Art. 13. Will this district-meeting ask the Annual Meeting to adopt suitable measures to enable the church to co-operate actively with the peace association of America?

Answer: Our church itself being a peace association, we need not, as a body, co-operate with others, but we may, as individuals, give our influence in favor of peace.[16]

Perhaps one reason for the general decline in interest among Brethren on the subject of pacifism was the arrival of considerable numbers of Civil War veterans in the church. On two occasions problems related to these veterans reached the halls of the Annual Meeting. In 1888:

10. Does the general ruling of the Brethren church allow a brother to attach himself to, and become a member of, the association of the Grand Army of the Republic? And if it does not, what course should be pursued in dealing with a brother who is a member of that organization? This District Meeting does not admit of it, and any brother doing so should be dealt with according to Matt. 18:17.[17]

In 1890:

22. Since there is a growing tendency among our Brethren who were soldiers in the late rebellion to attend soldiers' reunions, to march with and participate in their exercises, we petition Annual Meeting to say whether it is right for Brethren to do so. And if wrong, would Brethren be allowed to visit old soldier friends?

Answer: We decide that it is wrong to attend such places.[18]

Evidently the church was willing to accept Civil War veterans as members and occasionally as leaders, but it did not want them to display their previous military experience.

As the era of the First World War approached, Brethren became increasingly concerned about the actions of the United States government. In 1909 the Annual Meeting agreed to ask its officers to write to the government expressing the Brethren concern about increased military expenditures.

9. The Fairfax church, Second District of Virginia, petitions Annual Meeting, through district meeting, to protest to the Congress and President of the United States against the ever-increasing expenditures for the navy and the enlarging of the same.

Answer: Request granted, and the officers of Annual Meeting of 1909 are empowered to draft such memorial in behalf of the church.[19]

In 1911 the church took an additional step by creating a new national committee, the Peace Committee, to keep Brethren well informed and to express the concerns of the church in this area.

6. Whereas, Among the various governments of the world, and between the different societies of these governments, there are continually arising differences which ofttimes result in the destruction of life and property, and

Whereas, Jesus Christ was heralded to the world as the Prince of Peace, and his followers are enjoined to follow after the things that make for peace, and

Whereas, the Church of the Brethren has ever held to the principle of nonresistance,

Therefore, We, the Wichita, Kansas, church, ask Annual Meeting through District Meeting, to appoint a committee of three brethren whose special business, it shall be,

First: To propagate and aid in the distribution of such literature as may be helpful to the better understanding as to the sinfulness and folly of resorting to arms in the settlement of differences;

Second: To use every lawful gospel means in bringing about peaceful settlements of difficulties when such may arise between governments or societies;

Third: To keep the Brotherhood informed, from time to time, through our publications, as to the true status of the peace movement.

We also petition Annual Meeting to appoint a brother who shall represent us at the next Universal Peace Conference.

Passed to Annual Meeting.

Answer: We grant the request to appoint the committee asked for, but do not think best to appoint a brother to represent us at the next Universal Peace Conference.

Committee: J. Kurtz Miller for three years, D. Hays for two years, W. J. Swigart for one year.[20]

The Annual Meeting Minutes of 1912 and of 1913 did not include any report of this committee, although the report included in the Minutes of 1914 was identified as the "Third Annual Report." In their first printed report of 1914 the committee acidly commented: "having thus far received no contributions, we, therefore, have no financial statement to make." The report indicated that the committee had written two letters to President Wilson commending him for his "peaceable methods . . . respecting the troubles now existing in the Republic of Mexico."[21]

By the time of the Annual Meeting of 1915, the problems in Mexico had become something of a sideshow for the United States as it watched Europe become involved in the First World War. The Peace Committee's report to the Meeting of 1915 included a series of resolutions.

Whereas, The Church of the Bretheren is holding its Annual Conference this year at a time when more than one-half of the world's population is engaged in the most terrible war of the ages, thus threatening the peace and happiness of the whole human race; Therefore Be It Resolved,

First, That we do regard this as a most opportune time to express our abhorrence of war, with all of its train of evils.

Second, That we do not consider this a fitting time for our government to increase her armaments and thereby arouse the suspicion of other nations. We hereby pray and beseech all who are in authority to resist the influence of militarism in our land.

Third, We stand for peaceful pursuits and pray that our President and his cabinet shall earnestly endeavor to keep this country out of the throes of war.

Fourth, We look with profound sorrow upon this war of wars, but prophesy that God will turn the wrath of man to praise him by giving to the whole world a higher conception of human brotherhood and the doctrine of peace and good will towards all men.

Fifth, We express the hope that the day may not be far distant when all of our prayers for peace may be gloriously answered in the name of our Great Prince of Peace![22]

In spite of such resolutions Brethren were really not very well prepared for the coming of war to the United States in 1917. Among the reasons for this lack of interest in pacifism was the fact that not

very much had been written on the subject in the years since the Civil War. The many debates in which Brethren had been involved considered baptism and doctrinal issues but not pacifism. A rare article in the periodicals discussed pacifism, but it was not a subject of general interest among the Brethren. About the only lengthy discussion of the subject was written in 1876 by J. W. Stein, entitled, "Christianity utterly Incompatible With War and Retaliation, being one of Twenty Reasons, for A Change in My Church Relations." As the title suggests, he had been for most of his life a Baptist and a minister at that, but he explained in the introduction his change to the Brethren. In a sixty-eight page treatise, he identified seven reasons for his conclusion.

I.
WE URGE THE DOCTRINE OF THE UTTER INCOMPATIBILITY BETWEEN CHRISTIANITY AND WAR, UPON THE GROUND OF THE VERY PACIFIC NATURE AND DESIGN OF THE GOSPEL OF CHRIST. . . .

"Blessed are the peace-makers for they shall be called the children of God," (Matt. v. 9). Peace is one of the essential fruits of the Spirit of God in opposition to the lusts of the flesh, (Gal. v. 22). One of the peculiar characteristics of the wicked is their proneness to violence and war. "Their feet," said Paul, "are swift to shed blood; destruction and misery are their ways; and the way of peace have they not known" (Rom. iii. 15–17). Some one has truly remarked, that, "to return evil for good is fiend-like;—to return evil for evil is beast-like;—to return good for good is man-like, but to return good for evil is God-like." "One grand design of the gospel is to transform men from the likeness of wicked spirits and perishing beasts, into the likeness of God—to confer upon them through the agency of the Holy Spirit a divine nature and image, and make them like unto Christ, the second Adam, "the Lord from Heaven," who is a "quickening spirit," whose mission was not to destroy men's lives, but to save them, (Luke ix. 56). The design of the gospel is to save; while war destroys. "Christianity elevates men; war debases and degrades them. Christianity blesses men; war curses them." Christianity promotes love; war promotes hatred. Christianity enjoins forgiveness; war inculcates retaliation and revenge. Christianity teaches virtue; war encourages vice. Christianity overcomes with good; war overpowers with evil. Christianity strengthens the bond of confidence between man and man; war destroys confidence and promotes distrust and suspicion. Christianity teaches gentleness and humanity; war produces intolerance and pride. Christianity promotes the financial, physical and moral condition of any people; war leads to famine, pestilence and crime. No mind unbiased and unprejudiced by false theology, can read the Saviour's sermon on the mount, and feel justified in feelings and indulgences of revenge and retaliation under any circumstances whatever. . . .

The gospel, with its constitutional principles and imperative requirements, is addressed to all men without distinction, exception or reservation. It enjoins (as a fundamental rule—an eternal and unchangeable principle,) universal, complete and uninterrupted love to both friends and enemies. The wilful disobedience or known rejection of this law, by *individuals,* or *nations* of individuals, or *governments* of the nations of individuals, is rebellion against God. Its obedience precludes all possibility of wars of any description or species whatever—hence the positive and inevitable conclusion i.e., *the utter incompatibility between christianity and war.* . . .

II.
WE URGE THE DOCTRINE OF THE UTTER INCOMPATIBILITY BETWEEN CHRISTIANITY AND WAR, UPON THE GROUND OF THE UNSCRIPTURALNESS, SELFISHNESS, CRUELTY, IMMORALITY, COWARDICE, BASENESS, INEXPEDIENCY AND INEFFICIENCY OF THE LAW OF RETALIATION AS A METHOD OF SELF-DEFENSE.

Many seem to regard the law of non-resistence as subversive of the first law of our nature, viz: Self-Defense. But by no means is it true. While the laws of nature are the laws of God, he has, and demands, a right to superintend and regulate them, not according to the wild and fiendish passions, suggested by his enemy and man's, but according to his own pleasure and wisdom, and in his law he has provided for the most effectual defense against aggression. "If thine enemy hunger, feed him; and if he thirst give him drink, for in so doing thou shalt heap coals of fire on his head." (Rom. xii. 20). If by appealing to the faculties and emotions, or by fleeing from crime rather than perpetrating it, or by employing physical force without inflicting injury upon an assailant, one may repel his attacks, it should be done; otherwise a martyr's death should exemplify the Saviour's law, and vindicate the pure principles of his holy religion. . . .

1st. *The law of retaliation is unscriptural.* According to Christ's law, the Christian cannot resent an injury, though it be death. No Christian should suffer as an evil doer, (such persons should suffer justly at the hands of civil law) but if engaged in his legitimate sphere whether seeking the good of others in disseminating truth, or by honest labor providing a temporal support, he be called to suffer, it will be for the sake of the truth and right, and then according to the special directions of the divine law, he cannot "return evil for evil, nor railing for railing." In doing such a thing he takes his life into his own hands and forfeits his Master's protection. . . .

2d. The law of retaliation is supremely selfish, cruel and immoral. While the child of God is prepared for the realities and solemnistics of death, the one who seeks his destruction is not, and to kill him would be to hurl him beyond the reach of all the means of grace peculiar to man's present probationary state, hence not only the selfishness but the extreme cruelty of the design and act. Is it not better for the Christian to die prepared than the sinner unprepared! Not withstanding the Christian might be more beneficial to society, yet in God's wisdom and goodness (and his children must imitate that goodness), he giveth life to the wicked here that they may repent and removes many from the stage of action, at times when it seems to us we are but poorly prepared to spare them. Yet his providences, however, inscrutable to us, are just and right. . . .

III.
WE URGE THE DOCTRINE OF THE UTTER INCOMPATIBILITY BETWEEN CHRISTIANITY AND WAR, UPON THE GROUND OF THE INEFFICIENCY OF WAR AS A JUDICIAL REDRESS OF INTERNATIONAL GRIEVANCES.

We do not expect to see war banished from the earth, until, the "God of this world" "the prince of the power of the air, the spirit that worketh in the children of disobedience," shall be deposed from his usurped throne by the approaching glorious advent of the "Prince of Peace." Hence we are not astonished nor dismayed when we "hear of wars and rumors of wars." We expect the bloodiest and most fearful of all wars, whose withering, blighting curses have corrupted and polluted the earth, to be in the future, but we want to warn our beloved ones lest they assist the "prince of darkness" and reap the threatening penalties which shall befall the ungodly and the votaries of anti-Christ, and to urge the unspeakable benefits which may accrue to the nations by substituting as far as possible international legislation for the arbitrament of the sword, through the benign and peaceful influence of Christianity, until the kingdoms of this world shall "become the kingdoms of our Lord and his Christ." In discussing my third proposition, I remark:

1st. *War is entirely unlike all the judicial processes of civil government.*

Such is war, and now we ask, wherein consists its resemblance to a process of Justice? Let us examine the question somewhat in detail; and first, the law, or rule of decision. In all controversies there must be some standard recognized by both parties; such a standard society has provided in the codes of law; and to these laws every dispute must be referred. The law is common to all, known beforehand to all, and ready for every one that may need its protection, or deserve its penalties.

Here is the hinge or helm of justice in society, whether civilized or savage, but is there any thing like it in war? I know we talk about the Laws of War; but what does the phrase mean? A set of principles to determine right between nations? No! they are only a string of rules to regulate their fighting, to prescribe how they shall inflict on each other all the nameless evils of war. Well do they call them laws of war; not laws of right or justice, but by-laws of crime, mischief and blood; rules to regulate violence and outrage, theft and robbery, murder and rapine, and conflagration. War acknowledges no law as an umpire. It appeals to the sword alone, to might as the only arbiter of right, and all its laws, like the rules adopted by a court just to guide its proceeding in the application of law, or like the etiquette of dueling which prescribes how the parties shall fight, merely determine the mode of appeal to this blind, brutal standard. Laws of War! as well might we talk of the laws of piracy, or of pandemonium! . . .

Glance next at the principle of reference, so essential to justice. Not the rudest court on earth allows a man to be judge in his own case; even savages insist on the reference of disputes to a third party. The maxim is universal. Expunge this principle, and there remains no security for justice. If you lay claim to what I regard as my own, we can settle the dispute only by referring it to umpires. Does war proceed on this principle? Does it forbid nations to decide each its own case, and demand a reference of their disputes to arbiters? No! They spurn the thought of submitting to the decision of others, and indignantly exclaim, "we can judge for ourselves; we understand our own rights, and shall assert them too at whatever hazards to those who may dare to cross our path." Just put this language into the mouth of a mob, or a gang of blacklegs, or a horde of pirates; and you see at once how it scouts all justice and claims a reckless, illimitable impunity in crime. . . .

3rd. *War multiples rather than recovers losses.*

Many have tried to justify the late civil war of 1861–5, upon the ground that it resulted in the emancipation of 4,000,000 slaves. But if we admit that the thing was good in itself, was there no better method for its accomplishment? It has been estimated that the government spent four times as much in waging the war, as it would have required to have paid the masters a good price for every slave and colonized them in good homes, while the south spent at least twice as much as it would have cost her to have accomplished the same, to say nothing of the precious lives sacrificed on either side of the fearful contest. A comparatively small part of the means expended on the whole, would have furnished homes, implements of industry, a year's provisions, good church and school buildings with faithful ministers and teachers to the whole colored population, and with tears of affection they would have given their masters the parting hand, while confidence, peace and prosperity would have pervaded the nation.

But, instead of this, the fearful loss of life, the wails of widows, the cries of orphans, the desolation of thousands of peaceful and happy homes, the desecration of many a holy altar, the loss of confidence, the development of vice, immorality and crime, the almost universal bankruptcy and the almost ceaseless feuds and strifes which from time to time agitate, threaten and embitter different sections, are the sad consequences of cruel and barbaric war. "But" objects some one "the Southern people could never have been induced to have abandoned slavery, not even for the best financial remuneration." I think differently, but suppose they could not. Has Christ ever authorized his people to put away sin and promote moral excellence by sin? by the sword? I know God permits sinners to punish each other thus. But suppose we should propose to a congregation of sinners, "If you dont do right we'll make you" and set about killing them in order to convert them to Christianity. How well, think you, we would succeed? Set up such a precedent and at once you subscribe to all the intolerant and oppressive measures of state churches which have driven our persecuted fathers to the asylums of America. Moral persuasion and spiritual force are God's instrumentalities for converting men from error. . . .

4th. *War is both unnecessary and impracticable.* Many persons who admit the correctness of the anti-war theory from a moral standpoint, turn right over and reject it upon the false plea of impracticability. A gentleman who recently listened to me discourse on the subject, said: "The theory is sound, but what can we do? If we disband our armies, call our fleet from the seas, and abandon all defensive measures as a nation, other nations will immediately overrun us." But I must insist on the fallacy of his objection. Divine truth and law cannot be impracticable, since infinite wisdom, goodness and power are engaged to supervise and sustain them. Man is but a worm; and every appeal from the wisdom of God, as in this case, only illustrates and proves his own madness and folly. Many appeal to our frontier settlements, and the depredations committed by the natives in the absence of protecting armies, to illustrate the absurdity of a nonresistant policy. But they overlook to a great extent the numberless, savage provocations, insults, outrages, and barbarities, which have been perpetrated against these untutored sons and daughters of our forests, by those who, under a cloak of religion and civilization, have often defrauded them, and in many instances driven them from the happy hunting grounds of their fathers, without the least remuneration. Had civil authorities made as strong efforts to bring to justice the mean white men who have incited them to deeds of violence and crime, as the military authorities have to punish them for such deeds, we believe the effects would have been much happier. Even the millions of dollars expended in subjugating the little tribe of Modoes, would have delighted every tribe in America with valuable presents, and have secured at once their confidence for a sufficient number of faithful ministers and teachers, whom the same wasted means would have amply supported. The former success of Wm. Penn's policy with the natives, proves how much more effectual Christian methods would always have been.

5th. War should be superceded by international legislation. This is worth the consideration of all nations and civil functionaries not only on account of reasons already submitted, but of those yet to follow. In fine, since the arbitration of international disputes is just, rational, possible and practicable,—since belligerents when exhausted by the sword, resort to arbitration as a final expedient—since the moral, intellectual and physical weal of nations are secured and promoted only by peace—since war involves all the ills that can afflict the human family, dethroning religion, conscience, reason and judgement, and developing all the vile passions of a depraved nature, trampling down morality, confidence, life and property, and utterly failing to secure the results at which its votaries aim; therefore by consulting the welfare of nations, rather than the honor of dynasties,—by looking after the good of subjects as well as sovereigns,—by encouraging and rewarding honest and productive industry—by urging kindly but faithfully and uncompromisingly that fundamental principle of our holy religion, viz: "Peace on earth, good will toward man,"—let us urge as far as our influence goes, at least the reduction of offensive and defensive measures, and the substitution in lieu thereof, of a "High Court of Nations" in which international differences shall be fairly and publicly adjusted as individual differences are, in common courts of justice. By such means the pre-millennial state of the nations can be at least greatly benefited and incalculable good be accomplished in behalf of precious souls.

IV.
WE URGE THE DOCTRINE OF THE UTTER INCOMPATIBILITY BETWEEN CHRISTIANITY AND WAR, UPON THE GROUND OF THE DREADFUL EVILS WHICH WAR INVOLVES. . . .

1st. War unbridles all the lusts and passions, of depraved and carnal nature. Hence it may be considered a combination of all evils and all crimes. Man, of whom it has been said, "How noble in reason, how infinite in faculties! in form and moving, how express, and admirable! in action, how like an angel! in apprehension how like a God!" is by war, transformed into a shameless, ravenous beast. There is no evil of which he is susceptible that war does not develop. Murder, theft, robbery, arson, rape and everything that is base and vulgar are indulged. When we think of burning cities, pillaged towns, savage lust, beastly intemperance, cruelty and murder mingling with groans and shrieks and piteous lamentations of the oppressed, and the fiendish shouts and imprecations of the oppressing, the peculiar attendants of invading armies, the heart sickens at the very thought; and I think the world may be safely challenged to furnish an invading army which is an exception to this general rule. I know that there have been many noble exceptions of individual character, whose virtues have been too pure, to allow the tarnish of a single stain, except the brutal work of slaughter in the hour of deadly conflict; but an army of virtuous men, equipped for human slaughter, has never yet been found. . . .

2d. War produces bereavements, without mitigations of any true consolation. Here foes hate, friends are forbidden to administer comfort in seasons of greatest extremity and suffering, while God, the source of all consolation, cannot look with any degree of approbation upon the dismal scene. . . .

But when we turn to the drooping, fainting, dying soldiers, far from home and friends, made the subject of derision even by his comrades who in their blunted and brutalized feelings, allude to him only in coarse and vulgar epithets, left on the march by his command, to perish and become food for beasts of prey or devouring vultures, or see him expiring in the crowded hospitals amid the mimicing jests of his wounded companions, or taken mangled from the field of slaughter and cast into the ditch without sympathy or decency, we have a spectable loathsome and harrowing in the extreme. Yet this is only a spectacle with which war and warriors are familiar. Such are the cruel mercies of war. . . .

V.
WE URGE THE DOCTRINE OF THE UTTER INCOMPATIBILITY BETWEEN CHRISTIANITY AND WAR, UPON THE GROUND OF THE INCALCULABLE MISCHIEF WHICH WAR PRODUCES.

1st. *War produces an enormous financial waste.* War and war equipments are crushing the nations with insuperable burdens. Millions upon millions of men, are not only thus taken from the pursuits of productive industry and transformed into mere consumers, but the enormous expenditures in preparing engines of death, to say nothing of prostituted time and talents, are involving the nations in hopeless bankruptcy. Working men with the hardest labor and closest economy can hardly provide a comfortable subsistence for their families because the governments are taxing them to their utmost capacity to support devouring armies, and the sovereigns of the nations, watching each other with suspicion, and, ever and anon, increasing their respective armaments, so as to be prepared for any emergency, know not where the evil will end, and can only hope for deliverance by each other's conquest, by which the plundered spoils of battle may be appropriated to the payment of the conqueror's debt, while the creditors of the vanquished must go away empty. . . .

2nd. *War imposes its heaviest burdens upon the Producing and Working Classes.* Under this thought I will simply transcribe the remarks of Prof. Washburn, of Harvard University. He says "It is the working men who constitute the rank and file of an army. It is their labor and industry that supply the sinews of war,—their money that is spent and wasted in carrying it on, and it cannot be impertinent to ask these men what they get for this expenditure? Take any of the wars which have been carried on in our day in Europe where such immense armies, under such renowned Generals have been engaged in slaughtering each other, in battering down cities and ravaging the country, and who, of all the hard-working, industrious classes, have been benefitted to the amount of a dollar? . . .

. . . Whatever is lost, by way of material consumed, railroads destroyed, fields wasted, and towns and villages burnt, are to be met and restored by new taxes and new levies, which the industry and bone and sinew of these working men are to supply. The King goes home in triumph, and carries with him glory and fame and accession of territory. The soldier goes home wounded and broken in health, to live on public charity, or, if he escapes these, to go to work again to help pay the debt of the war. . . .

3d. *War makes an appalling havoc of human life.* What are the pecuniary costs of war compared to the dreadful loss of life. . . .

. . . Dr. Dick, in continuing his review of the dread casualties of war estimates that eighteen times the present population of the earth have fallen in battle. O, earth! hast thou fallen but once in the flood of Divine vengeance and eighteen times by thine own suicidal hand? Again he estimates that since the creation of the world, fourteen thousand millions of human beings have fallen in the battles which man has waged against his fellow creature man. "What a horrible and tremendous consideration?—to reflect, that 14,000,000,000 of beings endowed with intellectual faculties, and furnished with bodies curiously organized by divine wisdom—that the inhabitants of eighteen worlds should have been massacred, mangled and cut to pieces, by those who were partakers of the same common nature, as if they had been created merely for the work of destruction! Language is destitute of words sufficiently strong to express the emotions of the mind, when it seriously contemplates the horrible scene." . . .

4th. *War destroys the morals and confidence of mankind.* In proportion, as man's intellectual and moral nature are superior to his physical being, so do the dread waste and degradation of moral character, and the awful havoc of principles of rectitude and truth, exceed all conception of bodily misery and the loss of life. War is demoniacal in its very nature, transforming men, not simply into beasts, but into fiends, and only demonstrating the scripture proposition that for the time being Satan is the "God of this world" the "prince of the power of the air, the spirit that worketh in the children of disobedience." We shall not dwell on the discussion of this thought here, as the moral evils of war have been discussed under our fourth general proposition. . . .

VI.
WE URGE THE DOCTRINE OF THE UTTER INCOMPATIBILITY BETWEEN CHRISTIANITY AND WAR, UPON THE GROUND OF THE VIEWS AND PRACTICE OF THE PRIMITIVE CHRISTIANS.

The immediate successors of Christ and the Apostles, for several centuries, abominated war as unchristian. . . . Such a sentiment, during the reign of Constantine, indicates that, even then, there was a general opinion that war and a high standard of Christian morality were inconsistent with each other. Until Constantine himself introduced among the churches of the Roman empire, a secularizing spirit, casting the treasures of the State into the lap of the church, and marshalling her armies in defense of religion, such an idea as Christians going to war, was held in horror and treated with solemn contempt by those who claimed to be the followers of Christ. Constantine may be regarded the instigator of that blasphemous idea, viz: "Christian Wars," and his posterity felt its smart. . . . Alas! that so many have followed Constantine's example; but the pure Christians of every age have refused the sword. . . . The same is true at this day of the Mennonites, Friends and others, as well as our own Brethren. But with shame, by way of contrast, we pause to record the humiliating fact that many of

2. *The professing Christians of our day are largely responsible for the withering, blighting curse of war.* Many of the ministers of Christendom are among the most zealous advocates of war and violence, most ready to resent indignities, and often lay aside the clerical garb for official uniform and distinction in military life. Many of the

churches are no better, educating their sons in military schools, teaching them the *science of murder,* patronizing war literature in the day school, the Sabbath school, and domestic circle, and applauding the wholesale murderers and plunderers of the human race as glorious heroes, justly deserving the praise and suffrage of mankind. Professing to be followers of the "Prince of Peace," they worship at the shrine of the first great murderer, the demon of war. Such a Christianity is greatly responsible for the wars that now devastate the nations. They teach war, they preach it, they advocate it, they practice it. If they would veto all its policies, and have nothing to do with the cruel designs of wicked and blood-thirsty men, and exemplify in word and deed and influence the gospel which they profess, vice would begin to hide its head, the battle-flag would be furled by nations called Christians, the olive branch of peace would pervade the nations; they would beat their swords into plow-shares and their spears into pruning hooks, nation would no longer lift up sword against nation, neither would they "learn war any more." . . .

The positive duty of God's children. Many are ready to admit the correctness of the peace theory, "but what can we do in the midst of this warlike world?" is the anxious enquiry of many a convicted mind. To this I reply that if we are Christians we must follow Christ and do our duty. Our words, deeds and influences must go against war. We must labor to promote peace and appeal to the governments to which we pay tribute, to grant us the privilege, as our government has kindly done hitherto, of exercising our faith unmolested. If this privilege is denied us, we must follow in the wake of prophets, apostles, and martyrs, "Counting all things but loss for the excellency of the knowledge of Christ Jesus, our Lord," and cheerfully submit to whatever destiny a Father's hand may guide, ever being careful to "obey God rather than Men." "What!" perhaps, asks some astonished reader, "die rather than fight?" Certainly. Was ever a Christian's life as dear to him as truth and principle? Shall the common soldier throw away his life for his king, and the "soldier of Jesus Christ" not count all things but loss for his divine Sovereign? Shall they risk *all* for a corruptible inheritance, and he not risk a *little* for one incorruptible?" He who esteems anything, life included, more than Jesus, is not worthy of Him, and he who will not deny himself, and take up his cross and follow Jesus, cannot be his disciple. (Luke, xiv: 26, 27, 33.) Let us, therefore, dare to know and do right, whatever it may cost, relying upon our divine Lord and His sovereign grace, remembering that "the sufferings of this present time are not worthy to be compared with the glory which shall be revealed in us," and when the bauble thrones, dominions, diadems, and sceptres of warriors and monarchs shall smoulder with their memories in oblivion, we may possess through grace, for Jesus' sake, "a far more exceeding and eternal weight of glory." Our *afflictions,* our *light* afflictions, which are but for a *moment,* shall work out for us, as one has truly paraphrased it, *glory;* shall work out for us a *weight* of glory; shall work out for us an *exceeding* weight of glory; shall work out for us a *far more* exceeding weight of glory; shall work out for us a far more exceeding and *eternal* weight of glory. . . .

VII.
WE URGE THE DOCTRINE OF THE UTTER INCOMPATIBILITY BETWEEN CHRISTIANITY AND WAR UPON THE GROUND OF THE CHARACTER OF EARTH'S UNIVERSAL EMPIRE, WHEN "THE PRINCE OF PEACE" SHALL REIGN.

When the debasing lusts of carnal nature, which produce war, will be greatly subdued, and hearts polluted and rendered satanic by demoniacal influences, will be purified by God's sovereign spirit, redeeming love, and transforming truth, then the true nature of the Christian religion will be generally understood and embraced by the inhabitants of our globe; and its pure principles, doctrines and precepts operate in regulating all international intercourse. Then shall be realized the poet's enraptured vision:

> "One song employs all nations and all sing,
> Worthy the Lamb, for He was slain for us.
> The dwellers in the vales and on the rocks
> Shout to each other, and the mountain tops.
> From distant mountains catch the flying joy,
> 'Till nation after nation taught the strain;
> Earth rolls the rapturous hosanna 'round."

"Then righteousness shall be the girdle of his loins, and faithfulness the girdle of his reins. The wolf, also, shall dwell with the lamb, and the leopard shall lie down with the kid; and the calf and the young lion and the fatling together; and a little child shall lead them. And the cow and the bear shall feed; their young ones shall lie down together; and the lion shall eat straw like the ox. And the sucking child shall play on the hole of the asp, and the weaned child shall put his hand on the cockatrice's den. They shall not hurt nor destroy in all my holy mountain; for the earth shall be full of the knowledge of the Lord, as the waters cover the sea." (Isa. xi: 5, 9.) "And he shall judge among the nations, and shall rebuke many people; and they shall beat their swords into plowshares, and their spears into pruning hooks; *nation shall not lift the sword against nation, neither shall they learn war any more.* (Isa. II:4.)[23]

BLACK BRETHREN

The black population of the United States during these years was often referred to as "colored people." A very small number of them became Brethren. A difficult problem arose with the use of the salutation, or holy kiss, which was universally observed among the Brethren as a greeting similar to a handshake. Consequently, relations between white and black Brethren were strained in some areas. The problem was sent to the Annual Meeting two years in a row, 1874 and 1875.

Art. 21. As there is not a uniformity of practice among the brethren in reference to saluting our colored members, will not the brethren in Annual Council give us a decision that will enable us to be one in practice, and not respecters of persons?

Answer: We think it best to make no change in this matter.[24]

Art. 27. Since the Annual Meeting has left it optional with brethren whether or not to salute colored brethren with the holy kiss, designing men are making capital of it against us. To obviate this, let the Annual Meeting reconsider that decision, and say that we make no difference on account of race or color; and this district-meeting asks the Annual Meeting to make no difference on account of race or color.

Answer: We grant the request, but should have regard to the former minutes of Annual Meetings upon the subject, and advise the brethren to bear with one another.[25]

Former decisions in 1835 and again in 1845 had stated that "if colored persons are once received as members into the church, the members should be at liberty to salute them in like manner as (we do) white members; at the same time having patience with those who may be weak in the faith, and cannot do so." Basically, the Brethren "considered, that inasmuch as the gospel is to be preached to all nations and races," then the colored person should be accepted on the same basis as a white person.[26]

On occasion a black brother was asked to preach. Related was the question of his status as a minister in the church. A problem of this type came to the Annual Meeting of 1871.

Art. 6. Whereas, the eastern district of Maryland has decided that our colored brother, Elias Fisher, be authorized to preach the gospel to the colored people, and since he was installed there have been exceptions taken to the manner of his promotion, will this Annual Meeting confirm the decision of the eastern district of Maryland?

Answer: In relation to the above case, it appears, from what this Annual Meeting has learned, that there has been a failure on the part of the elders in the district to authorize Bro. Fisher to preach, and owing to said failure, a brother in the second degree installed him, by the laying on of hands. As this was a departure from the practice of the church, we think it was very improper; and, while we recognize Bro. Fisher as a minister among us, we consider him only in the first degree, regarding the laying on of hands as conferring no official authority whatever.[27]

Another black minister in the Church of the Brethren was Sammy Weir, whose early life among the Brethren was described in an earlier source book. His ministry was to black Brethren in southern Ohio. To complete the story, Landon West described Sammy's ordination and death.

We have already noted many changes and events for one short life, but we have yet a few more, and they are of greater importance than those already given.

The first we name is that of the choice of Brother Harvey Carter to the ministry, on Wednesday, February 9th, 1881. The meeting was held at the residence of Brother Carter, in Frankfort, and was conducted by Elders Thomas Major and the writer; and while all seemed to enjoy it much no one present enjoyed it so much as did Brother Sammy Weir. And it is not at all to be wondered at, for after a period of thirty-two years in the ministry, separate and alone, he now felt that he had an assistant in the work. None of us can know what the poor brother's feelings were, and none but God can tell how grateful he felt in the thanks he gave.

And it was at the same meeting, and on the day above given, that Sammy was ordained an Elder and was given the full ministry. This position—the highest and best the Church can bestow—was here given to one as well worthy to receive it as we need now to look for. This gave to Sammy the oversight of the colored members in the Scioto Valley, and while he lived but a short time to enjoy his position, yet we feel that none who may ever enjoy a membership in that district, need ever to feel ashamed of their first elder. . . . After his ordination, in 1881, he did but little more in public life, for his days were ending. He, with Brother Carter, kept up their meetings regularly at Frankfort, and occasionally at Circleville, where the work had begun; but Sammy's desire now was to leave his house and lot as a donation to the colored people for a church. But there being a debt unpaid and a mortgage on the lot, and his health failing, he felt that he must give up in despair unless God would aid him in this also. And so here, as all along the way, the Strong Arm was seen just at the right time, and Brother William D. Mallow of Ross County, assumed the debt, and Sammy's life was left to close in peace, and at his old home.

Of his Bible, he at one time spoke to me as follows: "After I had learned to read, I got a large Bible, and read it through several times. And the Methodist preacher here having no Bible, I loaned him mine, and he POUNDED IT TO PIECES." The Bible was in scraps, and the matter being stated to the sisters of the Lower Twin Church, of Preble County, Ohio, they made him the gift of another Bible. And at the close of the Love Feast held at Frankfurt, November 9th, 1883, and the last one Sammy attended before his death, the gift was presented to him, with a statement as to the ones sending it. He accepted it gladly and with tenderness said: "I am very thankful to them for it, and all I can do to pay them is, I can pray for them."

I now pass on to speak of his death, the greatest event of his life. His time was full of important changes, and all for the better, but this, the greatest of all, I have no power to describe, for I know not yet the glory to which he has gone. But I feel that that change was also for the better, for Sammy had nothing to lose by dying; it was all gain to him.

His last illness was Gangrene, and began in December, 1883. And learning of his sickness, Brother Henry Frantz and the writer, with Brother Mallow, visited him several times in February, 1884, giving him farewell March 1st, and did all that was possible to cheer him in

Fig. 7. *Advertisement in the* Brethren's Family Almanac, 1897.

Fig. 8. *Daniel P. and Sarah Rohrer Sayler. (BHLA)*

Fig. 9. *E. Landon West. (BHLA)*

Fig. 10. *James May, an early Black Brethren minister. (BHLA)*

his last days on earth. And during these calls, many of the items herein given were obtained directly from him.

Brother Mallow met him last on the morning of his death, and gave him Farewell for the last time. Brethren Carter, Jones Sowers, and Sister Carter, were his attendants night and day until his death, besides many others in and around Frankfort, who visited and cared for him as the day of his life was drawing to its close.

He seemed at all times fully resigned to the will of God, and left the world, being at peace with all its people. He went down slowly, but patiently and fell asleep at 9:00 a.m., on Saturday, March 15th, 1884. His age was 71 years and 11 months.

His funeral on Sunday, March 16th, was attended by many friends of both Races and the sermon was delivered by Brother Mallow, from the words: "Thou shalt come to thy grave in a full age, like a shock of corn cometh in his seasons." Job v. 26. The Brethren at Frankfort, not yet having a church house, the colored Methodists gave theirs for the occasion.[28]

Landon West, the author of the story of Sammy Weir, had a longstanding interest in black people. At about the same time that the Weir tract was being printed at the Normal School Steam Press in Tuskegee, Alabama in 1897, West was also having printed a broadside calling for Brethren assistance in ministering to the needs of black people.

OUR APPEAL

TO THE BRETHREN AND SISTERS, WHO WISH THE KINGDOM OF GOD TO COME, BOTH IN OUR LAND AND IN ALL THE WORLD, I SEND GREETING AND ASK:—

That in as much as the Mission Work among the colored people, has, by our church, been left for years almost entirely in my hands, therefore I now call for helpers, either Brethren or Sisters, or Friends, in any of the states or nations, to aid in showing forth the way of Truth and of Life to that long-neglected Race. And needing aid for the printing and sending forth of Tracts to the many names now sent me and from nearly all the states and from Africa, I ask that all who can aid me spread the work, write as to what they can do and where they can work, and those who feel to aid with gifts for this work, for the nation and for the Redeemer's Name, let them send to the undersigned, for eight millions of souls are an item in any nation.

With love to all,

I am yours as ever,

LANDON WEST.

Lanier, Preble Co., Ohio.[29]

Evidently West's appeal did not go unheard and during these years Brethren responded in a variety of ways. For example, A. W. Vaniman was sent to Atlanta, Georgia, about 1898 to establish a mission among black people. In 1899 the Vanimans were recalled because the General Missionary and Tract Committee wanted further guidance on what policy to follow. Nothing happened in response.[30]

In 1903 specific action was taken by the Committee to open a mission among black people at Palestine, Arkansas. A black woman named Mattie Cunningham was attending Manchester College, and her father was contributing each year to the Committee to make possible a Brethren mission to his people. According to the minutes of March 13–14, 1903:

Colored Mission

That Sec. & H. C. Early be appointed to formulate plan and arrange for sister Cunningham to take up the work.[31]

At this location a Brethren elder, J. H. Neher, was presiding over a white Brethren congregation and would be available to oversee the work. The proposal was expanded in September by recruiting a black Brethren minister from Ohio named Mays to accompany Miss Cunningham. His place was soon filled by a local recruit, D. C. Clark, and the Committee agreed in August, 1904, to provide financial support for his work.[32]

The next step was the decision to establish an industrial school. In 1905 the Committee took the necessary action:

Industrial Work for Negro

Decided that bro. H. C. Early with suitable assistance, and sister Mattie Cunningham raise at least $15,000, which amount shall be used to open up a christian industrial school for the negro.

That S. F. Sanger, H. C. Early and T. C. Denton be committee on location.

That H. C. Early prepare a plan for opening and developing the school.

That the Secretary be authorized to get out suitable blanks and stationary for the prosecution of this work.[33]

The evidence indicates, however, that not very much money was secured for this project and it never got beyond the planning stage. The return of Miss Cunningham to her home and the death of Clark resulted in the closing of the mission in 1909 and the sale of the property.[34]

At the same time that Brethren were closing the project in Arkansas, they became interested in another project in Colorado. Galen B. Royer was asked to investigate the matter for the General Mission Board and reported in a letter to the chairman.

Yesterday, I went carefully over the colored situation for which I was called. I was out to see their "shak" quarters in Denver and took several photos. The situation is this. About seven years ago Mr. Rhodes, now 35 yrs old opened up a Home for orphan and old colored people in Denver. He made it a matter of prayer and labor. He gets between $12 and $15 per week in Shipping clerk in a wholesale jeweler store. He lives on as little as possible and puts the balance in the support of his Home. He took elementary educational work at Roger Williams in Tennessee and finished his Normal work at Louisville, Ky. His work grew very well. Friends supported it. Four years ago he needed a matron and secured a woman, Mrs. Campbell, a grass widow as I understand and a woman of splendid talent and good face. She directs the home successfully. Starts it in the morning, then goes out and does a day's work and brings that wage home to support the Home—"give them daily food," as she says. Today they have 23 children and 4 old helpless people in their home. One old lady sick for two months, blind, is there under their Christian care. Something over two years ago Bro. Crist who was in Denver dropped in on these people and they asked him to speak to them. He was urged to return. These people accepted our faith and we now have 21 colored members.

Denver has about 10,000 colored people. It is a northern town and necessarily these people must show more thrift than is necessary say in Alabama, and they do. This is especially true of the two who are educated. There is an intelligence and humility in both that impressed me much. Bro. Rhodes has it in his head to give a Christian education to these orphans with the hope that some of them will go to Africa to redeem the race there. Indeed I was deeply impressed with the wisdom of such a course, slow as it may appear to me at first. Further, he is affording an open door to secure workers for the colored field in America. The district board seeing this opportunity as you know wants one of two things; the Board take and foster this movement or else give permission and encourage the brotherhood to take up this work. What they need is a small farm out of Denver for their orphans and a mission station in Denver to carry on their work among the colored people. Our Board will have a chance to spend our opinions at least on the matter in hand.[35]

At its December 21, 1910, meeting, the General Mission Board responded to the situation in Denver:

Colored Work—Denver

(a) That we cannot, as a Board, establish the Institution petitioned for by N. W. Kansas & N. E. Colorado.

(b) That the matter be deferred until April Meeting and Secretary to corresponde with N. W. Kansas & N. E. Colo. Board and report at that meeting.

(c) We allow $300.00 for the Denver colored work.[36]

To which, A. C. Daggett, chairman of the district mission board, responded:

We have arranged with Sister Camble (Matron) to give three days per week to Mission work among the Negros. I surely think the good Lord directed this, so as to get this matter before our Board meeting Feb. 14. I wrote Sister Camble and to my surprise she had been working out some this winter to help support the home.

She seemed to be overjoyed at the thot of her doing Mission work among her people. She had been praying for that opportunity. You remember your Board gave us 300 for Collored work. We are paying Sister Camble 1.00 per day and expences so she will have something to turn in at the home. Can you arrange to send her some tracts? 873 Zuni St., Denver, Colo.

Bro. Rhodes is so worried about their location[.] when he heard of our Board meeting he came to Quinter Kans to meet us[.] it seems those runing that building realize our Church is helping and they are demanding more money. City water must be used. You see they use lots of river water and the health officer has taken the matter up, and then those boys are idle.

I tell you Bro. Royer when you have some one come before you and plead for his people, and then we not able to help, it made us ask God for help. . . . We feel sure that your Board will place this before the Brohood. I am quite sure our Bre[thre]n will respond, if we have a chance to send some one to them who they can trust.[37]

The General Mission Board did indeed respond at the April, 1911, meeting:

Denver Colored Work

Bro. A. C. Daggett, of Kansas, was present and presented the work at that place.

Decided that the District Mission Board of N. W. Kansas & N. E. Colo. be authorized to solicit the General Brotherhood for $15000 for Colored orphanage and Mission Training School at Denver, Colo., and if plan should fail, the money received is to be returned to General Mission Board.[38]

The district board accepted this challenge, and by July, 1911 "40 acres of land in the suburbs of Denver" had been purchased and "their family of some twenty or thirty" had moved to this tract which had "a house and some fruit." This report, written by J. H. B. Williams in the Elgin office, concluded that "This promises to be a permanent establishment and we think will count for much in time to come."[39] Williams' prophecy, unfortunately, did not prove to be correct. Evidently the project was more than the district could handle on a permanent basis. In 1913 the district asked the General Mission Board to take over the project, which it refused to do, and the project subsequently closed. The final chapter was written at the Board meeting of August, 1914:

Denver Colored Work

The Board takes over the Denver Colored House Property at $8000.00.[40]

After these two abortive attempts to establish missions among black people, the General Mission Board was convinced that this type of project was not workable. However, the Board received additional requests for work among blacks. In 1913, it responded to a request to establish a mission in Texas, for there were black people desiring to be baptized as Brethren.

It is our policy to try and care for those who desire baptism, but we are not in a position to take up mission work among the colored people, further than to administer baptism to those desiring it.[41]

Finally, the attitude of the Brethren toward blacks seemed to have been well sumarized by Galen B. Royer in a personal letter.

. . . There is no question about the bible being that all are equal both in race, color and so on. That takes no argument. But while created equal and our ideal is equality thru Jesus Christ, two things follow.

First. Equality does not necessarily mean a mingling in social lines. Intermarriage is regretted by all and yet your arguement would advocate that. The very nature of the case means in a sense separation within certain bounds for the better progress of the good to be accomplished.

Second. It is very rare that the colored man wants to mingle with the white man any more than the white with the black. It may be the blacks are as far wrong as the whites; but shall we destroy the good accomplished because of this absolute stand to be taken? Bro. Rhodes is a fine man, has a good view of life and its problems. He says that race distinction is inherent and the best progress is made when we submit to that which cannot be removed. . . .

Would you recommend going into Alabama as a white person to do mission work among the colored people, salute them, mingle with them socially as one of them, when this very act would destroy your influence among both blacks and whites? I believe not. It is the ideal I know. It cannot be worked now; perhaps some day it can be, and then you and I will welcome that day if we are still alive.

Your view is not one of error. My reply is not wrong in this. I do not reject the ideal but work towards it on the plan that a soul begotten into the kingdom under the recognition of racial lines is better than that soul lost because the lines were not recognized. . . .[42]

SECRET SOCIETIES

The question of Brethren relations with American blacks was primarily racial, but another issue—how Brethren should deal with members of secret societies—was clearly a white issue. As was the case with most questions involving Brethren relation to society, the Annual Meeting on several occasions was queried about the Brethren and secret societies. For example, in 1869:

Art. 6. As our fraternity disapproves of its members joining the Masonic order, and all secret societies, when a report is in circulation that some of the brethren belong to some such society, and the nature of the case being such that it is very difficult, if not impossible, to obtain testimony to prove the charge, has the church, under such circumstances, a right to question the brethren charged relative to the truth of the report, and if it has a right to do so, and exercises that right, and the brethren refuse to answer, what shall the church do?

Answer: Under the circumstances alluded to, we consider that the church has a right to question the brethren, to ascertain whether the report is true, and we think such brethren owe it in honor to themselves, and in justice to the church, to give a direct answer upon the subject, and failing to do so, they throw themselves liable to be dealt with as offending members.[43]

Apparently one reason for the problem in the church was that people were being taken into membership who were already members of secret societies. To solve that problem, the church decided in 1870 to make certain that individuals being baptized as Brethren were not members of secret societies.

Art. 12. Would it not be prudent, since secret orders, such as Freemasons, Odd-Fellows, etc., are becoming more and more prevalent, to ask every applicant for baptism whether he belongs to any secret order?

Answer: We consider it necessary and prudent to do so.[44]

Another question was the determination of what groups were secret societies. For example, were the Patrons of Husbandry, popularly known as the Grange, such a forbidden group?

Art. 8. Can the church tolerate a member in the body that is a member of the society or order called Grange or Patrons of Husbandry?

Answer: No brother or sister should have any thing to do with such an order, it being a secret-bound, and from appearance, a political association; and members who have united with it, and persist in it, should be dealt with as transgressors. (See Minutes of the Annual Meeting of 1870.)[45]

What probably happened over the next forty years was a relaxing of the restraints on Brethren activity in some secret societies according to the decisions of local congregations. Now and then some congregation or its leaders would become disturbed by what was happening in its own membershp or in that of a neighboring congregation and petition Annual Meeting for a reconsideration of the issue. In 1895 the Meeting restated its position on secret societies.

13. We, the members of the German Baptist Brethren church at Brownsville, petition Annual Meeting through District Meeting to say what shall be done with Brethren who aid and abet secret societies, and let their houses for lodges for Freemasons and sympathize with them generally.

Answer: Brethren who do so shall desist, and if they refuse shall be dealt with according to Matt. 18:17. See Eph. 5:11.[46]

PUBLIC PLACES OF ENTERTAINMENT

In addition to the temptation of joining a secret society, Brethren were also influenced by the availability of all kinds of public places of entertainment. The Annual Meeting had established a policy of prohibiting Brethren from going to "places of merriment" which was restated in 1871.

Art. 24. Whereas, it is generally understood by the brethren, that members of the church are not permitted to attend places of merriment, such as state and county fairs, celebrations, circus shows, mass-meetings, and political conventions, etc., and as we can not find any thing in the minutes on the subject, a decision from the Annual Meeting is desired.

Answer: We consider that the answer given by the Annual Meeting of 1859, Art. 14, covers and applies to all the cases referred to in the query. The answer to Art. 14, in the minutes of 1859, reads as follows: "Such brethren should be admonished not to attend such places; and if they still persist in doing so, they should be dealt with according to Matt. 18."[47]

On occasion the Meeting was asked about specific types of entertainment. For example, in the 1880s it was the skating rink.

II. Whereas the Skating Rink has become a popular amusement throughout the country, Resolved, that we look upon it as an evil endangering the morals of those who frequent them, and that our ministers are urged to warn the people against them.[48]

In the 1890s, it was the Chicago World's Fair.

We petition Annual Meeting through District Meeting to advise all our members not to attend the World's Fair at Chicago.

Answer: Petition granted.[49]

An interesting problem was the private party which Brethren might hold in connection with a work-day, like wood-chopping or quilting.

4. Since members are not to attend fairs, political meetings, etc., (p. 293 Classified Minutes), and since some brethren have wood-choppings and quiltings on the same day, and these gatherings lead to a party in the evening, at which various plays are engaged in, will District Meeting ask Annual Meeting to give us a decision? District Meeting decides that it is wrong for members to allow or take part in such plays. 1 Cor. 10:7.[50]

By the twentieth century the county and state fairs were becoming increasingly educational in value because of the large number of exhibits. Consequently it seemed desirable to some Brethren to attend such fairs to learn from their exhibits. The Annual Meeting was concerned about the entertainment features of the fairs and was convinced that in order "to maintain the purity of the church" Brethren should avoid such places.

5. Indian Creek church requests Annual Meeting through district meeting, that inasmuch as there are features about county and state fairs that are not objectionable, and many members wish to avail themselves of their benefits, can they be allowed to do so, if they avoid the foolish and unbecoming?

Answer: We renew our protest against members going to county and state fairs (see Minutes of A. M., Art. 29, 1853, Art. 14, 1859, page 124 of "Revised Minutes of Annual Meeting"), and include World's Fairs as well, and therefore, in order to maintain the purity of the church, we urge upon our faithful ministers everywhere to teach and admonish members not to attend such places.[51]

PERSONAL RELATIONS

Finally, the Brethren's relation to society in general was reflected in many aspects of their personal life. The use of tobacco and of alcohlic beverages was frequently a matter of concern of the Annual Meeting. The Annual Meeting of 1870 continued the condemnation of the use of tobacco.

Art. 20. Since the Annual Meeting has, at different times, decided against the excessive use of tobacco (See Minutes of 1864, Art. 19), but the object desired has not yet been realized, we therefore ask this district-meeting to suppress its use altogether, except for medicinal or mechanical purposes, and to deal with such as use it according to Matt. 18, as we consider it proper to deal with members for wearing fashionable garments. Minutes of 1863, Art. 3, and Minutes of 1866, Art. 27. The district-meeting favored the request, and sent it to the Annual Meeting.

Answer: This Annual Meeting renews its disapprobation of the use of tobacco, and especially at the time and in the place of divine worship, and believes it should be classed with other vain and useless things.[52]

In 1886 the Meeting explained why the use of tobacco was condemned and also asked Brethren to refrain from selling it.

XI. Since the use of tobacco is acknowledged to be a waste of the Lord's money, productive of disease, and degrading the functions of the body so as to shorten life, would it not be in conformity with the spirit of the Gospel lovingly to admonish and advise all our brethren to abstain from the sale of that which is decidedly injurious, thus showing a proper light to the world, and throwing their influence on the side of right and of God? District Meeting asks Annual Meeting to so advise.

Answer: Annual Meeting grants the request.[53]

In 1889 the Annual Meeting took somewhat more drastic action with regard to the use of tobacco at Annual Meeting.

10. Berkley church, Western Maryland, petitions Annual Meeting through District Meeting that no delegate to Annual Meeting or member of the Standing Committee be accepted as such unless he abstain from the habit of using tobacco.

Answer: District Meeting grants the requests and Annual Meeting passes the same.[54]

This decision was extended to buyers and sellers of tobacco in 1896.

7. (Salem church, Southern District of Ohio.) We petition Annual Meeting through District Meeting to reconsider Art. 10 of Minutes of Annual Meeting of 1889, and so amend, that no delegate to Annual Meeting or District Meeting, or member of the Standing Committee be accepted as such who uses, raises, buys or sells tobacco.[55]

Thus the Annual Meeting was doing about as much as possible to control the personal habits of the Brethren in the use of tobacco.

The personal use by Brethren of alcoholic beverages was also a concern. Because of the increasing condemnation of the use of alcoholic beverages, some Brethren wanted to join temperance societies; however, the Annual Meeting did not see any need for such action.

Art. 13. Inasmuch as the church of the brethren has always endeavored to maintain the principle of temperance, will the brethren composing this Annual Meeting admit that members may join a temperance society, in the present form such societies take, outside of the church?

Answer: As our brotherhood has, again and again, taken decided ground against intoxicating drinks as a beverage, and recommended

Fig. 11. *Cigar making near Harleysville, PA, ca 1900–1910. (BE)*

Fig. 12. *Youth group of the Covina congregation, southern CA. (BE)*

to the brethren to abstain from their use as such, we see no necessity of joining ourselves to any other organization; and, therefore, we cannot allow brethren the privilege of doing so, but renew our solemn protestation against the use of intoxicating drinks as a beverage, and consider it the duty of every member of the church to use his influence against them.[56]

In addition to refusing to allow Brethren to join temperance societies such as the Women's Christian Temperance Union, the Annual Meeting also initially rejected the idea of officially petitioning the United States government to enact any kind of prohibition law.

VII. In as much as the use of ardent spirits cause much trouble and misery in our country, and we as a body of Christian believers advocate temperance and oppose the use of intoxicating drinks. Will not this District Meeting ask Annual Meeting to petition the General Government to enact a law to prevent the manufacture of ardent spirits, and to prevent the importation of the same into the United States.

Answer: Considered best not to petition Congress as requested, but we should continue to labor earnestly in the church against this and all other evils.[57]

Since the Brethren officially refused to associate with temperance societies and the prohibition movement or to put pressure on the national government to enact prohibition laws, they were sometimes accused by outsiders of not believing in temperance. This problem was considered by the Annual Meeting of 1889.

5. Consideration of Prohibition query was taken up, and the following unanimously passed: Whereas, in the consideration of query No. 2 from Western Maryland, there unfortunately obtained a misunderstanding among our brethren, producing very unsatisfactory results by creating a wrong impression as to our position on the subject of Temperance, therefore, Resolved, that this Annual Meeting recommend that all our brethren carefully maintain our position against the use, or toleration of intoxicants, whether to manufacture, to sell, or use as a beverage, and to the extent of our influence contribute our part to secure practical prohibition; but that we advised against taking part in the public agitation of the subject.[58]

Although the Brethren tried to make as clear as possible their opposition to the use of alcoholic beverages and their support of prohibition, as late as 1900 they were refusing to engage in any kind of political pressure.

5. Will not District Meeting of the Southern District of Indiana ask Annual Meeting to reconsider Art. 7 of 1884, page 215 of "Classified Minutes," and change answer to read, "We petition the General Government" as requested in said query?

Answer: While we do not make the change asked for, yet we do reaffirm the temperance principles of the church and put ourselves on record again as opposed to the manufacture and sale of intoxicants for beverages, believing that it is the duty of the Christian church to mould temperance sentiment, without which no law can become operative. We urge the greatest possible efforts of the church to create such sentiment. We also pray that our civil rulers may rise to the Gospel standard on this question.[59]

Brethren finally came to believe that some type of action needed to be implemented with regard to the prohibition movement, which was gaining ground rapidly in the United States in the early years of the twentieth century. In 1907 the Annual Meeting agreed to establish its own temperance committee.

12. Believing that the general opposing sentiment of the Brethren church toward the evil known as "intemperance" is right in its principle, and, believing that a further organized and concerted effort on the part of the church as a whole, can accomplish still greater results favorable to its sentiments; therefore,

We, the Altoona church of Middle Pennsylvania, petition Annual Meeting, through district meeting to appoint a committee of three, to draft a plan for creating and maintaining, through the approval of Annual Meeting, a permanent temperance committee, for the purpose of rendering service to the Brotherhood in defending their homes against the invasion of this evil, by providing for a temperance sermon at Annual Meeting, encouraging district organization in order to awaken and strengthen expression among our members, young and old to select and distribute tracts and helpful literature or any method looking to the end contemplated that meets the approval of the committee and Annual Meeting.

The committee named at this meeting, to report its proposed plan one year hence.

Passed and sent to Annual Meeting.

Answer: Petition granted. Committee: W. J. Swigart, J. W. Lear, J. A. Dove.[60]

The committee submitted a detailed plan of action to the Annual Meeting of 1908.

Report of Committee

To the Annual Meeting of the German Baptist Brethren in Conference, assembled at Des Moines, Iowa, June 9–11, 1908, Greeting:

We, your Committee, appointed by Annual Meeting of 1907, to formulate a plan for creating and maintaining a permanent temperance committee, realizing that it is the duty of Christians to endeavor to suppress all forms of evil that imperil the morality of the people, as well as the sacred interests of the visible church, and realizing that the present use of intoxicating liquors, as a beverage, constitutes such evil, therefore we beg to submit the following recommendations:

I. That a permanent temperance committee be appointed, consisting of three members, whose term of office shall be three years, with the exception of two in the first appointment, which shall be one and two years respectively, each recurring vacancy to be filled by appointing a member thereto for three years:

II. The duties of this committee shall be:

1. To diligently inquire into the conditions as they exist in the Brotherhood concerning the different phases of this evil; and select, write, or cause to be written, terse, helpful tracts in favor of temperance.

2. To constitute a bureau for procuring information as to the general temperance movement, and secure, and cause to be given to our membership, from time to time, through our church publications, such information as may be helpful in creating a more concerted action in dealing with the temperance question.

3. To assist State Districts and local congregations to organize and maintain aggressive movements toward counteracting and stamping out the evil of intemperance.

4. To render such personal assistance in holding district or local temperance meetings as may be deemed practical.

5. To create and quicken, in the minds of old and young, sentiment against this evil; to warn against the personal use of intoxicants of all grades, and to awaken opposition to the partnership of our State and National Governments in the traffic, by sharing the unrighteous profits and protecting, licensing, and fostering this great peril to all that is righteous and desirable to human life and hope.

6. To report annually to the General Conference the progress of their work, their methods of operation, etc., and suggest any further plans for approval, that may appear favorably to them.

7. To create a treasury to provide means for defraying expenses incurred, through a plan—embracing contributions from the different congregations, subject to the approval of Annual Meeting.

8. To arrange and have executed at time and place of each Annual Meeting a temperance program, consisting of either a temperance sermon, or such discussions of temperance topics as may tend to quicken interest in the cause, and emphasize our long-established temperance principles before our membership and the world.

III. That all these recommendations be carried out in accord with gospel principles, and subject to the directing care of the church.[61]

According to the report of the committee to the 1909 Annual Meeting, a major function of the committee was to secure and to distribute literature "upon some phase of the issue." Another important function was to encourage the organization of committees in the districts of the church:

Why should prohibition districts organize? A number of the duties of the committee, passed by Conference of last year, cannot be carried out unless the Districts perfect these organizations. We, therefore, urge upon the delegates of this body the importance of taking up the matter at once in their several Districts and report their action to the secretary of our committee.[62]

One of the continuing goals of the General Temperance Committee was to have organized temperance committees in each district. It was not until 1913, that it reported being "in touch with all the State Districts in this country through District representatives. . . . It cannot be said that the District Committees are all active, but interesting reports are frequently received from brethren and sisters in all parts of the Brotherhood who have the cause sincerely at heart."[63] The

General Temperance Committee continued the longstanding Brethren conviction that the Brethren should avoid cooperation with other temperance agencies. The report of 1912 emphasized this point.

We fully realize that to recommend a method of procedure for the furtherance of the temperance movement, so as to meet with the approval of all, is a tremendous task; neither shall we endeavor to do so.

Nothing short of the wisdom of God can map out a way by which the most good can be done.

After fervent prayer for guidance and much deliberation, and after seriously considering the numerous reform movements, as well as the many organizations at work in the temperance cause and our federation with them, we feel constrained to say that in our judgment the greatest care should be exercised in linking arms with these organizations if, indeed, it be ever advisable to do so.

Our work is the salvation of souls and the extension of God's kingdom in the world rather than aid in organizing forces to drive the enemy from the face of the earth, even if such a thing were possible.

The Church of Jesus Christ is complete within itself; her resources sufficient to do a mighty work if properly inspired and organized.

Our money can do no more good, and probably not nearly as much, as when used by our own temperance committee in a way that will eventually bring results for God.

We therefore urge our own beloved people to fully consecrate themselves in this great work instead of inviting speakers of organized bodies into our pulpits, causing our money to be used by organizations foreign to the church and not infrequently in the great cause we espouse.[64]

In spite of their refusal to cooperate with other groups involved in the temperance movement, Brethren were willing to recognize that results were being achieved. The report of 1914 noted:

Temperance seems to be growing everywhere. Commercial and industrial enterprises are legislating against the business of the liquor interests. The colleges are sowing seed that ought to yield a heavy crop of temperance fruit in the not distant future. This work will undoubtedly make a cleaner world in which to live here, but we should not fail to emphasize the fact that the best that reform can do is to make social conditions better. It does not prepare for the other world. The only work that can be put to our account for the world is re-creation. Regeneration of heart and transformation of life is eternal, and is the enduring temperance labor which will be gold, silver and precious stones to our account. Let us not forget our brother for whom Christ died, and bring him the message of the cross. We should not allow our hatred for sin to cause us to operate in such a way that compassion for the sinner will be covered.[65]

One of the most significant steps in the development of Brethren action regarding prohibition was the election of Martin G. Brumbaugh, a prominent Brethren minister and educator, as governor of Pennsylvania in 1915. As a part of the resolutions adopted by the Annual Meeting of 1915, the church commended Governor Brumbaugh, especially for his action dealing with prohibition.

Be it resolved, That we, the Church of the Brethren, which from its earliest inception has been an active advocate of temperance to the extent of prohibiting its members from the distillation of, as well as the traffic in, intoxicating liquors, commend Bro. Brumbaugh and his administration for the high ground he has taken upon all moral issues. We especially commend him for his efforts to secure local option in Pennsylvania as a stepping stone to the speedy elimination of the legalized traffic in intoxicating liquors from our nation.[65]

After this turning point Brethren now became enthusiastic supporters of the nationwide prohibition movement, which eventually led to the adoption of the Eighteenth Amendment in 1919.

The Annual Meeting had much to say about the personal life of Brethren regarding their use of tobacco and alcoholic beverages; the Meeting also had much to say about their personal life in terms of their homes—what they did to their homes and what they did in their homes. For example, was a church member permitted to use lightning rods to protect property from the danger of fire from lightning? This issue had been before the Meeting in the 1850s and now was brought up again in 1866.

Art. 20. Inasmuch as the subject of lightning-rods has been before the Annual Council, and brethren have only been advised to bear with one another, which we consider is no decision at all; for, if right, why not recommend it to all, and, if wrong, why tolerate it at all?

Answer: As we have no command to erect or forbid lightning-rods, we would not advise brethren to put up such rods, but the brethren should bear with one another in love in such matters. (Minutes of 1851, Art. 7, and of 1856, Art. 25.)[67]

Evidently this matter did not come to the Annual Meeting again, and Brethren were allowed to work it out according to their own convictions and needs. The same type of solution seemed to have been the answer to the issue of using carpets in one's home.

X. Will this District Meeting petition the Annual Meeting of 1878 to reconsider Art. 8, of Annual Meeting 1827, and Art. 11, of the Annual Meeting of 1828, and give us a more definite answer, or show by the Gospel that if we have common plain carpets on our floors, it will lead to elevation (pride)?

Answer: We consider the above queries and decide that plain carpets have no tendency to pride and elevation, and that they may be enjoyed by us; but fine and fancy carpets are not consistent with our humble profession, and should not be in our houses.[68]

An issue which was not quite so easily solved as the carpets was the use of musical instruments in a Brethren home. This problem was considered by the Annual Meeting on at least five different occasions.

In 1866:

Art. 34. Is it considered conforming to the world for ministering brethren, or others, to have musical instruments, such as melodeons, pianos, etc.; in their houses, and for their children, who are members of the church, to spend their precious time in playing on such instruments?

Answer: Considered, that it is tending too much in that direction, the world being largely engaged in it, and we have no example in the New Testament that it was ever indulged in by Christians. Yet, if strictly confined to sacred music, we can not positively prohibit it, but advise all the beloved members to deny themselves of this indulgence, believing that it is attended with dangerous consequences.[69]

In 1870:

Art. 23. Is it right for brethren or sisters to have musical instruments in their houses, such as melodeons or organs?

Answer: We think it not expedient to have them in our houses, when they cause offense, and we think, under such circumstances, every brother and sister that have them ought to be admonished, in love, to put them away, agreeably to Eph. 5:19; Col 3:16; James 5:13.[70]

In 1873:

Art. 15. Is it agreeable with the gospel, or the old order of the Brethren, for members to have musical instruments in their houses, such as organs or a fiddle, for their amusement, or for the amusement of the young people, and to play on them on the Lord's-day, after they return from worship?

Answer: We think it unauthorized by the gospel, and clearly opposed to the order of the old brethren, and the doctrine of self-denial, and not calculated to promote vital Christianity.[71]

In 1877:

XIV. Inasmuch as the Annual Meeting has decided that it is wrong for members to have and use musical instruments in their houses—what is to be done with members that will not put them away? Can we make it a test of church fellowship? And what shall be done with elders that justify musical instruments, and consequently make no effort to put them out of their congregations?

Answer: Inasmuch as the use of musical instruments has been the cause of trouble among our brethren in some places, and has been frequently brought before Annual Meeting, we would readopt the decision of 1873, and advise our brethren to put them away where they cause offense and trouble in the church; and members who would not do so should fall under the judgment of the church. And as many of our brethren have them where it is not opposed by their church, and as the evil of them is more in the improper use of them than in the instrument itself, we cannot decide the simple keeping and use of such musical instruments shall be made a test of fellowship. The great evil being in the improper use of them and in the trouble they produce we advise the brethren to be careful to avoid offence and trouble by keeping them when they wound the brethren, and elders should be dealt with as transgressors when they encourage the brethren to do so.[72]

In 1894:

5. Inasmuch as Art. 14 of Minutes of Annual Meeting of 1877, concerning the use of musical instruments in private houses is differently understood and differently interpreted by our brethren, some understanding said article to justify a test of fellowship in congregations where they cause offense and trouble, while others contend that it does not, we, the members of the Manchester church (Indiana), earnestly request Annual Meeting of 1894, through District Meeting of Middle Indiana, to tell us whether local congregations have the authority, according to the article referred to, to make it a test of fellowship where the use of instruments, such as organs and pianos, causes offense and trouble.

Answer: While this Conference does not mean to justify or encourage the use of musical instruments in private houses, we do not consider that the decision referred to justifies expulsion, only in case of an improper use of the instrument.[73]

By the beginning of the twentieth century a new problem related to music was the use of the phonograph. Probably its use in the home was taken for granted by this time, but the Annual Meeting did hear a query in 1904 about its commercial use.

5. We ask Annual Meeting through district meeting to say whether it is right according to the Gospel for Brethren and especially ministers to purchase phonographs and stereopticon outfits and hold entertainments in schoolhouses through the different churches, post bills for such entertainments and charge admittance thereto, thereby causing hard feelings.

Answer: We think it wrong, according to the tenor of the Gospel, for a minister to do as stated in the query, and we recommend that, inasmuch as it is the abuse and not the use of the instruments named in the query that is wrong, all of our brethren should exercise great care in their use.[74]

Presumably one of the values of musical instruments and phonographs in a Brethren home was to keep young people entertained at home and thus not looking for entertainment somewhere else. A related issue which came to the Annual Meeting of 1892 was the playing of various games. What was acceptable and what was not?

Is it right for our members to play such games as cards, checkers, authors, croquet, etc? Is there more harm in one of these games than in another, and what is the harm? Is it right for our members to have these games in their homes to keep their children from going away from home to seek other amusements?

This query was referred to a committee. The following report was submitted and adopted by Annual Meeting: We decide that card playing and like games are unquestionably wrong, and should not be indulged in by members or allowed in their homes; and we most earnestly admonish all our members to refrain from indulging in other games that may seem evil in their tendency, or give offense to members.[75]

Entertainment could take many forms. Self-gratification and pride could accompany a family portrait being made. The development of the camera and of commercial photography in the second half of the 19th century created a new set of problems for Brethren, who were noted for their humility and rejection of any form of pride. As early as 1849 the Annual Meeting had rejected the taking of portraits by the new process. However, Brethren persisted in getting pictures taken, as the countless pictures of Brethren leaders of the 19th century make clear. The Annual Meeting continued to discuss the matter after the Civil War. In 1867:

Art. 7. Is it consistent with the gospel for members of the church to have their profiles or miniatures taken; and, if inconsistent, how shall the church deal with such members who do so?

Answer: As the brethren, in Annual Council in former years, decided it to be wrong, or inconsistent, for members to have their profiles or miniatures taken, we advise them not to do so.[76]

In 1869:

Art. 21. Whereas, it has been repeatedly decided at our Yearly Meeting, that it is wrong for members of the church to have their likenesses taken, what then is to be done with members that have their likenesses taken?

Answer: We consider it not right for members to have their likenesses taken, and if they have done so, they should be admonished to put them away.[77]

In 1872 some Brethren wanted to know what it meant to "put them away."

Art. 10. Does this district understand the Annual Meeting to mean that we should dispose of our likenesses entirely when it advises us to put them away? (See Minutes of 1869, Art. 21.)

Answer: This Annual Meeting understands the phrase "put them away" to mean to put them out of public sight.[78]

For the next twenty years the issue was allowed to rest; in fact any rejection of the taking of portraits was "generally disregarded." In 1892 the Annual Meeting refused to act on a new clarification of the issue.

(1) Inasmuch as Annual Meeting has decided that it is not right for a brother to be engaged in taking likenesses (see Classified Minutes, page 295), how shall the church proceed with a brother who is engaged in that business, and will not stop when admonished to do so?

(2) Inasmuch as the decisions of Annual Meeting in reference to the taking of likenesses are so generally disregarded, we ask Annual Meeting through District Meeting to say what shall be done.

On motion both queries were deferred.[79]

Somewhat surprisingly perhaps, two further decisions in the 1890s perpetuated the policy of rejecting the taking of portraits. In 1894:

2. Whereas the order of the German Baptist Brethren concerning the taking likenesses of and by members seems to be disregarded by many of our members, even such as are prominent in the missionary cause, and by sad experience we learn that such behavior has a tendency to cripple the efforts to raise money for missionary purposes in those churches that have still been loyal to the non-conforming principles of the Brotherhood; we, therefore, ask District Meeting of Eastern Pennsylvania to urge the elders of their respective churches to enforce Art. 21 of the Minutes of the Annual Meeting of 1869. Classified Minutes, p. 295.

Answer: Whereas decisions now on the Minutes are so full and conclusive on the likeness question, we cannot see the propriety of adding to or taking from decision already made; therefore we advise and urge all members, and especially elders and ministers, to so reverence the advice of our old brethren that they give no offense.[80]

In 1895:

11. Whereas Annual Meeting has decided that it is wrong for members to have their likenesses taken, and that those that have them taken shall put them away,—put them out of sight; and whereas some of our members, either as authors, compilers, or publishers, have likenesses of members put in books and advertise that such portraits are in the book; therefore we ask Annual Meeting through District Meeting to say whether these authors, compilers or publishers are an exception to said decisions, and if not, to say that they shall stop doing so.

Answer: We do not consider them an exception, and therefore grant the request.[81]

In 1904, the longstanding issue was finally concluded.

4. Whereas the decision of Annual Meeting concerning the taking of likenesses of and by members is not heeded, neither reverenced, and

Whereas Annual Meeting has decided that there is sufficient legislation on this question (see Minutes of 1894, Art. 2 "Revised Minutes," page 131), we therefore ask district meeting of Eastern Pennsylvania to petition Annual Meeting to decide that the same course be pursued as is taken in the tobacco, dress and gold questions, making it a test of delegateship to District and Annual Meetings.

Answer of District.—We ask Annual Meeting so to decide that delegates to Annual and district meetings shall be asked if they have their likenesses taken, and if so, if they have them out of sight.

Answer: The following committee was appointed to take up the entire question of likenesses and pictures and report at next Annual Meeting: John Herr, D. M. Garver, Andrew Hutchison.

We, your committee on photos or likenesses, beg to submit the following in the fear of God:—

Whereas, Scripture references given in support of decisions on the likeness question, as they now stand on the minutes, refer to images of worship, we now decide to repeal all former decisions on this question, and at the same time refer to Rom. 8: 5–7; Luke 16: 15; Ga. 5: 24, 25; 1 John 2: 15, 16, as standing strongly against the practice.

We, therefore, in good faith, file our most earnest protest against the present extravagant use of likenesses, photos, and reproductions of crayon, and enjoin upon elders and ministers to labor in harmony with this decision.

John Herr,
D. M. Garver,
Andrew Hutchison.

Answer: While not unmindful of the good intentions of the Conferences passing the decisions regarding likenesses, we now decide to repeal these decisions, and at the same time enter our protest against the extravagant use of money for photographs.[82].

Thus by the end of this half century the basic issue of using a camera to take pictures of people had been settled.

Another question which was not settled to any degree until near the end of the century was the personal appearance of the Brethren. This issue of the "garb" worn by Brethren probably took more time at Annual Meetings than any other topic between 1865 and 1910. Not all of the discussion is included in this examination. The 1866 Meeting summarized the policy at that point in time.

Art. 27. Inasmuch as pride and an inclination to follow the fashions of the world are still increasing among us, in wearing fine apparel, frock and sack coats, dusters, shawls, etc., with the hair parted off to one side, or shingled and roached, moustaches, etc.; the sisters also wearing fine apparel, going without caps, wearing hoops, hats, veils, overcoats, jewelry, etc.; and, as admonition, in some cases, has not effected any thing, can not this Yearly Meeting propose some plan by which this growing evil may be arrested?

Answer: We think members of the church, conforming to the fashions of the world as above stated, should be admonished again and again, and if they will not hear the church, the Savior has given directions in Matt. 18 how to deal with them.

Resolved, by this Annual Meeting, That the churches throughout the brotherhood enforce plainness of dress, and a plain manner of wearing the hair and beard, upon the preachers and officers of the churches. By plainness of dress, we mean the common order of giving shape to dress, as practiced by the old brethren and sisters generally, and by plainess of hair we mean the hair parted on the top of the head, or all combed back in a plain manner, or combed straight down all around the head, and not having the hair and beard trimmed according to the custom of the world.[83]

It was one thing to establish a policy; it was another matter to enforce it. The Meeting of 1871 went into detail in terms of enforcement.

Art. 22. We desire an explanation, with an answer, on the words "again and again," used in answer to Art 27, of the Annual Meeting of 1866, as the word or words, "again and again," is or are not scriptural language. Hence, how often must an offending member be admonished to be admonished again and again, before an action can be taken against it?

Answer: We feel, as the brethren have always felt, that it is difficult to lay down a definite rule to apply to all cases concerning the subject alluded to in the query. We think that the wisdom of the churches should dictate the proper method of treating such cases. Where the general conduct of members is such as becomes the gospel of Christ, and there seems to be no inclinations to follow the fashions of the world, and their apparel is modest and not gay, forbearance should be exercised toward such members, hoping they will in time adopt the plain garment, as this is considered one of the peculiarities of our fraternity, and in accordance with the Christian grace of simplicity taught in the gospel. In cases, however, where members, instead of conforming to the order of the brethren in plainness of dress, conform to and follow the fashions of the world, such should be dealt with more rigorously; and, if after several admonitions, there seem to be no improvement, they should be dealt with according to Matt. 18; and in dealing with such cases, both the salvation of souls and the purity of the church should be kept in view.[84]

A further step in enforcement was taken in 1881 when leaders of the church who did not put on a correct appearance were prohibited from carrying certain responsibilities in the church.

XVI. We request Annual Meeting through District Meeting to send only such brethren as delegates and members of the Standing Committee and to settle difficulties, who are sound in the faith, and who carry out and advocate the order of the church in wearing the clothes, hair and beard, as well as in everything else, with the understanding that they will be rejected if not sent in harmony with the above.

Answer: Brethren who opposed the established order of the church are not suitable brethren to settle troubles in the church, or to represent as delegates.[85]

And in 1886 additional procedures were outlined to bring about a greater degree of enforcement of the plain dress policies of the church.

VI. As there is an active tendency on the part of some elders, minister, deacons, and churches toward discarding our order on plainness of dressing, as also the appropriate head covering worn by our devoted sisters; also consenting that sisters may wear hats in disregard to Art. 16, 1877, and thus rapid strides are made towards the ever-changing, and sinful fashions of the world, and the teaching of the Gospel of plainness of wearing apparel is disregarded; will District Meeting therefore petition Annual Meeting to authorize that the Standing Committee if ascertained by it through any reliable source, that adjoining elders to churches which tolerate departures from our general order on any subject have failed to undertake, or to set in order such officers or churches, as above named. It shall appoint with consent of the Annual Meeting faithful brethren to visit such church or churches, to set them in order. . . .[86]

Three major issues relating to the personal appearance of Brethren may be identifed—the use of gold and jewelry, the coat and hair-style of the men, and the hat vs. bonnet worn by women. Let us examine, first of all, the gold and jewelry issue. The Annual Meeting of 1889 stated:

2. Should the carrying of gold watches be made cause for expulsion of members from the Church? We consider that 1 Tim. 2:9; 1 Pet. 3:3, and Art. 7 of Annual Meeting of 1864 is sufficiently clear against the carrying of gold watches to enforce discipline on the subject. [87]

Suppose, however, Brethren had to wear glasses to improve vision. Could they have a gold frame? The 1891 Meeting did not accept any kind of gold.

19½. The Spring Run Church petitions Annual Meeting through District Meeting, to say whether it is right for members to wear gold spectacles.

Answer: Inasmuch as the wearing of gold is forbidden in the Gospel, 1 Tim. 2:9, 1 Pet. 3:3, we decide that wearing gold in any way that has an appearance of violating the Gospel shall not be allowed.[88]

One way of enforcing this decision was "to ask the delegates to District and Annual Meetings whether they are wearing gold in any way of appearance, thereby violating the Word of God."[89] This petition from the White Oak Church of Lancaster County, Pennsylvania was granted by the Annual Meeting of 1897. Since not many Brethren became delegates to the Annual Meeting, there needed to be some type of enforcement at the congregational level. How this enforcement might work out was illustrated in an episode that was recorded in the church in North Dakota; in this case, a family that did not have a Brethren background joined the church because of proximity.

MOTHER'S WEDDING RING

I remember how Mother cried when a solemn delegation came and told her she must get rid of her wedding ring. That was jewelry and the members of the Church of the Brethren were plain people, they were not to wear jewelry.

I'm sure my father was hurt by that demand of the church. He must have considered the idea piddling and unfair—that the symbolic value of a wedding ring was far more important than this restriction of the church.

However, Dad and Mother agreed to comply. The wedding ring was a massive gold band. Mother's finger was swollen around the ring until it couldn't be pulled off. Dad had to use a file to cut through and bend it open before it would come off. It was a slow and painful job.[90]

By the twentieth century many Brethren, whether they had only recently joined the church, as in this case in the Dakotas, or whether they had grown up in the church, had become storekeepers. What they sold in their stores was a concern of the Annual Meeting of 1906.

1. We, your committee, to whom were committed the following papers beg leave to report as follows:

(a) We, the Monitor church, of Oklahoma, in regular council, petition Annual Meeting, through district meeting, to prohibit members from engaging in the sale of playing cards, dice, diamonds, gold rings, gold watches and other articles of display, and refer to the following: "Revised Minutes," page 180, Art. 15, 1892; and also page 125, Art. 19½, 1891.

(b) Good Hope church, Sterling, Colo., in regular quarterly council, asks Annual Meeting, through district meeting, to prohibit members who are engaged in mercantile business from selling such articles as playing cards, dice, dominoes, and such articles of display as diamonds, rings, and gold chains.

The following committee was appointed to consider above papers and report to Annual Meeting of 1916: T. C. Denton, D. F. Hoover, I. J. Rosenberger.

We consider it inconsistent and we prohibit members from engaging in the sale of articles such as named in the queries, thus encouraging their use in violation to Rom. 14:13, 1 Peter 3:4; 1 Tim. 2:9; Rom. 12:1.

T. C. Denton
I. J. Rosenberger
David F. Hoover

Report accepted.[90]

Thus Brethren continued to forbid the use of gold and jewelry. Two major restrictions developed and were enforced for men. First of all, the cut of the coat collar was significant because the coat was to be worn without a necktie. In 1876 the Meeting refused to pin down the form of collar to be used.

Art. 11. We wish the Annual Meeting to say whether we shall have a rolling or standing collar on our coats.

Answer: While we can not positively say which of the above forms of the coat should be worn, we would advise the brethren to try to become more uniform and plain, rather than to depart from the order of plainness, not only in our coats, but in every thing else.[92]

At this time such a degree of freedom was not acceptable in some local churches, and the following year the Annual Meeting reconsidered its decision.

IX. We petition Annual Meeting to reconsider Article 11, of 1876, and so amend its answer that it make the standing collar on the coat the old order as recognized by the Brethren.

Answer: This Annual Meeting reconsiders the above article and grants the request.[93]

The second major type of restriction set forth by the Annual Meeting related to the hair on a man's head. Shaving of the face had become popular, while at the same time men frequently left some hair for decorative purposes. In 1874 the Annual Meeting was queried about a mustache.

Art. 5. Since it is fashionable for the world to wear the mustache, the brethren are adopting it and claim for it liberty of conscience, saying that it is good for the eyes, are brethren compelled to salute such if they can not do it without doing violence to their conscience?

Answer: Brethren should never wear a mustache only, or fashionable beard, according to the fashion of the world; and if they do, they will fall into the council of the church.[94]

Perhaps the other extreme to wearing a mustache was wearing a full beard on the face without shaving any part. Such an approach was also offensive to some Brethren as the Annual Meeting of 1888 recognized.

2. Inasmuch as Annual Meeting has granted the liberty of conscience to wear a full beard, also granted the liberty of conscience not to salute such brethren, will not the District Meeting ask the Annual Meeting to decide that brethren should clip their mustache so as not to hinder in the salutation of the kiss?

Answer: Brethren who do not trim the hair on the upper lip so that they may be decent and orderly shall be considered as offenders and dealt with accordingly.[95]

The style of cutting the hair on the top of a man's head was also an issue of the Annual Meeting. The resolution of 1866 had outlined three acceptable patterns of cutting the hair. By the 1880s new styles had been developed, as the Meeting of 1888 learned.

3. Since Annual Meeting has granted brethren three different ways to wear their hair, and has forbidden them to shingle their hair, will not the District Meeting ask Annual Meeting to stop the fashion of shingling the hair among the brethren?

Answer: Brethren should not follow the fashions of the world in the cutting or wearing of the hair or beard. 1 Peter 1:14.[96]

Finally the Annual Meeting of 1893 summarized issues related to a man's appearance and outlined again the measure of enforcement.

4. Since Annual Meeting has defined the cut of coat for our brethren (especially official brethren), we ask Annual Meeting, through District Meeting, what shall be done with brethren who disregard the order of the church by wearing the straight-cut, popular frock coat usually worn by popular clergymen? Rom. 12:2; 1John 2:15,16; 1Cor. 8:12,13; 1Pet. 1:14. Sent to Annual Meeting with a request to place in the Minutes the decision of Art. 47, 1866.

Resolved, by this Annual Meeting: That the churches throughout the Brotherhood enforce plainness of dress, and a plain manner of wearing the hair and beard, upon the preachers and officers of the churches. By plainness of dress, we mean the common order of giving shape to dress, as practiced by the old brethren and sisters generally; and by plainness of hair we mean the hair parted on top of the head or all combed back in a plain manner, or combed straight down all around the head, and not having the hair and beard trimmed according to the custom of the world.

Considered, that this Annual Meeting unanimously adopt this resolution, according to Rom. 12:2; 1 Pet. 1:14; 1 John 2:15,16, and that all preachers and officers that follow the fashions of the world in the foregoing particulars, violate the order of the Gospel by doing so, and render themselves liable to be brought under the counsel of the church.[97]

The restrictions of the Annual Meeting regarding personal appearance also applied to the women of the church. The issue that was most crucial was the wearing of "fashionable hats," according to the Meeting of 1876.

Art. 21. Is it wrong for sisters to wear fashionable hats instead of bonnets? and where is the Scripture forbidding the wearing of such hats?

Answer: We decide it is wrong according to Rom. 12:2; 1 Tim. 2:9.[98]

Not only were women wearing hats; they were wearing them to the Love Feast. The Annual Meeting of 1877 decided that the presiding officers of the church were responsible for not allowing such behavior.

XVI. How is it considered by the brethren in Annual Council in regard to sisters wearing fashionable hats while surrounding the communion table? Can the officiating brother consistently break the bread to such?

Answer: Inasmuch as there has been advantage taken of the decision of Annual Meeting of '76 on the subject of sisters wearing fashionable hats; we decide that the sisters shall not wear any hats at all at communion meetings or at any other time, and our brethren should not break the bread of communion to a sister with a hat upon her head, and elders or ministers who encourage and allow sisters to wear hats should be promptly dealt with as transgressors.[99]

Some Brethren persisted in wanting to know if there might be some kind of a crack in the door which would allow "modest hats" on the heads of the sisters instead of bonnets. The Annual Meeting of 1880 was not ready to tolerate such a deviation.

XIV. Inasmuch as the Annual Meeting decided in 1872, Art. 5, that the Gospel is a perfect law to govern the church in all things necessary to salvation, is it contrary, therefore, to the perfect law of the Gospel for sisters to wear modest hats? If so, give the Scripture forbidding sisters to wear them, and the Gospel authority for enforcing them to wear bonnets.

Answer: Inasmuch as the wearing of hats by our sisters is following the fashions of the world, it is in violation of the apostle's precept. "Be not conformed to the world," Rom. 12:2, and of the following: "Abstain from all appearance of evil," Thess. 5:22, and again, "know ye not that the friendship of the world is enmity with God? Whososoever, therefore, will be friend of the world is the enemy of God."—Jas. 4:4.[100]

Unfortunately not every local officer of the church accepted these decisions of the Annual Meeting, and the result was inconsistency in enforcing them. The Annual Meeting of 1881 examined this problem.

XXI. Whereas, There is much dissatisfaction expressed by many because of the inconsistencies they see in the general Brotherhood in the matter of wearing hats by the sisters; some localities being compelled by committees and decisions of Annual Conference to make it a test of fellowship by which many have been expelled from the church, while other localities or districts are admitting that for which others are being expelled, hence the just cause for complaining of inconsistencies in the Brotherhood. We therefore ask this District Meeting to say whether the wearing of hats by the sisters shall be made a test of fellowship; if so, to see that the same be enforced in all places in the Brotherhood, thereby removing the inconsistencies referred to.

Inasmuch as the Annual Conference has decided that sisters shall not wear hats, elders and officers should see that this decision is carried out.

Answer: Elders who do not do so, shall be dealt with as transgressors.[101]

The problem of inconsistency in application was not solved by this decision of the Annual Meeting of 1881. A number of years later in 1898, the Annual Meeting again examined this problem at considerable length.

3. Inasmuch as the wearing of hats by the sisters is made a test of fellowship, while the brethren are allowed to wear many of the styles and fashions, and still retain their membership; and, whereas, the above apparent inconsistency is causing dissatisfaction in parts of the Brotherhood, therefore, we, the Milledgeville church, ask Annual Meeting, through District Meeting, to devise some means whereby this inconsistency may be removed.

Answer:

(1) The inconsistency exists to some slight extent, resulting from a violation of the decisions of Annual Meeting. Upon examination seventy-four decisions covering the various phases of nonconformity to the world in dress and in adorning the body are found on our Minutes. In these decisions very little distinction is made between brethren and sisters. The fault lies in our practice. It must be apparent to all that more decisions will not remove the inconsistency complained of, but rather tend to weaken the authority of our Conference. Not more decisions, but a more intelligent understanding of the important Gospel principles of non-conformity to the world, plain dressing and plain living is what is needed.

(2) We therefore beseech all elders, ministers and teachers to teach these important Scriptural doctrines earnestly, intelligently, and fully in all their charges, and to make every possible effort to carry them out, so that the church may not depart from these principles that have been so dear to all our faithful members since she was first organized. With these Gospel principles established in the hearts of the people, the desire to conform to the foolish fashions of the world will disappear.

(3) That more teaching may be done in private, elders and ministers are required to carry out fully the decisions of Annual Meeting as to pastoral visit; and the congregations shall assist in the work by giving such financial aid as circumstances may require.

(4) Gospel plainness requires that sisters attire themselves in plainly-made garments free from ornaments, ruffles and all unnecessary appendages. Plain bonnets and hoods are in harmony with Gospel plainness, and are adopted as the head dress for our sisters. The brethren likewise should dress themselves in plain attire, not wearing fashionable hats and neckties, gold for adornment or other superfluities. 1 Tim. 2: 9, 10; 1 Peter 3: 3, 4, 5. It is the duty of all housekeepers to see that the brethren and sisters are properly instructed concerning the necessity of Gospel plainness and it is also their duty to see that the order of the church respecting plainness, is properly carried out in their respective congregations.[102]

The first step in the final solution of the "dress question," as it was becoming known, was taken at the Annual Meeting of 1909, by the appointing of a special committee to study the issue and report back to the Annual Meeting of 1910. Its assignment was outlined carefully.

5. (a) Inasmuch as there is a growing tendency in the Church of the Brethren to disregard the distinctive principles of nonconformity, causing much confusion, we, the Monocacy church, in council assembled, this third day of April, 1909, petition Annual Meeting, through district meeting, to devise some plan by which the churches may work in harmony.

Answer by district Meeting of Eastern Maryland: We endorse the sentiment of this paper, and request Annual Meeting to take such steps on the dress question as will keep us united on gospel principles and will maintain peace and unity in the Brotherhood.

(b) In consequence of the unrest at present existing in different parts of our Brotherhood in reference to the dress question, and with a desire to avoid further divergence in the minds of our brethren and sisters, the New Enterprise congregation asks Annual Meeting, through district meeting, to appoint a committee of seven representative brethren, who shall consider the existing inconsistencies resulting from the different interpretations of the present decisions on this subject. Also to take cognizance of all scriptures relating to this question, and the view of the founders of the Church of the Brethren, as they are on record or can be acquired, and report, as soon as possible, a plan by which the gospel principles of plain dressing and plain living can be accepted and exemplified in all our local congregations.

Answer: The following motion was offered and passed:

In view of the fact that these queries clearly touch the vital problem of the dress question, now disturbing the peace of the brotherhood, I move that a committee of seven faithful, intelligent, conservative brethren be appointed, to whom these papers shall be submitted, to be reported on at a coming Annual Meeting.

That the committee be instructed to examine carefully and exhaustively the scriptural ground on the subject of Christian attire, that the practice of the primitive church be investigated, and the position and teaching of our own church fathers and the Minutes of our Conference be examined, with a view of giving us a clear, concise restatement of our position on this vexed question, so that all may understand alike and be unified and dwell together as becometh children of the family of God—in love and peace and harmony.

During the time the committee, so appointed, is considering the queries, the dress question shall not be considered an open one for discussion in the Messenger, but those having suggestions of a helpful character to make, are invited to write the chairman of the committee; and further, in the meantime, elders, ministers, and teachers are exhorted to teach earnestly and intelligently the scriptural doctrine of plain dressing and plain living as set forth by our Annual Meeting, so that the Church may not depart from these principles that have been so dear to all our faithful members since she was first organized.

The following committee was then chosen: D. L. Miller, L. W. Teeter, Daniel Hays, A. C. Wieand, L. T. Holsinger, B. E. Kesler, G. W. Lentz.[103]

An interesting insight into the operation of the committee was provided by Galen B. Royer of the Elgin staff in a letter to H. C. Early, the moderator of the 1910 Annual Meeting.

I have carried a weight on my heart ever since committee adjourned. Strained conditions existed. D. L. was put in the chair which practically tied his mouth. Keslar and Lents are fair minded as it develops but not aggressive in such work. Bro. Hays was a "knocker" and nothing else. Anything that did not meet his view was from a "weak-kneed" person no matter who or what his experience was. The only thing that could be done was what was done. This is better than a divided committee. But it is not what the church is hoping for and expects. It puts a discouraging phase to church work. If the church is drifting worldward under past conditions this is an endorsement of that drifting. If in some localities the church is ruled over by a rod of iron, that rod to that person is endorsed. It does not improve things one bit only in this light and you are on the right track. We want to reject that report and have the work recommitted. In doing this we get rid of one of the most unreasonable men we have to deal with. I speak kindly but truely. A new committee can hardly find another like our dear brother Hays who is so uncharitable to every one's views who does not accord with him. This new committee may have a chance to deal with the question squarely. It is our hope. I have written to members of the standing committee on that score already. And there must be some tactful work done or we will certainly plunge ourselves into a pretty plight. I. J. Rosenberger writes that there is no use, the others won't give in and we will have to lop off some as we did thirty years ago. I. J. seems not to realize that he belongs to the one side of the lopping off. Bro Hays was strongly seconded in all his positions by D. W. Teeter and there you have it.[104]

Royer's prophecy regarding the Report proved to be correct. The Annual Meeting of 1910 heard the Report and recommitted it.

Report of Committee

Pursuant to the foregoing instructions, as given in the second paragraph of the answer, we proceeded as follows:

I. We examined carefully and exhaustively the scriptural ground on the subject of Christian attire and found, in all the teachings and examples of Christ and the apostles, in letter and in spirit, that the followers of Christ are to be a people separated from all worldliness, vanity, and sin (John 17:11–16; 2 Cor. 6:14–18; James 4:4; 1 John 2:15–17). We found that the New Testament teaches:—

1. General nonconformity to the world and transformation from

the world, which includes giving shape to the outward personal appearance (Rom. 12:1,2; 1 Peter 1:14,15);

2. Christ's followers are conformed to his image (Rom. 6:5, 8:29; 1 Cor. 15:49; 2 Cor. 3:18);

3. Christ's followers are to dress plainly and modestly (Matt. 3:4; John 19:23; 1 Tim. 2:9,10; 1 Peter 3:3–5);

4. Dress should not be extravagant (Philipp. 4:5; 1 Tim. 2:9,10; James 2:2);

5. Dress may become an abomination in the sight of God (Luke 16:15; Mark 12:38; Rev. 17:4,5; 18:16);

6. Garments worn for display or to attract attention are disapproved (Matt. 11:8; 23:5; Luke 7:25);

7. All Christian characteristics require modesty and plainness of the outward appearance and a corresponding meek and quiet spirit within (1 Peter 3:3,4).

II. We investigated the practice of the Primitive Church, following closely the Apostolic Period, and found the Early Church Fathers exceedingly strong and pointed in their teaching against pride and superfluity to dress. They taught much against the inconsistency and folly of a people of so high an order as Christians to stoop again to the low order of worldly fashion-mongers.

III. We examined the position and teaching of our own Church Fathers and found a remarkable unity of teaching that separateness from the foolish fashions of the world in dress must be maintained as taught in the New Testament.

IV. We examined the Minutes of our Conferences on dress and found that the full and unwavering purpose has been to maintain and exemplify gospel simplicity in apparel and personal appearance. It is also manifest in the Conference decisions, from first to last, that the church was constantly on the alert to adopt such gospel rules and means as would direct its members in the midst of the ever-changing fashions of the world, and save them from the spiritual damage and still preserve gospel simplicity in dress.

The general tenor pervading the four preceding lines of investigation impress the Committee, that the position of the Church of the Brethren on dress, in nonconformity to the world, is quite consistent with all New Testament principles.

We therefore offer the following:

After a careful and prayerful investigation of the Scriptures and the writings of the Primitive Church Fathers on dress and adornment of the body, we recommend the decisions of Annual Meeting, as given in the Minutes from year to year, as the best interpretation and application of the Scriptures on nonconformity to the world in dress, in a practical way, as the rule for all the brethren and sisters in all the churches of the Brotherhood, as the means to a greater union in Christian fellowship and the simplicity of the Gospel.

Committee: D. L. Miller, L. W. Teeter, D. Hays, B. E. Kesler, G. W. Lentz, L. T. Holsinger.

Answer: This Annual Meeting accepts the report of the Committee and decides that the questions involved in the queries and also the committee's report be recommitted to a committee of five faithful, intelligent, conservative brethren, who are hereby instructed to take the whole matter under advisement and to make a restatement reducing all the teachings of the Conferences on Christian attire to one plain and concise minute, to be reported to next Annual Meeting.

During the time the committee is preparing the report, no phase of the dress question shall be open for discussion in any of our publications; but all suggestions shall be sent to the chairman of the committee; and further, in the meantime, all elders, ministers, and teachers shall teach earnestly and intelligently the doctrines of plain dressing and plain living, as found in the Scriptures, so that the church may maintain the principle of nonconformity to the world.

We authorize the treasurer of the Annual Meeting to pay the expenses of this committee.

Committee: H. C. Early, John Heckman, Galen B. Royer, C. D. Bonsack, J. W. Lear.[105]

So an entirely new committee had been appointed to consider the dress question! The position of this committee was well represented in a letter from Early to Royer in July, 1910.

One of the most serious considerations with me in the whole question is whether or not what the Committee recommends as the rule should be made a test of fellowship; or whether it should be made advisory as all that the Conference teaches on all other questions of this large class of questions is simply made advisory, and not compulsory or mandatory. To be fair with the Scripture, I am unable to understand why one question of a class of questions should be carried further than the rest, when they all have about equal gospel authority and all stand in the same relation to Conference action. Do you understand me? The point is this: Is the Conference justified in making a matter of method on one question a test of fellowship and not do the same thing on all questions of method that have equal gospel authority? That's the point, and it is a serious one.

If the church could grow to be spiritual as Jesus intends, there would be no need of legislation on dress and a hundred other things with which the Conference is occupied. And too, a matter of this sort forced on one against his own free choice is of no benefit to the individual. But apart from this view of it and coming back to the original point, it seems to me if the dress is to be made a test of fellowship, then the Conference, to be fair with Scripture as well as fair with men, will have to move up a few notches on a good many other things.[106]

After the committee's work had been completed in the spring of 1911, Royer wrote a few of his observations in a letter to Frank Crumpacker.

The Dress Committee report I enclose you an advanced proof sheet. It is the best we could do considering the restrictions imposed by Conference and the spiritual development of the church. It is not ideal but we hope it will lift towards the ideal as it is in Jesus. The report is the final unanimous conclusion of over four days deliberation. It does not look like it would take that much work to write it out, but we discussed its application by the liberal and the radical, and if any phase of life was missed it was purely short sightedness on our part. We now await the criticism of an exacting fraternity who are screwed up to the highest tension on the subject and commend the entire to the Lord for his keeping and direction.[107]

The Annual Meeting of 1911 heard and accepted the report of the committee.

Pursuant to the foregoing instructions "to take the whole matter under advisement and to make a restatement" we proceeded as follows:

I. We examined prayerfully the scriptural ground of Christian attire, and found that Jesus and the apostles taught honesty and simplicity of life and modesty in dress and manners.

The scriptures bearing on the subject of dress and adornment are of several classes:

First. Jesus condemned anxious thought for raiment (Matt. 6:25–33; Luke 12:22–31).

Second. The direct teachings, such as 1 Tim. 2:9,10; 1 Peter 3:3–5.

Third. Teachings on nonconformity to the world in general, and that apply to dress on general principles, such as Rom. 12:1,2; 1 Cor. 10:31; 1 Peter 1:14,15; 1 John 2:15–17.

II. Investigation shows that the early church Fathers and our own church fathers taught strongly and uniformly against pride and superfluity in dress, and constantly in favor of gospel plainness.

III. The Minutes of Conference show that the Church of the Brethren has, throughout her entire history, stood firmly against the fashions of the age, and extravagance in all manner of living, and on the other hand has taught faithfully the principles of simplicity of life and personal appearance. And, furthermore, the Conference has, from time to time, adopted means and methods with the view of maintaining gospel simplicity in dress in the church body.

Now, since the Gospel teaches plain and modest dress and since this is taught in the form of an obligation, without rules and methods of application further than to exclude plaiting of hair, the wearing of gold, pearls and costly raiment, and believing that a form that agrees with the spirit of the teaching is helpful in maintaining the principles of plainness and simplicity in dress and adornment in the general church body, "it seemed good to us" to submit the following restatement:

1. That the brethren wear plain clothing. That the coat with the standing collar be worn, especially by the ministers and deacons.

2. That the brethren wear their hair and beard in a plain and sanitary manner. That the mustache alone is forbidden.

3. That the sisters attire themselves in plainly-made garments, free from ornaments and unnecessary appendages. That plain bonnets and hoods be the headdress, and the hair be worn in a becoming Christian manner.

4. That the veil be worn in time of prayer and prophesying (1 Cor. 11:1–16, R. V.). The plain cap is regarded as meeting the requirements of scriptural teaching on the subject.

5. That gold for ornanment, and jewelry of all kinds, shall not be worn.

6. That no brother be installed into office as minister or deacon who will not pledge himself to observe and teach the order of dress.

7. That no brother or sister serve as delegate to District or Annual Meeting, nor be appointed on committees to enforce discipline, who does not observe the order of dress.

8. That it be the duty of the official body of the church, to teach faithfully and intelligently the simple, Christian life in dress; and bishops who are the shepherds of the churches, are required to teach and to see that the simple life in general is taught and observed in their respective charges.

9. That those who do not fully conform to the methods herein set forth, but who manifest no inclination to follow the unbecoming fashions, and whose life and conduct is becoming a follower of Christ, be dealt with in love and forbearance; and that every effort be made to save all to the church until they see the beauty of making a larger sacrifice for Christ and the church. But if, after every effort has been made, they, in an arbitrary spirit, refuse to conform to said methods, and follow the foolish fashions of the world, they may be dealt with as disorderly members: and in dealing with such cases, both the salvation of souls and the purity of the church should be kept in view.

10. That all are urged and implored, in the bonds of brotherly love and Christian fellowship, to teach and exemplify the order of the church in dress as a suitable expression of "the hidden man of the heart, in the incorruptible apparel of a meek and quiet spirit, which is in the sight of God of great price."

11. That upon the final adopting of this report it shall supersede all else in the Minutes on the subject of dress.

Answer: Report adopted.[108]

The adoption of this report by the St. Joseph Conference of 1911 has been considered a revolution in Brethren history because, for the first time, the wearing of the garb was not considered a test of membership. But not all of the leaders of the church in 1911 were prepared to make such a drastic change in their responsibilities for the members of the church. Galen B. Royer's response to one of the inquiries he had received asking for an interpretation of the report has been preserved.

I am getting a good many letters asking me to explain this that and the other on the Dress report. For instance one brother wanted me to explain what is meant by "dealing with them in love and forbearance." The great trouble is going to be in trying to read into that report many things that are not there. I tell each one that as a Committee member I have nothing to say. As a member of the church I have no more right to interpret Conference decisions than any other member but that the report has no hidden meaning but if each member will take it for just what it says, no more or not less. It is this eternal disposition of reading into decisions, yea reading into the Word itself what is not intended that is tearing things up. Look at the first committee's report. Where was there ever such a list of misappropriated scriptures as was applied there in the dress report. And such things always do injury to the cause we love. I told our members the other evening that now there was more laid upon the member to see that his life was plain than ever before. The Conference does not interpret and so the individual must interpret and there is room for improvement among us. Elders feel they must regulate the member,—and in a sense they should. Elders want to lodge the responsibility some where else and ask that Conference says where and where not. Now the happy medium of Conference regulation is all right but when a thing goes into such intense extremes that everything turns on a necktie and a bonnet and nearly all else is unnoticed the plane of living the simple life is most dreadfully warped. A few complain at Sec. 9 but bless you it is '71 repeated and it was the stiffheadedness of both sides following that ten years that brot the unbrotherly split.[109]

As is frequently the case, the Annual Meeting of 1912 received a number of queries regarding the dress decision of 1911. Actually, only one was accepted, and it simply asked for a series of articles in the **Gospel Messenger** *"in favor of plain dressing and plain living."*[110] *The moderator of the Meeting, H. C. Early, concluded:*

Personally, I feel quite well with the actions of the Conference, especially so in regard to the queries on the Dress Question. It was certainly a great victory for the Dress Committee, if there is such a committee in existence.[111]

To which Galen B. Royer responded:

I note your comment on the recent conference. You did well in handling the meeting and the Lord blessed us thru you. As far as results of conference are concerned I feel good. To have the Ohio papers dealt with as they were in an environment so strongly on the other side apparently, means much in dealing with the question as it was passed. Had the same action occurred at Winona the defeated ones would have said it was the location. But for the most part location was decidedly conservative on the matter and yet the victory is signally encouraging.

The more I study the past which we pretend to follow so closely.—I mean the days of Christ and the apostles the more I am assured that such a thing as "order" and "form" was absolutely unknown. And why as a people in the light of this fact we should hold so tenaciously as some do, is unexplainable to me. I trusted our fathers of my generation on the truthfulness of their position of forms for form's sake, and no one will ever know the disappointment I have suffered when apparently willfully they have suppressed the facts to maintain a point of custom. I look ahead and do not see the way to refrain from all kinds of worldliness, but again I see about all kinds are here and we have simply emphasized one point or two and let all others go. If there ever was a time when simple life should be pressed home to the heart of every believer it is now.[112]

The Annual Meeting had refused to change the basic decision of 1911 regarding the dress question, and the next problem was the application of the decision in the local congregations. Although the application varied from congregation to congregation, one elder of a city congregation reported the development in two letters to one of the most conservative leaders in the church.

Yes, we have a few hats in the Elgin Church. Compared to our membership they are quite numerous. Compared to our membership there are more than there should be. Personally, I dislike to see the order go from our sisters. But it has gone from many of them. I believe I can truly say that I have endeavored to do constructive work in our church here and I believe that something has been done in holding us from a division in our local work. When I became elder we would have come near splitting in the middle if the matter had gotten into the church as some desired.

I will admit that things are not handled here as they would be in many of our country churches. And I will admit that I have tried hard to go according to the ninth section of the 1911 dress decision,—to save all to the church. But I have no doubt that my efforts in method would be severely criticised with many of our brethren. This I cannot help. Our church stands loyal to the Brotherhood in those fundamental principles that we hold dear. I do not want to see us get away from them; but it is in methods where we can be easily understood and methods have always caused more heartaches than principles. . . .

As for the dress question. It is like the man said about the poor,—ever present with us. I do not know how long we shall be bothered with that question. Possibly if I could tell how long you and I will live and exercise as elders, then I could tell you to the day just how long we would be pestered with the problem. It is not a pleasant picture to contemplate. I sincerely believe in the simple life; it will be very serious to our spiritual lives when we depart from that; but we are moving towards the departure from our present mode of dress. Personally I believe the pendulum is moving towards the other extreme; and I believe that we should scent the thing afar, and begin to do constructive teaching on the plain principles of the simple life. To legislate against the hat, with the present tendencies and unrest, only tends to hasten the day of the bonnet's doom,—that is unless we legislate all hats out of the church. But that would also hasten the day. The great trouble is that the dress question has been trimmed down on this side and that side until it has come to be almost altogether localized in the bonnet on the heads of the sisters. Beneath the bonnet, they can dress pretty much as they please and the bonnet itself has as many styles as there are general styles of hats today; the brethren have very wide latitude in their apparel,—even elders of good repute do not always need to wear the standing collar coat in some places, where a sister would be summarily dealt with if she departed from the head dress now recognized. If we had been as scrupulous in maintaining the same standard of separateness on the part of our entire membership of brethren,—ministers, deacons and laity,—as we have been on our entire membership of sisters, I am wondering just where we would be on the dress question now.[113]

These letters in 1915 regarding Brethren dress symbolized the drastic changes that were taking place at the end of this half-century in Brethren relation to society. Changes in relation to government included a willingness to vote and to hold office and an uncertainty about the historic pacifism of the Brethren. Also, Brethren were more willing to turn to the government for action on such issues as temperance. In effect, Brethren were becoming much more active participants in the total society.

III

FOREIGN MISSIONS

INTRODUCTION

In the decade before the Civil War, some Brethren leaders evinced an interest in the development by the church of a foreign mission program. For example, the Annual Meeting of 1852 was asked "Whether the commission of our Lord and Savior Jesus Christ (Matthew 28:19–20; Mark 16:15) does not require the church to send brethren to preach the Gospel where the name of Christ is not known?", to which the Meeting replied: "the Brethren acknowledge the great commission of Christ to its full extent, and that it is the duty of the church, the ministers, and every private member to do all that is in their power to fulfill the commission in accordance with apostolic practice." This idea was discussed by Annual Meeting on a number of occasions during the next quarter of a century. Enoch Eby, one of the most mission-minded Brethren of the day, summarized the developments in an article in 1880.

Since 1852 the question of greater and more general effort in the Brotherhood, for the spread of the Gospel, has been before our Conference some twelve different times; and every time received its approval and hearty encouragement, and while, in the meantime, there was a steady growth in the interests of the missionary cause among us, no very definite or extensive measure has ever been adopted till our late Annual Meeting. Districts have been recommended to labor in that direction, and many of them have done well, and we are glad to notice a constant growth in the interests of missionary work; and especially were we pleased to see our late Annual Meeting, for the first time, take hold of the reins in good earnest, and adopt a system which, if carried out, and worked up with the enthusiasm that the cause demands, and which becometh the children of God who have the salvation of the world committed unto them, will certainly work well and accomplish much good. But the best system in the world will amount to nothing if left dormant.[1]

Elgin Moyer, in a study of the development of Brethren foreign missions, suggested five reasons for the missionary awakening of the third quarter of the nineteenth century among the Brethren: (1) The extensive growth of the church in the United States gave Brethren an assurance of permanence and a feeling of national influence. (2) New leaders of the church were introducing many new ideas through the newly organized denominational periodicals. (3) Brethren were making new contacts with their social milieu and were realizing how small their contribution had been. (4) Specifically, their contacts included relations with other churches which maintained mission programs. (5) They became aware of the needs of others and the fact that such needs could be met without compromising the basic Biblical principles on which the church was grounded.[2]

At the same time that some leaders were becoming interested in the development of a foreign mission program, other leaders were vigorously opposed. Consequently, it was only in certain sections of the church that it was possible to encourage the idea of foreign missions. That the districts of the church were allowed to make their own decisions regarding foreign missions was outlined by the Annual Meeting on several occasions and confirmed by Enoch Eby in his article in 1880. Whether it was the will of God, or pure coincidence, it was Enoch Eby's own District of Northern Illinois that first got the Brethren involved in foreign missions.

BEGINNINGS IN DENMARK

A young Danish immigrant, Christian Hope, was searching for a religious group that fitted his own personal ideas. His story begins in Denmark, as he later related it to a close friend in America, M. M. Eshelman.

He had strong faith that God would sustain him and enable him to find a people who would fill the measure of God's requirements. He came in contact with the different sects, mixed with them freely, gave advice and direction to inquiring souls—but alas! the work was again found too destitute of the real, and he suffered from friends and foes alike.

Before this took place he and a friend had almost resolved to sail across the great Atlantic for free America, and in casting lots it was determined they should go. During the interval between his arrest by the government for the "Scaffold" publication, two more were issued entitled, "The Mark of the Beast" and "Redemption." These created a storm of indignation and a reward of 20 crowns was offered for him. Every means was used to arrest and imprison him. The mail and telegraph were brought into use for his apprehension, and he several times barely escaped capture. The way of escape was opened, and he reached Norway in safety.

Here he proclaimed the gospel, as he then understood it, in low and in high places for a month or more to great crowds of people who thronged to hear the young defender of the Bible. From here he started to America, reaching the central part of Iowa about harvest time in 1870. Here the same great struggles and trials bore down on his heart, and it seems that Satan followed him to sift him as wheat.[3]

In America, Christian Hope's religious search continued. He describes it:

In those long years of labor, and sacrifices, and God-given grace,—in those years of honest motives, yet so full of error, I had one clear and distinct idea of duty. I knew it to be the duty of a sinner to be taught, and the duty of the church to do this work. I saw that a great deal of wrong, and error, and wickedness had entered into the world because those who had espoused Christianity had not submitted to the church as their teacher, but either before or after they joined exalted themselves and ran ahead with their own ideas and divers doctrines. I knew, too, that I had never been taken in and taught, because I had no Brethren to warn me, to keep me, stay me,—because I had no man to advise me, hence often erred, not knowing better at the time.

Often had I been urged to organize a church on the basis of what I regarded gospel principles; but I could not.

I felt a willingness to hunt for such a people until death rather that set up a church. I felt sure such a people existed and that I would be permitted to see them.

Such was my state of mind—such my humble position; yet there rested upon me great responsibility. I must now judge whether these people whom I long have sought, are truly the children of God, for I do not wish to be deceived.[4]

Hope read a lot of religious material and asked a lot of questions. Eventually he learned about a group called Dunkers, whose ideas seemed to fit his own ideas. But he had difficulty finding them. Finally he succeeded in locating a group of Brethren in Illinois led by George Zollers.

Failing here we went on to Bro. Geo. D. Zoller's home. We were surprised at the plainness of his wife. This home, being clean, neat, and plain, is a type of the many I found everywhere among the Brethren. This sister, so kind, lovely, and pleasant, with a plain white cap on her head reminded me of the women in my native country, and especially brought to memory my mother when in my childhood days I beheld her in such saintly loveliness. This scene left a lasting impression on my mind, and I wished all the women everywhere would dress as does this dear sister. I wished that my wife could see her, believing that if she could she would cast away her hat and never more buy another.

Sister Zollers told us her husband was in the harvest field, but would soon come in. She, too, was a little alarmed, but kindly asked us to be seated; and we rested under the shade trees in the beautiful yard. We here saw Musselman, their deacon, as he passed by, and J. Y. Heckler, a minister, called in while we were there. Finally "George" came in smiling and seemingly happy. His wife told him of us, and soon we were engaged in relating our simple story. Surely we were repaid ten-fold for our hardships, for we found a man with an open, loving heart who himself once had been away on the distant ocean among scoffers and unbelievers. He at once understood our condition, sympathized with us, prayed for us and certainly was heard by his Father in heaven.

IN MEETING

We remained with him that night, and the next day being Sunday, we went with him to meeting. That morning Bro. Heckler put into my hands Moore's pamphlet, "The Perfect Plan of Salvation." This I read through before I reached the place of meeting. It's tone and manner of reasoning made a more favorable impression on my mind than any other tract I had ever read. I wrote a letter to its author for several other pamplets and books in order to learn more concerning the position of the Brethren. They were promptly sent by Bro. Moore, whom I never met, though I love him dearly.

Reaching the place of meeting we listened to the earnest, powerful preaching of brethren Zollers and Heckler. The hymn, "Am I a soldier of the cross," deeply impressed me. . . .

About four weeks afterwards we prepared to move to Mt. Carroll, Ill. and on our way stopped to see relatives in Clinton, Ia. We soon reached Hickory Grove, five miles west of Mt. Carroll, where three of us were baptized by the Brethren October 25th, 1874. Remained with the Brethren here a little while and found them kind, loving, plain and faithful. I still regard this little church as "my home."

We settled down to work in Mt. Carroll where we remained a few months, and then at the solicitation of kind friends moved to Lanark where we continued working at the harness trade. Here, shortly after our arrival, the Danish Mission project was brought forward, and the churches in Northern Illinois were pleased to put me to work where I now am.

The Lord does not delight in the death of a sinner, hence patiently worked with me to make me one of his children. He can use the poorest, and simplest man, after he has remolded him to do good and save others. O ye "little ones" take courage, look up; no longer feel poor and insignificant, for God can make you a "chosen vessel" fitted for his use. . . .

Later I moved to Lanark where, by kind brethren, I was enabled to set up in business. Well do I remember the love and kindness of those dear brethren and sisters whose lovely faces stand before me to this day. Here I commenced to translate brothers Moore and Eshelman's pamphlets into Danish, thinking that perhaps some day I would be able to have them printed at my own expense and have them distributed in Denmark. At this time the love between me and brother Eshelman was kindled, and which has kept us as one to this day. Little did I think that he would be the Lord's instrument to inaugurate the Danish Mission; and little did I then think that I would ever be sent to my native country to teach the people the way of the Lord. Had this been known to me then, I would likely have tried to hide myself like

Jonah; but what followed was wisely kept from me when translating those pamplets. I must here note brother Eshelman's part in the work of originating the mission. Somewhere I had learned that there were about 100,000 members in the United States; and as I worked on the translation, I thought what a great work could be done if each member would donate one cent towards printing these pamphlets in the Danish Language. I felt that if I had them printed, I could easily get them distributed all over Denmark; but I did not dare to ask this of my brethren and sisters, for evil-disposed persons would have misconstrued my motives, and injured the cause; and as the missionary plea was then just taking hold of the Brethren, I felt I must do nothing to discourage the church. But one day brother Eshelman came in to visit me, and our conversation soon drifted toward tract work. I reluctantly opened my writing desk and took out an article which I had prepared to send to the *Pilgrim.* I read it to him and then he said; "You must send this to the *Pilgrim,* brother Christian." I told him I could not and gave him my reasons. He replied, "Let me have that article, and I will make it work." I handed it to him and then went on with my work. Bro. Eshelman said, "I will begin the work by giving twenty-five cents; will you give the same?" We did so; and he called on others through the papers to give, and soon $400 was donated to publish the translated pamphlets.

THE CALL FROM DENMARK

While this was going on I wrote to my old friend Christian Hansen in Denmark concerning the Brethren, and sent him Moore and Eshelman's pamphlets, as he could read English. I prayed God to give him grace to know the truth and obey it. By the time the $400 for the tract fund was in, I received a letter from my friend Hansen to the Cherry Grove church, Carroll County, Illinois, asking to have the gospel preached in Denmark, and wishing to be received into the church. This brought the church to action; and after the request was read, it was agreed by the Cherry Grove church to seek the counsel of all the churches comprising the Northern Illinois District.[5]

Enoch Eby, who was directly involved in much of what was happening from this point on, described the events.

In the mean time, however, through brother Hope's answering letters of inquiry from Denmark, a very urgent request was sent to him from Christian Hansen desiring some one to come over and baptize him, and preach the gospel in its original purity. There were also others inquiring for the true bread of life. The matter now having assumed an important form, some of the Elders of Northern Illinois were consulted in reference to the Scandinavian cry for help; whereupon it was decided expedient to call a special District Meeting at Cherry Grove, Carroll Co. on the 12th, day of Nov. 1875, with a request that each church in Northern Illinois should, if possible, be represented by two delegates. The churches having responded accordingly (with the exception of one) and a general interest manifested by the large meeting was fully explained by referring to said call and the causes leading thereto, it became very apparent to the assembly generally that the call was worthy of a favorable notice, and that the gospel required their request to be granted, but while that point seemed plain, it was an important question as to whose duty it was to send men to Denmark; the District, or the general brotherhood. . . .

Therefore in the midst of all these uncertainties and the call being urgent, the meeting finally decided to prosecute the work according to her best judgement and ability. And as the call was from Southern Denmark and a good portion of the inhabitants being German it was decided that a German brother be sent, and one English (or English and German,) and one that could speak the Danish Language. And as there was no Danish brother in the ministry in the brotherhood that we had any knowledge of and only two lay members, it was decided that one from among those two should be chosen to the ministry and sent to Denmark to preach the gospel. The vote was taken, and brother Hope elected to the first degree with the privilege to baptize. The meeting also chose two more, Enoch Eby and Paul Wetzel. It was thought best that the two brethren last named should not go immediately. Bro. Hope accordingly made immediate preparation and left for Denmark about the first of January 1876.[6]

Christian Hope, however, went through some agonizing soul-searching regarding the assignment to go back to Denmark.

I was still certain on this memorable day, that I would not need to go to Denmark as a minister; but when brother Enoch Eby announced to the congregation that since they were chosen, it became necessary to send with them some one who could interpret and aid in the work, and that the church would necessarily be required to choose one to accompany them. When he announced this, and that there were only two in Northern Illinois who could speak the Danish Language, myself and another brother in Lee county, I began to fear that I might be called; so I went to my wife and asked counsel what we should do in case I should be chosen, whether to accept or refuse; for I knew the time to consider would be short if I should be the choice of the church. We thus reasoned: Since Brethren Eby and Wetzel were to go, I would only be required to interpret for them, hence the responsibilities would not be very great, and we could endure it in that way. I felt that by God's assistance we could do a little, while the other brethren would stand as representatives of the church; and as it was understood that only one year should be devoted to that, we concluded we would go if chosen.

It was then agreed that Christian Hope should prepare immediately and go in advance to begin the work, to secure a house for the others and find a room for meeting purposes.

By January, 1876 Hope was ready to begin the new venture.

Finally we arrived at Aalborg, Denmark, where Mary had some relatives. Their chief fear was that they would have to provide for us and keep us, and it was a lesson of study between their joy to see us, and their fear of having to feed and clothe us. But we soon betook ourselves away to the north to see Christian Hansen, who had for some time been calling for help to obey the Lord. He rejoiced to see us. . . . He was baptized May 5th. He informed me that in the northern part of Denmark there was a girl who was seeking the Lord and would likely come among the Brethren; so we went to see her, and on the 27th of May, she, too, was baptized. This finished the harvesting for 1876. . . .

The year 1877 found the work more prosperous, our membership being increased to eight. We also learned that brethren Eby and Fry with their wives would come to our help, and perform the work assigned to them. I secured a house in the northern part of Denmark and took up my residence there, in accordance with directions, as the mission was established in that part without doubt.[7]

Enoch Eby, one of the elders selected to make the trip, described some of his experiences.

At the Annual District Meeting of Northern Illinois in the Spring of 1877 the question was asked, Should not those two brethren appointed, go to Denmark and organize a church? It was decided they should, and that the different churches should raise a certain proportionate amount of the funds required, and that a special District Meeting should be called at Waddam's Grove, Stephenson County, August 13th, 1877 for the purpose of making more definite arrangements necessary for the anticipated voyage. And among the different items considered at this meeting was, the necessity of both brethren going, being ordained Elders, (or Bishops) or not. It being decided in the affirmative, brother Wetzel not being ordained, resigned his appointment. It now became necessary to elect another. Brother Daniel Fry was therefore duly chosen. In submission to this appointment, we, with our wives, at once began to make the necessary arrangements to enter upon our long and perilous journey, to start from a Love-feast at Waddam's Grove, Stephenson County on the 26th and 27th of September 1877 which was done amid the tears and sobs of a vast multitude of sympathizing friends, brethren, and sisters, and children. Some bade the last farewell, for before we returned they were in their graves. The feast and the separation, both at the meeting-house and at the depot in Lena, presented the most solemn and affecting scene we ever witnessed, fully demonstrating the love which does not only characterize brethren and sisters in the flesh, but that which unites the children of God in one common brotherhood.

We give the following extract from the *Lena Star,* descriptive of the parting. The Editor was present and wrote as follows:

"Elders Enoch Eby and Daniel Fry of the denomination of Brethren, left Lena on Thursday afternoon, on the 1:45 P.M. train on their way to Denmark, where they go at the direction of their church, to establish a mission in a field where there is now one minister of the above mentioned denomination, C. Hope. On several days before the gentlemen started, a Love-feast was held in the church at Waddam's Grove, the interest in which was, of course, deepened by the course the services took, bearing upon the subject of the departure of the brethren. About four-hundred members communed, and one was baptized. On the day of the ministers departure a very large delegation, we think at least three-hundred, accompanied them from the church to the station at this place, to bid them farewell. The scene at the depot was truly affecting and moved many hearts outside of the fold of the church directly interested. The wives of the missionaries accompanied them, and they will remain as long as they in their judgement see proper. These persons are sent in answer to the call from the missionary already in Denmark for help. And the expense is borne by individual subscriptions by the brethren of the Northern District of Illinois, assisted by those throughout the United States who feel disposed to contribute. . . ."

About noon we arrived at Wandrup, a village near the south line of Denmark. Here we had our first experience in the Danish language, and currency. On the 29th we left for Bronderslev, Denmark, our place of destination and arrived about noon much wearied of a journey of about eighteen days on land and sea, but felt to praise the Lord for his preserving care over us. At this place we shall ever remember the heart-beating joy we experienced in meeting our dear brethren C. Hope and C. Hansen, the latter living in this place and with whom we ate our first meal of black bread and cheese made of goats milk, and coffee, which had the relish of an American turkey roast; for the welcome which we received seemed to season the food with heaven's choicest blessings. After a little rest and brotherly greetings, we pursued our way five miles west by wagon to the house of Bro. Hope and had another joyful meeting with sister Hope and children and a Danish sister. Here we remained several days as members of the family, attracting much notice and curiosity among the people, and admiration among the members. Some said, "Well they did not send boys over here," others said, "They just look like the apostles," and others perhaps like the Athenians said, "what will these babblers have to say? They bring strange things to our ears because they preach except ye repent and be baptized, and then keep the commandments of Jesus, we cannot be saved. We must not go to war, but love our enemies. We must not swear by any oath; we must not conform to this world. We cannot put away our wives by divorce and marry another."

At the time of our arrival there were ten members in Denmark, one more added in a few days; then by the desire of all the members, arrangements were made at once to hold the first Love-feast in Denmark on the 18th of November in Bro. Hope's house, at which time two more were added, making in all nineteen communicants, including brother and sister Hope, and ourselves. There was a remarkable interest at this meeting by all; for none present ever before saw the ordinances of the church practiced according to apostolic order, (save we who went from America) and never did I witness a more enjoyable feast to the members, nor more admired by all present. At this meeting by the unanimous consent of all present brother Hope was ordained to the Eldership, and an election held for one minister and one deacon. After the scripture was read and briefly commented upon, which sets forth the qualifications of the elder and the deacon, the members were requested to cast their vote; and the result was brother Eskildsen was chosen to the ministry, and brother C. Neilsen to the deaconship.

We then continued to preach by interpretation (brother Hope being interpreter) as time and opportunity would permit; and as some more were added to the church, it was unanimously desired to have another Communion season before we returned to America which was held at the place of the former one, on the 6th of January 1878, with the same degree of solemnity and interest as the former one. At this meeting brother Eskildsen was also ordained an elder without a dissenting voice, when the reason was fully explained, which was to have the church prepared to perform any business without official aid from America.[8]

And so the visiting Brethren returned to America.

When brothers Eby and Fry left for Germany and thence home, brother Hope was absent preaching the Gospel; for the field is large and the work abundant; so that when he came home, the loved ones had gone, and instead of finding the good, sweet associates, he found the members weeping and sorrowing because they never more, in this life, expected to see their dear brethren and sisters. He says to this day the Danish church feels the effects of their leaving, and especially the good work done by them. Hear Bro. Hope on the sending of those brethren and sisters.

"It was wise and prudent that Northern Illinois sent two brethren and two sisters over to us. They were a great help to the church here, though they could not speak the Danish language. The brethren alone would never have done what they and their wives together did; hence no one should blame the District for sending them."[9]

For the remainder of his life Christian Hope continued to represent the German Baptist Brethren in the United States among the people in Denmark and Sweden. He almost literally worked himself to death; in 1886 he and his wife had to return to the United States to recover. Between then and his death in 1899 he made three additional trips to Scandinavia in efforts to encourage and strengthen the church that was developing there.

One of Hope's major problems in his work in Scandinavia was the support of his family. For a variety of reasons he found it necessary to depend almost entirely on assistance from America. In the United States, however, most Brethren did not believe that any minister of the Brethren anywhere ought to receive his entire support from the church. Therefore, the question arose as to who was primarily responsible for the support of Christian Hope. The district mission board of Northern Illinois had sent him to Denmark. In 1876 this board through the district meeting turned to the church as a whole for support.

In 1876, at the A. M. held in Logan county, Ohio, brother Enoch Eby, the member of the Standing Committee from Northern Illinois, introduced the following to the meeting:

"Will this District Meeting agree to send the decision of District Meeting of November 12, 1875, at Cherry Grove, to Annual Meeting for approval or reflection?" To this the meeting replied:

"We unitedly agree to send it to Annual Meeting for approval and reflection."

After considerable discussion, by request of the Moderator, H. D. Davy and a few others, it was withdrawn. This showed that those in charge of the meeting were unfavorable to the brotherhood giving its co-operation.[10]

Evidently the supporters of foreign missions in the church in the United States had not done sufficient homework, for the more conservative elements which opposed foreign missions controlled the Standing Committee in 1876. However, the supporters of missions were persistent, and in 1877 they again presented a query, which evidently was accepted by the Standing Committee, because it was eventually accepted by the Annual Meeting and became a part of the official Minutes.

VII. This District Meeting requests Annual Meeting to inquire into the missionary work now begun in Denmark, and if it thinks it advisable to recommend it to the sympathy and support of the general brotherhood.

Answer: Whereas from what we know of the success of the Danish Mission, we do grant the request of the Middle District of Pennsylvania. The following resolution in regard to the Danish Mission was also passed by the Annual Meeting:

Resolved, That this Annual Meeting approve of a collection being made while in session, for the Danish Mission.[11]

The Minutes do not indicate how much, if any, of a collection was made at the Meeting. A later report noted that "with all patient waiting up to October 13th of that year very little money from the 'general brotherhood' had fallen into the treasury." The result was action by the Brethren in Northern Illinois.

At a special meeting of the Northern District of Illinois held at Waddams Grove, Stephenson county, Illinois, August 13, 1877, it was unanimously agreed that the churches composing the District would contribute $2,000, one half of this sum to be paid into the Treasury by September 27th. With characteristic promptness the churches contributed, and on the day mentioned a draft for $1,000, was handed to brother Eby.[12]

Three months later in December, 1877, a group of Brethren leaders who were interested in evangelism and mission work in general and in foreign missions in particular met in Myersdale, Pennsylvania and established an organization known as the Brethren's Church Extension Union. The leading spirit in the movement was Howard Miller, a progressive-minded young Brethren minister. He had previously sent out a questionnaire to attempt to determine how much interest the Brethren had in missions. He also publicized the idea in the church's papers; he claimed to have received 2500 letters with no dissenting voices.[13]

Another meeting of this Union, which included any interested Brethren, was held at the Ogan's Creek church in Indiana on the Saturday preceding the beginning of the Annual Meeting of 1878. Further work was done to clarify the organization, which included "a General Organization, District Organization, and Local Organizations." Also, the name was changed to the Brethren's Work of Evangelism. An editor of the ***Progressive Christian,*** *J. W. Beer, reflected on the importance of this program and its impact on foreign missions.*

In another column of this issue will be found a correct report of the plan of the Work of Evangelism, as adopted at the meeting at Ogan's Creek, Ind., on Saturday preceding our last Annual Meeting. Our brotherhood was well represented by brethren and sisters from a number of the States. The whole plan was read and then re-read, article by article, and, after some amendments were made was unanimously adopted. It is just to conclude that there was a fair representation of the wisdom, piety and zeal of the Church, and it was gratifying to see the harmony that characterized the meeting. It shows that, as a church, we feel the importance and necessity of making a greater and more united effort in the spreading of the truth; and now we do not want the work to stop, but to move steadily and rapidly onward. We are sorry that the A. M. of 1878, on account of a little informality, hesitated to sanction this plan. It may have its imperfections, but it certainly has some advantages over every other plan that has yet been proposed. . . . This plan provides for

GENERAL MISSIONARY WORK

in which all the districts and churches are to be united. It is the privilege of any district, or congregation, or, even, individual member, to send out a missionary, and to support him in his work; but it is the duty of the entire church to see to it that the work is not neglected. Here we have a plan by which we may unite in the most free and equitable manner: there is not compulsion, but there is universal liberty. This is God's plan.[14]

Because the Brethren's Work of Evangelism organization had not followed the established procedure of being approved by a District Meeting, it did not secure a hearing at the Annual Meeting of 1878. However, the District of Northern Illinois did have a petition prepared for that Meeting.

XVII. Whereas Annual Meeting has heretofore left the Danish Mission to the care of Northern Illinois, recommending it to the support and sympathy of the entire brotherhood, and

Whereas, a Church has now been fully organized in Denmark, does this Annual Meeting consider it advisable for that Church to remain under the care of Northern Illinois, or does it properly belong to the direct care of the Annual Meeting?

Answer: The Church in Denmark shall be under the care of the

Northern District of Illinois, but it is the duty of the whole brotherhood to help defray the expenses, that the said District does not have to bear more than its part or proportion of the expenses that must be met and provided for.[15]

This decision in 1878 did not satisfactorily settle the matter of what was the District's "proportion of the expenses." Apparently, the other districts did not do their share, and the District of Northern Illinois returned to the Annual Meeting for further clarification.

III. Inasmuch as it was decided by last Annual Meeting that the expenses of the Danish Mission shall be paid by the general brotherhood, will not the District of Northern Illinois request Annual Meeting of 1879 to tell each district what its probable portion will be?

Answer: We agree to petition Annual Meeting to grant the above request.

Answer as given by Annual Meeting. As $800 are needed to meet the expenses of said mission for the present year, this Annual Meeting requests each church in the brotherhood to pay $2.00 the wealthier churches more and the poorer ones less, to make up said amount that amount from each church being necessary the money to be sent to the treasurer of the Northern District of Illinois, C. P. Rowland.[16]

Editorial comments in the ***Progressive Christian,*** *although supportive of foreign missions, was not pleased with the decision of the Annual Meeting.*

The Northern District of Illinois again petitioned Annual Meeting to help pay its expenses in the Danish Mission. A tax of two dollars for each congregation was levied. This we consider an imposition, and we hope the matter will be brought before the next Annual Meeting in such a shape that conference will either assume control of the mission, or compel Northern Illinois to pay its own expenses.[17]

Another important decision of the Annual Meeting of 1879 dealt with the new organization promoting missions and evangelism.

XVII. We, the Elk Lick congregation, ask the District Meeting to instruct the delegates to Annual Meeting to urge the mission work of evangelism upon said body, and that they be instructed to use all fair means to have the Annual Meeting accept and encourage the work. This was agreed to by the Western District of Pennsylvania.

Deferred by Annual Meeting.[18]

Obviously, the most conservative elements in the church, which opposed foreign missions, had succeeded in postponing the action of the church as a whole regarding missions. Silas Thomas, one of their spokesmen, commented:

. . . Most of the periodicals among us are persistent in their praise of the new missionary scheme, and in their calls upon the members to further it with their money, while they refuse, point blank, to publish anything in opposition to it or commendatory of the pure old apostolic mode of evangelizing thru which the Brotherhood has attained her present state of prosperity. "Coming events cast their shadows before them," and this work of the papers is a sure precursor of what will happen when the missionaries of the new order have taken the field.[19]

The basic issue of whether the foreign mission program would be solely the responsibility of individual districts or the responsibility of the entire brotherhood finally reached a conclusive climax at the Annual Meeting of 1880. The church as a whole accepted the responsibility.

III. A request from the Western District of Pennsylvania to call up and protect the petition of that district sent up to Annual Meeting of 1879, urging the work of evangelism upon said meeting, and instructing the delegates to use all fair means to have the Annual Meeting to accept and encourage said work, but which was deferred by Annual Meeting of 1879.

Upon the presentation of the above request, the following resolution was offered and passed by the Annual Meeting: Resolved, That we appoint a committee of five, whose duty it shall be to present a plan that will harmonize with other plans that have been favored by Annual Meeting and the one now in operation among us; but Annual Meeting shall not be financially responsible for any plan.

The committee reported the following plan which was adopted by the Annual Meeting:

1. We recommend this Annual Meeting to appoint five brethren, sound in the faith and fully alive to our missionary interests, to super-

intend the Domestic and Foreign missionary work of the general Brotherhood.

2. That those five brethren appoint out of their number such officers (Cor. Sec'y, Treasurer, etc.) as the nature of the work requires.

3. That the brethren be instructed to interfere in no way with any present individual church or district missionary efforts among our brethren.

4. That Annual Meeting advise that any Domestic or Foreign mission work of a general nature, like the Danish mission, now under the care of district council, be committed to the supervision of this Board.

5. That this meeting recommend that the fund now in the hands of the "Brethren's Work of Evangelism" be committed to the treasury of the Board of the General Conference.

6. That this Board be instructed to proceed no further in its appointments, etc., than the means in its treasury will justify.

7. That the officers of this Board be required to make an official report of their work, its condition, operation and wants, to each session of our General Conference, and that said report go into our regular minutes.

8. That every church in the Brotherhood be requested to appoint a solicitor in its own congregation to raise funds for this work and forward the same to the treasurer of this mission Board, at least every six months.

9. That this board be instructed to proceed to its work at once as opportunity permits.

10. The Standing Committee of Annual Meeting be required to fill any vacancy that may occur in the Board from time to time, and that its members be elected every four years.

J. W. Stein,
John Metzger,
Hiel Hamilton,
J. D. Livengood,
J. W. Fitzgerald,
Committee.

In connection with the foregoing, the following resolution was passed: Resolved, That the Danish mission be transferred to the Domestic and Foreign mission Board.[20]

In this way, Brethren established their first nationwide board to coordinate the activities of the Brethren in the area of missions and evangelism. Enoch Eby became the first chairman of the Board, indicating the emphasis that would be placed on foreign missions. As expected, the anti-mission leaders in the church were distressed and came to the Annual Meeting of 1881 requesting a rescinding of this action.

XXIV. Inasmuch as the Foreign and Domestic mission is causing trouble and confusion in the Church of the Brethren, we ask Annual Meeting to consider all its decisions on this subject since 1868, Art. 21, and to re-adopt the decision of that year.

Answer: We do re-adopt the decisions of 1868, but to save the Danish mission and the arrangement of 1880 from being disorganized, we leave them stand at least one year.[21]

The leaders of the Annual Meeting attempted to be conciliatory in dealing with the conservatives, but they were not in a reactionary mood and refused to terminate the board which had been established in 1880. By the following year the more conservative or Old Order group had departed (see chapter on Divisions), and the supporters of foreign missions were able to move forward more aggressively. One change was a restructuring of the board in 1884, which will be considered in the chapter on policy and organization.

The final chapter on the story of the Brethren in Scandinavia was written in the twentieth century. Gradually Brethren withdrew from the area, ending work in the 1940s. By that time many of the Scandinavian Brethren had emigrated to the United States. Several significant results of this initial Brethren foreign mission effort may be enumerated: (1) It affected the lives of a number of people who were brought to a new recognition of their relationship with Jesus Christ. (2) It encouraged the state churches of the area to undertake a more aggressive church program for the benefit of the people. (3) It served as a laboratory in which the Brethren gained some valuable lessons in the administration of foreign missions, and it served as the pioneer and forerunner in getting the Brethren interested in foreign missions.[22]

INDIA

As a pioneer and forerunner, the Danish mission prompted a group of Brethren students in the 1880s to become interested in serving in areas of the globe that had never been exposed to Christianity. The individual who stood out in this group was Wilbur B. Stover. He developed an interest in India during his student days at Mount Morris College. John S. Flory, who entered Mount Morris in September following Stover's departure in June, recalled "how the atmosphere of the place was still full of what Wilbur Stover had said, and how he had exalted the cause of missions in the church."

Almost through his entire school career Brother Stover was a leader among the students in religious work. He was early imbued with the spirit of missions. A call to serve the Master meant to him to accept his program of teaching and work. Especially during his last several years at Mount Morris he became noted for the insistence with which he talked missions. It was his hobby. No matter whether the occasion was a prayer meeting, a meeting of the literary society, a conversation among a group of students, a private walk with a fellow-student for exercise,—no matter what, Brother Stover talked incessantly about the missionary duty of the church.

The phase of missions that especially impressed him was the duty devolving upon the church to carry the Gospel message to all the world. He did not have a particular plan of work, nor did he urge individuals to offer themselves for the service; he was not a volunteer himself; but he was impressed with the importance of the missionary enterprise as a part of the church's duty to the world.[23]

After Stover's graduation from Mount Morris he spent several years as the pastor of the Germantown, Pennsylvania church, where he continued to emphasize the need of the Brethren to become involved in foreign missions. On one occasion a member of his congregation, after hearing another of his missionary sermons, is supposed to have asked whether the pastor expected someone from his congregation to become a missionary. Stover responded in typical fashion: "Somebody's got to go." Evidently he also preached in other Brethren congregations, for the Waynesboro congregation in Pennsylvania agreed to provide $800 to support Stover and his wife in India.[24]

Something of a climax came in October, 1892, when Wilbur B. Stover made a proposal to the General Missionary Committee at its regular meeting at Mount Morris.

At this point, Eld. J. H. Moore and Sister Lizzie Miller came in to be present at the discussion of the India Mission Question, and the Board upon motion decided to drop unfinished business and proceed.

Bro. Wilbur B. Stover presented a proposition to go to India as a missionary. After due deliberation the following was decided upon: That in view of the proposition made by the Waynesboro Church to assist in sending Bro. Wilbur B. Stover as a missionary to India, We agree to send him on the following conditions.

1. That he conform fully to the order of the church in dress.

2. That he agrees to remain at least five years subject to and under the direction of the General Mission Board. Also that the Foreman write him fully concerning conditions and the Secy telegraph him our decision. Telegram, "Go this fall on conditions. Letter explaining coming from Vaniman." Further, the Board recommends that Bro. G. N. Falkenstein of Mt. Morris, Ill. take his place at Germantown, PA.[25]

"This fall" evidently meant immediately, but for a variety of unidentified reasons, Stover could not go immediately. It was reported to the January, 1893 General Missionary Committee meeting that "Bro. Wilbur Stover did not go to India" with no "definite reasons why Bro. Wilbur failed to go."[26] However, this failure of Stover to leave immediately did not end the discussion of an India mission, for in February the General Missionary Committee held a special meeting.

The question of opening a mission in India came before the Board in the form of Bro. Albert W. & Sister Alice Vaniman of McPherson, Kan. offering themselves to go to heathen lands, wholly under the control of the Board. The merits of the case were carefully discussed and finally decided to ajourn until 7 a.m. Feb. 28 [the next morning] and in the meantime prayerfully to consider the question.

Feb. 28, 1893

All present, but the Secy one half hour late.
Decided to accept Br. Albert W. & Sister Alice Vaniman as missionaries to India.

Also to publish in the Gospel Messenger the following official call.

The Opening of an India Mission

At a meeting of the General Missionary Committee, February 28, the pressing need of a mission in India was presented and after prayerful and careful consideration, the Committee decided on the following:

1. That steps be taken towards opening a mission in India.

2. That Brother Albert W. and Sister Alice Vaniman, having offered themselves to labor in a foreign field, wholly under the control of the Committee, their application was accepted.

3. That the Committee desires to send another suitable brother and his wife, or a brother, or a sister, as circumstances direct, to accompany them.

4. That the Committee will need means to carry on this work, and now calls upon the Brotherhood for contributions. It is necessary, to carry out the present plans, that sufficient funds or a guarantee for the same, be in the hands of the Committee by Annual Meeting.

5. That the Board proposes to have the missionaries sail about October 1, 1893.

6. That all money for this work should be designated as "India Missions" and sent to the Secretary of the Committee, Mt. Morris, Illinois.

7. That the Committee suggests that all the churches and Sunday-schools in the Brotherhood hold special collections for this work on the first Sunday in May, or as near that time as convenient. There will also be an opportunity to contribute at Annual Meeting.

8. That applications with full particulars from members desiring to accompany Brother and Sister Vaniman, should be in writing and in the hands of the Secretary no later than time of Annual Meeting.

9. That the following are the qualifications for missionaries:

(a) That [they] must be sound in the faith.

(b) They must be willing to submit themselves wholly under the control and advice of the Committee.

(c) They must be able and willing to teach and defend the principles of the Gospel, and the doctrines and peculiarities of the church, as defined and applied by Annual Meeting and must manifest the same in their conversation, life and character. If married, the missionary must have a wife who is to him a true helpmeet, possessing, so far as may be, similar qualifications, and who is ever ready to carry forward the Lord's work.

(d) The Committee agrees that such missionaries shall be furnished steady employment, so long as they prove to be the right members in the right place, and while thus employed they shall be supported. An itemized report of expenses is to be submitted to the Committee quarterly, by all missionaries in their employ.

The above is to be signed by both the Committee and those who go.

By Order of the Board,
Daniel Vaniman, Foreman.[27]

Although Brethren seemed to be responding favorably to this notice in the **Gospel Messenger,** *the Missionary Committee decided at its meeting held during the Annual Meeting in May, 1893 to defer the India Mission until the July meeting. Again in July the proposal was deferred "in view of the decision of last A. M." That decision was in answer to a query.*[28]

2. Will the District Meeting ask Annual Meeting to reconsider Art. 10 of Minutes of 1892, and so change that no brother or sister be sent to foreign countries to do missionary, or church work, without first obtaining a favorable assent of the local District in which they live, as to their qualifications, and then also obtain the consent of Standing Committee and approval of Annual Meeting, and that no brother or sister be allowed to go for the above purpose in the name of the Brotherhood without being so sent?

Answer: Decided that the request be granted.[29]

Finally, at the October, 1893 meeting of the committee, more definite action was taken.

On motion, the India Mission question was reconsidered. The following was decided upon:

1. In view of the pressure brought to bear upon the Committee, it was decided to open a mission in India.
2. Decided to send two brethren and their wives.
3. For the present to send ministers only.
4. After some deliberations on application of bro. Wilbur Stover and Wife, decided to defer action until next meeting, and brethren S. F. Sanger and S. W. Hoover were appointed to visit them to investigate more fully their qualifications as missionaries to India.
5. Decided to recommend A. W. Vaniman and Alice Vaniman, his wife, as missionaries to India, to our next Annual Meeting.[30]

After further investigation the committee was prepared by the time of the Annual Meeting of 1894 to make a decision.

Decided to present the following to Standing Committee: Brother W. B. Stover and Sister Mary Stover, his wife, of Waynesboro, Pennsylvania, Brother A. W. Vaniman and Alice Vaniman, his wife, of Topeka, Kansas, and Sister Bertha Ryan, of Chicago, Illinois, having been properly recommended by their respective churches, and having been examined by the Standing Committee and the General Missionary and Tract Committee, as applicants for the India Mission field, are considered suitable for the work. Therefore, we hereby recommend them to Annual Meeting for approval, with the understanding that for the present the Missionary Committee will send only three of them.[31]

It is puzzling that the Missionary Committee approved five missionaries for the consideration of the Standing Committee and then the Annual Meeting delegates, and then turned around and proposed to send only three. Obviously, Bertha Ryan, as a single person, was being accepted; either the Stovers or the Vanimans would have to stay in the United States. To answer the question, the following letter was sent to the committee.

To the Mission Board:—

Whereas, it has been decided to select three of the five applicants for the India Mission, we present to you the following for your consideration: Being much impressed with the importance of our church opening a mission in India, we offered ourselves for the work, willing to be used if the Lord should so direct, and while all the applicants are much interested in the work, we feel to say to the Committee that any former decision of yours, in our case, should in no wise be a barrier to your full and free action in the matter now, and we, in accordance with the Scripture which says, "In honor preferring one another," cheerfully accord the preference to Brother and Sister Stover and Sister Ryan. This is further based upon the following consideration: Brother Stover was the first applicant. The church at Topeka needs our services. Praying that the Lord may guide the Board aright, in this important and far-reaching enterprise, we submit the above.

Signed: A. W. Vaniman, Alice Vaniman[32]

Eventually the Vanimans devoted their lives to the Brethren mission in Scandinavia. In the meantime the Annual Meeting of 1894 had officially approved the sending of missionaries to India.

India Missionaries Approved

Bro. W. B. Stover and sister Mary Stover, his wife, of Waynesborough, Pa., Bro. A. W. Vaniman and sister Alice Vaniman, his wife, of Topeka, Kans., and sister Bertha Ryan, of Chicago, Ill., having been properly recommended by their respective churches, and having been examined by the Standing Committee and the General Missionary and Tract Committee, as applicants for the India Mission field, are considered suitable for the work.[33]

The Stovers and Bertha Ryan departed from New York City in October, 1894 on their way to India. After stopping in London, they arrived in Bombay. Following careful study and investigation, they decided to locate in the town of Bulsar. Although it had about 12,000 people, the total area of Brethren responsibility included more than a million inhabitants. Becoming accustomed to the living conditions and learning a different language proved to be slow processes. A report to the Annual Meeting of 1896 follows:

India Field.—It has now been two years since the three who have been working in this field were approved by this meeting. The years have been full of experience. The missionaries are acquiring the language, and becoming more fully acquainted with the people, and the difficulties they have to meet. Affliction was heavy upon one of them, but he was raised up, and is, with the others, earnest in the work. A number have made inquiry concerning the faith, but none have been received into fellowship. Eld. D. L. Miller and wife spent some weeks in this field and were deeply impressed with the great need of mission work. They found the missionaries of one mind and faith and desirous to be in full sympathy and harmony with the Brotherhood at home.[34]

On one of his numerous visits to India, D. L. Miller described some of the cultural differences that Brethren encountered in their efforts to bring Christianity to India.

This morning Wilbur and I went to the home of one of our native teachers. They have a new baby, a boy three days old. I had the honor of naming the tiny bit of humanity "Samuel," a good old Bible name and the one borne by Brother McCann. The house has two rooms; the floors, the usual cow-dung mixture so common in this country, The teacher insisted on giving us tea. Teacups were set on the floor and the spoons were also laid by the side of the saucers. The tea was poured, the spoons taken from the floor and used for stirring the tea, and I drank mine without even closing my eyes. You can easily get used to things if you have to.

For two evenings I have had a lot of Hindus to consult me as to religion. They all talk good English. I rather upset their faith when I told them I had traveled around the world and found nothing but salt-water oceans. Their books teach that there are seven seas, or oceans, one of salt water, one of sweet water, one of clarified butter, one of milk, one of honey, etc., etc. When I asked them if they believed me, they said, "Yes, we saw you three years ago and you have been all over the world."

"Well," I said, "if you believe me, then you cannot believe your sacred books, for they tell you there are seas of butter, milk, honey, etc., and I say there are none." They had to believe this. These Hindu youths from eighteen to twenty are of the upper caste, one of them a Brahmin. I found they actually worship the idol and not the god through the idol.

We also had a call from two Hindus of the Baunia caste—merchants—one a money lender and the other a maker of fireworks. They wanted to see the "Padre Sahib" (that's me). Wilbur is "Stover Sahib" to them, but I am Padre, father of the whole business. They want to be baptized, and say that they are ready to do all that is required of them. But if they become Christians, they lose caste, and none of their people will have anything to do with them. Nobody will borrow the money lender's few rupes, and no one will buy fireworks from the other. Now they say, "What shall we do?" And this is the greatest problem we have to solve in India.[35]

In addition to all of the cultural differences, one of the major problems the Brethren had to encounter was the bubonic plague, which was brought into India from China in 1896. By the spring of 1897 around twenty to thirty people were dying each day in Bulsar; altogether about twelve hundred perished before the plague had ended. Many of these were adults, which meant that the number of orphans had increased drastically. The missionaries appealed to the Brethren at home for additional support to establish orphanages.[36]

Fig. 13. *Christian and Mary Nielson Hope in front of the mission house, Bethel Hordum, Denmark. (BHLA)*

Fig. 14. *Early baptismal scene at Bulsar, India. (BHLA)*

The Brethren responded with more than $25,000 over the next several years. The annual meetings of 1899, 1900, and 1901 received reports on the work that was being conducted in India.

[1899]

The report for India closes with April, 1899. From the beginning of the mission in 1894 to this date, 42 have been received into church membership, 1 has been disowned, 3 died. The present membership is 45, of which 32 are Hindoos, 1 Parsee, 1 Syrian, 3 Eurasian, 8 American. As organized into a congregation there are 2 elders, 1 minister in the second degree, 1 deacon, 2 lay evangelists, 1 colporteur, 2 day teachers, 3 Sunday-school teachers. One outstation at Navsari is occupied. Three love feasts have been held. The orphanage has a present enrollment of 34. 11 have died and 12 have been baptized. The response of the churches to donate for the orphans' home in India has been prompt and liberal, and the workers in India are using due caution to expend the consecrated amount judiciously.

[1900]

During the past year a suitable orphanage home was built by the funds so liberally donated one year ago for this purpose and about two hundred famine children are being cared for and instructed in the ways of the Lord. The India Famine Fund, so freely contributed, has been promptly forwarded and is being used by our missionaries in the most advantageous manner. Of the $15,631.99 donated up to April 1, not one cent was used to pay any clerical help or expense in this country and none of the missionaries in India. And it was the good fortune of the Committee to purchase gold at par, or a little below, so that not even did the expense of remitting decrease the fund one cent. The results of this relief work will be felt for a long time to come.

[1901]

Brother S. N. McCann sends this report for Anklesvar where he and his wife have been located since November 15, 1898:

"The famine began to be felt the following December after we moved and in January we commenced to care for some orphans. The year was largely given to famine work. We have at present five outstations, where regular work is done. Fifteen have been baptized during the year, eight of whom are our boys in the orphanage. In all there are twenty-one members at this place. We have sold about 500 gospels, exact record not kept. The field is large and much work is required."

The total of the famine fund sent to India by the church within the last two years amounts to $26,058.11. This has all been placed in the hands of the workers over there and they have labored hard to make good use of it, as intended by the donors.[37]

In some ways the establishment of orphanages typified the work of Brethren missionaries. They had not come to India for the sole purpose of preaching the Christian gospel but also of ministering to the total needs of the Indian people. One of the results was that the people were favorably impressed by the Christianity of the missionaries. Elgin Moyer in his study of Brethren missions described this impact.

While the orphanage work was hard, and the famine which caused the need of orphanages was a calamity, they seemed to the missionaries not to have been without some profit to India. Many people were reached for Christianity through the kindness and help of the missionaries. The Christian spirit had opportunity to permeate further into Indian life. Openings were made for more Christian work. Some of the foundation stones of the wall of caste were loosened. Some of the customs and superstitions that accompany non-Christian religions and primitive cultures lost their hold. The girls, as they grew up, made better wives and mothers. The boys as they went out from the orphanage, were more intelligent, possessed higher morals, and were more nearly self-supporting.

The most of the orphans became Christians. One of the missionaries said:

"They can become Christians without any of the objections which lie in the way of the Indian masses. They have no caste to fear; they have no employment to lose; their friends cannot say them no; they are free to do according to their own desires."

From among these Christian orphans, there were trained some of the early workers of the India mission. Some of the "orphan boys" are numbered among the successful preachers in the Indian Church of the Brethren today.[38]

In the first twenty years of Brethren activity in India, down to the beginning of the First World War in 1914, Brethren poured extensive human and financial resources into India. Approximately fifty mis-

sionaries had been sent to India from the churches in the United States. Each missionary required extensive financial support in travel and living expenses in India, for the work had to be supported from the United States. The result was converts to Christianity beginning with the first baptisms in April, 1897. D. L. Miller was responsible for the organization of the First German Baptist Brethren Church of Bulsar on one of his visits in February, 1899.

The Church of the Brethren, as it soon became known in India, had come to stay.

CHINA

For a number of years individuals here and there throughout our Brotherhood had been looking to China as our next mission field. In 1906 at the request of the General Mission Board Brother D. L. Miller had made a trip to China, calling at Hong Kong and Canton and going interior from Canton as far as the railway was finished. He was making inquiry as to the place where the Brethren should first open work in China. He also came up to Shanghai and had intended to go up the river to Hankow, but about this time there was an uprising in that part of the country and he did not get to complete his contemplated trip. He made inquiry as to the possibilities and advisability of opening work in China. He returned home, made report to the Board and urged that the Church of the Brethren begin work in China as soon as men could be found.

At Brother Miller's suggestion the General Mission Board asked Bro. McCann to investigate this field on his way home from India in the early part of 1907. He stopped at Hong Kong and came inland as far as Hankow. During the investigation he found that Shansi in the north and Yuan in the south were the least occupied of the provinces.

Thus began a brief pamphlet of eighteen pages entitled, ***A History of the Church of the Brethren in China,*** *written about 1915. The desirability of sending Brethren missionaries to China had been discussed occasionally in the years since the opening of China's doors to foreign missionaries in the 1850s. The interest developed steadily after the sending of missionaries to India. In 1900 John R. Snyder wrote in the* ***Gospel Messenger*** *that some of the members of the church were praying "that the day might be hastened when the whole gospel might be taught to the benighted souls in ancient Sinim." The*

March, 1903 issue of the ***Missionary Visitor,*** *another Brethren periodical, was devoted entirely to China.*

Brethren interest in China was slow in developing, if the contribution of funds for that purpose is an accurate indication. As early as 1901, the General Mission Board was accepting "gifts for a China mission." By March, 1906, it had received $1,125, which was not a very encouraging amount. However, by 1904 young Brethren were volunteering to go to China, and the Annual Meeting of 1906 responded to the demand for a mission in China and the availability of volunteers by approving F. H. Crumpacker and his wife, and Emma Horning, as missionaries to China. This action was taken in response to the recommendation of the General Mission Board at its meeting of May 26. At this point the Mission Board evidently dragged its feet. According to its secretary:

They did not sail that fall, for it was thought best to spend some time on the home base, developing a stronger interest in China. To this end Brother Crumpacker spent his energies in working among the churches and doing all he could for the new field. At the meeting of July 24, 1907, the Board did not think it prudent to send the three approved, alone to that far-away field, and asked the party to remain in the homeland for another year, with the hope that others would join the party in another year.

This came to pass, for at the Conference of 1908 Geo. W. Hilton and wife were approved. The party of five began preparations at once, and sailed from Seattle, Washington, in the latter part of August on the steampship, "Minnesota," arriving in Shanghai, China, on September 25.[39]

The missionaries in China now tell their own story.

When F. H. Crumpacker and wife, G. W. Hilton and wife, and Emma Horning were sent to China in the fall of 1908 the location was left entirely in their hands. After a thorough study of the "Atlas of Missions," by H. P. Beach, and much prayer they decided on Shansi Province. This decision was encouraged and strengthened by Bishop Bashford, who came over with us on the same boat.

Learning the name of the senior missionary, Rev. Sowerby, at the capital of Shansi, we wrote him a letter from Japan, asking him to rent us a house. At Shanghai we learned of two people who had been to Shansi—Dr. T. Richards and Mrs. Morgan—who gave us a great deal of information as to what we should take with us. At Hankow we received a letter, saying Rev. Sowerby had rented a house for us. Thus the Lord was leading us step by step in the darkness, and we were indeed thankful, for His answer to our prayers.

From Hankow on the real difficulties of a foreign land were upon us, for they could speak no English and we could speak no Chinese. By packing everything in a freight car, eating, sleeping, and riding here most of the way, we at last arrived at Tai Yuen Fu, the capital of Shansi. Here we were welcomed by the English missionaries and entertained for the night. The next day we moved into our rented compound and began the study of the language. Thus the first step in the location was accomplished.

To find the least occupied and the most needy part of the field several investigating trips were made. In March, 1909, F. H. Crumpacker and Geo. W. Hilton made a trip to the east mountains with our friend, Mr. Corbin, of the American Board Mission. On this trip they visited Liao Chou and the surrounding country. In April they made a trip west towards the Yellow River in company with Mr. Corbin and Mr. Pye, also from the American Board. A third trip was made north in September, but of the three places we decided that the east mountains were the best. Bro. Crumpacker visited Ping Ting and Le Ping in February, 1910, was favorably impressed, and proceeded to secure property. No one would rent, for they were afraid of foreigners. After repeated visits and much difficulty an old house was bought for about seventy dollars, gold. The owner, not being a native of the province, wanted money very badly so that he could return to his home, but as soon as the people of the city heard that he had sold to us, he was forced to stay in hiding as they intended to give him a good beating. But Bro. Crumpacker began repairing the house and making friends. The people soon found that he had come to do them good rather than evil, and the storm quickly blew over. April 25 Bro. Crumpacker's took full possession and moved in and have lived in this house ever since. This was the real beginning of our China Mission.

The second station was opened by Bro. Hilton in June, 1912.

Ping Ting Station

Bro. Crumpacker, now having a working knowledge of the language, moved to Ping Ting May 25, 1910, bringing with him his wife and baby, Frantz, who came to brighten their home July 2, 1909.

Fig. 15. *Annual conference of the China Mission, 1914. (BHLA)*

Fig. 16. *Daniel L. and Elizabeth Miller leaving India, ca 1905. (BE)*

They began work at once among the people by holding services in their home. At the first service about forty were present. A service was held also in the afternoon. These have continued regularly from that date, being the fountain of life which many are continually drinking of the water of salvation. In the autumn, property was rented in the east suburb, and Sept. 11, 1910, the services were moved to this place. The audience has long outgrown the seating capacity, for we have about two hundred each Sunday. The overflow fills the yard, many standing through the services. All of us are rejoicing over the new churchhouse that was dedicated in December, 1915.

Aug. 31, 1910, Emma Horning came from Tai Yuen Fu to help with the work among the women. Oct. 5, 1915, Minerva Metzger arrived from America and began at once the study of the language. In February, 1911, the midweek prayer meeting was begun and has continued to increase each year since. April 17, 1911, two men were baptized in the river about a mile south of the city. Two others were baptized before we left Tai Yuen Fu. May 10, 1911, we had our first love feast, held in Bro. Crumpacker's upper room. There were three Chinese and us four missionaries.

The later part of this summer our joy knew no bounds when we received news that six new workers were coming with Bro. Hilton that fall—Bro. B. F. Heckman and wife, with their two children, Esther and Lois, Bro. J. H. Bright and wife, with their two children, Esther and Cathryn, also Sister Anna Hutchison and Sister Winnie Cripe. In October, 1911, just as we were making the last preparations to welcome them to Ping Ting, we received a telegram stating that the revolution was on and it would not be wise for them to come interior. A couple of days later we received a letter from the United States consul, summoning us at once to Tientsin for protection. That night we packed the few necessary things and the next morning found us on the way to the coast. Bro. Crumpacker accompanied us, but returned after a couple of weeks under great difficulties, for he had to pass through the war line. He received a great welcome by the people of the city on his return, the officials even sending protection to his house and urging him to stay by them. The work continued much the same during this winter, for the direct effects of the war were not very great here.

The party at Tientsin were busy studying the language, which the war could not hinder. Towards spring Mr. Yin was received into our church. He had been a Christian and had received his training in a mission school, but position and money were leading him from the straight path, so when he became one of our language teachers he was brought back and has since become one of our best workers. In March, 1912, Emma Horning left for America for special medical treatment. In April of the same year Sister Crumpacker again joined her husband in Ping Ting. Early in June, 1912, Bro. Hilton's and Sister Hutchison came interior, and Bro. Hilton opened the work at Liao Chou. The rest of the Tientsin party spent the summer at Peitai-ho, a summer resting place, especially for missionaries, on the coast north of Tientsin. Here they continued the study of the language until September, 1912, when the whole mission gathered at Ping Ting for a general mission meeting. At this meeting much business was transacted and many plans laid for the progress of the mission. The two churches were organized, Ping Ting having eight members and Liao Chou nine. In July the first inquirers' class was organized, containing six members. In September, 1912, seven were baptized, reminding us that truth was impressing these people.

While everything seemed prospering in the mission suddenly great sorrow came upon us. Brother and Sister Heckman and little Esther took the smallpox, from which Bro. Heckman did not recover. He died April 9, 1913,[40] and was buried on a terrace overlooking the city. In the spring Sister Heckman and her two children, bearing their sorrow with sweet resignation, returned to America. In September the ranks were again lessened by the return of Bro. Hilton because of poor health. Thus the work was weakened by the absence of five from the field at the same time. But the Lord was hearing our prayers, for that fall eight workers arrived to give strength and hope—Dr. O. G. Brubaker and wife, with their two children, Leland and Edythe, Dr. F. J. Wampler and wife, Bro. Ernest Vaniman and wife, Sister Anna Blough; also Emma Horning returning. Giving still more encouragement, two representatives of the Mission Board, Bro. H. C. Early and Bro. Galen B. Royer, arrived with the party. The next day after the arrival sixteen were baptized, two being our first women received into the church. The same evening we had the love feast, when thirty-nine consecrated themselves anew to the cause of the Lord.

Work is not confined to the common people, for the teacher and official classes also are being reached. Christian papers and other literature are being sent to the leading men of the district. Bro. Crumpacker teaches English twice a week in the city high school, and their physical director gives our boys physical training in return. This puts us in touch with the educational work of the city. The Bible is in the school now and the superintendent is reading it.

Large crowds of business men, students and teachers come on invitation to any of our special services, such as we have at Christmas, laying of cornerstones and special days of prayer. At these services the official always speaks, also the superintendent of the high school and other prominent men. We have given them Bibles, and they eagerly awaited the completion of the new church, so we will have a suitable place to invite this class of people to regular services. The large Sunday-school will also be glad to occupy this building, for we have had to hold it in the various departments because of lack of room.

The missionary must be prepared for any kind of occupation, so not the least of Bro. Crumpacker's duties has been the buying of land, repairing and building. The Boys' School building was finished the fall of 1913. The Girls' School, church and sisters' house are being finished this fall (1915). The planning of those buildings from native material and the overseeing of a hundred workmen is no small matter when the other mission work must be looked after at the same time. This coming year Bro. Crumpacker goes home on furlough, leaving the work in charge of Bro. Vaniman and Dr. Wampler. Although they have not finished their language study, we know the Lord will bless their efforts in continuing the work.[41]

By 1915, the mission in China had taken its place, alongside the missions in Denmark and in India, as an area in which the Brethren were investing human and physical resources in the development of a foreign mission program. This type of activity was new in the life of the Brethren in the years following the Civil War. Evidently, they had developed the stability in their domestic life and the resources to make possible an expansion program into new areas outside of the United States. The result was that the Brethren took their place alongside other Protestant denominations in the field of foreign missions.

IV

EDUCATION

Introduction

By 1865 most Brethren accepted the need to provide some level of education for their children. However, they were not agreed on how much education their children should receive. Generally, Brethren in the pre-Civil War years had opposed a college education, for they mistrusted its moral level. Even the common, or primary, grade of education was usually taught by non-Brethren, and those teachers sometimes posed problems for the Brethren. Consequently, it seemed desirable to have some Brethren teachers and some Brethren schools. A few such schools were established before the Civil War, but generally they were temporary in nature.

After the War, the Brethren evinced a new interest in higher education at the college level, which is the major thrust of this chapter. The first part of the chapter concentrates on the relation of the church to these schools, according to the actions of the Annual Meetings; and the second part considers the formation of several colleges, most of which became a permanent part of the life of the church.

Policy Regarding Higher Education

In 1871 the church was confronted with questions regarding a new school, named Salem College, established by a group of Brethren in Indiana. Annual Meeting provided some definite answers to questions about the policy of the church on higher education.

Art. 3. Does the Annual Meeting of 1871 claim Salem College of Bourbon, Indiana, to be under the auspices of our brotherhood?

Answer: It does not regard it as a church school, or conducted by the general brotherhood, though it is under the auspices of members of the church, and is supported by those who patronize it, and not by donations of the church. . . .

Art. 27. Is it advisable for a brother to serve as manager or teacher of a college or high school, as the tendency thereof is to lead many of the brethren from the simplicity that is in Christ, and also to divide the brotherhood?

Answer: Inasmuch as the Annual Meeting has admitted the propriety of a high school, as a private enterprise (See Art. 51, 1868), we can not prohibit a brother from engaging in teaching in such an institution; and as it regards the fears that many entertain of the tendency of such an institution to lead brethren from the simplicity of the church, this will depend upon the character of the institution. And to guard the Salem College against any such tendency, this Annual Meeting advises the elders of the church district, in which the college is located, to take into its charge all the teachers and scholars of said college, who are members of the church, and require of them to conform to the general order of the brotherhood.[1]

Evidently it was acceptable for Brethren to establish a college, or any level of school, but it would have to be a private enterprise because the brotherhood was not going to be involved in sponsoring any institution of learning in the United States. Furthermore, the Annual Meeting refused to allow any group of Brethren to use the term "Brethren" in connection with a school, a policy that was emphasized at the Annual Meeting of 1874.

Art. 10. Inasmuch as the brethren, when assembled in Annual Council in the year 1831, decided it not to be advisable for a brother to have his son educated in a college; "inasmuch," they say, "as experience has taught us that such very seldom will come back afterward to the humble ways of the Lord," what will the district-meeting and our Annual Meeting say when a combination of brethren are trying to get up a high school for more thorough education of the brethren's children, and term it the "Brethren's School"?

Answer: Referred to the minutes of the Annual Meeting of 1858, Art. 51. But the brethren shall not call the school the "Brethren's

School," or by any other name that would involve the general brotherhood.[2]

In the next two decades Brethren established a considerable number of colleges, and some Brethren who may, or may not, have been involved in higher education deemed it necessary to provide some type of control or regulation of these schools. This issue was presented to the Annual Meeting in 1890.

14. We, the brethren named in connection with query No. 5, Minutes of Middle Missouri, offer the following substitute:

(1) Standing Committee shall, by approval of Annual Meeting, appoint a Committee of three elders for each of the Brethren's schools, living as near as suitable brethren can be obtained, whose duty it shall be to watch over the moral and religious influence of the schools, and see that the principles of the Gospel and church government be carried out as defined by Annual Meeting, and report annually to Annual Meeting the condition of the schools, and they may serve so long as they give general satisfaction to the Brotherhood.

(2) All members of the Faculty, who are members of our church, shall be in full sympathy with the principles and doctrine of the church, and shall conform to the order of the Brotherhood in their personal appearance.

(3) At least once each year the doctrines of the church shall be specially held forth in a series of doctrinal sermons.

(4) These provisions shall apply to all Brethren's schools, and the right to establish additional Brethren's schools shall rest with the Annual Meeting, to which petition for such privilege shall first be presented.

Signed, Enoch Eby, John Wise, R. H. Miller, Daniel Vaniman, D. L. Miller, S. S. Mohler.

Answer: Passed.[3]

The basic tenet of having a group of elders of the church visit each of the colleges was widely accepted. However, the instructions of 1890 were not specific enough. The Annual Meeting of 1893, after studying the matter for a year, provided a much more detailed set of instructions for these "School Visiting Elders" of Brethren higher education.

2. Report of School Visiting Elders.

(a) (Query deferred from 1892.) We ask Annual Meeting to plainly define the duties of the visiting elders, who visit colleges, or schools of the Brethren, in making their visits to said schools. Can their report, at Annual Meeting, be objected to or criticised before the Annual Meeting?

Your committee begs to submit the following answer. The Annual Meeting has already decided (Art. 14, 1890) that it is the duty of the school visiting elders,

1. To watch over the moral and religious influence of the schools and colleges conducted by the Brethren;

2. See that the principles of the Gospel and church government be carried out as defined by Annual Meeting;

3. And to annually report the condition of the schools to the Annual Meeting.

It was also decided at the same time that,

1. All members of the Faculty, who are members of the church, shall be in full sympathy with the principles and doctrines of the church, and shall conform to the order of the Brotherhood in their personal appearance;

2. And at least once each year, the doctrines of the church shall be especially held forth in a series of doctrinal sermons.

To the above we add and recommend,

1. That the visiting elders, in a body, if practicable, visit the schools once each term, and make such suggestions and recommendations for the moral and religious guidance of the schools, as in their judgment may be deemed for the good of the school, as well as for the maintenance of the principles of the church.

2. In making these suggestions and recommendations, they shall confer with the principals as well as the trustees of the schools, and may also have all the members connected with the schools (teachers and students) assembled to hear such instructions, admonitions and encouragements as prudence may dictate.

3. It shall be the special duty of these elders to see that all necessary, reasonable and prudent efforts be made to maintain Gospel plainness and simplicity among the members attending and connected with the schools, and also to see that once each year our principles of church government, as well as the doctrine of the church, be clearly set forth before the school in one or more sermons on that subject.

4. They shall urge upon the managers of the schools the impor-

tance and necessity of keeping the Commencement Exercises, Literary Societies, as well as all other gatherings connected with or belonging to the schools, within the bounds of Christian propriety, and discourage everything and anything that tends to produce only levity, coarseness and light mindedness.

5. We also urge the importance of the visiting elders making themselves acquainted with the work and character of the Bible Terms connected with our schools, and make to the managers of these departments such suggestions as will tend to the maintaining of the doctrine, distinctive features and harmony of the Brotherhood.

6. In order to carry out these principles, for the good of the schools as well as the good of the church, we emphasize the importance of the visiting elders being men of broad views, who are in sympathy with our educational interests, as well as sound in the faith and doctrine of the Brethren church.

7. Nothing in these suggestions shall be so construed as to interfere with the business management or government of the schools.

8. The visiting elders shall submit, in writing, to the Standing Committee, an annual report of the condition of the schools with such suggestions and requests for advice as may be deemed advisable. These reports are entirely at the disposal of the Standing Committee.

9. The actual expense of the visiting elders, incurred by visiting the schools, shall be paid by the Treasurer of the Annual Meeting.

J. C. Lahman,
Jesse Stutsman,
S. F. Sanger,
J. F. Oller,
J. H. Moore.[4]

This arrangement of control by visiting elders evidently worked satisfactorily for a dozen years or so, but in 1905 a series of queries were received by the Annual Meeting and assigned to a special study committee of five Brethren. In 1906 the committee reported that it had not yet completed its work and was continued. By 1907 in response to several school related queries, the committee prepared a voluminous report in two sections: I. Local and State Management, which included nine points. Point one read "That the State Districts in which the colleges are located shall acquire the ownership of the college property in their respective districts by donation or purchase, or both, if at all practicable." This was followed by a section II. General

Management. The response of the Meeting to the report: "Report spread on Minutes for one year."[5]

So the Annual Meeting of 1908 was given the responsibility for acting on the report.

1. Educational Board.

A number of papers on the moral and religious guidance and control of the Brethren schools were referred to a committee; the following clauses of their report were adopted.

1. Standing Committee of Annual Meeting shall appoint an Educational Board of seven brethren, to be confirmed by the open Conference for a term of five years each, except those first appointed, two of whom shall serve five years, two four years, two three years and one two years, respectively, as indicated by Standing Committee.

2. Three members of the Educational Board shall be chosen from the schools, and four shall be chosen who are not connected with the schools; the majority of the board shall be ordained elders and they shall organize by electing a chairman, a secretary and treasurer from their own number.

3. The Educational Board shall be composed of brethren who are favorable to Christian education, broad-minded and who are working faithfully in harmony with the principles of church government as defined by Annual Meeting.

4. The Educational Board shall meet annually, or oftener if circumstances require it, and it shall visit, in body, each school once a year, or oftener if conditions demand it; or at the discretion of the Board, it may appoint three or more of its number to discharge this duty.

5. All questions arising as to teachers, textbooks, courses of study, athletics, church government, morals and religion, in connection with the several schools shall be referred to the Educational Board for decision.

6. The Educational Board shall have authority to make its decisions operative, and all appeals from its decisions shall be made to Standing Committee of Annual Meeting.

7. The Educational Board shall have the same moral and spiritual supervision over the several schools whose property is not owned by State Districts, but recognized by Annual Meeting, as those owned by State Districts and that such schools shall make full written report annually, to said Educational Board.

8. The Educational Board shall make written report annually of the condition of the several schools to Standing Committee of Annual Meeting, the report to be at the disposal of the Standing Committee.

9. The Educational Board shall be allowed $2.00 per day for actual time, and expenses incurred in its work, these expenses to be paid by Annual Meeting Treasurer out of a fund provided by Annual Meeting for this purpose.

10. All former decisions in conflict with this report are hereby repealed.

Educational Board.

A. C. Wieand, five years, 1913; S. G. Lehmer, five years, 1913; J. C. Bright, four years, 1912; W. B. Yount, four years, 1912; Edward Frantz, three years, 1911; L. T. Holsinger, three years, 1911; H. C. Early, two years. 1910.[6]

The most significant part of the accepted report was the establishment of a new committee in the life of the church, called the Educational Board, which would have an overall supervision of the schools established and related to the church. However, another important part of the report was the omission of the entire first part dealing with local and state management, which had been a part of the report in 1907. Evidently, some uncertainty existed then (and since) about the ownership of the colleges by the church. Also, in the second part of the report of 1907 three of the original thirteen points were omitted in the final report. Thus the introduction of the report of 1908 was quite correct: "the following clauses of their report were adopted."

THE BRETHREN COLLEGES AND BETHANY BIBLE SCHOOL

This new Educational Board was assigned the responsibility for supervising various aspects of the life of colleges established by the Brethren. The oldest of these colleges at the time of the establishment of the Board was Juniata College in Pennsylvania. An excellent description of its early years was written in 1882 by Howard Miller.

Huntingdon Normal College

This Institution is located at Huntingdon, the county seat, on the Main Line of the Pennsylvania Central Railroad, 198 miles west of Philadelphia and 153 miles east of Pittsburg. It is also the northern terminus of the Huntingdon and Broad Top Railroad, 75 miles from Bridgeport, where it connects with the Connellsville and Pittsburg Railroad, and 89 miles from Cumberland, Md., where there is a connection with the Baltimore and Ohio Railroad, thus affording the most ample facilities of access from every direction. The healthiness of the climate, good morals of the citizens, low cost of living, excellent railroad and mail facilities, and the beautiful scenery on every side, all recommend it as a most desirable place to attend school. The scenery as viewed from the building is striking, impressive and grand, and to the admirer of Nature, it will prove a continued source of enjoyment, which of itself, will be worth a trip from the prairies of the West.

The College building stands on high ground overlooking the town and the adjacent country. It is substantially built of brick, in the form of a cross, 84 × 102 feet, four stories, covered with slate. It is admirably adapted to the purposes of the Institution, and is a pleasant and comfortable "Normal Home" for Teachers and Students of both sexes. The basement story contains a large, convenient and pleasant dining room, pantry, kitchen, laundry, storeroom, for rooms for employees, etc. The cellar apartment lies in the rear, and is mainly under ground. Just outside are two large wells and a cistern containing excellent water for laundry and culinary purposes. On the main floor are the Library, Reception Room, two Recitation Rooms and the Chapel, a large room which will seat from 500 to 600 persons. The Chapel is the general assembly room, and here the students meet for devotional exercises, to hear announcements, receive their letters, etc. The next story is laid out into Recitation Rooms, Teachers' Rooms, Sleeping Apartments for lady students, and Book Room. There is a private stairway for lady students, leading up from the basement. The upper story consists entirely of dormitories for gentlemen students. From the top of the building there is a grand outlook over the town and surrounding country. The view is one that will delight the eye of any one who can appreciate the beauties of natural scenery. Many beautiful pictures have been painted on the canvas of Pennsylvania by the Great Artist, but our picturesque State contains few lovelier scenes than that which greets the admiring gaze of the students from the "Brethren's Normal."

History and Design

Although organized by the Brethren and by its charter placed forever under the control of members of the Church of the Brethren, for the special benefit of the children of the Fraternity, to be a home, church, and school for them, where they can receive an education free from the contaminating influences of fashionable life; yet the Brethren's Normal College is designed to give a good, thorough, practical education to all students, without regard to sect or creed. Starting April 17, 1876, in a very humble way, under the control of the late Prof. J. M. Zuck, in a small room in the *Primitive Christian* building, the school has been steadily growing in numbers and influence. Its patrons represent the States of Maryland, Virginia, West Virginia, Ohio, Indiana, Illinois, Missouri, Nebraska, Colorado, the Republic of Mexico, and New Jersey, besides a majority of the counties of Pennsylvania. Instead of the small room with its four inmates, the commodious building erected for its use, has been crowded with earnest students intent upon making the best possible use of their time and their talents. The work has met with Divine favor, and therefore has prospered.

Expenses

The aim is to bring expenses down to the lowest possible figure consistent with a fair compensation for the services rendered.

Tuition in Normal Course	$1.00 per week
Board in College Building..................	2.40 per week
Furnished Room	50 per week
Washing about..........................	25 per week

Light and Contingencies, $2.00 to $2.50 per Term

Tuition for a shorter time than a Full Term, or when not paid in advance, $1.20 per week.

Sessions and Vacations

The School Year consists of 43 weeks, opening Sept. 5, 1881, and closing June 29, 1882, and is divided into three sessions, at the opening of each of which the classes will be recognized, thus affording advantages to the students who may wish to enter at the opening of any session, while those who continue during the year, can do so without the interruption and loss of time occasioned by vacations.[7]

The second of the Brethren schools in Miller's survey was Ashland College in northeastern Ohio.

ASHLAND COLLEGE

Ashland College was founded in 1878 in order to promote the cause of religious education, and is placed by its charter under the fostering care of the Brethren Church, from whose members the Board of Trustees is chosen. The immediate object of the founders was to establish a first-class college for both young men and young women, which should combine the advantages of home and school, develop and cultivate the best powers of mind and body, instill a taste for simplicity, economy, and an aversion to vain show and extravagance; and afford the most thorough instruction at the least expense to the student. In short they seek to dedicate the Institution to the *highest interest of youth and to the glory of God.*

Location and Advantages

For beauty and healthfulness of location, Ashland College is not surpassed in the West. The grounds, comprising nearly thirty acres of land, were selected on account of their elevation, pure air, freedom from malarial diseases, and extent and beauty of landscape. The work of grading and improving the grounds about the College buildings will be continued until there shall be nothing wanting in the surroundings to please the eye and cultivate the taste.

Ashland is a thriving town of nearly four thousand inhabitants, situated in one of the richest and most beautiful farming districts in Ohio, and distinguished for the thrift, business enterprise, and high moral character of its people. Nearly all denominations of churches are represented here, a large and influential circle of the Brethren surrounding it. There are four large and flourishing churches of the Brethren within a few miles of the town.

Ashland is situated on the line of the New York, Pennsylvania & Ohio Railroad, a trunk line from New York to Cincinnati. Students coming by way of Pittsburgh, Ft. Wayne & Chicago, or Baltimore & Ohio roads, change cars at Mansfield, which is only a half hour's ride from Ashland.

Buildings

The main College Building is a very fine edifice, and is not surpassed by any college building in the State for convenience and comfort. It is one hundred feet front and the same in depth, four stories high, built of cut stone and brick, roofed with slate. There are school room accomodations for five hundred students, besides Library, Parlor, Office, Museum, Society Halls, six private rooms for the Professors, and a large Chapel, which will seat five hundred worshippers.[8]

After the schismatic divisions which the German Baptist Brethren experienced in the 1880s, Ashland College became affiliated with The Brethren Church, which also had its publishing house and center of operations in Ashland.

The third in Miller's survey of four early Brethren schools in operation by 1882 was Mt. Morris College in Illinois.

MT. MORRIS COLLEGE

This institution is located in Mt. Morris, a quiet, pleasant, and moral town, in Ogle country, Ill., about one hundred miles west of Chicago, on the Chicago & Iowa R.R. It is free from saloons, gambling houses, etc., surrounded by a beautiful and fertile country, with a generous, industrious, intelligent and thrifty people.

The College buildings are situated on a commanding site, and surrounded by a beautiful park of six and a half acres. The buildings cost about $40,000. All the windows have blinds; the inside is nicely painted and calcimined; the floors are carpeted in all rooms and halls; registers and ventilators are in every room, and a cozier, cleaner and more attractive set of students' quarters is not to be found in this country. The dining room is a model of neatness and order.

This immediate section is almost entirely free from ague and those malarious diseases so common to the Mississipi Valley. . . .

Students from the East can come to Chicago or Aurora, thence to Mt. Morris via the Chicago & Iowa R. R. Those coming from the West can either go to one of the above named places, or to Forreston, on the Illinois Central Railroad, and thence to Mt. Morris.

An examination of the following terms will show that the best of educational advantages are offered at extremely low rates. In all cases the money must be paid in advance. In cases of sickness the money for the unexpired part of the term will be refunded. Where money has been paid in advance by the year, and the student is prevented through sickness from attending school, there is a proportional reduction.

TERMS

Tuition Fall or Spring Term	$10.00 in advance.
Tuition Winter Term	$13.00 in advance.
Tuition per year	30.00 in advance.
Board in College	2.00 per week.
Room rent	.50 per week.[9]

In this instance Miller was not very studious in outlining the origins of Mt. Morris College. According to S. Z. Sharp, who was president of Mt. Morris College for a number of years in the 1880s, the school had been started about 1840 by the Methodists. When they established Northwestern University about 1855, they withdrew their support from a number of surrounding schools, including the one in Mt. Morris known as Rock River Seminary. In 1879 a group of Brethren, led by M. S. Newcomer, invested $6,000 to purchase the buildings and property in order to establish a Brethren school. Sixty students were present when the school opened on August 20, 1879.[10] *After a few difficult years the college prospered, but eventually in the twentieth century it was closed and merged with Manchester College, which had been established by Indiana Brethren in the 1890s.*

The last of the four Brethren schools described by Howard Miller was located in Virginia and later became known as Bridgewater College.

VIRGINIA NORMAL SCHOOL

Though originated for the special benefit of the Brethren (or Tunkers) and under their immediate control to be a home, church, and school for their children, where they can receive an education free from the contaminating influences of fashionable life; yet the Virginia Normal school offers a hearty welcome to all those who seek knowledge regardless of sect or creed.

In point of location the Virginia Normal School will compare with any other institution in America. The Shenandoah Valley, so widely known for its beauty and fertility, has a climate distinguished for its equability,—its summers being seldom too warm and its winters much milder than in the more mountainous sections of Virginia.

In this salubrious climate none of the diseases which infect many portions of the South are known. The Valley apparently encircled by mountains forms a scene of surpassing beauty and interest.

Situated in this romantic region and healthful climate is Bridgewater in which is located the Virginia Normal School.

The town has a population of about 1000 which is rapidly increasing. Bridgewater is one of the most thriving towns in Virginia—the enterprise of her citizens having recently placed her in the front rank of improvement.

There are here few of those temptations which often lead young men into habits of dissipation and ruin; but on the contrary a wholesome influence is constantly exerted by the School and community to restrain them from the cultivation of evil habits.

Parents sending their sons and daughters to the Virginia Normal School may do so, fully assured that they will not only have the constant care and attention of the Faculty; but that they will, also, be surrounded by the best influences and associations.

Bridgewater is situated four miles from the Valley Branch R.R., and on the proposed line of the Atlantic and Ohio R. R., which will possibly be completed at an early day. It is also on the Warm Springs Turnpike, seven miles south of Harrisonburg, with which there is daily connection by stage.

These advantages with daily mail, leave but little to be desired in the location. . . .

Two large and commodious buildings have been rented for the use of the School. The Boarding Hall is a large, substantial frame building. Arranged expressly for the students of the Virginia Normal School, it is admirably adapted for a comfortable and pleasant home. The Boarding Hall is under the supervision of a competent and experienced caterer, who will make everything as pleasant as possible for them, but will demand a strict observance of all the requirements of the Hall.

The Dining room will be in charge of an experienced matron, who will spare no pains to supply the tables with an abundance of well cooked food of the greatest variety that the season permits.

The young ladies' apartments are separate from the Boarding Hall. They are placed under the special care of a matron who will endeavor to make them as comfortable and happy as possible. All things considered, we can truthfully say that the Virginia Normal School offers to the students superior advantages in point of good board, comfortable rooms, and low prices.

Expenses

Tuition . . . . $3.25 per month
Board, including fuel and light, ... 9.00 per month
Washing . . . . 1.00 per month

A contingent fee of $1.00 per term is required of all day students. All non-resident pupils will be required to board in the Boarding Hall, unless parents or guardians desire them to board elsewhere.

From the above it will be seen that students can attend the entire session of forty weeks at a cost of $132.50.[11]

Over the next century the comparable cost of attending Bridgewater College for one year had increased to more than $6,000. But, of course, other prices and costs had increased also. Thus Bridgewater had become one of the permanent colleges of the church in the twentieth century.

Another of the permanent colleges was McPherson College in Kansas. It began in 1888 and thus was not included in Miller's survey of 1882. S. Z. Sharp, the founder and first president, recorded some of the early events.

McPHERSON COLLEGE, KANSAS

In 1887 the Annual Conference was held at Ottawa, Kans. An educational meeting was held in the tabernacle, composed of several thousand interested members. S. Z. Sharp was chosen moderator and H. B. Brumbaugh, secretary. The most important subject discussed was the location of a college in Kansas, to be owned and controlled by the State Districts.

This meeting was informed that a number of Kansas towns were eager to have the Brethren locate a college in their town. Consequently a committee was appointed to select a location. It visited seventeen towns in the summer of 1887 and concluded:

Aug. 22 the committee met at McPherson and carefully reviewed the offers made by the several cities, and decided in favor of McPherson as having made the best offer and being most favorably located.

The next step was the organization of a corporation, which included the preparation of a detailed charter and by-laws. A number of provisions made clear the close relationship to the church, including the statement of purpose:

That the purpose for which this association is formed is to establish and maintain an institution of learning in harmony with the principles of the German Baptist (Tunker) Church, and, as far as practicable, to be under the control of the District Conferences of said church in Kansas.

Furthermore, the instructors, "as far as practicable," were expected to be members of the church. Finally, the charter by-laws outlined certain specific requirements.

[Article VII—Requirements] Sec. 1—All members of the German Baptist Brethren Church, whether officers, students or employees, shall observe the general order of the Brotherhood in the manner of dress and general non-conformity to the world, as understood and defined by Annual Conference.

Sec.2—Instructors who are members of the German Baptist Brethren Church, before assuming their respective duties in the college shall be required to subscribe to the following:

1. Faithfully to discharge the duties devolving upon them.
2. To maintain in apparel, general life and character the principles of the Gospel as defined by the Annual Conference of the German Baptist Church.
3. To give no aid or encouragement to those who strive to subvert the Gospel or the order of the church.
4. Students who are not members of the German Baptist Church shall not be permitted to make any unnecessary display in the use of jewelry, the improper and injurious manner of wearing the hair and apparel, but shall be required to observe the laws of simplicity and health.
5. The use of tobacco in any form shall be prohibited upon the college premises.

Officers of the corporation were elected, funds were raised, and

Oct. 19, 1887, the contract was let for the building of the dormitory, in dimensions 40 by 100 feet and four stories high, now called Fahnestock Hall. This building was divided to accommodate both ladies and gentlemen students, and space was left for chapel and several recitation rooms. . . .

By the middle of the summer of 1888 the dormitory was finished and furnished, and the first story erected of the main building now called the Sharp Administration Building. In order to have a kind of dedication service for the first building on the campus, it was decided to have a love feast. The churches of the Brethren in Kansas were not then large as they now are, but the college sentiment among them was strong, and they came from far and near and filled the spacious dining hall in the basement of the dormitory. About two hundred were seated around the Lord's table, and among them a number of the leading elders in the Church of the Brethren.

Sept. 5, 1888, school opened with sixty students present the first day, and closed the term with two hundred and one students enrolled.

The religious character of the school was made prominent. There being three ministers on the faculty, they held a revival meeting, and every student in the dormitory, not already a member of some church, united with the Church of the Brethren, except one whose parents did not allow her to join then, but she became a member later and wife of a prominent elder. Of the students in attendance during the first year, ten became active elders in the Church of the Brethren and one of them a college president.[12]

In spite of many difficulties, such as financial problems brought on by bank failures and drouths, and the death and/or illness of presidents, the college did survive. A final step of significance in the life of the college during these years occurred in 1913 when ten districts of the church in the area between the Mississippi River and the Rocky Mountains agreed to appoint trustees and in effect "to place McPherson College into the hands" of the state districts of the Church of the Brethren. Even this step did not end all of the problems, but it did help to make possible the permanence of McPherson College.

It was easier to establish a college in Pennsylvania, Illinois, or Virginia, where there were many Brethren, than it was in Kansas in the 1880s. It was even more difficult to establish a Brethren college in California. Nevertheless a group of Brethren gave such a project their best effort; the result was Lordsburg College—after 1977 the University of LaVerne—in California. In 1891, a group of Brethren purchased the Lordsburg Hotel in the town of Lordsburg for $15,000.

They at once organized for the opening of the school. . . . a small faculty was engaged and the school opened. These beginnings were small, for most of the students were in the grades and none in the college department, but the foundations were laid for larger work.

The founders of the school learned from the beginning that deficits are among the most persistent factors in the promotion of an

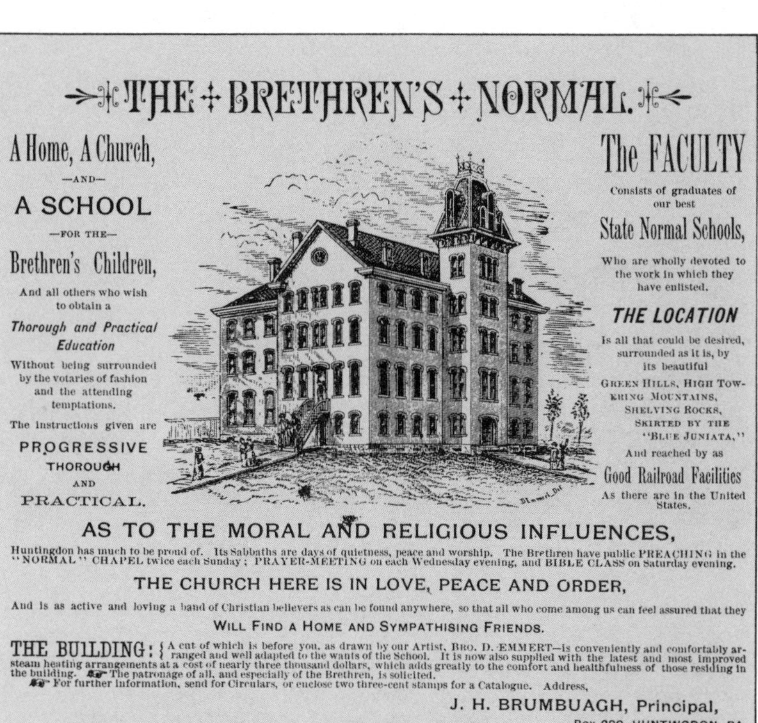

Fig. 17. *Advertisement appearing in the* Brethren's Family Almanac, 1880.

Fig. 18. *First building (formerly a hotel) of Lordsburg College, now the University of La Verne, ca 1898. (BE)*

Fig. 19. *(Old) Founders Hall, Ashland College, ca. 1881. (BE)*

Fig. 20. *McPherson College building, late 19th century. (BHLA)*

educational institution. . . . The problem of placing the school on a solid basis seemed to be an insurmountable one. On the coast the membership of the Church of the Brethren had not grown large enough to support the school, had it been ever so good. The financial depressions, the uncertainties of the citrus industry, in which many of the Brethren were engaged, the unavoidable differences because of the conditions, both in and out of the school, and the increasing demands on the part of the State University and the State Normal School, had a tendency to discourage those who were not vitally connected with the college. The trustees, on the other hand, knew no discouragement in the matter. They gave their loyal support to the school, and in the face of almost certain defeat continued their efforts for the upbuilding of an institution in which they had faith. . . .

In 1908 the District of Southern California and Arizona accepted a proposition to receive the property and conduct the school, proceeding at once to elect a board of directors. . . . The reorganization of the school was now made. . . . A strong effort was made to increase the student body, and solicitations were made for financial support. The problem that confronted the board was not a new one, but different from the former ones, in that now the District had to be reckoned with in addition to the former problems. . . . Through it all the college had to struggle, which is common to all new denominational colleges.[13]

Through all of its struggles, the University of LaVerne did survive to become a stable institution in the twentieth century.

The next in the list of permanent Brethren colleges was Manchester College in Indiana. Like all of these Brethren schools, it did not begin as an official venture of the church, but rather began under the sponsorship of a group of interested Brethren. In this case, as in California, the Brethren purchased an established property, and in comparison with Mt. Morris, it was a college property. In 1889, the United Brethren Church built college buildings in the town of North Manchester, but after five years they gave up the effort. In May, 1895 the local newspaper reported:

Articles of incorporation for the Brethren's College and for the Bible School, which is to be run in connection with the college, were filed with the secretary of State last week. . . . School will open Sept. 11, 1895.

So classes began on September 11 at Manchester College. According to S. Z. Sharp's understanding:

The opening of the school seemed quite auspicious. The enrollment was considered good. . . . The records of the first year show a remarkable attendance. Two hundred and seven students were enrolled, one hundred and twenty-four being in the Bible department. During the year, many ten days' Bible institutes were held in local churches. In these local schools one thousand and fifty students had been enrolled. . . . As yet the school belonged to private parties, who held the property and bore whatever responsibility there was. The Brethren in charge of the institution found many financial difficulties to meet. Support did not come as it seemingly should. Some differences arose in the board of trustees.

In order to meet the variety of problems that had developed, it became essential for the districts of the Church of the Brethren to take over the school.

The pledges were given on the absolute condition that the school was to become the property of the church. . . . The transfer was made from the old trustees to trustees chosen from the State Districts of Northern Indiana, Middle Indiana, Southern Illinois, Southern Ohio, and Northwestern Ohio. . . . Southern Illinois decided to discontinue official connection with the college in 1904. Southern Indiana joined the college family in 1905. . . . The year 1916 was also marked by additional members in the ownership of the school. Michigan and Northeastern District of Ohio have united in the ownership of the college and have appointed trustees.[14]

Thus, Manchester College had also made the transition to ownership by a number of Church of the Brethren districts, which helped to assure the permanence of the institution.

The last of the six Brethren related colleges which became a permanent part of the life of the church in the twentieth century was Elizabethtown College in Pennsylvania. In this case, in contrast to some of the other schools, Brethren built and organized this college from its beginning. Also in contrast, this college was surrounded by many strong Brethren congregations. Quoting again from S. Z. Sharp:

Some years before the formal founding of Elizabethtown College, there was felt the need of an institution in Eastern Pennsylvania where the children of members of the Church of the Brethren might have an opportunity to obtain a more extended education than it was possible to acquire in the public schools, and at the same time make it possible for them to remain loyal to the Church of the Brethren, chiefly along the line of non-conformity to the world. It was further decided to extend the facilities for higher education to such members as would obtain the same education at State institutions unless such opportunities were afforded by schools in the church of their choice, where they would have a Christian environment, free from atheistical and other influences that make shipwreck of a religious life. Withal there existed many good schools in this territory, so far as intellectual training is concerned, but upholding wrong ideals and tolerating, if not fostering, pernicious features, such as intercollegiate athletics, hazing, students' fraternities, class rushes, etc. Those interested in promoting a school for higher Christian education were moved by a lofty purpose, which may be concisely stated in a constitution adopted later on by the trustees and friends of the college, as follows: "The object of this school shall be such harmonious development of the physical, mental and moral powers of both sexes as will best fit them for the duties of life and promote the spiritual interest of its patrons. While under the control and management of the Church of the Brethren, and while primarily intended for the education of our own children, the school shall be open to all such as desire to avail themselves of its advantages."[15]

In the winter of 1898 meetings of interested Brethren were held, and steps were taken to locate a site for a school. At least half a dozen towns were interested in securing the college in their town; a special locating committee visited each of the towns and eventually decided unanimously on the town of Elizabethtown. By the summer of 1899 the trustees had organized, and plans were made for opening the school in 1900. Funds were raised and the first building was constructed in 1900.

The educational work of this institution, so modestly yet auspiciously begun, had its trials and difficulties to overcome. The fate of the institution, so untried and so young, was unknown and its future success not fully assured. It passed through a period of growth that may well be called the *experimental stage.* In this critical period it was carried through by certain staunch trustees, some self-sacrificing teachers and numerous devoted friends.[16]

Indeed it was carried through by its many devoted supporters and eventually became a strong, prosperous college among the Brethren in eastern Pennsylvania.

In spite of the earlier debate about whether or not Brethren schools would be designed to educate ministers who would then want to receive a salary for their ministerial work, these Brethren colleges did provide courses in religion. In addition to such courses, some Brethren wanted to secure more specialized training in ministerial leadership, and some Brethren agreed that such training was desirable. The result was the establishment of Bible schools. The only one of these Bible schools to achieve permanent status among the Brethren was Bethany Bible School.

A. C. Wieand and E. B. Hoff, after becoming friends and associates, and after a long period of study and preparation, were ready to open a Bible school (which they had decided to call Bethany during a trip to the Holy Land) in Chicago in 1905.

Obviously a great demand had developed among Brethren for training in a Bible school of this type, and the leadership of Bethany Bible School moved as rapidly as possible to keep up with that demand.

The Work Begun

After these years of special preparation it was decided that the time had come for the beginning of Bethany Bible School. The time for opening the school was set for Oct. 3, 1905. A curriculum had been prepared and a very modest circular had been distributed privately. This was about all the general advertising that was done. It was thought best to begin in a quiet way, for "the kingdom of heaven is like a grain of mustard seed."

Bro. Hoff's private house, across the street from the mission church on Hastings Street, was slightly altered to accomodate the students. A room was set apart for a library, and in this the classes were formed. The basement of the house was fitted up for a dining-hall. On the opening day there were twelve students present, and twenty-one at the close of the term, while the entire enrollment for the year was thirty-seven.

The opening services were conducted in Hastings Street Church by Eld. J. H. Moore, then editor of the *Gospel Messenger.* He mentioned the fact that when he was a young man he longed for exactly such opportunities for Bible study and preparation for the ministry as were here being afforded to the young people of our church and he greatly rejoiced to see this day.

During the first year all the students were in the freshman class. While there was no classification of students, plans were constantly being perfected for a large attendance in the future.

After consulting with many Brethren of wide experience and skill in handling such matters, an attempt was made to secure a fairly large number of Brethren of wide influence and experience to become trustees of the institution, but the effort failed, and as a last resort, Albert C. Wieand, Emmanuel B. Hoff, and James M. Moore associated themselves together and obtained a charter, dated June 6, 1906, and outlined a constitution.

Constitution of Bethany Bible School of Chicago, Ill.

Article I

The name of this institution shall be BETHANY BIBLE SCHOOL.

Article II.—The Purpose (Same as in Charter)

The purpose for which this association is formed is to provide for the study and teaching of the Bible and for the preparation and training of the various kinds of Christian workers in harmony with the principles and practices of the Church of the Brethren.

Article III.—The Authority

The authority of this association shall be vested in a Board of seven or more Directors.

Article IV.—Board of Directors

Section I.—Duties of Said Board of Directors

Sub-Sec. 1.—To own, to control and to manage to the best of ability; viz., real estate, chattels, mortgages, notes, moneys, endowments, etc., of said institution for the highest good of the same in strict harmony with the purposes as declared in the charter of incorporation and set forth in Article II above.

Sub-Sec. 2—To provide professors, instructors, and other helpers necessary for the maintenance of the instruction, research, and whatever is requisite to the carrying out of the objects of the institution above mentioned, in full harmony with duties and qualifications of professors, instructors and helpers, etc., as set forth in Article V, Section 1.

Sub-Sec. 3—Neither the board of directors nor the executive committee shall have power to contract any financial obligation in any way to encumber the institution or its property, excepting as they make themselves personally liable as private individuals.

Sub-Sec. 4.—Said directors, by act of accepting office, pledge themselves to hold said institution and all the appurtenances thereof in trust for the Church of the Brethren, until such time as the General Conference of said church shall take the necessary steps for the full ownership and control of said institution, in harmony with the declared purposes of said corporation as set forth in the charter.

Section 2—Qualifications of Directors

Sub-Sec. 1,—All the members of the Board of Directors shall be members of the Church of the Brethren in good standing and faithful to all her principles.

Article V.—Qualifications of Teachers and Helpers

Section 2

No one shall be eligible to election or appointment as teacher in said institution unless distinguished for high moral excellence of character, adequate intellectual and scholarly attainments, deep spirituality, aptness to teach, faithful devotion to the Bible as the Word of God, eminent devotion to the distinctive features of the Church of the Brethren and to her highest interests.

Fundamental Principles

The following are the fundamental principles on which the school is based and which give form to its curriculum:

1. The *sine qua non* of religious success, and therefore the primal in the training of the Christian worker, is the development of spiritual power.

2. Second only to spiritual power in importance is a thorough and practical mastery of the Sacred Scriptures—to know the materials as they exist—to understand them in their deepest meaning, to know how to use them in helping and saving men.

3. To overlook or neglect to provide adequate and varied clinical

practice and experience, under wise guidance, is as fatal in spiritual as it would be in physiological therapeutics.

4. Thorough discipline in teacher-training, according to the most practical and scientific pedagogy and psychology, is at least as important in the making of the religious as of the secular teacher.

5. Teacher-training, however, is sadly lacking efficiency if it is not complemented and reenforced by psychological development of expression, oral or written.

6. The primary business of the training school and of religious leaders and workers is to furnish and equip practical, effective workers and secondly and mediately to produce technically and critically learned scholars. Besides, the rational foundation for true theological scholarship is spiritual perception and practical widsom.

7. In developing this curriculum, the endeavor has been, constantly and strenuously, to apply rigidly the educational principles of induction, correlation and expression, and to make the curriculum an organization in which progress is according to pedagogical requirements.

During the summer vacation of 1906 some of the best students of the first year were sent out into the various churches and Districts to collect data and to talk to the people about the ideals of the school, the needs in a financial way and otherwise. An illustrated booklet was prepared and circulated among the members of the Church of the Brethren in the States nearest to Chicago. Bro. Hoff and wife personally paid for the campaign fifteen hundred dollars. In this way the people were made aware of the existence of the school, its character and the nature of its work. A constituency was now beginning to be formed of people who were willing to pay for the school and in some way consider its needs. Very little financial support, however, was received from this venture.

The second year of Bethany Bible School began Sept. 25, 1906. A. C. Wieand and E. B. Hoff composed the faculty, with four assistants. Brethren, Methodists, Mennonites, and Friends were enrolled as students, but mostly Brethren. Up to the close of the year, students were enrolled from seventeen States and from Canada.

One of the greatest difficulties in the early life of the school was to obtain a faculty, so few members of the Church of the Brethren, at this time, having been theologically trained. It was found necessary to look out for promising young men and women, with proper literary attainments, spiritual growth and studious habits, and then to direct their training for the positions they were to fill. Happily this difficulty by this time has been overcome.

During this year the scope of Bethany's usefulness to the church was enlarged. James M. Moore, Galen B. Royer, I. B. Trout, and Mrs. Catherine B. Van Dyke were engaged to assist the faculty. The course of study was extended; correspondence and expression courses were added. The students were classified and started on practical mission work, such as Bible instruction in homes, work among ex-prisoners, Sunday school for the Chinese, etc.

Prospecting for a Home

Not only were ten years spent in studying the character of other institutions of learning, their methods of instruction, and in personal literary preparation for the work of Bethany Bible School, but diligent search was made for a home for the school when it should materialize. During the years 1899 to 1902 considerable time was spent in searching out a location for a Bible school. It seemed that the west side of the city would best afford the location, because it was nearer to the members in the city and the membership outside. Since it was impossible to obtain a large piece of ground for a campus, it would be best to locate near a park. Garfield Park afforded the greatest inducement. The block of ground bounded by Van Buren and Congress Streets and Trumbull and St. Louis Avenues was selected. Of course there was no money to buy this land, but much prayer was offered that the Lord would in some way provide the means to secure it.

After the first two years of school, during the summer of 1907, a campaign of solicitation was started to obtain the money to buy this block of ground. This was, perhaps, the hardest task undertaken in connection with the school. To go to our country people and talk to them about buying an acre and a half of ground for twenty-five thousand dollars seemed almost hopeless, but with due effort the money was secured and the land bought.

The two previous years were marked by great blessings, which could be explained only as being special divine provisions in answer to prayer. This enabled the management to enlarge the scope of usefulness of the school and to extend its curriculum by adding the following departments:

The *Sunday-School Workers' Course;* The *Musical Department;*

The *Department of Practical Work* and that of *Mission Training*. This last department was in existence from the beginning, but the growth was so pronounced that an additional teacher had to be provided for it.

Missionary Bible Classes—For this work forty-five students were organized to take charge of forty-nine classes in institutions for the blind, rescue homes for girls, and for boys gathered from the streets and in homes. House-to-house visits brought statistics from more than fifteen hundred homes.

The Gospel Song Service.—This afforded work for another group of students.

Practical Mission Work for the Chinese.—Brother and Sister Hilton, missionaries to China, were placed in charge of this work. Nothing in practical mission work so stirred up the enthusiasm among the students at Bethany as this work among the heathen at our door.

A School of Health and Physical Help for Mission Fields.—Bethany Bible School was exceedingly fortunate in securing such eminent specialists as Dr. William Sadler and Dr. Lena K. Sadler for instruction in this department.

Not fewer than thirty-three Sunday-school Teachers' Institutes, Christian Workers' Institutes and Bible Institutes were held by the faculty and assistants during this year.

From the above it will be seen that Bethany made a tremendous forward movement this year by way of enlarging its usefulness. In addition, by means of a vigorous campaign, the $25,000 was raised and the block of ground bought for the new building.

The fourth year at Bethany began by adding B. F. Heckman as instructor in Hebrew. New fields for practical mission work were presented. An unlooked-for opportunity was afforded at the very door of the school in the Jewish quarter, containing about two hundred and forty thousand inhabitants. A friendly relation was established with this people. The *Life-Boat Mission* also solicited help from our students.

The most important forward movement of the year was the securing of the money and the erection of the first building for the permanent home of the school on the plat of ground purchased the year before at 3435 West Van Buren Street. Here the first building was erected, 40 by 60 feet and three stories high, at a cost of $26,000.

Sept. 11, 12, 13, 1910, ushered in the beginning of the fifth year of the school. These were days of great rejoicing. Here faculty and students raised their Ebenezer as they looked over the trials and perplexities they had encountered, the unmistakable leadings of Providence all the way, and the great blessings received. This was the time of the dedication of the new building. Eld. J. H. Moore delivered the dedicatory sermon, taking the school of the prophets, 2 Kings 6, for his subject. After the installation, it was found that there were only about half enough accommodations for the demands of the school.

Among the important events of the year was the conversion of Moy Wing, the first Chinese student. Later two other Chinamen were received, promising much for the future. Large openings also were afforded in the Jewish mission.

The teaching force at the beginning of the sixth year was increased by the addition of Franklin Byer, instructor in Bible and hymn reading; Roy Dilling in music; and R. H. Nicodemus in Hebrew and homiletics. The large increase in the number of students made it imperative that another building be erected. Liberal responses were made to appeals for means. Great blessings were reported in all the missionary activities, and the students were enthusiastic over the results. Eight conversions were reported from the Chinese mission. The Rescue Mission has been of great advantage to the Bethany students as they saw the power of the Gospel able to save from all forms of sin.

The school year of 1911–12 began with a teaching force of fifteen instructors. E. E. Eshelman, for New Testament epistles, and Laura Gwin and Ezra Flory for Sunday-school teacher-training, were added. The seminary curriculum was extended from a three to four-year course, placing the training and scholarship on a level with the other learned professions. Encouraging progress was also made in all the missionary activities. Four Chinese members and one Jewish lady were recevied by baptism.

During the summer of 1912 the second building was begun, in dimensions 44 by 113 feet, four stories high above the basement, and costing $65,000. This gave thrice the accommodations for the students, yet was scarcely more than half sufficient for the needs of the school.[17]

During the half century from 1865 to 1915 Brethren had established more than two dozen institutions of education at different levels from high school academies through normal training schools for teachers and colleges for various professionals. S. Z. Sharp in his sig-

nificant study of Brethren education identified twenty different schools. Most of these schools did not survive early difficulties, financial and otherwise. In fact, only six Church of the Brethren colleges and one seminary, now known as Bethany Theological Seminary, and one Brethren college (Ashland) have survived the wide variety of problems. Certainly, however, those eight have proven to be valuable enough to have made the entire effort worthwhile.

V
ECONOMIC ACTIVITIES

INTRODUCTION

In spite of their emphasis on separation from the world, Brethren had never been completely able to remove themselves from economic activities. Certain products had to be purchased from someone else, and in exchange certain products had to be sold. Even the most remote Brethren farmer could not remain isolated permanently. However, in the years following the Civil War, Brethren became much more openly involved in the economic world around them. Some of them found occupations away from the family farm. They moved to the cities and became industrial managers or workers. Some wanted to join labor unions, which created problems for the Brethren leadership. The more prosperous Brethren farmers sought new forms of investment which also created a variety of problems.

Railroads were a very important form of transportation for Brethren, as for all Americans. They enabled ministers to move from one area to another, on preaching missions or permanently. They also enabled groups of Brethren to migrate from one area to another, and such action sometimes created major problems for the congregation from which they emigrated. Advertisements by the railroads, and by other businesses, in Brethren periodicals sometimes caused dissatisfaction. Railroad accidents and other industry-related accidents occasionally caused deaths; these accidents, as well as traditional farm-related accidents, brought a new emphasis on the importance of life insurance. Whether Brethren could insure human life had not been conclusively decided by Annual Meeting by 1865, nor was it settled by 1915. The question of life insurance and a variety of other economic activities which created problems for Brethren are considered in this chapter.

WORK ON SUNDAY

A fascinating problem which concerned some Brethren was the fact that certain types of economic activities, whether rural or urban, had to continue on a seven-day-a-week basis, for example in rural areas where Brethren had dairy farms. The Annual Meeting of 1876 considered this problem.

Art. 16. A brother has a dairy, and objections were made against him for furnishing his customers milk on Sunday, claiming that brethren would do no more harm to work on their farms on Sunday. The brother claims that his customers, many of them are ministers, and ministers of Sabbatarian churches, who say they must have their milk; besides, he furnishes milk for the sick, and for children raised by the bottle; and he says not to be allowed to furnish the milk would ruin his business, and subject him to heavy loss. What is to be done in the case?

Answer: We can not grant a brother liberty to furnish milk on the Sabbath to his customers, only to the sick and to the children, and we advise him to get out of the business as soon as possible.[1]

Even at a "heavy loss," the Brethren were not allowed to engage in business on Sunday. By the end of the century a more frequent problem in the cities was working on Sunday. The Anderson, Indiana congregation raised the question in 1899 about members employed in the postal service and fire departments.

10. (Anderson church.) We ask District Meeting of the Southern District of Indiana and Annual Meeting of 1899, is it according to the Gospel and the order of the Brethren church for members to engage in a work where they are compelled to work on Sunday and to wear the uniforms, such as are worn in the mail service and fire department or any other work?

Answer: We decide that the working on Sunday has been fully covered by former decisions, and that brethren working for the Government and for corporations where the uniform is required to be worn, should wear such uniform only when engaged in such services.[2]

And in 1907 the South Bend, Indiana congregation was even more specific in asking about Sunday work in factories and for corporations who demand it.

8. South Bend Church (First Brethren).—Owing to the fact that many of our brethren work in factories and for corporations who demand their services on Sundays as well as on other days, thus making it very embarrassing to refuse; and not complying with their demands often jeopardizes their situation and causes them to lose their employment; therefore, we petition Annual Meeting through district meeting to say to what extent, if any, brethren may be allowed thus to labor on Sunday.

Answer: Passed to Annual Meeting.

Answer: (1) We desire to raise our voice in earnest and emphatic protest against the growing tendency to desecrate the Christian Sabbath.

(2) We condemn all mere pleasure-seeking on this day.

(3) We urge diligent and specific teaching on this subject in the churches, in the Sunday schools, and the homes.

(4) We urge that our people refrain as much as possible from the use and patronage of those institutions, the running of which require other men to work on the Lord's Day.

(5) That our members in selecting their vocations should seek such work as will give them liberty therefrom on this day.

(6) That our brethren in pursuit of their occupations and labors and our sisters in the management of household affairs, are admonished to refrain as much as possible from secular labors, that they may give the day to physical rest and religious exercises, according to the Scriptures.[3]

Actually the Annual Meeting decisions of these years around the opening of the twentieth century were quite consistent with long-standing Brethren opposition to work on Sundays, including some seven different decisions before the Civil War which date back to the Annual Meeting of 1810. On this question, at least, Brethren demonstrated a clear reluctance to come to terms with one of the demands of industrialization.

BUSINESSES AND INVESTMENTS

By the 1870s a number of Brethren were becoming involved in a variety of non-rural activities connected with the economic activity of the Reconstruction period following the Civil War. Because some of these activities were objectionable to some Brethren they reached the floor of the Annual Meeting. In 1871 the Meeting examined two problems:

Art. 9. Is it in accordance with the gospel for brethren to belong to the building and loan associations now organized in different parts of the country?

Answer: We advise the brethren not to unite with such associations until they understand them properly, and are satisfied that uniting with them does not conflict with the gospel.

Art. 19. How is it considered for members of the church to attach themselves to the Washington Mutual Live Stock Insurance Company?

Answer: We consider that brethren should not join any society by which they jeopardize their non-resistant principles.[4]

Evidently the Meeting was not certain whether such activities violated traditional Brethren interpretations of the New Testament. If not, then some types of investments might be acceptable.

In 1872 the Meeting examined another form of investment. The problem of banking and taking interest was a matter of concern for the Meeting.

Art. 11. What is to be done with a district of the church that tolerates its members in taking illegal interest for money loaned, after the Annual Meeting has decided again and again that it is wrong to do so?

Answer: This Annual Meeting thinks that that church should be visited by the elders of the adjoining churches, to set in order the things that are wanting.

Art. 21. Will this meeting allow brethren, and especially ministering brethren, to engage in the banking business?

Answer: Not advisable for brethren to engage in such business. (See Matt. 6:3)[5]

In 1873 the Meeting was asked about buying railroad stock.

Art. 9. Is it according to the gospel, or is it conforming to the world, when brethren subscribe for railroad stock?

Answer: We know of no direct Scripture forbidding it; but inasmuch as it brings us into associations in which we are liable to violate our Christian principles, we would advise brethren not to engage in it.[6]

These quite brief responses by the Annual Meeting in 1872 and 1873 elicited a demand for a more thorough explanation, which the Annual Meeting of 1874 provided.

Art. 6. Inasmuch as the answer to Art. 21, of the minutes of 1872, in reference to brethren engaging in the banking business is considered indefinite, and as some take advantage of this circumstance and do engage in the business, will not this district-meeting request the Annual Meeting to reconsider said query, and give a more positive answer? We agree to ask the Annual Meeting for a reconsideration of said query.

Answer: We, according to the above request, are willing to reconsider the query alluded to; but we do not see our way clear to make any decision more positive than we have already made. But we would admonish brethren to be very careful in engaging in all kinds of business, and especially in business done by incorporated bodies, such as railroad and banking companies, since by so doing they may be brought into dangerous associations with ungodly men.[7]

Obviously the Annual Meeting was becoming more tolerant of Brethren who were engaged in business activities. However, the Meeting could grant only a cautious acceptance, because by such activities members might become involved in "dangerous associations with ungodly men." Finally, in 1890, the Meeting was asked again about Brethren working "as directors or presidents of banks." The Meeting responded by referring to Article 6, 1874, and quoting the final sentence of that answer. That decision just about completely answered the issue.

"As directors or presidents of banks," some Brethren were apparently becoming economically successful in non-farming pursuits. One of the outstanding success stories among the Brethren was the Studebaker family of South Bend, Indiana, who produced automobiles for a number of years in the twentieth century. In background, they were evidently a typical Brethren family.

"Father and mother [John and Rebecca Studebaker] were devoted members of the denomination of Dunkards, and their primitive log house in the early days of Ashland County became renowned as the place where the ministers of that denomination of Christians resorted to hold their meetings, on which occasions the furniture of the audience room was removed to the woodshed for the better accommodation of those who attended the meetings. . . .

The fervor of their faith was so great and their opportunities for worship and religious exercises so limited that protracted meetings, prayer meetings, class meetings and Sunday school as well as the occasional services held in some settler's cabin by an itinerant minister of the gospel were regarded in the light of special privileges and served more than any other factor to relieve the monotony of their simple life. . . ."

From 1820 to 1840 was a time of turmoil on the American frontier as armies of preachers, invariably recent converts themselves, roamed the countryside in search of the unsaved. The young in Dunkard settlements were special targets, itching as many were to escape an evermore unfashionable concept of good and evil. Those familiar with German Baptist theology will appreciate that men of great wealth cannot be accommodated in that faith. This no doubt figured in the eventual abandonment of the Dunker religion by all the brothers except Henry. Yet its ethos remained at the center of Studebaker commercial policy through all the years the company was in family hands. . . .

Presumably the father spent most of the daylight hours in his shop, a log structure with thatched roof which stood "to the west of the house, across the north and south road," making and repairing metal items in the custom of blacksmiths. In that day, smithies were community gathering places, and the proprietor often filled such additional roles as constable, doctor, and undertaker.[8]

The Studebaker family was also typical in its dissatisfaction with life where it was and its desire to look for better economic advantages somewhere else. In this case the call of the city plus the call of relatives plus the call of the church helped to determine where the Studebakers would go.

With ever larger responsibilities and ever smaller resources, John Studebaker in 1849 decided that it was time to move again.

"That constitutional tendency to financial prostration," his son's biographer writes, "heretofore remarked as one of the leading traits of John Studebaker's character, did not disappear with the increasing years and wider experience."

Things had not worked out in north central Ohio and each passing year yielded little beyond crushed hopes. So John hung up his tools, saddled his horse, and rode west.

"The trip covered a distance of over three hundred miles through sparsely settled and little improved country. He went and returned by way of South Bend, where he had relatives, and stopped for a short visit each way. His relatives in South Bend and a number of other people residing in the vicinity were members of the German Baptist or Dunker Church, and this circumstance, added to the arguments of his friends decided him to locate among them instead of going to Chicago."

On his return home, John set in motion the preliminaries of migration. This must have been a simple evolution, probably centered on a public sale of the more cumbersome furnishings of the house and shop. Many of the items kept for later use are now in the Northern Indiana Historical Society collections in South Bend.

Sally, or Sarah Studebaker Welch, the oldest child, with husband and family were already in the South Bend area and her letters home no doubt influenced the decision to move. But Sally's reasons for leading the way are lost in the mist of time. Henry, the eldest, had been there even earlier, but reports upon his return to Ashland must have been anything but encouraging. Clem went to South Bend in 1850 and found work teaching school while Henry followed shortly thereafter. Clem later wrote: "I decided to go west and grow up with the country. From Ashland I went to Sandusky and there took the boat to Detroit. In that city I found those new-fangled conveyances called steam-cars by which I came to Niles Michigan, and from there by stage to South Bend. The journey occupied about three days."

John engaged George Meyers and together they built a new wagon for the trip. Then, when the roads dried in 1851, the family abandoned "Pleasant Ridge," a place of so much heartache to John and Rebecca and of so much joy to their remembering children.

A neighbor, apparently William B. Allison later recalled: "One day, to the surprise of everyone, old man Studebaker loaded his family and a few household goods into a covered wagon and started west. All the neighbors had confidence in his honesty and were sorry to see him go." A subsequent return seems to have been an even greater surprise. "In a year or two he came back to Green Township and paid every debt that he had left behind him. I remember how proud the old man was of his ability to do this and how glad his former neighbors were to see him prosper."[9]

Out of the work in a blacksmith shop and the work with machinery in general evolved the skill of building wagons which was evidently picked up by some members of the family. The military use of these wagons apparently caused some concern among the leadership of the local congregation. According to a Studebaker family history:

In the early years, and probably at the time Clem and Henry were building military wagons in partnership with Milburn, a committee of deacons from the local church stopped at Henry's home. Those acquainted with Dunker theology will know that such a call, in itself, has ominous overtones. There is no record of what the visiting churchmen said to Henry or what he may have said in reply. But minutes of the Annual Meeting of the Brethren, dating back to 1778, show that "going to the muster ground" or otherwise cooperating in military doings was anathema to any true Dunkard. Building army wagons destined to help kill Mormons, Indians and slave holders was a clear-cut example of such prohibited cooperation. There is no record of what Susan, as major shareholder, may have added. She, too, from a Dunker background as strong as Henry's, probably criticized the brothers' recent war contracts.[10]

This event took place in the 1850s at South Bend and involved two of the best known sons of John Studebaker, who had moved the family from Ohio to Indiana. Eventually Henry's conscience caused him to withdraw from the business.

"Under the influence of the persuasion of his Dunker brethren and yielding to the inclinations of his own heart, Henry expressed a desire to retire from the business which he and Clem had established, and which had already begun to yield good returns, and to go to farming."

It is possible that similar considerations figured in the failure of the father to resume his lifelong trade in partnership with his sons. He was then age 53 and ostensibly in good health, but he is not mentioned

Fig. 21. *Advertisement appearing in the* Brethren's Family Almanac, 1899.

Dr. Peter's Blood Vitalizer

is not a so-called patent medicine—not a cure-all—but a reliable household remedy, carefully compounded from medicinal herbs, leaves, roots, barks, etc., according to the prescription of a learned Swiss-German physician, which has been handed down from father to son for three successive generations.

Many a discovery in medicine has been hailed with delight, only to be thrown aside because it could not stand the test of time. Not so, however, with **Dr. Peter's Blood Vitalizer,** the old blood-cleansing remedy. It has been in constant use for over one hundred years, and thousands have gladly testified to its curative properties.

Dr. Peter's Blood Vitalizer is an article of acknowledged merit. It is distinctly different from all other medicines. It may have its imitations, but it has no substitute. It not only expels the disease from the body, but it creates new, rich, red blood, and sound, solid, healthy flesh. It has won its way into popular favor without gaudy newspaper advertising, solely on its own merits.

It Purifies the Blood. **It Promotes Digestion.**
It Acts upon the Liver. **It Regulates the Bowels.**
It Acts upon the Kidneys. **It Quiets the Nervous System.**

It Nourishes, Strengthens and Invigorates.

It Opens the Pores of the Skin and Induces Healthy Perspiration.

In short, it is a family medicine in every sense of the word, and ought to be found in every household. It is pleasant to take and absolutely harmless. It is not sold by druggists, but only by local **Vitalizer** agents or the proprietor direct.

☞ Persons living in localities where there are no agents for the **Vitalizer,** and who have not previously ordered any, can obtain a trial box, containing twelve 35 cent bottles, at the special price of $2.00. Address at all times

DR. PETER FAHRNEY,

112-114 South Hoyne Ave. **CHICAGO, ILL.**

Fig. 22. *Advertisement appearing in the* Brethren's Family Almanac, 1898.

thereafter in connection with the shop in South Bend. His picture, however, was later used in company advertising.[11]

Perhaps one of the ironies of the day was that Henry also became wealthy. He purchased relatively inexpensive farmland, which soon became expensive residential and industrial land in the South Bend area. He was also closely related to his family. "Although not directly identified with his brothers in the larger and more prosperous growth of their business, his fealty to them was a marked and pleasing feature of his life. . . . He frequently counseled with them, and in various ways rendered the company and its individual members valuable aid." Henry was "essentially a man who avoided contention and cultivated relations of peace and goodwill with all men. His sympathies were easily aroused, his benevolences were large and his generosity responsive and helpful."[12] An obituary of Henry Studebaker published in the ***South Bend Daily Tribune,*** *March 4, 1895, remembered him:*

"Mr. Studebaker was a member of the denomination of Dunkards, the faith of his parents and the church to which his wife and sisters, Mrs. Welch and Mrs. Witwer belong. Mr. Studebaker was very fortunate in his home relations. His first wife was a woman of excellent Christian graces and homely virtues, a faithful helpmeet in his earlier years of privation and toil. His second wife also has been a devoted mother to all of his children by whom she is unitedly and heartily respected and loved in return. Their home has always been the abode of peace and good cheer and bountiful hospitality. Mr. Studebaker was never so happy as when an opportunity was afforded to entertain his friends. His roof tree has been the natural resort of every preacher of their church."[13]

Henry's brother Clement Studebaker also prospered through the making of wagons and carriages for the American people. He became very active in political and business activities, including membership in the Masonic Order. By that time, however, he was no longer a member of the Brethren. According to one account, he did live according to many Brethren ideals.

"As a devoted Christian, he spent his life living up to the ideals of his Christianity. He was raised as a Dunkard and belonged to the German Baptist Church which assimilated the Dunkards. His second wife was a Methodist and he joined that faith in 1868. Mrs. Studebaker erected Milburn Chapel as a memorial to her father, and in 1889–1900 they began building St. Paul's Memorial Church in South Bend. Its dedication came after Mr. Studebaker's death in 1901.

"They quietly and privately aided many in need, and their financial contributions to the city were numerous. They were contributors to the building fund of nearly every church in South Bend, but perhaps the most important was their donation of land and money for the completion of the new Epworth (Memorial) Hospital.

"In a eulogy Timothy Howard wrote that Clement Studebaker was 'not only a man of strength, but one of magnetism, with a sympathetic outflow toward all suffering. He was charitable in spirit, and his benevolence manifested itself in countless good works. . . An ideal business man, a good citizen, a helpful friend, a broad philanthropist and a man of the world, eager to aid in its best progress. . . . He was a practical man of rare ability and tireless energy, coupled with an iron determination and a manly ambition to excel in life work.'

"Perhaps his own attitude toward life was best summed up in a letter to his brother Peter in which he said, 'Life at the longest is too short for anything that is unkindly meant or ungenerously intended.' "[14]

LABOR UNIONS

The policy of the Studebakers regarding labor unions was not identified in the passages quoted above. In some areas of industrializing America it was desirable, if not necessary, to become a member of a union in order to secure employment. This question reached the Annual Meeting in 1882.

XXVIII. Will this District Meeting ask Annual Meeting to say what shall be done with members who attach themselves to worldly organizations? Such as Life Insurance companies and United Workmen.

Answer: Considered that brethren cannot unite with such associations as above named, and those who belong are required to leave them or be dealt with as transgressors.[15]

The Annual Meeting of 1889 again rejected the idea of Brethren joining any kind of labor unions, even carpenters.

17. Is it right, according to the Gospel, for members of the church to join the Brotherhood of Carpenters, Farmers' Alliances, or other similar organizations?

Answer: No. See 2 Cor. 6: 14–18; 2 Tim. 2: 4.[16]

The issue was dormant for the next fifteen years, but then the European Brethren raised the issue in their particular context for the Annual Meeting of 1904 to reconsider.

1. We ask Annual Meeting whether Brethren may unite with the Swedish workmen's union, and we present the following for your consideration:

(1) They are in no sense secret societies.

(2) It is almost impossible for Brethren to get employment in the cities if they do not unite with a union.

(3) If it is not allowable for Brethren to unite with a union, how shall we provide for Brethren who suffer because of not uniting with such an organization?

Sent to Annual Meeting.

Report of Committee.

Labor unions as now conducted often lead to violence, and sometimes to riot and bloodshed, and as these are contrary to the spirit and teaching of the Gospel of Jesus Christ, we cannot allow our members to unite with or belong to them. John 28: 36; Philpp. 2: 15.

As to providing for those in need, see Art. 18, Conference Minutes of 1888, page 137, "Revised Minutes."

D. L. Miller
D. C. Campbell
A. C. Wieand

Answer: Report Adopted[17]

Thus the Swedish Brethren were to be treated on the same basis as the Brethren in the United States. However, it was almost certain that the Brethren in the United States would continue to question this policy. The Annual Meeting of 1908 was again queried on the issue.

9. The Macoupin Creek church asks Annual Meeting, through district meeting of Southern District of Illinois, to reconsider the report of committee in Article 1 of 1904, and so amend that brethren

may belong to such labor organizations as do not require them to violate any gospel principle.

Answer: Since the church has ever held sacred and inviolate her Gospel principles against secret and oathbound organizations, and all labor unions, and inasmuch as there is so much trouble between labor organizations and capitalists, we consider it unwise and exceedingly dangerous for our brethren to unite with any labor union. See John 18: 36; Philpp. 2: 15; and Art. 1, 1904, Annual Meeting Minutes.[18]

This policy continued to be questioned. The Annual Meeting of 1911 decided to appoint a committee to study the matter.

8. Whereas, Annual Meeting has advised strongly against members uniting with Labor Unions, but has not strictly forbidden it, in its last decision (see Art. 9, 1908), therefore, we, the Reading church, ask District Meeting:

(1) Whether some leniency can be shown members who, in the judgment of the local church, have joined the Union, not because they were in sympathy with the Union, but for the sake of obtaining work in a city where labor is closely organized?

(2) Is it allowable for brethren who are contractors to sign the "Union Wage Scale"?

(3) Are brethren justified in belonging to relief associations or beneficiary societies?

If District Meeting is not disposed to answer the above, then forward to Annual Meeting.

Answer by District Meeting—Sent to Annual Meeting.

Answer: Referred to a committee of five to report to next Annual Meeting.

Committee: H. C. Early, A. P. Blough, I. H. Crist, G. B. Royer, A. L. Wright.[19]

The committee reported to the Annual Meeting of 1912.

Answer by the Committee

After a careful consideration of the above queries your committee submits the following:

(1) We consider the first two questions answered satisfactorily in Annual Meeting Minutes, 1908, Art. 9.

(2) Members may belong to relief associations and beneficiary societies when by doing so they violate no gospel principle.

Signed by H. C. Early, A. P. Blough, I. H. Crist, Galen B. Royer, A. L. Wright, Committee.

Answer: Report accepted and committee continued.[20]

No explanation was offered for the unusual answer of accepting the committee's report and continuing the committee. Part of the answer was provided by the Annual Meeting of 1913 which restructured the committee: A. P. Blough, I. H. Crist, A. L. Wright, G. H. Bashor, M. C. Swigart. This new committee reported to the Meeting of 1914 that it had not finished its work and was continued. By the following year, however, their assignment was completed.

Report of Committee, 1915

After a most careful investigation of all the issues involved in the above queries, your committee submits the following report:

1. Members may belong to Labor Unions, relief associations and beneficiary societies when, by doing so, they violate no gospel principle.

2. Members desiring to have the benefits of labor organizations, relief associations, and beneficiary societies shall, before affiliating with such organizations or societies, request the local church to investigate said organizations and societies, to see whether any gospel principle may possibly be violated by affiliating with such organizations and societies.

3. All former decisions conflicting with the above, are hereby repealed.

Committee: A. P. Blough, I. H. Crist, G. H. Bashor, A. L. Wright, M. C. Swigart.

Answer of Annual Meeting, 1915

While this Conference cannot sanction membership in any of the Labor Unions, yet we do not see our way clear to wholly forbid a necessary affiliation of members with Labor Unions, relief associations and beneficiary associations when by so doing they violate no gospel principle.[21]

The Church of the Brethren had now placed officially a rather grudging toleration on membership in labor unions by members of the church. It was a somewhat similar approach to other relationships to society, such as political action and use of modern clothing.

LIFE INSURANCE

Brethren ownership of life insurance, like Brethren membership in labor unions, was given a grudging toleration by Annual Meeting by the first quarter of the twentieth century. In the 1860s Brethren had made a distinction between property insurance and life insurance. The former was accepted but the latter was prohibited. Then, in decisions in 1869 and in 1870, the Meeting had hedged on the issue of life insurance by refusing to make a definite statement. However, in 1873, the question was raised again and the Meeting was more definite.

Art 1. Is it consistent for brethren to have their lives insured? and how shall we proceed with those who have their lives insured?

Answer: It is inconsistent for brethren to do so.[22]

In the 1880s the Brethren were inconsistent in dealing with this issue. For example, in 1882 the response was clear.

XXIX. As the Annual Meeting has decided that it is inconsistent for members to have their lives insured, (Annual Meeting 1873, page 379, Art. 1st) What is to be done with a brother who has his life insured, especially ministers and ordained elders who persist in so doing?

Answer: Those who do so shall be dealt with as transgressors.[23]

But in 1883:

8. Inasmuch as Annual Meeting has granted the Brethren the privilege of insuring their property, and as we fail to see the difference between property and life insurance, and whereas Brethren are indulging in life insurance thereby causing trouble, we then ask Annual Meeting of 1883, to either repeal all decisions favoring insurance, or to grant the privilege of life insurance.

Answer: Whereas there are different views on the subject of insurance, therefore resolved that we defer this query indefinitely.[24]

And in 1886:

. . . Whereas, of late years life insurance companies have become more numerous, and many persons have had their lives insured; and whereas, there is a probability that some of those persons will make application to come into the church by baptism, will this District

Meeting give us instructions how to proceed? If members are required to withdraw their life insurance policy, surely we can not take in applicants without withdrawing their policy. Therefore, when visiting applicants for membership, when we ask them if they are members of any secret order, and if so, they must withdraw, ought we not also to ask them if they have their lives insured, and if so, ask them to withdraw their policy?

Answer: Annual Meeting decides as requested.[25]

As far as Annual Meeting action was concerned, the issue of life insurance did not come up again for another ten years. In 1896 the Meeting was asked to appoint a committee to study the subject.

10. The Pine Creek church petitions Annual Meeting through District Meeting to appoint a committee of five brethren to investigate the subject of life insurance, to find out whether or not there are any life insurance companies who issue policies which the Brethren may accept without violating any Gospel principle. This committee to report to next Annual Meeting.

Answer: We cannot grant the request.[26]

Five years later in 1901 the Annual Meeting agreed to appoint a study committee in response to two queries. The first asked about the desirability of some kind of beneficiary society in the church, and the second asked for "scriptural reasons and references" why Brethren could not have life insurance. A committee including D. L. Miller, L. H. Dickey, C. Fritz, John Heckman, and H. C. Early was appointed to prepare a report for the Annual Meeting of 1902. At least two of the members, Miller and Early, were outstanding leaders of the church at this time. The committee did its homework well and prepared a report for the Annual Meeting of 1902.

1. A Beneficiary Association conducted by the church would involve intricate business problems and financial responsibilities which it would be unwise for the church to assume. We therefore report against such organization in the church.

2. Our members should not unite with any Secret Beneficiary Society, or Secret Mutual Life Insurance Association. In uniting with such organizations they are led into alliance with secret societies, which are contrary to the teaching of the Scriptures. "Be ye not unequally yoked together with unbelievers." 2 Cor. 6:14.

3. There are some forms of investment in Life Insurance Companies that do not seem to us to be wrong, either from a moral or scriptural standpoint. Among these may be named, Annuities, Endowments, and Employees' Accident Insurance, and while we do not encourage investments in Insurance Companies we do not find scriptural authority to make them a test of church fellowship.

D. L. Miller
L. H. Dickey
John Heckman
C. Fritz
H. C. Early

Answer: In view of the importance of this subject, we recommend that this report be spread on the Minutes for one year for general study before final action is taken.[27]

So final action was to be delayed, probably because some important leader of the church, either on the committee or off of the committee, was not prepared to make the change called for in the third point. It is even more interesting that the issue was not resolved in 1903—or in any year following. It simply is not mentioned in the Minutes of the Annual Meeting until 1920.

The actual practice in the church regarding life insurance was well stated in a letter written by Galen B. Royer from his Elgin office in 1910.

Concerning life insurance I have this to say. I once thot as you did. I preached a sermon to a crowded house in Bridgewater one afternoon and while on my knees and some one else was leading us in prayer all my insurance came up before me in such a light that I laid it all away before the Lord. I could not preach the life of faith I did that day and carry insurance. I have no insurance on property or life in any way.

As a district we are consistently trying to hold to the conference in not ordaining any one to the eldership who carries life insurance. Further than that I hear little of the subject. I know of no cases of discipline because members carry life insurance, that is all that I know about it. To me it is a matter of spiritual development and with less of the commercial spirit and more of the Christ spirit we will all drop all kinds of insurance and trust the living God and press on in the work of the kingdom.[28]

RAILROADS

One business activity in the United States that affected virtually all Brethren in some way or another was the railroad. Members invested in its stock, traveled over it, and shipped products over it. It was a crucial part of their lives and it was hard for them to imagine how they had gotten along without it. For some Brethren, who had enough surplus funds to invest in other than agricultural pursuits, the railroads provided an attractive opportunity. The result was that the question of owning railroad stock reached the floor of Annual Meeting on several occasions. As early as 1849 the Meeting studied the matter and concluded that "brethren had better not engage in such investments," because "the business of such companies is often much involved in obscurity, and persons dealing with such companies may be liable to be deceived." Since this decision dealt with both banking and railroads, the Annual Meeting of 1860 was asked to divide the question. The answer was: "We advise brethren not to invest their money in bank stock at all, and would advise them to be cautious of all incorporated companies." The problem of investing in railroad stock was settled by the Annual Meeting of 1873, which advised Brethren "not to engage in it," but conceded that it could not find any "direct Scripture forbidding it."[29]

Most Brethren probably did not have enough spare funds to invest in railroad stock, but they did have enough money to travel on the railroads. Recall that one of the Studebaker boys "decided to go west and grow up with the country" by traveling from Ohio to Indiana; part of his trip was made on "those new-fangled conveyances called steam-cars." What was happening in this instance was a migration, which also happened to countless thousands of Brethren during these years. Many of them went farther than from one state to the next. A large-scale migration involving an entire train of freight cars and passenger cars is described in a previous chapter on geographical expansion.

As was true in this settlement in the Dakotas, the western railroads needed to secure settlers to buy their land or government land and to use the railroads in relocating and shipping agricultural produce. In order to secure settlers the railroads employed recruiting agents. These agents found that Brethren made excellent settlers or "colonists," and frequently attempted to secure Brethren leaders who would recommend western land to other Brethren. This practice had reached serious proportions by the 1890s and was considered by the Annual Meeting of 1899.

9. (a) We petition Annual Meeting through District Meeting, that no brethren shall serve on "Standing Committee" or as delegate to "District Meeting" or "Annual Meeting," or as a member of any "Mission Board," who receives a remuneration from a railroad corporation or land speculators, for assistance in locating families in new countries, thus weakening the influence of their holy calling. This shall not be so construed as to prohibit brethren from accepting free transportation, for the purpose of going to see new countries for themselves. By order of the Beaver Dam church. District Meeting grants the petition.

(b) Inasmuch as some of our brethren have been employed by immigration agents and land associations to canvass, and others have given their influence by allowing their names to be used in circular letters, and thereby many have been influenced to leave comfortable homes and to seek homes in new countries, much to the dissatisfaction of many and also causing much severe criticism on our Brotherhood, therefore we ask District Meeting to petition Annual Meeting to decide that brethren shall cease thus giving encouragement to such schemes, or declare them ineligible to represent the church as delegate at District Meeting or Annual Meeting.

Answer: We grant the petitions, and decide further that, if Brethren will persist in exercising undue influence to induce emigration, they shall be called to account.[30]

Certainly, this discouragement by the Annual Meeting did not end the emigration of Brethren from the eastern states to the western states of the United States. Another practice of the railroads and land companies which came to be questioned was the use of the church periodicals for advertising. One illustration of such advertising was placed by Max Bass in the September 1896, issues of the ***Gospel Messenger.*** *Bass was the agent of the Great Northern Railroad and an important element in the colonization of the Brethren.*

Who Should Go West

The following thought has no doubt occurred to all Eastern people who contemplate a change. Can I improve my circumstances by going West? In some cases benefit would result, but if a man is well fixed financially, in good health, himself and his family, and contented with local conditions, there is no good reason why he should try his fortune elsewhere. There are people however, who can better their lot by going west, and among these are the following:

1. All persons in poor health. A change of climate, air, water and food will give a new lease of life to those enfeebled by damp or malarious conditions in the East or South. The air of the Northwest is dry and invigorating. Summer heat never depresses and winter cold never chills.

2. Farmers with large families.

3. Farmers who are heavily mortgaged and cannot see their way out.

4. Farmers who can get together $500–1000. This will give the possessor plenty of means to improve a homestead, or a farm bought on scrip payments or any other agreed method.

5. Young married people just starting in life.

6. Any man who has livestock and implements and knows how to work.

7. All men who rent land in the East.

8. Any farmer at work on worn out land and paying out for fertilizers per acre each year as much as land costs by the acre in the West, should by all means expend his energy on the fertile soil of North Dakota.

9. Any farmer whose home place is too small to divide up and give his children enough land to provide them a living. He should go West where there is elbow room.

10. Any merchant, mechanic, or manufacturer who is being overcrowded by too close competition in the East.

Any person included in the above classes, or others who may have a desire to visit and investigate to the West, can get printed matter and information about rates, routes, etc. by addressing:

Max Bass
Chicago, Illinois
220 South Clark St.[31]

It was this type of advertising, as well as other advertising which might be even more colorful, that led to a query to the Annual Meeting of 1897.

2. We petition Annual Meeting through District Meeting that all land advertisements be excluded from the Gospel Messenger, as it has a tendency to mislead some.

Answer. We consider that it would not be proper to exclude all land advertisements; but to admit such only that will bear the strictest scrutiny as regards being for the good and use of all, whether of land or anything else.[32]

There is no doubt that advertising had become an important source of income for the ***Gospel Messenger*** *and other church periodicals, which may be one reason why the Annual Meeting did not take stronger action. Shortly after the turn of the century, however, railroad land advertisements in Brethren periodicals did cease.*

Much of the advertising in the ***Gospel Messenger*** *was intended to appeal to Brethren farmers by illustrating and describing various kinds of farm machinery. If a farmer purchased machinery, it was delivered by the railroad. If a farmer produced wheat with the machinery, the wheat was transported by the railroad. Thus farmers were very much interested in the procedure by which the rates were established. The* ***Progressive Christian*** *of January 3, 1879 noted in fine print under "Secularities" that a group of railroads had met in Chicago in December to pool traffic and rates.*

The Railroad Combination—Chicago, Dec. 19

The Railroad Convention to-day unanimously adopted the report agreed on last night by the joint committee. This report provides that Chicago roads leading east shall pool their business on the same plan as roads out of Cincinnati, Indianapolis, Peoria, and St. Louis; that the arrangement shall go into effect immediately; that rates shall be restored to the basis of the tariff of Nov. 25, viz; 35 cents per 100 pounds on grain and 40 cents on fourth-class freight to New York; that all rates from all points be restored at once; that none of the roads here represented shall hereafter be parties to any contract or agreement, or allow rebates below the agreed tariff, and that all existing contracts shall be reported within a week to the chairman of the joint committee. An apportionment of freight was made. . . .[32]

This action, coming as the United States was recovering from the economic depression known as the Panic of 1873, probably tended to increase the rates on grain shipped by railroad. Also it is doubtful if any of the Brethren profited from rebates, which were payments by the railroads, usually made secretly, to their biggest customers. It is more likely the case that Brethren farmers, like most American farmers, were treated unmercifully by the railroads. Rarely did any farmer have access to more than one railroad to ship his products.

However much Brethren disliked the railroads because of their unreasonable freight rates, they loved their passenger cars. They used the railroads extensively for traveling to Annual Meeting. Evidently the railroads loved the Brethren, too, for they gave them special concessions. The Annual Meeting of 1858 had considered the appropriateness of accepting concessions from the railroads.

Art. 28. Is it consistent with the Word of God for the followers of our Lord and Savior Jesus Christ to make arrangements with railroad companies to obtain the benefit of half-fare, in going to and returning home from the Yearly Meeting?

Considered, that it is right for brethren to avail themselves of the privilege offered by the railroad companies, but we would advise all our brethren to comply with the rules of the companies, and if a misunderstanding should occur, not to contend, but rather pay full fare.[34]

Over the years Brethren developed the practice of appointing special agents to negotiate with the railroads for passenger fares. For example, in 1870 the Meeting "resolved that Bro. John Buechly, of Illinois, be the agent for obtaining railroad privileges west of Pittsburg and the Ohio River, and Bro. Christian Custer, of Philadelphia, for obtaining such privileges east of Pittsburg."[35] As the number of railroads increased along with the number of Brethren utilizing the railroads, several men were appointed to obtain these special rates. In 1889 the Meeting apointed a Railroad Arrangements committee:

The following brethren were appointed on Railroad Arrangements for next year: D. L. Miller, General Agent, to be assisted by the following brethren residing in the several Passenger Associations: John Wise, Trans-Missouri Association; S. S. Mohler, Western States Association; J. G. Royer, Central Association; E. W. Stoner, Trunk Line Association; Geo. C. Bowman, Southern Association.[36]

Brethren periodicals each year printed detailed instructions from the various agents regarding the best routes to follow on the way to the Annual Meeting. Once in a while they noted that a particular route was not cooperating with the Brethren and should be avoided. For example, in 1869 the ***Christian Family Companion*** *included this report from D. P. Sayler:*

I have made arrangements with the Baltimore and Ohio R. R. Co. for all the members who have been in attendance at Annual Meeting and have paid full fare going, to be returned free of charge. I also made the same arrangements with the Cumberland Valley R. R. Co. from Harrisburg to Hagerstown and there strike the Baltimore and Ohio Road. In consequence of the arbitrary demands of the Northern Central from Harrisburg to Baltimore, I have made no arrangements with that road. Hence Brethren following the directions of Brother Moomaw may lose the benefit of half fare from Harrisburg. I have requested the Pennsylvania brethren to attend to the Pennsylvania Central, and Va. brethren to attend to the roads south of Washington, D. C., north of that they are too far off, and better leave to others nearer by. So far as the Baltimore and Ohio, and Cumberland Valley roads are concerned, you will pay your fare going, asking no questions, and at Annual Meeting you will procure a ticket by me, which will return you free of charge to all points you may take the road east of Columbus Ohio. But Brethren coming from via Pittsburg must at Harrisburg take the Cumberland Valley road to Hagerstown, (and not to Baltimore.) This is the correct route, (but the difference is not much,) but I could not accede to the unreasonable demands of the Northern Central road.

D. P. Sayler[37]

Although the Brethren requested, and usually received, special rates from the railroads, they still expected to enjoy the best of accommodations and comfort. Members were encouraged to make their feelings concerning their treatment known to those in charge, so that something could be done about it. An article in the ***Primitive Christian*** *expressed this sentiment:*

As the different railroad companies have promised to give our brethren and sisters, going to Annual Meeting, good coaches and the best of accommodations, we will be glad to hear from such, if there should be any, who will be disappointed in this respect. We will expect them to do just as they have promised, and if they do not do so, we shall be glad to learn it and put such roads on record, so that we may know what roads to advise our brethren to travel over hereafter. If our members are willing to give the different railroad companies, a hundred thousand dollars and more, for the privilege of riding over their roads to A. M., they will expect to realize, at least, a reasonable amount of enjoyment from the outlay.[38]

The Brethren expected much from the railroads with their demands for half-fares and the best of accommodations, and they usually received excellent treatment. Occasionally Brethren expressed their appreciation, as in a ***Gospel Messenger*** *article in 1890.*

The officials of the different railroad companies, over whose lines it was our pleasure to travel, were certainly very courteous towards our people and went to some trouble to make their trip to Annual Meeting and return both safe and pleasant. We take pleasure in naming the Baltimore and Ohio, the Ohio and Missouri, and the Missouri Pacific. They were all very considerate and obliging and we believe that our people were well pleased with the manner in which they were treated. The Missouri and Pac. had an office on the Meeting grounds which was a great convenience. How they bore up under the thousands of questions asked, we don't know but they did it bravely and deserve considerable credit for the Job-like patience exercised.[39]

A major problem faced by committees making arrangements for the Annual Meeting was getting Brethren from the railroads to the Meeting grounds. Sometimes the railroads were very helpful. The report of the 1874 Annual Meeting in the ***Christian Family Companion and Gospel Visitor*** *explained the arrangement.*

The Railroad accommodations were excellent. The place of meeting was about two hundred yards from the Railroad. And to accommodate the meeting, the Company made a temporary station, calling it Filbruns Station. Here all the trains stopped during the meeting. There was also a temporary Telegraph Office connected with the station. And from the station to the meeting, there was a plank walk made to guard against mud in case it should rain. In short, the arrangements were wisely made by the brethren, and all done by them that well could be done to promote the comfort of those attending the meeting. And their labor was appreciated, at least by many, and the results of it enjoyed.[40]

One other illustration of the importance of railroad connections is taken from the planning for the Hagerstown Annual Meeting of 1891, which was reported in the ***Gospel Messenger*** *in November, 1890.*

To-day it [Hagerstown] is one of the leading cities, and the most important railroad center in Western Maryland. Its population has

Fig. 23. *Meeting Brethren at the Salford Station, Lower Salford Township, Montgomery Co., PA, 1903. (BE)*

Fig. 24. *Henry Lorenz with peddler's wagon ca. 1912 from his general store in Plevna, IN. (BE)*

grown to about 12,000 souls. It has six railroads, and is directly connected with the great trunk lines North and South, East and West, and it is fast becoming a great manufacturing center. This prosperous city has been selected as the place for our next Conference, and the numerous railroads, centering here, will afford ample means for reaching the place of meeting. When our Annual Conference is located on any one line of road, as is sometimes the case, no matter what its facilities for handling the people may be, much inconvenience is experienced, owing to overcrowded cars, and delays.

At Hagerstown the railroad facilities are all that can be desired. . . .

The Meeting Grounds

Are located in the South-eastern part of the city, and in its corporate limits. They are within ten minutes' walk of the Western Maryland depot; the other depots being much nearer to the ground. The Baltimore & Ohio depot is but a few blocks away. This is a convenience that will be much appreciated by all who attend the meeting. Very often the meeting grounds are located at a considerable distance from the railroad, and it is on this account very inconvenient.[41]

In addition to providing a variety of services for the Brethren, the railroads also gave them stop-over privileges, which allowed them to spend time visiting relatives or friends along the route of their travel to and from Annual Meeting. An account from the **Gospel Messenger** *in 1890 illustrates this practice.*

The Wabash R. R., including all its branches, will sell tickets to Annual Meeting at the rate of one fare for the round trip, good for thirty days, to all who wish to attend. Good connections with the Missouri Pacific R. R. at St. Louis are made via the *Popular Wabash Route.* Stop-over privileges will be granted to all who wish to visit friends living on Wabash R. R.—within the limits of their tickets. Tickets will be on sale at all Wabash stations by notifying the agent in time. The Missouri Pacific is the only railroad leading to Annual Meeting. Good accommodations and close connections will be the leading features of these two lines. To visiting members who desire to visit friends farther west than Warrensburgh, the Missouri Pacific R. R. will sell tickets at one fare for round trip to all points in Southwestern Missouri, Kansas, Nebraska, and Indian Territory. . . .

Application was made for a longer extension of time on the tickets but it was decided that the limit given above was all that could be granted. . . . We trust this will be satisfactory to those who wish to go to the Meeting.[42]

One of the requests made by the railroads was that as far as possible Brethren should travel together. This stipulation aided the railroads and the Brethren, who were encouraged to become acquainted and to travel together. One of the Brethren railroad agents discussed this in the ***Progressive Christian.***

The concessions that R. R.'s make are on the assumption that business will be condensed and not scattered. If any sufficient number, say thirty-five people can be got together, I will have a car ready for them and they may occupy it themselves to the exclusion of all others, except brethren. If Huntingdon Co., Somerset, Bedford, Blair or any lot of brethren can agree as to their coming and going, they can have a car—one of the best—and go in the best style. The parties going, if they address a card to this office stating about the time they want to go, can have it published, and the brethren can then arrange together. Sometimes friends go in the same train and never know it.[43]

Traveling together provided opportunities for fellowship, often a means of spiritual growth for Brethren. The railroads also provided much material for articles and sermons by Brethren writers and preachers. An experience by one editor, while witnessing an attempt to avoid paying train fare for two children, inspired an article concerning honesty. J. S. Mohler preached a sermon entitled "Railroad Sermon. Just the Thing for Travelers from Earth to Heaven," which was later printed as a tract. His text was taken from Matthew 7:14, and began:

The term strait as used in our text, means narrow, somewhat difficult of entrance; the gate of the same width as the way. Whatever cannot be taken through the gate, cannot be taken on the way. The way here spoken of, may appropriately be compared to a railway. Of these there are two kinds,—the wide and narrow gauges.

His outline included the topics: The Narrow Gauge and The Broad Gauge, Safe Way to Travel, On Time, Through Ticket and Stop-Over Ticket, Up Grade All the Time, Down Brakes, Side Tracks,

Baggage Car and Sleeping Car, Conductor, Engineer, Costs Money, Lightning Express, Grand Excursion, and Destination. In his conclusion he wrote:

Since the destination of these two roads is so different, the narrow gauge ending in eternal happiness, while the broad guage ends in eternal misery, we should carefully examine our ticket to see whether we are on this heavenly road. If not, make an effort to get on board as soon as possible. See that your tickets are stamped with the seal of the Holy Spirit. Keep a careful look-out for counterfeit tickets, for they will be refused by the great Conductor of the train. The great Conductor says that "many will come unto Him in that day saying, Have we not cast out devils in thy name, and in thy name have done many wonderful works?" Then He will say, "Depart from me, ye workers of iniquity, I never knew you." They all had counterfeit tickets. The great Conductor further says, "He that doeth the will of my Father which is in heaven, shall enter the kingdom." Then let us see that our tickets have stamped on them not only the seal of the Holy Spirit, but also full, unreserved obedience to all the precepts of the Gospel. May our tickets also have the additional mark or evidence that we were not ashamed to follow the Captain of our salvation through evil, as well as through good report; and so shall an abundant entrance be administered unto us into His everlasting kingdom above.[44]

Whether in preaching sermons or traveling or shipping, it is obvious that the railroads did have a great impact on Brethren, as a church and as individuals, during the fifty years following the Civil War. One of the ways by which the Brethren attempted to show their appreciation was in the form of resolutions adopted by the Annual Meeting. In each year following 1881, the resolutions included reference to the railroads. The resolutions in 1903 were particularly interesting because of the reference to a rebate.

5. To the several railroad companies for reduced rates and safe transportation, and especially to the Big Four, the Toledo and Ohio Central and the Wabash lines, who have pledged a rebate to the Committee of Arrangements.[45]

The relationship between Brethren and the railroads was largely one of mutual cooperation that reaped mutual benefits. As a result of the work of the railroad agents, the Brethren spanned the continent

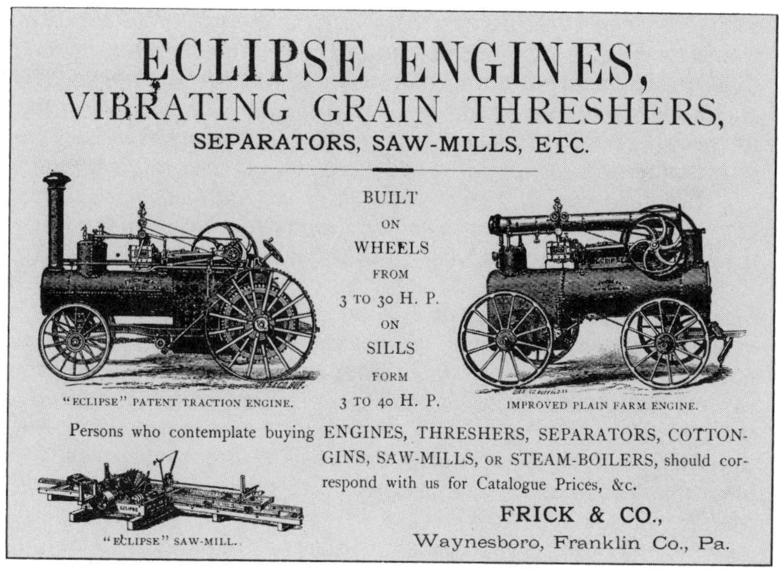
ECLIPSE ENGINES,
VIBRATING GRAIN THRESHERS,
SEPARATORS, SAW-MILLS, ETC.
BUILT ON WHEELS FROM 3 TO 30 H. P. ON SILLS FORM 3 TO 40 H. P.
"ECLIPSE" PATENT TRACTION ENGINE.
IMPROVED PLAIN FARM ENGINE.
Persons who contemplate buying ENGINES, THRESHERS, SEPARATORS, COTTON-GINS, SAW-MILLS, OR STEAM-BOILERS, should correspond with us for Catalogue Prices, &c.
"ECLIPSE" SAW-MILL.
FRICK & CO.,
Waynesboro, Franklin Co., Pa.

Fig. 25. *Advertisement appearing in the* Brethren's Family Almanac, 1884.

Fig. 26. *Threshing machine near Lima, OH, early 20th century. (BE)*

and added many to their membership. It is doubtful that the church would have expanded as rapidly as it did within such a short period of time, if the transcontinental railroads had not been completed, thus making inexpensive agricultural land available. The low rates offered by the railroads to encourage excursions to the western lands enabled potential settlers to view the land before taking the step of emigrating.

The quick and efficient operation of the railroads made it possible for Brethren preachers to embark upon preaching tours, ministering to lonely and isolated members, as well as established congregations. Also, the railroads made it possible for more Brethren to take part in annual meetings, as well as local love feasts and district meetings, because less time was needed for travel. Clearly the railroads influenced the spiritual, private, and business lives of Brethren, making profound changes in their lifestyles and altering the future of the church.

In summary, the economic activities of Brethren provided another illustration of the extent to which they had departed from their traditional isolation from society by 1915. Their extensive involvement in American railroads, their involvement in industry, both at the management and the common laborer level, and their overall attitude toward participation in business reflected the changes that were taking place among them.

VI

POLITY AND ORGANIZATION

INTRODUCTION

The organized life of the German Baptist Brethren, later the Church of the Brethren, developed at two basic levels—the local, or congregational level and the national, or brotherhood, level. In some cases, as in the examining of material for the Annual Meeting, the in-between level, the district, played a role. For example, the districts were assigned responsibility for mission work in the cities. Most of the action, however, occurred at the congregational or brotherhood level.

One of the most significant changes during these years was the organization of a number of permanent brotherhood committees, the most important of which was the General Mission Board. A number of these committees will be identified in the section of this chapter dealing with brotherhood activities. These specialized committees helped the church make a number of changes at the congregational level, such as the addition of Sunday schools to congregational activities.

CONGREGATIONAL ACTIVITIES

By 1865 very few Brethren congregations had established a permanent Sunday school program. As early as 1857 the Annual Meeting had given the congregations permission to establish Sunday schools, a decision that was reiterated in 1862 and explained further in 1868.

Art. 14. As the Annual Meeting has given the liberty to hold Sabbath-schools, it is particularly requested that this Annual Meeting give a full and definite answer to the last question in Art. 1, minutes of 1862, that there may be a uniformity of practice among the brethren who hold, or who wish to hold, Sabbath-schools.

Answer: We advise that, where the nature of the case will admit of it, for brethren to hold Sabbath-schools, and such schools should be opened by singing and prayer, and closed by singing or by prayer, as it may be thought proper, and they should be superintended by brethren. And we advise the brethren to be very careful in introducing books, to introduce none that inculcate doctrines contrary to the gospel. And we further advise that brethren avoid taking part in or encouraging the Sabbath-school celebrations, common in the world.[1]

Since Brethren meetinghouses had not been built to include Sunday school classrooms but for worship purposes, the question arose as to whether or not meetinghouses should be used for classrooms. The Annual Meeting of 1870 considered the question.

Art. 25. Does the Annual Meeting consider it wrong for the brethren to hold their Sunday-schools in their meeting-houses?

Answer: We consider it not wrong, if such schools are conducted according to order, and by the consent of the church.[2]

The final phrase of the decision of 1870 attracted attention, especially among groups of conservatives in the church who did not approve of the establishment of Sunday schools. The Meeting of 1871 was asked:

Art. 17. Will not this Annual Meeting recall the privilege granted to establish Sunday-schools, especially where the church is not entirely unanimous?

Answer: We do not recall the above privilege, but where the establishing of Sunday-schools would cause trouble or division, brethren had better desist from introducing them.[3]

The Annual Meeting of 1873 was asked for further clarification regarding the holding of Sunday schools.

Art. 11. As the Annual Meeting has given the liberty to hold Sabbath-schools, if held according to the gospel, this district-meeting thinks the Annual Meeting should give the order for holding Sabbath-schools.

Answer: This query is answered in, or designed to be answered in, the Answer to Art. 14, of the minutes of 1868. And in addition to said answer, we would say that our Sabbath-schools should be held, as all our meetings should be held, to the glory of God. (1 Cor. 10:31.) And as the object of our Sabbath-school is to teach children Christianity, Sabbath-school teachers should observe the directions given by Paul to parents, in which he admonishes us to bring up our children in the nurture and admonition of the Lord. Eph. 6:4.[4]

Evidently this attempt to clarify the issue in 1873 did not satisfy all of the opponents of the Sunday school movement; the phrase in the decision of 1871 which indicated that if the Sunday schools caused trouble or division, then the "brethren had better desist from introducing them," meant that a relatively small minority could prevent the majority from establishing a Sunday school in a congregation. At least that was the problem which the Annual Meeting of 1879 considered.

IX. Inasmuch as the Annual Meeting has advised brethren to desist from holding Sabbath-schools where it causes trouble; and in some instances a few brethren have prevented even a large majority from holding Sabbath-schools, upon the ground that they would not be reconciled to it, and, therefore an organization could not be effected without causing much trouble, will District Meeting consent to ask Annual Meeting to modify this restriction in such a way that a portion of local church cannot prevent us from holding Sabbath-schools according to the direction of Annual Meeting, provided such schools are held according to gospel order and for the honor and glory of God. This District Meeting asks Annual Meeting not to let a small minority prevent a large majority from organizing Sunday-schools.

Answer: We advise the small minority to yield to the majority for the sake of peace. And we also would advise the majority to not overrule the minority in a way that shows no regard for their feelings.[5]

The obvious next step in asking Annual Meeting for answers was to determine the percentage that made up a minority. In 1886:

VIII. Where there is a two-thirds vote in favor of a Sabbath-school, will not Annual Meeting authorize that the minority shall not hinder the school?

Answer: We decide that the minority of a church should not hinder the majority from organizing and conducting Sunday-schools in harmony with the principles of the Brotherhood.[6]

The final question which the Annual Meeting considered in relation to Sunday schools was the matter of various attractions designed to encourage the growth of Sunday schools. The Brethren in 1882 understood that such attractions as conventions were not approved because they were a part of "popular Christianity."

XXII. Does District Meeting consider Sunday-school Conventions a means to promote the interests and peace of the church, —a means to maintain the simplicity of the Gospel of Christ, and a means to encourage the principles and practice of non-conformity to the world?

Answer: No; and since holding conventions is not authorized by Annual Meeting, we ask Annual Meeting to advise against them.

The foregoing is the answer of the District Meeting, the following is the answer of Annual Meeting:

Answer: However much we are in favor of Sunday-schools, and believe they are promotive of good and enhance the cause of Christianity, yet the Annual Meeting cannot allow the unnecessary appendage of Sunday-school Conventions which follow the course of popular Christianity and are contrary to the principles of the Gospel and contrary to the Scriptures. See Rom. 12:2.[7]

Fifteen years later the Meeting had decided that some kinds of conventions were desirable to improve the Sunday school program.

7. The Bethel church asks Annual Meeting through District Meeting, if Minutes of 1882, Art. 22, deprives the Sunday-school workers of a District from meeting in conference to discuss Sunday-school interests? If so, will Annual Meeting reconsider said query and grant the members the privilege of doing so?

Answer: We reconsider and decide that Sunday-school meetings, to advance the Sunday-school cause, may be held, provided they be kept within the bounds of Christian propriety, and be conducted in harmony with the principles held by the Brotherhood.[8]

However, this same Meeting rejected the use of various kinds of gifts to attract and reward Sunday school children.

6. As the Brethren give Sunday-school treats in various parts of the Brotherhood, such as books, cards, candy, oranges, etc., causing some dissatisfaction, and as there are no decisions on that question, we, the Fort Scott church, ask Annual Meeting, through District Meeting, to say if it is right to give such treats.

Answer: While we do not object to proper Sunday-school presents, we do object to making a public display of such presents.[9]

The final step in supporting Sunday schools in the congregational program was taken by the Annual Meeting of 1895 in establishing a permanent Sunday school committee.

1. We ask Annual Meeting through District Meeting to appoint a committee of five or more brethren, to be taken from different parts of our Brotherhood, and who are well informed in regard to the history and needs of our Sunday school work. Let this committee furnish information and otherwise assist the Missionary and Tract Committee in obtaining statistics and proper information in regard to the needs of our Sunday school work and let the Missionary and Tract Committee report the result to next Annual Meeting.

The petition was granted by the Annual Meeting of 1895 and the committee appointed. The committee reported as follows:

Ottawa, Kans., May 25, 1896.

To Annual Meeting, Greeting:—

We, your Sunday School Committee, appointed by Annual Meeting of 1895, by instruction of the General Missionary Committee, submit the following:

Art. I.—We mailed circulars of inquiry to all churches within our knowledge. While a majority of these circulars have been returned with satisfactory information, yet not a sufficient number from which to gather correct statistics and information in regard to the condition of our Sunday schools. If desired and so directed by this Annual Meeting, we will, as soon as practicable, within the coming year, publish in the Gospel Messenger the most interesting features of the information gathered.

Art. II.—(1) We recommend that this Annual Meeting appoint a committee of three brethren who are in sympathy with our Brotherhood and her Sunday school work. This committee to sustain a relation to our Sunday school literature similar to that sustained by the

Advisory Committee to the Gospel Messenger, and to be amenable to the Annual Meeting through the Standing Committee. This committee shall assist the publishers of our Sunday school literature in keeping our quarterlies, papers, etc., sound in the doctrines of the Scriptures, as understood by the General Brotherhood, and in raising the standard of our Sunday school literature as rapidly as possible.

(2) We further recommend that this Sunday School Committee conduct a Sunday school meeting in the Tabernacle at each Annual Meeting, the program and arrangements for such meeting to be subject to the approval of Standing Committee.

(3) The term of office of this committee shall be three years, except those first appointed, one of whom shall serve one year; one, two years, and one, three years.

(4) Should it become necessary for this committee to incur some expenses, let such expenses be paid from the Sunday school missionary contributions, or by public collection at annual Sunday school Meeting.

Signed: I. Bennett Trout, C. E. Arnold.[10]

Another important activity of the local congregation, in addition to the Sunday school which was designed primarily for children, was the Sisters' Aid Society (with various later names) for the women of the church. This activity developed in the late 1880s. The Annual Meeting of 1895 was asked for its approval.

6. We ask the District Meeting to ask Annual Meeting whether it is right, according to the spirit of the Gospel, to have sewing societies in the church.

Answer: Yes. If the sisters labor in union with the church as expressed in the council and according to the principles of the Gospel.[11]

A specific illustration of the establishment and work of a Sisters' Aid Society in the local congregation was the activity in the Bridgewater, Virginia congregation. At the February, 1899 congregational council meeting the "request of Sisters Fanny Miller and Sallie Holsinger for permission to organize a local Sister's Aid Society" was granted. In the May 6, 1899 issue of the ***Gospel Messenger,*** *it was reported by Mattie V. F. Wayland:*

On March 4 a number of our sisters assembled at the home of Sister Susan Floyd for the purpose of organizing an aid society.

Twenty-three enrolled their names for active membership and two others were made honorary members by payment of the required fee. . . .

All, as a committee of the whole, have agreed to labor for "the cultivation of church benevolence, the assistance of the poor, the encouragement of the sick and lonely, the welcoming of strangers to the place of worship," etc. . . .

A regular meeting is held on every fourth Saturday afternoon, at the home of one of the members. The meetings are opened with singing, reading of Scripture, and prayer, and are closed with the Lord's Prayer. . . .

Work has been begun on a number of useful articles, and from this encouraging beginning we hope to report the accomplishment of much good later on.[12]

Indeed the Sisters' Aid at Bridgewater and everywhere else has done much good across the years. Certainly the sisters of the Aid Societies and the children of the Sunday schools and virtually everyone else in the congregation was involved in some way or another in revival meetings held during these years, which added large numbers of new members to the Brethren. The Annual Meeting became involved occasionally in various ways in encouraging this development. The Meeting of 1867 thought about ways of spreading the Gospel.

Art. 30. Should not our church adopt some general plan for the spread of the gospel, as the duty is enjoined upon her by the Savior himself? And does not an efficient plan imply some pecuniary provision?

Answer: This Annual Meeting hails the desire to have the gospel spread, and which is growing among the brethren as a favorable indication, and it would encourge this and recommend to the several states to take such measures as a prayerful consideration of the subject would suggest, to engage in this good work; and it would also recommend that such plans be adopted as would suggest themselves by such consideration, since no one plan can now be united upon, hoping that, as the work progresses, and as further light is elicited by reflection, observation, and experience, a greater and more efficient system may be adopted. In the meantime, let whatever is done be done according to the spirit and word of the gospel, as work done in any other way will not be approved by the Lord.[13]

Fig. 27. *The James M. Neff family in camp near Alva, OK, with their "Mission Wagon."* (BHLA)

Fig. 28. *Revivalist J. Edwin Jarboe, Sumner, NE, 1913.* (BHLA)

Several years later, in 1871, Annual Meeting was again challenged with the basic need to "introduce the principles of the brethren in the many sections within said district, which they have not yet reached."

Art. 7. Should not this district adopt measures to provide and supply ministerial aid for churches where there is no preacher? and also to fill calls, open missions, preach the gospel, and introduce the principles of the brethren in the many sections within said district, which they have not yet reached?

Answer: This Annual Meeting approves of the suggestions in the above query, as it is very necessary that churches or bodies of brethren, in which there are no resident ministers, should be assisted; and inasmuch as there are many localities where the gospel, as preached and practiced by the brethren, is not known, we think the gospel should be taken into such places. As it regards the measures necessary to accomplish these objects, we think the district should adopt such measures as it judges best calculated to answer its purpose.[14]

One method of evangelism which was slowly accepted by Brethren during these years was the revival meeting, sometimes called the protracted meeting because it lasted for longer than the old three-meeting limit. The Annual Meeting of 1874 seemed to assume that such protracted meetings were acceptable, but some local congregations had not accepted the idea.

Art. 17. Inasmuch as the Annual Meeting is favorable to the holding of protracted meetings, what right have the bishops and householders of certain districts of churches to limit such meetings to a series not exceeding three in number?

Answer: They have the right, if the meetings are not conducted in the order of gospel and of the church.[15]

By the 1880s such meetings had become so widely accepted that the Annual Meeting in 1887 agreed to advise the leaders of the local congregations to hold a series of meetings at least once a year.

4. Will this District Meeting request Annual Meeting to advise the elders of the churches to hold at least one series of meetings in their congregations each year? We do; and ask that this request be submitted to Annual Meeting by our delegate.

Answer: We do so advise.[16]

Fig. 29. *Publishing House exhibit at Bicentennial Annual Conference, Des Moines, IA, 1908.*

Fig. 30. *Tenting at the Winona Lake, IN, Annual Conference, 1913. (BHLA)*

Many excellent revival preachers developed among the Brethren, one of whom was S. N. McCann. On one occasion, McCann held a series of meetings lasting for four weeks in the Bridgewater, Virginia church. The result was forty-one baptisms which took place in the middle of the winter. The report indicated that it was necessary to cut four inches of ice off the river in order to conduct the baptisms.[17]

Having to cut ice in order to conduct baptisms was one type of problem which Brethren were prepared to solve; another problem related to receiving new members into the church was the lack of a satisfactory body of water in which to conduct immersions baptisms, as in urban churches. Again Brethren were able to find a solution in the building of a special pool, or baptistry, inside the church building. But was such a baptism acceptable in the interpretation of the New Testament? The Annual Meeting of 1875 answered the question.

Art. 2. Is it according to the gospel for brethren to make a pool in a meeting-house, for the purpose of baptizing?

Answer: As we have no authority in the Scripture for baptizing in the house, we consider it wrong to do so.[18]

So the question was answered by the Annual Meeting. The new problem was the question of those people who had already been baptized in such indoor pools. Specifically the Philadelphia church had built and used such a pool for baptizing. The Annual Meeting of 1877 had to deal with this matter.

XXX. How do we, the members of the Philadelphia church that have been baptized in the pool or baptistry stand in relation to the church at large; and does the church consider it a valid, christian baptism?

The above query was read and considered by the Philadelphia church and referred to District Meeting. District Meeting agreed to refer this query to Annual Meeting.

Answer: We decide that those who were baptized in the pool were baptized with a valid baptism and those who walk in the order of the gospel and the Brethren are recognized as members of the church.[19]

As a matter of convenience, when new church houses were built in the twentieth century most Brethren congregations added baptistries to the church's facilities. Once a person had been baptized as a Brethren, it was desirable to retain him/her as a member. One of the means used was the annual visit by the deacons of the church. The Annual Meeting of 1867 outlined their task.

Art. 2. Would it not be well to have the same questions asked throughout the brotherhood, on our annual visits?

Answer: We think it would, and the following form of questions is given: 1. Are you still in the faith of the gospel, as you declared in your baptism? 2. Are you, as far as you know, in peace and union with the church? 3. Will you still labor with the brethren for an increase of holiness, both in yourself and others? 4. Liberty should be given to members to bring any thing they may desire to, and that may think the good of the church requires, before the visiting Brethren.[20]

Twenty years later the Annual Meeting was asked for clarification of the visit by the deacons.

19. How is it considered in paying the annual or general visit to members before love-feast, is it right for the officers of the congregations to meet and visit each other before sending the visiting brethren, or deacons, on the visit? It is right, so that no one be sent on the visit who is not in peace and in the order of the General Brotherhood, and we ask that congregations be required to adopt this order of sending the general church visit.

Answer: Passed by Annual Meeting.[21]

The establishment of urban congregations created some new problems in carrying out the annual visit, according to a query in 1905.

8. West Dayton church: Whereas it is the established rule of the church that an annual visit be paid to all the members by the deacons, and,

Whereas, it is almost impossible to pay such visit in large congregations in the city, because Brethren are absent from home during the day;

Therefore, we ask Annual Meeting through district meeting to permit the elder or pastor of such congregations to call special meetings at the usual place of worship where the visit may be paid in a manner as private as possible.

Answer: We recommend that so far as possible the usual course of visiting be followed.[22]

In such urban congregations as in Dayton, Ohio the increasing tendency during this half century was to secure professionally trained

pastors who were employed at a stated salary per year. The Annual Meetings dealt with this problem on several occasions, beginning in 1866.

Art. 41. Is it according to the gospel for members, or any body of members, to pay a stated salary to our ministering brethren, for the support of their famlies, that they may give themselves wholly to their ministerial labors?

Answer: Not wrong to support the ministry, where it is needed. 1 Tim. 5:18; Luke 10:7. But we do not approve of paying a stated salary.[23]

Evidently by the 1880s some congregations were violating the basic principle of not paying a stated salary, for the Meeting of 1882 was asked:

XIX. Whereas there is a tendency in places in our brotherhood toward a salaried ministry, will this District Meeting ask Annual Meeting that there be no specified sum per day, week, month or year, paid to ministers on missions or any other work; but the Mission Board or Committee having control of funds may donate to ministers such sums as in their judgement their circumstances require.

Answer: Passed by Annual Meeting as requested by the District Meeting.[24]

In actual practice most of the congregations in the Church of the Brethren then were led by unsalaried pastors in the "free ministry." One of the most detailed explanations of the unsalaried pastor in the Annual Meeting Minutes resulted from the fact that railroads were reluctant to grant Brethren ministers reductions in rates normally granted to ministers, because the Brethren ministers made their living in some other way than preaching. The Meeting of 1894 appealed to the railroads.

1. Whereas, the railroad companies of this country propose to provide the minisiters of the different churches with orders for tickets at one-half the regular fare, and

Whereas, the ministers of the Brethren (German Baptist) church have been refused these orders on the ground that they have other occupations bearing remuneration, therefore:

Resolved, that the Huntingdon church ask District Meeting to petition Annual Meeting to appoint a committee to memorialize the

United Passenger Association, requesting it to change the rules governing the granting of these orders, or so modify them as not to exclude the ministers of our church, and set forth the following reasons or any other reason to Annual Meeting as the committee so appointed may deem best.

(a) That, although our labors are humble, we do not like to stand excluded from the Christian Ministry of America by said railroad companies.

(b) That we give our ministerial labors to the world free of cost, and without renumeration.

(c) That our occupations are not intended to supplement a salary for preaching, and thus add to worldly wealth.

(d) That the few ministers who have "no other occupation" and who can conscientiously sign the applications for orders, for these privileges generally have an independent competency; hence the discrimination is in favor of the rich and against the poor.

(e) That our duties as ministers frequently call us into remote parts of congregations, which cover large areas of country, and also into other congregations requiring frequent use of roads in performance of our church work.

(f) That although we have other occupations, our ministers have made it a rule when such orders have been granted, to use them only for purposes contemplated in the granting of the orders.

Answer: The petition was granted, and the following committee appointed to confer with the railroad associations concerning the granting of half-fare permits to all of our ministers: D. L. Miller, E. W. Stoner, and S. W. Hoover.[25]

By the early years of the twentieth century the leaders of the Annual Meeting recognized that a change was taking place in the church with regard to the employment and paying of congregational pastors. But they wanted the change to take place gradually and carefully in order to make as few mistakes as possible. At least that seemed to be the way the Meeting of 1908 described the situation.

2. Supporting Pastors and Evangelists.

To the district meeting of North Dakota, Northern Minnesota and Assiniboia, Canada, greeting: Inasmuch as the cause of Christ is suffering in our beloved Brotherhood, for the want of the proper support of the ministry, we, the members of the Berthold church, North

Dakota, petition Annual Meeting of 1906, through district meeting, to devise a plan or method by which the pastors and evangelists of our church shall receive a gospel support (1 Cor. 9: 14 and 1 Tim. 5: 17, 18), that they may give themselves wholly to the work (1 Tim. 4: 13–15).

Answer: We recognize that, under the present unequaled distribution of our ministry, too often needed help is not given, the work of the ministry is much hindered and the cause is made to suffer, because the ministry has these financial hindrances. But we also recognize that our ministry, as it stands in relation to the church today, is gradually undergoing material changes, and that any legislation or radical change, in advance of this movement we seem to be undergoing, would be injurious to the church and the sacred calling of our ministry.

We therefore recommend that our Brotherhood exercise the utmost care and patience, while this conscious change is taking place. We need to be exceedingly careful in attempting to effect improvements along this line, when there seems to be an entire transformation coming over us, that our ministry does not fall from the high standard it has always held among our people, and degenerate into a class of hirelings, and thereby lose our power.

We further recommend that our churches comply more with the gospel rule of giving. See 1 Cor. 16: 2. If our churches would reduce to a system the recommendations of the Gospel, as suggested in the above text, and the scriptures referred to in the query, very much of the want that is being felt today would be relieved.

We further suggest that the mission boards of the various districts of the Brotherhood study this question prayerfully, in relation to their several districts, and endeavor to encourage more the scriptural plan of freewill giving from every member in the district, having in mind this particular thing, of giving a worthy minister a proper support.[26]

BROTHERHOOD ACTIVITIES

Without question the most important activity of Brethren at the brotherhood or national level was the Annual Meeting. On numerous occasions the Meeting discussed its own development. Several of those occasions are considered in this context. For example, in 1879 the Meeting was concerned about the large number of visitors who attended.

I. As a committee had been appointed by the Annual Council of 1878 to devise a way to more effectually reduce or prevent the assembling of mixed multitude, and for the carrying out more fully of the plan of 1866, and to report to the present meeting the result of their labors. This being unfinished or deferred business, it was the first in order to be acted upon, and accordingly the committee made the following report:

The committee apointed by the Annual Meeting of 1878 for preparing and presenting to the Annual Meeting of 1879 some plan for holding the Annual Meeting by which that adpoted in 1866 may be more fully carried out, and the mixed multitude reduced, met at the house of Brother Christian Wine, on the 30th of May, 1879, in Rockingham, Va., and upon a prayerful deliberation of the work committed to us, have concluded to submit the following suggestions to this Annual Meeting:

First.—Inasmuch as there has been some difficulty in holding our Annual Meeting because of the amount of funds required to hold it, to obviate this difficulty, we recommend that each brother that attends the meeting shall pay one dollar; and though the sisters have nothing laid upon them, it is to be understood that they may do as they think proper in contributing to the support of the meeting.

Second.—We recommend that none but the brethren and sisters, and their special friends, shall receive their boarding in the general boarding tent, but that a tent, or if necessary or desirable, more than one be erected by reliable persons for accommodating such as are not members of the church with suitable boarding, and at a moderate price. And that this may be done, we recommend that the brethren have the oversight of all the boarding arrangements, and so fix them as will be most satisfactory to the church and to those for whose accommodations they are designed.

Third.—In order that a proper distinction may be made between such as are members and such as are not, we recommend that the members be furnished with tickets. Their tickets shall be furnished by the proper authority at the place at which the meeting is to be held. And each church shall obtain from that authority as many tickets as shall be wanted by members going to Annual Meeting from the church.

Fourth.—The members of the church in which the meeting is held, shall be exonerated from paying the amount that the others shall pay. And the committee of arrangements shall decide who are entitled to exoneration besides the congregation in which the meeting is held, for services rendered.

Fifth.—We recommend that the committee of arrangements acting for the church in which the meeting is held, shall decide whether there shall be any preaching at the place of meeting.

Sixth.—We recommend that good arrangements be made for the Standing Commitee and delegates, and that the tent for holding the council be no larger than will contain as many as can hear what is spoken. We also recommend that it be a sufficient distance from the boarding tent, that the council may not be annoyed by any noise. We also suggest the propriety of so arranging the council tent that the seats may be elevated from the center, but the seats only, and not the platform for the Standing Committee and delegates. We further recommend, that in making the boarding tent, that there be an aisle through the whole length of the tent, separating the brethren from the sisters; and that the tables run from the aisle to the sides of the tent, and that there be a door in the side of the tent to each table for admitting the brethren on one side and the sisters on the other. All of which is respectfully submitted.[27]

R. H. Miller
J. Quinter
D. Brower
E. Eby
S. Garber

This Annual Meeting was held in Rockingham County, Virginia in the area of the Linville Creek congregation. One of the local newspapers provided an interesting insight into preparations for the Meeting.

PREPARATIONS

For the Annual Conference of the German Baptists

The busy notes of the work of preparation for the Annual Conference of the German Baptists, to meet in the church near Broadway, next Tuesday the 2nd of June, are still heard in the surroundings of the place of meeting. A large number of the brethren of the church were on the ground Tuesday, engaged in completing the labors so auspiciously and energetically begun and carried forward. The work was being done quietly and systematically, but with the carefulness and thoroughness characteristic of our German friends. The grounds were being put in complete order by the removal of all obstructions. The rugged, and in many cases uneven surface was being rendered smooth and pleasant. The kitchen and dining place are well worth looking at, as models of almost perfect arrangements for cooking for and feeding an immense multitude. There are 200 persons, young men and young women, selected to wait upon the guests who will crowd the tables. This arrangement will prevent any confusion and enable the 700 or 800 persons seated at the tables at one time, to be quietly served. There will be, we are entirely satisfied, enough of food of the best kind to meet the wants of the vast brotherhood assembled at the Conference.

The Council Hall, in close proximity with the church, is all ready for use, seats for several thousand persons being placed near the great table in the center of the hall.

The trains with their loads of passengers will stop at Broadway as well as at the crossing, half a mile above Broadway, where a new platform has been fixed for the passengers who may wish to get on and off. The new stopping place is half a mile nearer the church than Broadway, and the road leading to and from the church, a very excellent, broad one, wide enough for the passage of two vehicles.

Everything looks as if the conference is to be one of the largest gatherings of religious people ever seen in the South.[28]

The number of people attending these meetings was one of the reasons for the concern at the Meeting of 1879. The "Conference Bulletin" of Thursday morning had these comments on the attendance.

The attendance at the Conference yesterday was variously estimated at from 8000 to 15000 persons. From all directions did people swarm. They came by hundreds and by thousands. The rolling stock of the railroad was taxed to its utmost, and some had to wait for later trains. We estimated the gathering at fully ten thousand. To-day the people will pour in again, for hundreds of those who were here on yesterday will come again, and the report they will have spread about the good times everybody is having at the Conference, will bring hundreds of others. It may be possible that Thursday's gathering will exceed the day previous. You chaps who said the Conference was going to be a small affair, are wanted to come help us to count the swarms of persons who will be here to-day.[29]

In addition to dealing with the large crowds, the Meeting periodically needed to deal with its own organization. One of the at-

tempts to clarify the organization was made at the Annual Meeting of 1882.

XV. The following Report, as amended by the General Council, of the committee to whom were submitted the papers asking for a change in the manner of holding the Annual Meeting was accepted:

1. We advise that there be no change in the manner of electing the Standing Committee, but no elder shall be elected to serve on Standing Committee more than two years in four.

2. We further decide that each congregation having a membership of 200 or less may send one delegate.

Congregations of over 200 members may send two. The Delegates thus sent with the Standing Committee shall compose the voting power of Annual Meeting.

All members present shall have the right to participate in the discussion of all questions before the meeting; and in case any query or queries cannot pass by unanimous consent, the Delegates and Standing Committee shall decide them by a two-third majority.

B. F. Moomaw,
S. C. Stump,
John Humberger,
L. H. Dickey,
E. W. Stoner
J. S. Snyder,
Edmund Forney,
John Brilhart,
Samuel Harley,
Geo. W. Cripe.[30]

The Meeting in 1885 turned again to the problem of providing adequate facilities and accepted a number of recommendations from a study committee.

III. As there were several papers before the Meeting relating to the management of the Annual Meeting, they were submitted to a committee which made the following report, and it was accepted by the meeting:

1. The meeting should be held where there are good railroad facilities, and where the Committee of Arrangements can procure sufficient and suitable lodging quarters at reasonable rates.

2. Meals to be furnished at the uniform price of 25 cents each.

3. The dining hall or halls to be so arranged and conducted that the Standing Committee and delegates may have the usual services at the table where they eat.

4. A lunch stand to be also provided for the sale of refreshments.

We also recommend economy in the management of the meeting, and caution our brethren against making the Annual Meeting an occasion of money making.

We further recommend that our members continue to perpetuate and maintain their well-earned reputation for Christian hospitality by opening their houses and barns free of charge for sleeping purposes to visiting members on their Pentecostal meeting.

All surplus funds should be turned over to the Church Erection and Missionary Committee.

All former decisions of Annual Meeting in any way conflicting with the above, are hereby repealed.

J. H. Moore,
Saml. H. Myers,
Danl. Vaniman,
S. W. Hoover,
S. S. Mohler.[31]

Two decisions by the Annual Meeting of 1897 indicated that Brethren were still struggling with problems related to keeping the Annual Meeting a religious and spiritual experience, rather than an economic opportunity.

10. A number of queries, pertaining to trafficking on the Annual Meeting grounds, were submitted to a committee, who presented the following, which was adopted by the Conference:

Your committee, appointed to consider a number of papers referring to unnecessary trafficking, etc., on and about Annual Meeting grounds, submit the following:

We decide,

(a) That photographing, in all its forms, the exhibition and sale of merchandise by the Brethren, on or about the grounds, except that necessary for the meeting and the ciruclation of the Brethren's literature, be not allowed.

(b) That the Annual Meeting enter her protest against those not Brethren in bringing their goods near the grounds for exhibition and sale.

(c) That Brethren be not allowed to use the influence of the

Fig. 31. *Mission Church house, at Weiser, ID, 1904. (BHLA)*

Fig. 32. *Ladies Aid Society quilting, Hagerstown, MD, ca 1909. (BE)*

church in emigration schemes, and that Brethren be cautioned against using undue personal influence in matters of this kind. . . .

12. Whereas the tendency of the times is to disregard the Lord's Day, and whereas our General Conference brings a large number of people together on the Lord's Day, previous to the opening of the council:—Resolved, that the Huntingdon church ask the District Meeting to request the Annual Meeting to make increased efforts to have this day more sacredly regarded; that nothing but the merest necessities be sold or furnished on the grounds; that the post-office be closed; that the sale of newspapers be prohibited; that our people, in coming, be urged to make their arrangements so that they need not arrive on Sunday, thus removing any encouragement, on our part, to the running of Sunday excursion trains, and that the general conduct of the day, in our social minglings, be as much in keeping with the intent of this Christian institution, as possible, that it may be a quiet, worshipful and spiritual Sabbath.

Answer: We are heartily in sympathy with this paper, and earnestly urge our members to make every possible effort to put into practice the suggestions made.[32]

In 1903 the Meeting took another look at the membership of the Standing Committee.

1. (a) We petition Annual Meeting through District Meeting to decide that all State Districts are entitled to one delegate on Standing Committee of Annual Meeting and that such Districts as have thirty-five hundred members or more are entitled to two delegates on said Committee.

(b) Will not this District Meeting ask Annual Meeting to reconsider resolution of 1889 ("Revised Minutes," page 13), referring to representation by proxy, and provide that all foreign Districts shall be represented by a member or members of their own Districts, or by letter through the Secretary of the General Mission Board?

(c) We ask Annual Meeting through District Meeting to reconsider resolution of Annual Meeting of 1889 referring to representation by proxy ("Revised Minutes," page 13), and change them so as not to allow any one to serve as a member of Standing Committee who does not have his membership in the District from which he is sent, but give District Meeting in foreign countries the privilege of selecting suitable persons outside of the District to present and explain to Annual Meeting such papers as they may decide to send.

(d) We, the members of the Highland church, petition Annual Meeting through District Meeting to reconsider minute of 1889, page 13, of "Revised Minutes," and amend so as not to permit any State District to be represented on the Standing Committee by proxy.

(e) Whereas under the present ruling some State Districts are entitled to more than one delegate on Standing Committee while others are not; we therefore ask Annual Meeting through District Meeting to reconsider and so amend her ruling that no State District be entitled to more than one delegate on Standing Committee.

Answer: The foregoing queries, referring to District representation, were placed in the hands of the following named brethren with instructions to report to Annual Meeting of 1903; S. S. Ulery, T. C. Denton, D. B. Eby, L. W. Teeter, and J. C. Bright.

Report of Committee on District Representation:

We, your committee appointed to take under consideration queries, Art. 2 (a), (b), (c), (d) and (e), Minutes of Annual Meeting, 1902, on the subject of District Representation, beg leave to submit the following report:

Resolved, That each State District in our Brotherhood be allowed a representative on Standing Committee.

Resolved furthermore, That each of such Districts having thirty-five hundred or more members may represent by two delegates on Standing Committee.

Resolved, That hereafter when new State Districts are intended to be organized, a full statement of the proposed organization be presented to general conference and recognized by her before they can represent on the Standing Committee.

Resolved, That every State District be represented on Standing Committee by a member living in the District he represents, or by letter.

Resolved, That the General Missionary and Tract Committee be authorized to assist foreign Districts in defraying the expenses of their delegates on Standing Committee, when said Committee thinks prudent to do so.

Resolved, That all former decisions conflicting with this report be repealed.

S. S. Ulery,
D. B. Eby,
L. W. Teeter,
J. C. Bright,
T. C. Denton[33]

One of the functions of the Standing Committee was the maintenance of order and discipline in the church. It was empowered to send investigating committees to local congregations, according to the Meeting of 1886.

VI. As there is an active tendency on the part of some elders, ministers, deacons, and churches toward discarding our order on plainness of dressing, as also the appropriate head covering worn by our devoted sisters; also consenting that sisters may wear hats in disregard to Art. 16, 1877, and thus rapid strides are made towards the ever-changing, and sinful fashions of the world, and the teaching of the Gospel of plainness of wearing apparel is disregarded; will District Meeting therefore petition Annual Meeting to Authorize that the Standing Committee if ascertained by it through any reliable source, that adjoining elders to churches which tolerate departures from our general order on any subject have failed to undertake, or to set in order such officers or churches, as above named. It shall appoint with consent of the Annual Meeting faithful brethren to visit such church or churches, to set them in order, but if a majority of a church will hinder the work, said elders shall proceed with the minority as directed by the second paragraph of Art. 4, 1882. And further, said elders shall have authority to call before them those adjoining elders to interrogate them, and if need be, go into their respective churches to complete their work as it may affect those adjoining elders, and the expense attending such services shall be met by the district in which the churches visited are located, for all which see Art. 47, 1866 and Art. 13, 1877, closing paragraph of plan for holding Annual Meeting adopted in 1866, Art. 4, 1882, and Art. 15, 1874.[34]

This particular item likely related to the dress question, for the Annual Meeting had been sending investigating committees for many years. The Philadelphia congregation, a very progressive congregation in many ways, was the subject of several investigations. In 1869 it was reported:

Art. 2 The committee appointed by the last Annual Meeting to visit the Philadelphia and Germantown churches, reported, and the following is the part of the report judged necessary to be entered upon the minutes, it being the result of the conference between the committee and said churches: . . .

The foregoing report is respectfully submitted to the Annual Meeting, with the hope that it will take such action upon the subject as will further the blessed cause of truth and righteousness. Signed by the committee: D. P. Saylor, H. D. Davy, J. Quinter, B. F. Moomaw, M. Miller.[35]

The issue in this particular investigation related to the observance of the Love Feast, particularly the mode of feetwashing. In 1876 an investigating committee reported its visit to Philadelphia; this time the issues involved were much more extensive, including the paying of a pastor, the worship service, the collecting of an offering on Sunday, the practices of the Sunday school, the use of a musical instrument, and the indoor baptistry.

Art. 27. The committee, namely H. D. Davy, Moses Miller, Jos. R. Hanawalt, Christian Bucher, and J. Quinter, appointed by the last Annual Meeting to visit the Philadelphia Church, to settle difficulties in said church, met in Philadelphia on the 27th of October, 1875, and organized by appointing H. D. Davy foreman, and J. Quinter clerk, and after devotional exercises proceeded to hear grievances from the grieved brethren. . . .

9. They (the majority are, in all the above new things, in unison with the popular and fashionable religion, having abandoned the nonconformity testimonies and practice of the brotherhood.

Considered, that from the foregoing grievance, and from the departure we see, we would most earnestly and affectionately urge the brethren and sisters of the Philadelphia Church to adhere to the doctrine of nonconformity to the world in dress, in spirit, and in every way that doctrine can be applied, as this constitutes such a prominent doctrine of the gospel, and one of the peculiarities of our brotherhood. H. D. Davy, J. Quinter, J. R. Hanawalt, C. Bucher, M. Miller.

In regard to the case of the Philadelphia Church, we accept the report of the committee sent to said church, and reappoint the committee first appointed to have the said report carried out.[36]

Perhaps the most unusual aspect of this report was that much of it was included in the Minutes. In 1880, for example, the meeting dispatched seventeen committees to visit congregations and districts to deal with local problems. However, none of the reports from these committees was included in the Minutes of 1881.

Another activity of the brotherhood which was carried out by the Annual Meeting was the distribution of large numbers of published and generally very brief tracts. As early as 1875 the Meeting heard this request.

Art. 29. Inasmuch as there exists a strong demand for tracts advocating the faith and practice of the brethren, we earnestly recommend a more united effort to carry forward this work, and facilitate the publication and circulation of works of this character, subject before publication to the examination and approval of competent and well-established brethren; therefore, we earnestly recommend that the brethren give this matter an earnest and prayerful consideration.

Answer: Approved by order of the district-meeting, and confirmed by this Annual Meeting.[37]

By the 1880s a number of Brethren writers were taking advantage of the numerous private printing establishments in various parts of the country to produce tracts. Some type of coordination or organization of these activities seemed to be needed. The result was the establishment of a new committee by the Annual Meeting in 1885.

VII. Requests having come before the meeting for a plan for a Book and Tract Organization, the following plan was accepted:

Art. 1. This Committee shall be called the Brethren's Book and Tract Committee; and shall have for its object the dissemination of the principles of the Gospel of Christ, through the distribution of tracts and other publications, both in this and foreign countries; in families, in cities, in towns, and country; in cars, depots and reading rooms; on board of outgoing and incoming vessels; in short, everywhere as means for publication and facilities for judicious dissemination can be secured.

Art. 2. The Standing Committee of Annual Meeting shall nominate and Annual Meeting approve and perpetuate, an Executive Committee of six members living sufficiently near each other for frequent consultation: to serve for a term of three years, except the members first appointed, two of whom shall serve one year, two, two years, and two, three years. Said Committee shall select its own officers, make its own by-laws, procure, and distribute tracts, and other publications upon best available methods; fill all incidental vacancies occurring in the Committee; inform Standing Committee each year whose time has expired, and make an annual report of its work including receipts and expenditures, with all necessary suggestions to Annual

Meeting through Standing Committee, which shall inspect, or cause said report to be carefully inspected.

Art. 3. The funds of the Committee shall consist of bequests, free-will offerings, money received on life interests and from sale of publications.

Art. 4. In order to promote the object of the Committee, each church in the brotherhood is hereby requested to appoint one or more home agents to solicit aid and assist in distributing the publications of the Committee. The home agents shall forward the means to the Treasurer as collected; fill out blanks furnished, and present them quarterly to the church for approval and then to the Corresponding Secretary of the Committee.

Art. 5. Each church shall be entitled to draw any of the publications of the Committee through her home agents, equal in value to half the sum paid during the year. All claims for publication not presented during the year shall expire May 1st of each year.

Art. 6. Any person paying at one time twenty or more dollars to promote the object of the Committee, shall be entitled to draw annually from the Committee a printed report of its work, and any other of its publications to the value of one dollar for each twenty dollars paid.

Art. 7. The S.C. shall nominate, and the Annual Meeting confirm, a committee of five, faithful and well-informed Brethren, whose duty it will be to examine and approve all works to be published and distributed by the committee.[38]

The report of the committee to the Annual Meeting of 1888 indicated something of its activity.

Number of Publications.

On hand from last year, all kinds,	44335
Tracts and Pamphlets, published,	115000
Golden Gleams [Biblical charts],	1000
Books,	1416
Total,	161751

Number of Publications Sold and Distributed.

Books and Gleams,	1002
Tracts,	99550
Total,	100552[39]

The establishment of the Brethren's Book and Tract Committee in 1885 was a part of the brotherhood activity which witnessed the establishment of a group of permanent committees. Probably the earliest of these committees was the Domestic and Foreign Mission Board, established in 1880 with special responsibilities for the mission in Denmark. Since the Brethren were also becoming interested in an urban ministry, this committee was succeeded in 1884 by a new committee which coordinated both interests.

II. The Committee on Missions and Church Building, appointed by the Annual Meeting of 1883, made the following report, which was accepted:

We, the undersigned Committee appointed by General Conference of 1883, to formulate a plan for general church erection and missionary work, respectfully submit the following:

1st. We recommend that a committee of five brethren be appointed, living sufficiently near each other for frequent consultation: part of whom shall be lay members, part deacons, and part ministers, and not more than two of either; and this Committee shall be known as, "The General Church Erection and Missionary Committee."

2nd. That said Committee be nominated by Standing Committee and approved by General Conference, and shall serve for a term of three years, except the members first appointed, two of whom shall serve for one year, two for two years, and one for three years.

3rd. That said Committee shall meet as often as necessary to carry on its work successfully, and shall elect its own officers, make its own by-laws, fill all vacancies that may incidentally occur in the committee and recommend to General Conference for adoption, anything necessary to forward its work.

4th. That the object of this committee is, and shall be, to build, or assist in building plain houses of worship, and to send suitable brethren to preach the Gospel, distribute tracts, and to organize and build up churches where there are favorable openings. All expenses, both of committee and of brethren sent out on church work, to be paid out of the funds collected.

5th. That each State District be urged to have some effective church erection and missionary plan of its own to assist weak churches in its own territory to build plain houses of worship, and to preach the Gospel where there are favorable openings; and the general committee may assist but shall in no way interfere with any building or missionary work carried on by any district or individual church, and any church situated in a State District, in order to get help through the general committee must apply to, and build under the directions of the district committee, and any district committee unable to meet all such calls may apply to, and receive help from the general committee.

6th. That the general committee shall, quarterly or oftener, circulate through the Brotherhood, a printed report explanatory of the nature and progress of its work, and shall annually submit a report of all its work to General Conference for approval.

7th. That Standing Committee shall annually inspect, or cause to be inspected, the report of the general committee before it is submitted to General Conference, and shall assist the committee in developing any necessary improvements for advancing the work.

How to Raise the Means

1st. Let each member, at all able to do so, give for general church erection and mission work, one cent, or more, if able, each week, according as the Lord has prospered him, upon the principle taught in 1 Cor. 16: 1, 2.

2nd. Let each congregation throughout the Brotherhood adopt some plan to solicit each member at least twice each year, and receive such offerings and forward the same to the treasurer of the general committee, who shall receipt for the amount, and report it through quarterly report, and to General Conference, in connection with the amount raised and expended by each State district in their district work.

Committee: Daniel Vaniman, W. R. Deeter, S. S. Mohler, Enoch Eby, John Zuck.[40]

The next logical step in the organizational structure of the committees was the consolidation of the Book and Tract Committee and the Church Erection and Missionary Committee. That action was implemented in the 1890s. A special committee on consolidation appointed in 1890 reported to the Meeting of 1893.

1. Report of Committee on Consolidation

Hagerstown, Md., May 27, 1891.

We, the undersigned Committee, appointed by Annual Meeting of 1890 to present a plan for the Consolidation of the General Church Erection and Missionary Work, and the Book and Tract Work, respectfully submit the following:

(1) That Standing Committee shall nominate and Annual Meeting approve and perpetuate a Committee of "five members as Trustees," to serve for a term of three years, except those first appointed, one of whom shall serve one year, two two years, and two three years. Said Committee shall be called the General Missionary and Tract Committee of the German Baptist Brethren Church, and shall be the successor of both the General Church Erection and Missionary Committee and the Book and Tract Work, to hold in trust, manage, control and use all the property rights and interests now vested in both the above-named organizations for the promotion of the objects for which they were designed.

(2) The Committee shall meet as often as necessary to carry on its work successfully and shall elect its own officers, make its own By-Laws, fill all vacancies that may incidentally occur in the Committee, inform Standing Committee each year whose term has expired and recommend to General Conference for adoption anything necessary to forward its work.

(3) The object of this Committee shall be to send suitable Brethren to preach the Gospel and to assist in building plain houses of worship, publishing and distributing printed matter, to organize and build up churches, and, when suitable arrangements can be and wisdom dictates, to own and control all the publishing interests of the church.

(5) The General Committee shall quarterly or oftener circulate throughout the Brotherhood a printed report explanatory of the nature and progress of its work, and shall annually submit a report of all its work to the General Conference for approval, and the Standing Committee shall annually inspect the report of the General Committee before it is submitted to the General Conference, and shall assist the Committee in developing any necessary improvements for advancing the work.

(6) The funds for this work shall consist of bequests, endowments, free-will offerings and money received as life interests, and from the sale of publications.

(7) We recommend that each member give for the Mission and Tract Work of the church as the Lord has prospered him, upon the principle taught in 1 Cor. 16:8.

(8) Let each congregation throughout the Brotherhood appoint solicitors to solicit all members annually and receive their offerings, and forward same to the General Committee, who shall receipt for the amount, and upon application shall annually forward tracts to such congregation to the value of ten per cent of the sum sent.

(9) Any person paying or obligating him or herself to pay twenty or more dollars, as a live membership, as an endowment of the work or otherwise, shall be entitled to draw publications annually to the value of one dollar for each twenty dollars so contributed.

(10) The Standing Committee shall nominate and Annual Meeting confirm a committee of five faithful and well-informed brethren, whose duty it will be to examine and approve of all matters to be published and distributed as tracts.

(11) All former decisions touching the general Church Erection and Missionary Work or the Book and Tract Work, in any way conflicting with this arrangement, shall upon the adoption of this report become null and void.

(12) Owing to the importance of the work and the interest involved, we recommend that this plan be placed on the Minutes and deferred for two years.

Signed by the committee,

Daniel Vaniman,
D. L. Miller,
S. W. Hoover,
Samuel Bock,
Enoch Eby,
D. E. Price,
Daniel Hays.[41]

Evidently the two-year delay did not seem necessary, for the report of the Church Erection and Missionary Committee to the Annual Meeting of 1894 included these two sentences: "This completes the work for the General Church Erection and Missionary Committee. Already its successor, the General Missionary and Tract Committee, has taken up the labor." This committee under a new name accepted in 1908, "General Mission Board," continued for many years into the twentieth century. These committees, by whatever name, represented a widespread movement in the church; a number of new committees, including the Sunday School Committee, the Educational Board, and the Temperance Committee, are considered in other chapters.

Most of these committees, especially the ones responsible for building churches, sponsoring foreign missions, and distributing tracts, needed money. Like most people in the United States, the Brethren were generally prosperous during this half century from 1865 to 1915. True, occasional panics, as the economic depressions were called, disrupted economic life. The Annual Meeting on numerous occasions dealt with the problem of raising money to support brotherhood activities. In 1879 it asked the congregations for $2.00 per con-

gregation, on the average, to support the Danish mission. Building meetinghouses in some areas also needed to be sponsored by the brotherhood. In 1883 the Annual Meeting came in with a much more detailed proposal for raising money.

13. Resolved. That the paper from N. W. Kansas and Colorado, in regard to general church work, be placed into the hands of the Committee nominated by Bro. Moore, and appointed by the Meeting, to form a plan for raising funds for building Meeting-houses, for their consideration in connection with other matter submitted to said Committee.

The following is the paper referred to in the above resolution:

There being a necessity for a more simple and effective system for the purpose of raising means for general church work, we request that District Meeting ask Annual Meeting to adopt the following plan, in harmony with the Scriptures. See 1 Cor. 16: 1, 2, 3, and 2 Cor. 11: 8.

First. Let the foreman of each church or congregation throughout the Brotherhood at the time of holding their church meetings, (say at least once a quarter) take up a collection or subscription for general church work.

Second. Let the amount so raised be sent up to Annual Meeting by the Delegates, or otherwise, and be reported to the Clerk of Annual Meeting.

Third. Then let the Annual Meeting appoint a Committee to whom shall be reported the amount brought up, and to whom all claims or requests for means to carry on general church work shall be made, such as Foreign or Home Missions, assisting in building meeting-houses, or any work that the general church may be disposed to assist in or do.

Fourth. Said Committee, after duly considering all such claims or requests, shall suggest an apportionment of the funds to the different branches of church work, as they may in their judgement think best for the furthering of the cause of general church work, and report the same to Annual Meeting before its close, for adoption, rejection or amendment.

Fifth. The Annual Meeting shall appoint a Treasurer to receive the funds sent in, who shall disburse the same in accordance with the instructions resulting from the last preceding clause. He shall hold office until the next Annual Meeting and make his report thereto, accompanied with his receipts.

Sixth. The report of the amount of money sent in from each church to be published in the Minutes.[42]

The report of 1885 indicated the progress being made in providing financial support for the outreach program of the church.

It will be seen by examining the foregoing report, that, of the whole number of church organizations in the Brotherhood (something over 500), only one out of five has responded to the call of Annual Meeting, to appoint solicitors for the missionary work of the church.

Illinois, with a membership of about 5,000, donates $857.19, or one-fourth of the whole amount paid in, and of this sum two churches in the State paid $520.97. The work done in these two churches shows what might be done in our whole Brotherhood, if all were willing to do their part.

Instead of one cent a week being paid by each of our members, as was suggested by our Annual Meeting last year, we have received less than one-tenth of a cent per week.[43]

Over the next fifteen years Brethren began to respond more generously to the needs of the church. One form of response was the establishing of an annuity program by which Brethren made funds available in return for interest on the money. By 1901 the General Missionary and Tract Committee was paying interest on more than $200,000 which had been made available for the use of the Committee. Appropriately enough, the Annual Meeting received annual reports in considerable detail, but also queries were received dealing with the handling of these funds. A special committee examined the matter in 1900–1901 and reported to the Meeting.

1. Report of Committee on Mortgages and Endowments:

To the Annual Meeting of 1901 Greeting:—The Committee to which was referred the subjoined queries by the Conference of 1900 respectfully submit the following report:

(3) We the Conestoga church, Lancaster County, Pa., ask Annual Meeting, to devise a better plan for the use of the money in the endowment and other funds than the present mortgage one, so that money may be loaned or donated to build meetinghouses in cities and such other places as they are needed and the churches are not able to build themselves, the General Missionary Committee holding the title until otherwise arranged.

(10) Will not District Meeting petition Annual Meeting to decide that no endowment funds belonging to the Brotherhood shall be loaned on mortgages in the future.

(11) We petition Annual Meeting through District Meeting, to prohibit the General Missionary and Tract Committee from soliciting or receiving endowment funds. See Matt. 6: 19, 20, 34. But this shall not be construed as to prohibit any person from giving any amount they may feel to donate.

Your Committee held a meeting at Elgin, Illinois, where every opportunity was afforded to make a careful and thorough examination of the present plan of investing and caring for the funds of the church. It was found that the very best that can be done was being done by the General Missionary Committee with the funds intrusted to its care. However, we recommend that the General Missionary and Tract Committee be authorized to investigate the advantages of purchasing farms as an investment, and if they find it practicable to so invest such sums as may seem advisable to them. Many of our brethren looking for money to invest very much prefer to pay interest to the church. It is found that the endowment fund cannot be diverted from the purpose for which it was given by the donors. It was found that every possible care is used in investing the funds. The Secretary and Treasurer is under adequate bonds, and vouchers are kept to show where the money goes. Every penny donated is expended in the most careful manner. The General Committee give their time free. Your Committee feel that it is due to say that the course pursued in the care of the funds in their charge is worthy of high commendation. It is the opinion of your Committee that no funds are more carefully guarded and more sacredly held than are the funds of the church placed in the hands of the General Missionary and Tract Committee.

We recommend that no hindrances should be thrown in the way of securing funds for the mission work of the church and that our members be encouraged to give as the Lord has prospered them. In presenting the duty of giving to the members of the church, solicitors should always give each one the right to choose this method, and in making endowments, as much as possible, the right of the General Conference to use the fund when thought best to do so, be reserved.

Report accepted.[44]

The brotherhood needed money for many causes. One long-standing concern of Brethren was to provide for their own members who were poor. If they were supposed to provide for their own members' needs, was it right to place a Brethren in government owned facilities? The Annual Meeting of 1875 considered this problem.

Art. 12. Whereas, it is not considered to be according to the Scriptures to keep our poor in the county poorhouse, is not the church under obligations to build a house to keep our poor in, providing the brethren petition the legislature to be exempt from paying our poor tax into the county treasury?

Answer: We refer this back as a matter of purely local interest.[45]

Presumably the poor members were adults, perhaps the aged. A new area of concern during these years was orphan children. The earliest reference in the experience of the Annual Meeting was in 1870.

Art. 8. Is it the duty of the members of the church to take special care of their orphan children in getting homes for them among the brethren, and in having them raised up in the faith of the gospel?

Answer: We think it is according to Eph. 6:4.[46]

This reference was, like the reference to the poor, a distinctive concern for those individuals who were related to the church, and certainly not a concern for members of society in general.

To some extent it was possible to find Brethren homes for orphan children, but if the number of children increased, it might be necessary to establish a special home. As in the case of foreign missions, the earliest action of this type occurred in one of the districts. Also, the district turned to the Annual Meeting for assistance. The response came from the Annual Meeting of 1873.

Art. 17. Since the district-meeting of middle Indiana, last year, had under consideration the orphan's home, or a home for orphan children, and expressed itself favorably, but laid it over for further consideration, will not this meeting take into consideration the propriety of erecting a home for orphan children, and members who are a church charge?

Answer: This Annual Meeting does not see the propriety of adopting such measures at present, but if the middle district of Indiana desires to do so, we will not oppose it.[47]

On the basis of this decision of Annual Meeting, the districts took whatever action seemed appropriate. Undoubtedly most of them followed the practice of the District of Oklahoma and Indian Territory, as it was reported to the Annual Meeting of 1905.

2. Whereas the method of saving orphan and homeless children adopted by the District of Oklahoma and Indian Territory has proven successful and economical, such children being gathered and placed in Christian families, where they are properly trained and educated, and much good is being done: Therefore, the district meeting of Oklahoma and Indian Territory, 1904, petition Annual Meeting of 1905 to recommend that a similar method be adopted by the various State districts, so that orphan and homeless children be gathered from both country and city and placed in select families; also, that the different districts cooperate with each other, in harmony with the laws of the State, so that the greatest amount of good may be done.

Answer: We heartily endorse the work of the district of Oklahoma and Indian Territory in saving the homeless children, and urge that our several districts awaken to this important work.[48]

According to a report in 1908, four districts had provided facilities for about 125 children.[49] The Annual Meeting of 1908 also received a request for more definite activity in "saving homeless children."

12. Whereas the Annual Meeting of 1905 heartily endorsed the work of saving homeless children, and urged that other districts awake to this important work, and inasmuch as some districts have now taken up this work under somewhat similar methods, while others have not taken it up: Therefore the district meeting of Oklahoma petitions Annual Meeting of 1908 to appoint a committee of five brethren from various portions of the Brotherhood, who are interested in the work of saving homeless children, to investigate the various methods of caring for such children, and present to the Annual Meeting of 1909 a plan or method so that all state districts can organize and carry on a similar system of caring for orphans and homeless children, and can cooperate together so as to accomplish the greatest good to the greatest number.

Answer: Request granted, and committee appointed.

Committee: Frank Fisher, George C. Carl, David Emmert. (Committee to organize themselves.)[50]

Due to "our arduous work and because of the many complications to overcome, and the undeveloped conditions of the question nationally," the committee asked in 1909 for a one-year extension. In 1910 the committee presented a detailed report.

The committee on orphanage work, after carefully canvassing the purpose in contemplation, submit the following:

1. We recommend that an orphans' agency be organized in every State District, where the sentiment strongly favors it.

2. We suggest that this agency be known as "The Children's Aid Society of the Church of the Brethren," and that it consist of as many members and officers as the State District may desire. All members are to serve without compensation except the secretary and traveling agent, which offices shall vest in the same person. All official members of the agency shall be elected by district meeting.

3. We do not recommend building institutional homes, but favor a hearty cooperation with those now in operation and with local churches and State Districts, in looking after needy children, and their placement into good, Christian homes by said agency.

4. All methods and regulations governing these agencies in receiving and placing children into permanent homes, and their after-care, shall conform fully to the laws of the State in which such agency exists.

5. We recommend that a fund be raised in each organized agency to meet the needs and transportation expenses, and continued after-care in giving proper attention to the children while in their foster-homes. Said funds to be raised through district meetings, churches, Sunday-school and Christian Workers' collections, by bequests, and by soliciting or any method that the District may adopt.

6. Each State District shall, in harmony with its own State laws and peculiar needs, draft its own constitution and bylaws, suited to its surroundings and best interests.

7. For the benefit it may have in fostering sentiment among the churches of the Brotherhood, we encourage that a yearly report of the number of children, permanently located by each District agency, be published in one of our church periodicals.

Committee: Frank Fisher, Geo. C. Carl, D. Emmert.

Answer: Report adopted.[51]

Probably some of these children were not from Brethren families, for by this point in the early twentieth century, Brethren were ministering to the needs of those outside the Brethren community.

By 1915 the polity and organization of the Church of the Brethren had become much more sophisticated. At the local level Brethren had accepted Sunday schools and other specialized agencies, such as Sisters' Aid Societies. They were employing pastors, particularly in urban areas, where a pastor could not make his living as a farmer. At the national level the Annual Meeting was becoming more formally structured with tenure rules for Standing Committee and officers of the Meeting, as well as more definite patterns for the logistics. Also some of the Annual Meeting responsibilities were being shifted to a group of permanent committees, beginning with foreign missions but also including church erection, tracts, Sunday schools, higher education, temperance, and homeless children.

VII
PUBLICATIONS

Introduction

One of the many significant changes among Brethren in the years following the Civil War was their enthusiasm for the publication of books, tracts, periodicals, hymnals, and just about anything that could be printed. In fact, any student examining this period is easily overwhelmed by the mass of material which the Brethren produced. The basic purpose of this chapter is to identify some of the periodicals that were published and to consider the hymnody of the Brethren during these years. Some of the ideas set forth in the periodicals, books, and tracts are identified in other chapters.

Periodicals

Howard Miller, in his survey of the Brethren in 1882 provided an excellent overview of periodicals published for Brethren at that time.

There is probably no organization of Christians in existence which has as many papers and periodicals as the Brethren have, considering the small number of members we have enrolled. The latitude of expression, both allowed and taken, is something remarkable, and he must be hard to please, indeed, who cannot find an expression of opinion congenial with his views.

For a long time, there were no papers published in the Church. For one hundred and forty-three years the Fraternity grew in grace and numbers when the first paper was published, by Henry Kurtz, in 1851, at Poland, Ohio. The GOSPEL VISITOR (its name) was first published in the loft of a spring-house, and had two hundred and forty suscribers to its monthly edition. By a combination of farm work and editorial labor, the paper was enabled to live.

The GOSPEL VISITOR had the field for thirteen years, when the CHRISTIAN FAMILY COMPANION was issued by Henry Holsinger, from Tyrone, Pennsylvania. This differed from the GOSPEL VISITOR by being a weekly, and met with great favor, on that account from the Brotherhood. The paper was moved from Tyrone to Meyersdale, or, as a large number of readers better know the place, to Dale City, Pennsylvania. An examination of the contents of these papers would provoke a smile at the difference between the issues of the press then and its product now—and the difference is not a favorable one.

In 1870, Henry Holsinger started the PIOUS YOUTH, a youth's paper, in Tyrone, Pennsylvania, but it was subsequently discontinued for want of patronage.

In 1870, the PILGRIM, a new aspirant for public patronage, appeared before the church, issued from James Creek, Huntingdon Co., Pennsylvania, by Henry B. Brumbaugh and his brother, John B. Brumbaugh. This was the first opposition paper in a business sense. It was then moved to Huntingdon, Pennsylvania. The PILGRIM was a paying paper, and, like all our earlier papers, was characterized by a mild tone, and was harmonious with the church at large.

In 1870, another publication, known as THE VINDICATOR, was undertaken. This paper is better explained by the following letter, received from the Editor, in answer to a letter of inquiry concerning its scope and results:

"THE VINDICATOR was established in the year 1870, with its present Editor, Samuel Kinsey. Elder Peter Nead—a father in the Church, and so widely known in his time, whose writings, several books, were so much admired, and do still exist—was its warm support and advocate down to his last labors on earth. A number of the old tried and faithful posts of the Church have always given their names to it as its advisers, &c.

"On beholding the downward course of the Church—her innovations and deviations—it was thought necessary to publish THE VIN-

DICATOR to call back, if any would hear, and to hold us in check, if possible, that the Church run not too rapidly into a popular and fashionable Christianity.

"This was the primary object and design of the paper, and, though it met with slurs and sneers, and a decided disapproval on the part of some, it nevertheless had its glorious effects, and accomplished the glorious results of bringing comfort to the hearts of many who were weeping for Zion, and uniting and strengthening all those who were yet favorably inclined to the time-honored order, faith and practice of the Church.

"THE VINDICATOR has always been, and is still, a faithful advocate of the old order and first faith of the Church, in holiness, sobriety and practice.

"Truly, SAMUEL KINSEY."

In 1877, the CHRISTIAN FAMILY COMPANION and the GOSPEL VISITOR were consolidated and the name changed to PRIMITIVE CHRISTIAN, James Quinter, Meyersdale, Somerset Co., Pa., Editor. The PRIMITIVE, as it was known in brief, had a considerable circulation, and was very conservative.

With a view to lessen the number of papers, the PRIMITIVE CHRISTIAN and PILGRIM consolidated their forces under the management of James Quinter, H. B. Brumbaugh and J. B. Brumbaugh, at Huntingdon, Pa. The object of the consolidation was to prevent a number of papers being started, and to concentrate our literary forces; but, in 1875, J. T. Meyers purchased and published the BREDERBOTE [i.e. DER BRÜDERBOTE], issuing it as an English-German paper, half in each language. It was soon merged into the BRETHREN AT WORK, at Lanark, Carroll Co., Illinois, under the joint editorship of J. T. Meyers, M. M. Eshleman [Eshelman] and J. H. Moore, in 1876. Bro. Meyers retiring, leaving the other two in possession, S. H. Bashor was taken in as a partner, and remained such until 1878. In 1879, M. M. Eshleman became the owner of the paper, with S. J. Harrison and L. M. Eby as partners. In 1881, the paper was moved to Mt. Morris, Ogle county, Illinois, and Jos Amick and D. L. Miller became partners with Robert Miller as one of the Editors.

In 1879, the BRETHREN'S ADVOCATE was published at Waynesboro, Franklin county, Pennsylvania, as a weekly. It was subsequently changed to a monthly, in 1881, and the price correspondingly reduced.

About this time, the GOSPEL PREACHER was published at

Ashland, Ashland county, Ohio—S. H. Bashor and J. H. Worst, Editors.

In 1877, THE DEACON was published in Montandon, Northumberland county, Pennsylvania, as a little monthly, compensating in its pugnaciousness what it lacked in size. It was published two years, paying its way. The Editor, P. H. Beaver, explains its demise on the grounds that distinctions came too consecutively, he having been elected to the ministry, arraigned by the A.M. for its publication and became a grand-father all in one day, June 5th, 1879, and THE DEACON was then suspended.

In 1878, the PROGRESSIVE CHRISTIAN was published at Berlin, Somerset county, Pennsylvania, by Henry Holsinger and Joseph Beer. The paper was started as a rostrum for the expression of all opinions regarding the polity of the Church. The paper soon passed into the hands of J. W. Beer, who soon transferred it to Howard Miller. The writer, having received an important appointment from the Government at this period, it was made over to Henry Holsinger, and S. H. Bashor was taken in as a partner and associate Editor.

The BREDERBOTE was next issued as a distinctively German paper from Grundy Center, Iowa.

FREE DISCUSSION made its appearance from Topeka, Kansas, advocating the peculiar views of its Editor, Lewis O. Hummer. Publication presently suspended.

Several other small papers were issued by different members of the Fraternity, but they can hardly be classed as Church papers, and they will not be mentioned in detail.

For the use of the Sabbath schools of the Brotherhood there was issued the YOUNG DISCIPLE, in 1875, from Huntingdon, Pennsylvania, by H. B. Brumbaugh and J. B. Brumbaugh.

The CHILDREN AT WORK was published in 1879, by J. H. Moore, at Lanark, Illinois. This paper was sold to S. Z. Sharp, and was finally absorbed by the YOUNG DISCIPLE, at Huntingdon.

The YOUTH'S ADVANCE was published by J. H. Moore and M. M. Eshleman, which included the CHILDREN AT WORK and this paper, the YOUTH'S ADVANCE, is now a part of the YOUNG DISCIPLE.

OUR SUNDAY SCHOOL was published at Ashland, Ashland county, Ohio, by S. Z. Sharp, in 1879, but was finally merged into the YOUNG DISCIPLE.

Fig. 33. *Office of the* Christian Family Companion, *Tyrone, PA, appearing on the cover of the* Brethren's Almanac, 1871.

Fig. 34. *H. R. Holsinger as a young man. (BE)*

Fig. 35. *James Quinter, late 19th century. (BHLA)*

Fig. 36. *Cover of the* Brethren's Almanac, *1876.*

THE PRESENT PUBLICATIONS

The Brethren's Advocate,

Waynesboro, Franklin Co., Pa., D. H. Fahrny, Editor. A Monthly of conservative character. Fifty cents per year.

The Primitive Christian,

Published at Huntingdon, Huntingdon Co., Pa., A Weekly. Price $1.50 a year. Subscriptions may begin at any time. Conservative.

The Progressive Christian,

Published at Berlin, Somerset Co., Pa., by H. R. Holsinger and S. H. Bashor. Price $1.25 a year. The organ of the Progressives.

The Gospel Preacher,

Published at Ashland, Ashland Co., Ohio. Address Edward Mason, one of the Editors, for terms and specimen copies. Progressive.

The Vindicator,

Published at Kinsey's Station, Montgomery Co., O. Price $1.00 a year. Monthly. Old order.

Brethren at Work,

Published at Mt. Morris, Ogle Co., Ill. Price, $1.50, Jos. Amick, D. L. Miller and Robert Miller, Editors and Proprietors. Conservative.

The Brederbote,

Published at Grundy Center, Iowa. Address THE BREDERBOTE, Grundy Center, Grundy Co., Ia., for terms. The only German paper. Conservative.

The Young Disciple and Youth's Advance,

Huntingdon, Pa. Quinter and Brumbaugh. Weekly S. S. paper. Single copy, 50 cts.; 10 copies, $4.00.[1]

As Miller suggested in his brief evaluation of each paper, some of them were more progressive than others in tone and content. One result was that some Brethren were irritated by the papers and appealed for redress to the Annual Meeting. On a number of occasions the Annual Meeting took action, as in 1873.

Art. 7. Whereas, the "Christian Family Companion" and "Pilgrim" have published articles with reference to decisions of questions of Annual Meeting, differing from the sentiments contained in said decisions; and, communications from others, even from those who are not members of the church, and even from expelled members, reflecting seriously upon the character of the Annual Meeting; therefore, resolved, that the editors of said periodicals be required to make acknowledgment of their offense, and to promise to be more guarded in the future in this respect.

The acknowledgment was made, and the promise given.[2]

Again in 1875 the Annual Meeting was asked to take action regarding the publication of "derogatory" material.

Art. 31. The southern district of Missouri petitions and entreats the Annual Meeting to restrict our editors in publication of matter derogatory to or militating against the advice, counsel, and decision, as given by our beloved brethren, at our Annual Meetings, from time to time, such as advocating high schools, salaried preachers, musical instruments, etc.

Answer: We caution our editors, and all our brethren, from writing or publishing any thing against the acknowledged doctrines of the church.[3]

And in 1879 petitions from five different districts expressed concern about "slanderous and schismatic articles".

XVI. Whereas petitions were presented from Northwestern Ohio, Eastern Pennsylvania, Middle Pennsylvania and Virginia, as well as from Southern Ohio, requesting this Annual Meeting to prohibit the slanderous and schismatic articles from being published in the Progressive Christian and Deacon; therefore it is required that the editors of the Progressive Christian make an humble acknowledgment to the Annual Meeting for publishing erroneous statements in regard to church members; charging a part of the church with idolatry; stigmatizing some of its members with terms of reproach; ridiculing some of the peculiar practices of the church, and admitting into the paper inflammatory and schismatic articles some even from expelled members.

2. The editor of the Vindicator and of the Deacon are also required to make satisfactory acknowledgments for writing or publishing similar articles as the Progressive Christian.

3. That elder John Harshey, brethren James Ridenour and Howard Miller, be required to render satisfaction to the Annual Meeting for writing schismatic articles.

4. That the editors of all our periodicals be required hereafter not to admit into their papers any articles that will assail the doctrine of the church in regard to non-conformity to the world, the personal character of ministers, or any of its peculiar tenets or practices.[4]

Without question, the most controversial figure in the editorial world of the Brethren was Henry R. Holsinger, the editor of the ***Progressive Christian.*** *Holsinger had been called to order by the Annual Conference on several occasions before 1879; now in 1879, as one of the editors of the* ***Progressive Christian,*** *he was again in hot water. In response, he resigned from the editorship and explained why in a lengthy editorial in the paper.*

GOOD BY BROTHER HENRY

With this number of the PROGRESSIVE CHRISTIAN I retire from the editorial columns and management of the paper. This announcement will surprise everybody, disappoint many and please a few. I participate in some degree with all. The query will arise in the minds of all of our readers, why? how? What brought about this change? And as I think it a proper question, and am opposed to all secret, underhanded schemes, and therefore do not believe in covering up anything, I will try to tell you.

1. It does not pay two men to spend their time upon the paper, and receive no compensation. I have given my time freely since last January, with a cash investment of at least fifty dollars, which is all that I can feel justified in donating to the cause for the present. Brother Beer had also made some sacrifices, and it was mutually agreed that one of us would retire. And as he preferred to keep the paper, and I was willing to withdraw, the present arrangement has transpired, with my consent.

2. My willingness to dissolve and retire, was the second and last cause of bringing about the result herein announced. Among the reasons that led to that willingness we may mention.

1. A conviction that a paper in the free and outspoken manner in which I have been characterizing my own writing and dictating to others, and the principles upon which alone I would take PLEASURE in conducting a public journal, will not become popular nor be liberally patronized among us in such time as I could afford to wait for it. Experience has proven this to my satisfaction. We have been publishing a good paper. This I say without feeling any conviction of egotism. It is admitted by friend and foe, in the church and out of it. Good and unprejudiced people among all denominations sympathize with our mission, and give us credit of skill and ability, and pray for our success. Many of our own brethren are heartily in sympathy with our cause, and have befriended and supported it to the extent of their ability. There are many more who secretly are in sympathy with our effort who care not to recognize us publicly. Of course we appreciate their motives, knowing the cause of their concealment. But there is much about such a business which is exceedingly unpleasant. I love to be on terms of friendship with all to whom I am any way related; and hence the idea of conducting a paper, to contribute to which subjects a brother to church discipline, and which will call forth such severe and unjust denunciations as were charged against us at the late Annual Meeting, does not contribute to my happiness. As, therefore, the publication of the paper does not afford me any pecuniary support, and subjects me to unpleasant reflections, and brings my friends into trouble, it will be seen it would be no hard matter to consent to refrain from continuing to issue it.

2. While I have no doubt in the justice and righteousness of our cause, I have thought, for reasons which I will try to specify, that I may not be just the best man to work in it. (1) It appears that an unaccountable degree of prejudice and jealousy has obtained against me. With all who have been possessed with such feelings my influence has been very much impaired. Unfortunately, too, for me this has reached men of high position in the church, and in some places has become very general. This matter presented itself very seriously to my mind lately while translating the minutes of last Annual Meeting from the English into the German language, this requiring me to carefully notice and ponder every word it contains, and especially when I went

to translate such words as "erroneous statements," "schismatic," "stigmatizing," "ridiculing," "inflammatory," and kindred expressions, showing the animus of the parties who drew them up. Then when I read the report of annual meeting, calmly and considerately, and noticed the ungenerous and uncalled for decisions which passed four different District Meetings, I felt that we are indeed performing a THANKLESS DUTY; nay, more, that bitter persecutions will be the lot of those who will be instrumental in bringing about the needed reform in the church. (2) That perhaps my views may be too radical, and too far in advance of those of our people to make a successful leader. Perhaps a man with the same views, but with a more compromising disposition, may do better.

Now all these things I have pondered. And while I am not a coward, and would like to work for the cause of truth and progression among the Brethren, I am also aware that I do not have to do so at the sacrifice of money, comfort and happiness. And so, in the capacity of editor of a paper, I will let the Annual Meeting and its Standing Committee alone, for a while at least, and will endeavor to work in such other ways as the Lord may open up to me: and my friends are assured that brother Holsinger will always be found in the discharge of what he believes to be his duty. But for the present I feel as though I had done my share of the thankless service of showing people their errors, and telling them how to correct them. Right at this point we beg leave to introduce a few extracts from private letters from friends. The first is from a brother, enclosing two dollars for the support of the cause, but wants the donor's name withheld. He criticises my writings (as he supposes them to be) very candidly, thinks we "are unnecessarily caustic in our criticisms," and cut off our power of doing good by the course we pursue and then remarks:

"You may ask, why, then, do you send us money, to continue the paper? I answer: 1. Little as I think of it as a means of grace, it is stirring up some of the old cess-pools in the church and giving them an airing, and showing up some of the errors and faults of the church. 2. It is the only paper in which all parties can be heard, and for that reason I do not want it to die out. Allow me to suggest to you that you try and cultivate a greater growth of love among your contributors. I live and move in one halo of love. Never is heard in our heaven of a home one cross word, one unkind word. And oh! could you feel and know its gentle influence as I do, you would be as great a contender for my doctrine as I am. When your paper first was announced, I subscribed at once, thinking I had found what I wanted, and so much was I in earnest that I contributed a few worthless articles, a thing I never thought of in any of the other papers. This much I have done, and mention it only to show my position. Love and kindness, in words and actions, is the lever that moves the earth, yea, the heavens also.

I know, should I attempt to govern my house on your plan, my own faultless (you can pardon that for it is literally true) would do anything else than what I wanted her to do. "I am sorry, pet, that you did it so," or something similar, will bring her as a penitent child goes to its parent for forgiveness.

But you must say: Would you have me compromise my position? by no means. Keep your position; but dip your pen in another place. Dip into love, not vinegar."

This letter shows the kinds of work that the writer thinks are necessary to be done in the church. There is a class which is called "dirty work," showing up the "errors and faults of the church." This is labor that every serious, intelligent Christian believes should be performed, but it is "cheap work," and few have the humility and courage to discharge it. Nor is reproof and correction desired by the church, especially from an individual in humble position. Its members would rather be flattered than corrected. It appears to me as if we had verily entered the time spoken of by the Apostle: "When they will not endure wholesome doctrine, but will accumulate teachers for themselves, according to their own inordinate desires, tickling their ear, and they will indeed turn away from the hearing of the truth, and be turned aside to fables." And one of the most serious objections I have to our beloved fraternity is the manifest disposition to hide our own sins, and expose those of others. Beecher is held up to the gaze of the world as a transgressor, while Davy and Long go unrebuked by the press. Those who practice infant baptism are denounced as following innovations, while we try to establish an ordinance in "uniformity of dress" equally unwarranted by the Scriptures; those who neglect the Salutation by the kiss of charity, are accused of neglecting to keep the all things of the Bible, while we ignore the ordinance of the Lord, that they which preach the gospel shall live of the gospel.

I have never attempted to establish any doctrine of my own, and yet I am accused of trying to create schisms. I challenge any man to prove that in one single instance I have advocated a measure that was not based upon plain scriptural teaching or good common sense. I have no dogma of my own, no ends of my own, and no interests of my own to establish—religiously—except the salvation of my own soul! With me when God speaks every man speaking contrary may be a liar.

From my childhood an opposition to "creeds," "disciplines," and "confessions of faith" has been cultivated, by parental instructions, and the public preaching of the Brethren; but now after I have accepted the Bible and the Bible alone, as my all sufficient guide, in religion, and having planted my faith upon the ever enduring word of God, I am asked to accept the OLD ORDER, and obey the "principles of our church according to the definitions thereof by the authorities of the Annual Meeting!" I am still willing to accept the principles of our church as defined by the Holy Scriptures. Why, the Minutes of Annual Meeting to-day make a larger volume than the Augsburg Confession. I am tenacious for nothing in religion but the plainly taught instructions and privileges of the Scriptures. I am in full accord with the church on ALL points of scriptural doctrine and practices. It is only in matters of tradition and commandments of men that I refuse obedience. I have been arraigned before Annual Meeting repeatedly, but never, thank God! (and I say it gratefully and not boastingly) for any immorality or crookedness. Nor has ever an accusation of scriptural heterodoxy been laid to my charge. I have been called before my own congregation a few times, but have never been accused of violating any scriptural injunction. Twice I was arraigned for speaking on temperance, a doctrine of the New Testament, but was acquitted and justified. I have also been "in perils among false brethren," who sought to obtain vengeance upon me by turning church powers against me. Through all the Lord has so far safely brought me.

While writing the above another letter came to hand from a brother whom we have always esteemed and though it is strictly a private letter, I will take the liberty of making a few extracts:

"My Dear Brother; As I have been long and intimately acquainted with you, I therefore take the liberty of writing these lines to you in a private way, and not for publication. We have often associated together in a religious capacity, in days gone by, and I always entertained a high regard for you as a man, as a brother in Christ, and as a minister of the gospel, and have often admired the ability with which God has blessed you for usefulness in the church. But when you announced your present enterprise and declared a "free rostrum" I had some doubts of the propriety of your course. I thought there might be danger in such a broad platform, and therefore did not encourage your paper. I however received an occasional copy and perused it carefully, and, I think, impartially, and many of the articles of the PROGRESSIVE I could heartily endorse, as being good and orthodox. Recently I have been receiving the paper. * * * The dress question has been so much agitated through your paper that I am perfectly disgusted with it. We as a congregation here have very little or no trouble with it, and we could move along harmoniously were it not for the continual agitation that is kept up through the papers. We have never expelled a young sister of eighteen years for wearing a plain hat, and I would question the right of the church to do so, if her conduct in all other respects was such as becomes a Christian lady."

I, too, am tired and disgusted with the dress question, and have been for years, and yet I am compelled to read it, and hear it, and feel it everywhere. In many places it is more preached than matters actually pertaining to religion. Not long ago I was present at a place where baptism was being administered by one of those dress Christians. He instructed the candidate before baptism to part his hair in the middle, and to wear a round coat with standing collar, to the utter disgust of many brethren and sisters and others. This anti-scriptural custom I want to see discarded before I sit down at ease. While the brother who wrote the above letter, (who by the way is an elder in the church), may have no trouble in his church, upon this subject, there are many others who do have, and who are suffering severely from it. A number of young sisters were expelled from the church for no other crime than wearing plain hats. They are not only well behaved ladies, but they are moral young women, and some of them Christian workers. And such outrages are being committed all over the brotherhood, and we must hear of them. We cannot stop the paper and thus close our eyes and ears against the sad news. We would love to rally the church to a higher spirit life, and our labors are to that end, but before we can enjoy the great passover feast of rejoicing, all traditional rubbish must be removed and we must unite upon the Book of the law; the "high places" that would usurp the power belonging to the word of God alone, must be "stamped to powder and burned." See 2 Kings 23. There are many good people who will go with us with the Bible as our guide, but who will not and should not unite in our traditionals.

In conclusion, I heartily thank the brethren and sisters who have so zealously stood by us in our effort to establish a free rostrum, and to throw off the iron rule under which our people have been suffering and still suffer. My retirement from the management of the paper need not, and we hope will not, impede its progress and influence. It is intended for its good and success in the mission for which it has been established. And while I feel that I may be excused from farther service in the capacity of editor, and gladly retire to private life, I shall not withdraw so far out of sight that I may not be recalled when I have been persuaded that the cause demands my service.

To Brother Beer, my successor, I confidently entrust the management of the paper, and have reason to hope that he will conduct it with prudence and ability, and I hope the friends of progression will stand by him, and encourage and support him, by contributing matter for its columns, and money for its support. And may the Lord lead, instruct, and save us all, is the sincere prayer of your brother.

H. R. HOLSINGER[5]

As his explanation of his decision indicated, Holsinger loved to write, and he was too ambitious to remain out of the journalistic world for very long. As Miller had indicated, Beer soon turned The ***Progressive Christian*** *over to Miller, who in turn returned it to Holsinger. Holsinger continued to edit the paper for some years. Eventually he became the leader of the Progressive group of Brethren and the* ***Progressive Christian*** *was its media.*

During the 1880s the conviction developed among Brethren that too many papers were competing for the available audience. This issue was considered by the Annual Meeting of 1882; the decision was to consolidate two of the major papers, The ***Primitive Christian*** *and* ***Brethren at Work*** *which appealed to the largest number of Brethren. This group was "middle-of-the-road" in twentieth century terms, or the "conservatives," as they were known in the 1880s. Both papers were private businesses not yet owned by the church.*

XXI. The committee to whom were submitted the papers asking for the consolidation of our periodicals, presented two reports. The following was accepted:

We the owners and publishers of the "Primitive Christian" and "Brethren at Work," have this day agreed upon a basis of consolidation on the following conditions:

Two papers shall be published, one East and one West, or one paper with a branch office, as Annual Meeting and the consolidated firm may think to be for the best interests of the church.

The Annual Meeting shall recognize this paper, or papers, as the case may be, as the official church paper.

We agree to make ourselves directly amenable to Annual Meeting for the contents and character of the paper or papers.

If the above is not acceptable to Annual Meeting, we hereby agree to sell our respective papers to any company that this Annual Meeting may designate at the price agreed upon between ourselves as the basis for our consolidation.

Quinter & Brumbaugh Bros.
Miller & Amick

Milford, Ind., June 1, 1882

Committee: D. L. Miller, H. K. Myers, H. B. Brumbaugh, R. H. Miller, S. T. Bosserman, J. Harshberger.[6]

*Evidently the "owners and publishers of the **Primitive Christian** and **Brethren at Work**" had not done their homework adequately, for the consolidation of the papers was delayed for another year. Finally, the June 19, 1883, issue of The **Primitive Christian** was able to report to its readers:*

TO OUR FRIENDS

A number of our friends have been urging consolidation, promising that if we would do so, they would go to work and greatly enlarge our list. We have now complied with their wishes, and the next paper will be published by the new firm with the incorporated name, "The Brethren's Publishing Co." We expect to unite our efforts to make the new paper worthy of the patronage of the whole church, and kindly ask our brethren and sisters to now go to work and see what they can do towards enlarging our list for the balance of the year. 75 cents will be the price for the remainder of the year. Let us see what you can do for us.

CONSOLIDATION

The subject of consolidation has been under consideration for several years, but on account of the many difficulties that seemed to be in the way, the matter was postponed from time to time until the present. We now inform our readers that hereafter the PRIMITIVE

CHRISTIAN and the *Brethren at Work* will be published together, and that next week you can expect the new paper. What it will be you will see when it comes. While some would have preferred the papers to have remained separate, a large majority, apparently, wished to have but one paper, thus enabling them to get all the church news by paying for only one paper. There are a number of other reasons that have been urged upon us, that we shall not name now. After having carefully and prayerfully considered the best interests of the church, and the wishes of our patrons, we have decided on consolidation, and we hope that this decision will meet the entire wishes of the church and insure to us its hearty co-operation, which we will need to make our work a success.

There are some who have subscribed for both papers, and as we believe that they did this to enable them to thus get all the church news, and as they will now get all this in the consolidated paper, we will be much obliged if they will donate to the new Co. the six months that will be due them. Those who will not feel like doing this can have the new paper sent the balance of the year to any one whom they may name. We hope that one of these propositions will be accepted, as we are anxious to have all such subscriptions closed with the year. All the other subscribers will receive the new paper until the expiration of the time subscribed for.[7]

The result of the consolidation was the merger of the two papers into one paper, which took the new name, ***The Gospel Messenger.*** *Its first issue was published on July 3, 1883. Three items in the first issue are of particular interest.*

OUR GREETING

In accepting the position here allotted to us we have no promises to make or changes to suggest, more than that we will continue to labor with the ability given us for the good of the church and for the promotion of the Master's cause. The peace, union and prosperity of the church lies closest to our heart, and everything that shall tend towards this most desirable end, we shall advocate. As the course pursued by the two papers, now consolidate, for the last year was so nearly alike, but little change need be expected for the future. The true journalist must be neither bought, nor sold, frowned nor flattered from pursuing the cause that his own judgment dictates to him as being right. Policy is said to be allowable for the politician, but for the Christian, never. The man who is willing to sacrifice for the sake of principle, always comes out best in the end. Upon this line we have started, and upon this line, by the grace of God, we expect to fight it out. But while we stand fast in our own convictions, we, at the same time feel it our duty to exercise due deference towards those who conscientiously differ from us. In doing this it frequently necessitates us to submit our judgment to respect the opinions of others, who may be equally conscientious of being right. This is the principle which enables us to prefer one another and at the same time cautious to labor with an eye single to the glory of God.

Our position is not only an arduous one, but it also entails upon us grave responsibility. Feeling this, we ask the aid, the sympathies, and the prayers of all those who have an interest in the welfare of our beloved Zion. Hoping that the union of our papers may result in the best of consequences, we remain your fellow-worker in the cause of Christ.

THE GOSPEL MESSENGER

We have the pleasure of laying before our readers the first number of the long-looked-for consolidated paper. It is not as large as we would like to have made it, but we have concluded to continue this size and shape to the end of the present year, with a view of other improvements. The GOSPEL MESSENGER now takes the place of the *Brethren at Work* and *Primitive Christian,* with the intention of supplying the Brotherhood with a mass of reading that will prove both instructive and edifying; especially will this prove true of the church news. Having one paper will tend to bring our people closer together, and unite them still more fully as a church and a band of Christian workers. They will become better acquainted with each other, know more of the doings throughout the whole Brotherhood, and thus be knit together by a kindred feeling which always results from reading the same class of literature.

Uniting the two papers gives the MESSENGER a large circulation, but we desire to still increase that circulation, for the more readers we have, the more good can be accomplished. If possible, we desire to get the MESSENGER into every family in the Brotherhood,

Fig. 37. *Editor J. H. Moore in the office of the Brethren's Publishing Company, Mt. Morris, IL, 1898, (BHLA)*

Fig. 38. *Composition room of the Brethren Publishing House, Elgin, IL, ca. early 20th century. (BHLA)*

and hope that all of our present readers will make a special effort to aid us in this part of the work. Proper efforts upon their part will double and even treble our circulation. To aid in thus increasing the circulation, and give the people everywhere a chance to become acquainted with the character of the paper, we have concluded to offer it to the end of the year for the small sum of fifty cents. Let it be announced to all of the congregations in the Brotherhood that the consolidated paper can be had to the end of the year for fifty cents, and some one appointed to take the names and money and forward the same to us. We trust that our agents and the housekeepers in the various congregations will see that this is promptly attended to. If sample copies are desired, drop us a card.

Address all communications to the Brethren's Publishing Co., Mt. Morris, Ogle C., Ill., or Box 50, Huntingdon, Pa.

AN ADDRESS TO OUR READERS

Our readers have noticed remarks in our paper from time to time in regard to the consolidation of the *Brethren at Work* and the *Primitive Christian.* To prevent temptation to improper competition between the two papers, and for some other reasons, the proprietors of the two papers made a partial consolidation—a consolidation of our interests, sometime ago. And from the action that the Annual Meeting of 1882 took upon the subject of consolidation, and from the feeling that was manifested among the brethren at that meeting in favor of consolidation, we have since that time been considering seriously and prayerfully the propriety of a complete consolidation of our publishing interests, and of our two papers. And things seemed to so open and so to work as to favor the consolidation, and it has been done.

The patrons of the two former papers will now receive the one consolidated paper. They perhaps have not been looking for this quite so soon, but we hope they will cheerfully acquiesce in what we have, upon mature consideration, thought would be best for our readers, for the church, and for ourselves. In looking at the subject under some aspects, we would have preferred to keep the papers separate. But taking all things into consideration, we concluded it would be best to consolidate. First, in having but one paper, we shall have all the church news, which is generally considered an interesting department of the paper, in the one paper which can be read by all. Whereas, while we had the two papers, the church news divided between them, and the readers of the one paper did not get to read what was in the other.

Secondly, there were often articles which appeared in one paper, that were of such a character that it was desirable that they should be read by as many of the members of the church as possible. But unless they were copied from the paper in which they first appeared, by the other paper, they would only be read by the readers of the one paper. Under the present arrangement such articles will be read by a much larger number of readers than they would be read by under the former arrangement.

Thirdly, by concentrating the writing talent of the church upon one paper, the paper can be made better in its contents of reading matter than when we had the two papers. Fourthly, by concentrating the writing talent of the church, a paper can be made that will be likely to accomplish more good in the world than the two papers would have done. Fifthly, those who took both papers before, will have less to pay and less to read than they had before, while they will have, it is to be hoped, nearly the advantage of reading as they had when they received two papers.

Sixthly, as there are several families that live upon the income of our business, it is very desirable that the business be conducted as economically as possible. And we think we can publish one paper more economically than we could the two.

In looking at the subject then, under such aspects, we think we can increase our usefulness to the church, and to the world, and also promote our own interests by our consolidation. But we are fully aware to accomplish the anticipated advantages of the change in our papers, there will have to be much wisdom, discretion, watchfulness, and caution used by all the editors. And this we hope will be done. The responsibility we hope is appreciated by us all. We all have had considerable experience, and that experience has added to our knowledge of and fitness for the business. We also hope that we all appreciate the present condition of the church, and the duties devolving upon us in view of our relation to the world, and to all bodies of professing Christians, and that we shall labor harmoniously and successfully, for the peace, the purity, and the prosperity of the church.

And we want to say to our beloved brethren, that our interest in our work as an editor has not abated in the least, and we shall continue to labor with the ability that God may give us, which ability we shall try to improve by experience, culture, and his divine assistance. We have hoped that our labor and responsibility would be somewhat lessened by our present arrangement, for we feel that this is very desirable. And if our desires are gratified, we shall feel relieved and pleased. Our position, however, on the editorial staff is such, being the senior editor, that we shall feel a great responsibility resting upon us, and relying upon divine help, we shall do our utmost to meet that responsibility.

We think we fully appreciate the kindness of our brethren in extending to us their patronage, the long time we have been connected with the press, and we take this opportunity of expressing our gratitude. At this juncture of our editorial life, and in making the change we are making, we have taken a retrospective view of that life. And we trust a little allusion to it here will not be out of place.

It is twenty-seven years since we become connected with the press. In his preface to the 6th volume of the *Gospel Visitor,* Bro. Kurtz makes the following reference to us: "This constant increase of labor became exceedingly burdensome and grievous to us, and long already we looked around for assistance. We durst not to make our own choice. We waited patiently for some token of Providence. The Lord graciously granted us such a token at the last yearly meeting. Then our dear brother James Quinter was nominated as our assistant in the clerkship, and performed the duties thereof acceptably, as we have reason to believe, to the whole meeting. From this we took courage to call him to our assistance in the editorship, as being pointed out by the finger of God, and we rejoice to say that he has accepted the call, and will shortly enter upon the active duties of the same." This was in January, 1856. In the following June we commenced our editorial work, and in the number of the *Gospel Visitor* for that month appeared our Inaugural.

In taking this retrospective view of the past, oh, how many things crowd upon our memory! Our heart is melted to tenderness, and we feel very humble before God, at what he has done for us, and for the confidence the beloved brethren have placed in us, though we have been so very unworthy. Well, though we have served the church twenty-seven years as editor, and labored in this capacity long enough to know the perplexities of the profession, and would gladly retire if duty and circumstances would permit, but as such a permission does not seem to be granted, at present, we shall continue to labor for the edification, the defence, and the prosperity of the church.

We entered upon the editorial work conscious of its responsibility. We feel that responsibility more at this time than we ever felt it. And we shall try to labor with the same caution hereafter, that we have labored with in the past. In our past editorial labors, while we have tried to the best of our ability, to maintain the truth as it is in Jesus, we have also tried to observe the apostle's admonition in which he says, "Give none offence, neither to the Jews, nor to the Gentiles, nor to the church of God." And we shall still try to do the same.

We hope our beloved brethren, will cheerfully accept the change we have made in our papers, and that when we get the work under the new arrangement fully under way, that it will prove satisfactory to our subscribers and to ourselves. In the meantime, we ask a hearty co-operation on the part of our brethren in our work. And let us all labor and pray that we may have a sanctified church literature, to promote the cause of Christian truth.

JAMES QUINTER.[8]

James Quinter continued to edit The ***Gospel Messenger*** *for the remainder of his life, and The* ***Gospel Messenger*** *continued to be the official periodical for the Church of the Brethren.*

HYMNBOOKS AND HYMNALS

Henry R. Holsinger was also responsible for the publication of the first Brethren hymnal that included music, in contrast with all of the previous hymnbooks without music. In 1872 Holsinger and Benjamin Funk published The ***Brethren's Tune and Hymn Book*** *at the Funk printing shop in Singer's Glen, Virginia. It used shape notes associated with gospel music rather than the round notes commonly used in twentieth century humnals. The Preface outlined something of the purpose of this volume.*

PREFACE

The true child of God ever keeps before his mind three great points—Truth, Duty, and Interest. These three points are so closely connected, that he cannot see any one of them, without, at the same time, seeing the other two. To be impressed with truth, to be animated to duty, to be awakened to interest, is the great sum of spiritual blessings attainable in public worship. It is to this end we engage in the three leading exercises of the house of God, viz: Preaching, Praying, and Singing. The minister of the Gospel may preach in such a way that

"Truths divine, come mended from his tongue"—He may pray with the fervor of an Apollos; but if the songs of Zion are left off, we feel that an indispensable part of the service has been omitted. Can this feeling be the result of habit? Habit may have something to do with it; but it mainly springs from our consciousness of the enlivening and edifying effect of good singing upon the heart. When do we gaze most rapturously through "opening vistas into heaven?" When do "our spirits most ardently long to rise, and dwell on earth no more?" When do the songs of the redeemed most joyfully thrill our hearts? Every true Christian's experience answers, as if with one voice, when we are imitating those blissful strains of adoration, love, and praise to Almighty God. The utility of sacred music in awakening and strengthening our devotional affections, will, perhaps, only be fully known and felt, when we once read the records of the Book of Life.

We now offer the Tune and Hymn Book to the Brethren, in the hope that it may greatly contribute to this desirable end. If it be desirable "that all be in the same mind, and speak the same thing," surely it cannot be less desirable that all likewise sing the same thing, that there may be a union in song as well as in doctrine.

When we visit distant branches of the church, and look in vain for one familiar face, how comfortable we are made, and what a home feeling we enjoy, and what a deep sympathy springs up in our hearts for those around us, when we join with them in singing some good old tune which we learned in our heart's first love!

The Tune and Hymn Book contains nearly all of those venerable airs that have stood the test of time; together with many of equal merit that are new, which will likewise soon take their place in the list of old tunes, and be equally dear to the lambs of the flock, when they become old, as those are now dear to us.

In the hope that this book may meet with a cordial reception from the Brethren everywhere, and thus promote the great objects of true devotion, it is affectionately submitted by the compilers.

Benjamin Funk
H. R. Holsinger[9]

This hymnal included all of the 818 hymn in The ***Brethren's Hymn Book*** *published by James Quinter in 1867. According to Nevin*

W. Fisher who wrote an important study of Brethren hymn books in 1950, "The printing of music with the hymns was an innovation and a departure from tradition."[10]

Some Brethren were not prepared to accept such a "departure from tradition," and the status of the new idea was questioned at the Annual Meeting of 1873.

Art. 20. Do the brethren not think it proper to exert their influence against the admission into the church of the new hymnbook with notes?

Answer: We advise all districts of churches to keep them out of the church in public worship.[11]

Probably one of the basic problems in introducing this new approach to the singing of hymns among the Brethren was the relation of Henry R. Holsinger to the new hymnal. James Quinter, by contrast, was a much more acceptable journalist and also just as much interested in the publication of hymnbooks and hymnals. Quinter had been responsible for the publication of the ***Brethren's Hymn Book*** *mentioned earlier. That this hymnal was widely accepted among the Brethren is indicated in an Annual Meeting decision of 1872.*

Art. 18. Whereas, both the new English hymn-book, and also the German, are now used in some few of the churches of our brotherhood; and, whereas, the use of the two books, the old and the new, causes at times considerable inconvenience, and for this and other reasons it is desirable that but one book should be used in our churches; and, whereas, the reason given by some brethren for not introducing the new book, is that the Annual Meeting has never given them its sanction; and, whereas, the English book had, before its publication, been presented to the Annual Meeting for an expression of its judgment upon the character of the work, but for want of time no expression was given: and, whereas, the new books, both the English and the German, have now been before the brotherhood for some time, and have given general satisfaction; therefore, resolved, that this Annual Meeting give the new books its sanction, and liberty to all the members of the churches to use them.[12]

Quinter was now convinced that the Funk and Holsinger ***Tune and Hymn Book*** *had a Brethren audience. In 1879, he collaborated with the Brumbaugh brothers in the publication of The* ***Brethren's Tune*** *and Hymn Book, which was "a thoroughly revised, and radically changed and improved edition of Funk and Holsinger's hymnal."*[13] *The Preface outlined the changes.*

PREFACE

The Brethren's Tune and Hymn Book was first published by Benjamin Funk and Bro. H. R. Holsinger, in the year 1872; but, as they did not have their work stereotyped, the edition was soon exhausted, and as the Church had learned the utility of the work, a demand was made for another edition of the book. By this time Bro. Holsinger had disposed of his interests in the publishing business, and his circumstances did not seem to justify him in publishing another edition. As there were a number of improvements recommended by those especially interested in good church music, we thought it best to have it thoroughly revised, making use of only such tunes as would best harmonize with the sentiment of the hymns. In order that our selections might be the best and most appropriate, we employed the services of Bro. J. C. Ewing, who has made music a study for years, and is also quite a successful teacher. He did principally all the selecting of tunes and placing them to the proper hymns. A number of the tunes are his own composition, some of which were composed and harmonized for some special hymns, for which no other suitable music could be found,

To the following gentlemen we tender our thanks for valuable contributions for our work. Dr. Lowell Mason, William B. Bradbury, J. William Suffern, J. H. Leslie, N. Coe Stewart, L. S. Leason, Dr. Geo. F. Root, I. B. Woodbury, Dr. Thoms. Hastings, and others.

The selection of tunes, we think embrace all of the best church music in use, both old and new, some entirely new, never having been used before. While we have labored to produce some good new music, we have been especially careful in not omitting any of the good old tunes that have gladdened the hearts of our venerable forefathers.

In the revision we have, also, changed the arrangement so the number of every hymn in this book corresponds to the number of the same hymn in the Brethren's Hymn Book and is set in the same order, so that they can be used together without the least inconvenience in any way.

We now offer the revised Tune and Hymn Book to the church with the hope that, by its use, life and spirit may be infused into that very important part of our worship, the service of song. Good singing adds greatly to the interest and life of worship, and without it much of the spiritual edification seems to be lost, no matter how good the preaching may have been. By its general adoption we will not only learn to sing, but we will learn to sing the same hymns, thus bringing about a most desirable uniformity in church music, throughout our great brotherhood.

The compilers now submit the humble result, of what has been to them a very arduous labor, to their own beloved fraternity, with unaffected pleasure, in the simple hope that it may be used in building up our Redeemer's Kingdom in the most holy faith, and that it may be accompanied by the fulness of his power and grace of his Holy Spirit.[14]

Although the hymnbook of 1867 and the hymnal of 1879 published by James Quinter were widely accepted by the Brethren, some Brethren were exerting pressure for the production of a new hymnal. By 1887 the Annual Meeting was hearing this concern.

A number of papers were presented in relation to the Hymn Book and Hymnal, which were referred to a committee who reported as follows:

"We recommend a revision of the Brethren's Hymn Book the revised Book not to contain over five hundred hymns, and the price of the best binding not to exceed fifty cents. The hymns in the new Book to be regularly numbered, and those taken from the old Book to have the number of the same hymn in the old Book. The classification of the new Book to be on the plan of the old one, with an additional class of hymns, suited to the wants of children. We also recommend the publishing of a missionary edition, containing about one hundred selections from the revised Hymn Book. We also recommend the revision to the Hymnal in character notes, conforming in numbering and classification to the new Hymn Book."

The report was deferred to next Annual Meeting permitting the General Missionary Committee to publish a small book for its use in mission work.[15]

Since the report was deferred for one year, the Annual Meeting of 1888 heard a more specific request for a revision.

We petition Annual Meeting through District Meeting to have our Hymn Book and Hymnal revised on the following bases:

1st. Above five hundred of the best hymns to be selected from our present hymn book.

2nd. A number of other good, familiar hymns, not to exceed one hundred, to be added, of which some shall be especially adapted to the wants of children.

3rd. The Hymnal to contain no duplicates of tunes, but as nearly as possible to contain the music of all the tunes used in the Brethren's congregational worship.

4th. The time and the music of the tunes to be used as nearly as possible as originally written, the same character notes to be used as those in our present Hymnal, the binding to be plain, good and substantial, and not to exceed two kinds for the hymnal, as well as for the Hymn Book.

Answer: The Revision of the Hymn Book is deferred two years.[16]

Evidently to defer the issue was not sufficient to kill it, for the matter was back in the hands of the Annual Meeting of 1890, which took a different approach to the question—it committed it.

The revision of the Hymn Book and Hymnal deferred by Annual Meeting of 1888. The following query was read:

"Appanoose church, Kansas, requests Annual Meeting to take action this year on the revision of Hymnal and Hymn Book query deferred two years ago."

All the papers pertaining to aforesaid revision were referred to the following committee, with instruction to report at next Annual Meeting: J. H. Moore, S. F. Sanger, L. H. Dickey, H. B. Brumbaugh, and Jos. Amick.[17]

This committee took the matter seriously and prepared a lengthy report for the consideration of the Annual Meeting of 1891.

The Hymn Book Committee appointed at the last Annual Meeting made the following report, which was accepted and ordered to be placed on the Minutes:

In the year 1888 there was a petition sent to the Annual Meeting asking for a revision of our Hymn Book and Hymnal. This petition was deferred until the Annual Meeting of 1890, when it was again taken up and submitted to us, with instructions to report at the Meeting of 1891.

Having carefully and prayerfully considered the work entrusted to us, we now beg to submit the following report:

(1) We do not see the way clear for either diminishing the size of, or improving the character, of our Hymn Book and Hymnal sufficiently to answer the various wants of our growing Brotherhood.

(2) We therefore recommend that the Brotherhood have prepared and published another book, to be known as the "The Brethren's Song Book".

(3) This book to contain, not to exceed 500 hymns, about three hundred of which are to be selected from our present Hymn Book and the remainder from other sources.

(4) The sentiment of the hymns to be in harmony with our faith and practice and suited to the wants of the Brotherhood for public worship, Sunday-schools, council meetings, revival work, missionary fields and family worship.

(5) The arrangement of the hymns to be miscellaneous throughout the book, and numbered consecutively from first to last, Hymns from our present book to also have old number printed in brackets.

(6) The first one hundred and fifty hymns, or thereabouts, to be selected, especially for use in the missionary revival and Sunday-School work, so that the plates may be used in printing a small book for use on the mission fields and in Sunday-schools, if so desired. This book is to be known as the Brethren Song Book, Part I.

(7) The book is to be printed in character notes, but no duplicates of tunes used.

(8) Several hymns may be arranged under one tune, provided they are on either the page with the music, or on the one facing it.

(9) The book also to contain the rudiments of music sufficient for good practical use in learning to sing.

(10) The work to be printed with and also without music. The book without music to have the same size page and type as the Brethren Hymn Book to contain good paper and to be substantially bound in arabesque and morocco, plain.

(11) The book with music to have the same size and shape page as the Brethren's Hymnal, to contain good paper, to be substantially bound in board, half leather and morocco.

(12) The Annual Meeting shall appoint a competent brother to superintend the compilation of said book, with four other well qualified brethren residing in different parts of the Brotherhood to assist in the compilation.

(13) The meeting shall also appoint a competent brother, well versed in the science of music, to superintend the selection and arranging of the music with four other well qualified brethren residing in different parts of the Brotherhood to assist him in this part of the work.

(14) To aid them in their work the compilers of the hymns are to call through the Messenger for each member who feels an interest in the work to send a list of such hymns as they desire to have in the new book.

(15) To aid them in selecting music well suited to all parts of the Brotherhood, the compilers of the music are also to make a similar call for selections of tunes for the new book.

(16) The book without music is to contain two indexes: (a) A general index, giving the first line of each hymn alphabetically arranged. (b) The subject Index, giving the first line of each hymn arranged under subjects, such as Opening hymns, Closing hymns, Sunday-school hymns, Missionary hymns, Funeral hymns, etc.

(17) The book, with music, is to contain the same index, with an addition of an index of the music.

(18) When completed the books are to be published by the Brethren's Publishing Co., who are to pay all expenses for compilation and copyright.

In view of the importance of the work we ask that this Report by spread upon the Minutes as deferred matter until the Annual Meeting of 1892.

J. H. Moore
H. B. Brumbaugh
S. F. Sanger
L. H. Dickey
J. Amick[18]

In 1892 the report of the committee was repeated and was adopted, but no immediate action was taken. The Annual Meeting of 1893 heard a briefer report from the Hymn Book committee, and reached a much different conclusion.

1. That a Sunday-school Book be published separate from the Hymn Book.

2. That a new Hymn Book and Hymnal be compiled and published to contain about nine hundred hymns. Five hundred of

these hymns to be selected from the present Hymn Book, and the remainder from other sources.

3. That the present Missionary Hymn Book be accepted upon a revision of the same and an addition of hymns thereto. But all the hymns for the Missionary Hymn Book are to be selected from the proposed new Hymn Book.

Report of committee, together with queries bearing on the Hymn Book, was disposed of over the following answer;

Decided that the old Hymn Book be continued as it is, and the committee be instructed to improve the Missionary Hymn Book, and also produce a book for Sunday-schools, as suggested by the committee.[19]

Evidently Brethren in general were not enthusiastic about the publication of a new hymnal, as recommended in the second point. Nothing happened for the next five years until 1898, when the Annual Meeting was again queried about the publication of a revised hymnal.

Query 11. Inasmuch as our Hymnals do not contain sufficient Sunday School and missionary songs, and as the introduction of additional books to supply this deficiency has a tendency to divide the song service; therefore, we, the members of the Oakland congregation, ask Annual Meeting through District Meeting, to so revise our Hymnals that this deficiency may be supplied within the compass of one book.

Petition from Solomon's Creek Church. As there is quite a diversity of song and hymn books in use among us, thereby preventing harmony in our song service, and inasmuch as the Brethren's Hymnal and the Sunday school Song Book do not meet the wants of the church, will not District Meeting ask Annual Meeting to supply this want and direct that all the churches use the same book in all our services?

These queries were submitted to a committee and answered as follows:

(1) Inasmuch as there is now forthcoming, by authority of Annual Meeting of 1896 (see Article 18), a No. 2 Sunday School Song Book, which will likely be published soon, and thus supply the demand along this line for the present . . .

(2) In view of the importance of this question submitted, and the limited time for its consideration, we ask for time until next Annual Meeting to carefully consider this question. But we suggest (1) that in the meantime the churches use the Hymnal and Sunday School Song

Book, as recommended by Annual Meeting. (2) That the Brethren Publishing House collect suitable hymns and music, as opportunity affords, as a stock to draw from when needed. Committee L. W. Teeter, L. H. Dickey, H. E. Light.[20]

In this case the committee asked for additional time to complete its report. The Annual Meeting of 1899 heard a more complete report but then deferred action for one year.

Article 2. After consideration of the question of the previous year's conference concerning the petitions of the Oakland Church and Solomon's Creek congregation the following was recommended:

1. That the publication of the Hymn Book and the Hymnal be continued in about the form and size they now are.

2. That a committee of three be appointed to revise both the Hymn Book and Hymnal according to the following outline:

(1) Revise the Hymn Book, expunging a sufficient number of hymns least in general use to admit a Sunday-school department, of sufficient compass that, by the use of some hymns from other departments, the book may be used for Sunday-school song service.

(2) Give special attention to the doctrine of all hymns, and arrange them topically, and fully indexed.

3. Revise the Hymnal (1) to contain the same hymns as those in the Hymn Book, and topically arranged and indexed. (2) To contain few, if any duplicates, thus giving us a greater variety of tunes without increasing the size of the book.

4. We recommend that the publication of the Hymn Book and Hymnal be turned over to the Brethren Publishing House, and that they should put them in substantial binding, and sell them as near cost as possible.

Committee: L. W. Teeter, L. H. Dickey, H. E. Light.

Answer: Decided to spread the report on the Minutes and defer one year.[21]

The Annual Meeting of 1900 considered this report, which was included in its complete form in the Minutes, and then finally accepted the report:

Answer: Report adopted and committee of three appointed, viz., D. L. Miller, L. T. Holsinger, H. B. Brumbaugh.[22]

Thus the Annual Meeting had approved the preparation of a new hymnal. The committee immediately moved into action. The result was the publication of The ***Brethren Hymnbook*** *in 1901, which was printed in editions both with music, and without music. This procedure helped to bridge the gap between the more traditional Brethren who were accustomed to having a hymn book and the newer Brethren who wanted music with their words. According to Nevin W. Fisher's evaluation:*

It is not difficult to understand why the membership of the Church of the Brethren desired a new church hymnal towards the close of the century. The new style in religious lyrics and music which was affecting the entire country was affecting the Brethren also. There was in the denomination a growing contact with people of other religious denominations, made inevitable perhaps by the influence of high school and college education. Sunday Schools, prayer meetings, evangelistic services, social gatherings in the churches, and many other ocassions seemed to demand a more informal type of religious song. . . .

It would be fair to say, therefore, that the new twentieth century Brethren hymnal was in part the fulfilment of the desire of the denomination for gospel songs. As everyone knows, the line of demarcation between a hymn and a gospel song can be quite vague, and there are many kinds of gospel songs, some possessing more worth than others; also, it is not denied that many of them have value and that there is an appropriate time and place for an informal type of religious song. . . .

The title page of the new hymnal was reminiscent of other Brethren hymnbooks. The word, "Hymnal" was new, and so was the designation for Sunday Schools. The full title and other information on the title page were as follows: "The Brethren Hymnal, a Collection of Psalms, Hymns and Spiritual Songs, suited for Song Service in Christian Worship, For Church Service, Social Meetings and Sunday Schools. Compiled under Direction of the General Conference of the German Baptist Brethren Church by the Committee. Brethren Publishing House, Elgin, Illinois." This title page demonstrates the new interest manifest by Brethren people in service, social life, and religious education.

The Preface was followed by a table of contents which included subtopics under the following main divisions of the hymnal: God; Worship and Praise; The Holy Scriptures; Christ; Church; The

Gospel; Christian Life and Experience; Death; Time and Eternity; Heaven; Meeting and Parting; The Family; Special Occasions; Miscellaneous, Sunday School, Prayer Meeting and Evangelistic Hymns. Then followed the 742 hymns.[23]

In addition to the committee of D. L. Miller, L. T. Holsinger, and H. B. Brumbauth, which was primarily responsible for the publication of the new hymnal of 1901, some specialists in music were needed, since none of these three was a noted musician. The Preface of the hymnal mentioned in addition to these three a "Music Committee" composed of George B. Holsinger, J. Henry Showalter, and William Beery, who are considered by Nevin Fisher as "Well known composers among the Brethren, and . . . undoubtedly the best musicians in the Church of the Brethren at the beginning of this century." An analysis of the 742 hymns indicated that Holsinger was responsible for the musical setting of fifty-three, Showalter for twenty-nine, and Beery for seven. "There were hymns by other Brethren poets and musicians in the hymnal of 1901, but these three persons were the most important and made by far the greatest contribution to the hymnal by members of the denomination."[24]

Finally, in this discussion of hymnals and hymnbooks, it should be noted that in addition to the more standard hymnals for worship services, the Brethren were also taking an increasing interest in other types of collections of music, designed for other purposes. The distinction between hymns and gospel songs has been noted. The Brethren published a number of song books during these years which were more informal than the hymnals, including:

Bible School Echoes and Sacred Hymns—Compiled by David F. Eby, and published by the Brethren at Work Publishing Co., Lanark, Illinois, in 1880. Contained 110 hymns, and ninety-seven tunes. It was intended for Sunday School use.

Gospel Chimes, for Sunday Schools and Religious Meetings—"A collection of new and standard songs and hymns". Compiled by William Beery. Publisher: Brethren's Publishing Co., Huntingdon, Pennsylvania, and Mt. Morris, Illinois. 1889.

The Brethren's Sunday School Song Book, for use in Sunday Schools, Prayer and Social Meetings—"Published by Authority of the Annual Conference of the German Baptist Brethren Church. The General Missionary and Tract Committee, Mt. Morris, Illinois. Copyright 1894, by Brethren's Publishing Company". From the Preface, we read: "The committee acknowledges indebtedness to Bro.

William Beery for valuable assistance rendered in the compilation and preparation of copy for the press." This book was authorized by Annual Meeting in Muncie, Indiana, in 1893. It included rudiments of music and some sight-singing exercises. It contained some standard hymns but mostly gospel songs which are generally no longer sung. There were a number of selections by J. H. Hall, J. Henry Showalter, George B. Holsinger, and others who were Brethren composers, and 25 songs by William Beery—183 songs in all. There was a "General Index" of first lines and a "Special Index" of nine topics. Advertisements of other Brethren books and tracts appear on the last few pages. The Brethren Publishing House has retained no record of the sales of this volume; however, it was probably widely used around the turn of the century.

Gospel Songs and Hymns, No. 1—"For the Sunday School, Prayer Meeting, Social Meeting, General Song Service. By George B. Holsinger. Forty-Fifth Thousand. Brethren Publishing House, Elgin, Illinois. Copyright 1898". Included some standard hymns, but most of the selections were composed by E. T. Hildebrand, A. J. Showalter, William Beery, Geo. F. Root, J. H. Fillmore, C. G. Lint, William J. Kirkpatrick, B. C. Unseld, Charles H. Gabriel, and others. There were thirty-four selections by George B. Holsinger. The book contained 237 hymns and songs. In the index titles were in capitals, first lines in Roman, and "Choruses" in Italics. Also printed in 1901.

Song Praises—Compiled by George B. Holsinger. Brethren Publishing House, 1906. Also printed in 1907, and 1909.

Practical Exercises in Music Reading—"For Sunday Schools, Day Schools, Institutes and Normals. By George B. Holsinger. Brethren Publishing House, Elgin, Illinois, 1908." Contained both sacred and secular songs in the last section of the booklet.

Kingdom Songs—"For Sunday School, Prayer Meeting, Christian Workers' Societies, and All Seasons of Praise. Published by Authority of the General Mission Board. Brethren Publishing House, Elgin, Illinois. 1911." Compiled by "The Committee". This book is included in the list of music works of his own editing, which J. Henry Showalter drew up, by request. Numbers 1–197 are mostly gospel songs. Numbers 198–281 are mostly standard hymns, printed in small type, two or three hymns to a page. Numbers 282–290 are suitable for choir, quartette, or chorus, rather than for congregation. These might be described as a poorer type of sacred music. This book, together with Kingdom Songs No. 2, was widely used in the Church of the

Brethren. Perhaps between the publication of this volume and Kingdom Songs No. 2, in 1918, gospel hymn singing was reaching its height among Brethren people.[25]

The publication of **Kingdom Songs** *is an illustration of the wide variety of publications that appealed to Brethren in the years following the Civil War in the United States. These included many volumes of periodicals, a large number of books and tracks, and hymnbooks, hymnals, and song books. One purpose of all of this activity was to keep Brethren well informed. Another purpose was to present Brethren ideas to the outside world, particularly in the matter of Brethren beliefs. And still another was to minister to the needs of the many people who were becoming Brethren during these years.*

VIII
DOCTRINES AND BELIEFS

INTRODUCTION

During the fifty years between 1865 and 1915 Brethren writers spent most of their time discussing Brethren doctrines and beliefs, if one may judge by the printed tracts and books. Most of the work was defensive, explaining how Brethren were different from other Christian groups. The major point of difference during these years was the Brethren practice of the sacraments of baptism and communion. The term "sacrament" was too liturgical for Brethren; they preferred the term "ordinance." In this chapter most of the emphasis is on these two ordinances. However, the chapter begins with a general overview of the beliefs of the church as seen by two prominent leaders. J. W. Beer wrote a tract of twenty-two pages in 1878 entitled ***A Summary of Religious Faith and Practice or Doctrines and Duties.*** *This tract is unusual among Brethren writings because it included a discussion of some of the more general beliefs of the Christian church relating to God and man. Included here are the sections dealing with religious faith and doctrines, not the parts dealing with practice and duties.*

I. Of God

There is one only living and true God, who is eternal, of infinite power, wisdom and goodness, just and terrible; and in the God-head are in unity the Father, the Word, or Son, and the Holy Spirit.

II. Of the Father

God, the eternal Father, is a Spirit, immortal, invisible, infinite and immutable in his being and perfection, immense and incomprehensible, almighty, most wise and holy, merciful, gracious and abundant in goodness, forbearing and forgiving, yet just and terrible, who will take vengeance on His enemies, and not acquit the wicked. He is the First Cause, the Designer and Creator of all natural things, the Source of all the laws and forces in nature, and the Giver of every good and perfect gift. He is not dependent on any creature nor governed by any necessity, but works according to the wise and immutable counsel of his own will, by which He manifests his own glory, grace and power.

III. Of the Word, or Son of God

In the beginning was the Word, who was with God and was God. But the Word was made flesh, assumed the form and nature of man, and was God manifest in the flesh, in the person of Jesus the Christ, who was miraculously conceived, and was born of the virgin Mary in Bethlehem of Judea; and hence in him are joined two perfect natures—the Divine and the human. In this mysterious union was Immanuel—God with us—the Son of God, who established his church in the world, revealed the will of God to man, was put to death on the cross, and was an acceptable sacrifice to make atonement for original guilt and for the actual sins of men; who, though he was dead and buried, truly arose from the dead, appeared to his disciples and instructed them in the things pertaining to the kingdom of God, and then ascended into heaven, where he is now interceding for God's people, and whence he will come again with power and glory, to reign till he has put down all opposing rule, authority and power; and when he has put all enemies under his feet, destroyed death and judged the world in righteousness, he will deliver up the kingdom to God the Father, who shall be all in all.

IV. Of the Holy Spirit

The Holy Spirit was eternally and incomprehensibly in unity with the eternal Father, brooded on the face of the waters before the creation of man, communed with and comforted man before the fall, and, after the fall, moved holy men to speak according to God, and by his word, he convinces of the truth, convicts of sin, leads sinners to Christ, renews man's nature, enlightens, guides, directs and comforts

God's people, communicates and distributes spiritual gifts, and sanctifies and prepares the children of God for an inheritance with the saints in light.

V. Of Creation

In the beginning God, in the exercise of his wisdom, power and goodness, created the heaven and the earth; and, in his own time and order, he created all things "that are in heaven, and that are in earth, whether visible or invisible," and all very good. God created man in his own image, male and female created he them, with reasonable souls; endued them with knowledge, righteousness and true holiness; wrote his law in their hearts, and gave them power, according to the exercise of their own will and choice, either to obey or disobey. He also commanded them not to eat of the tree of the knowledge of good and evil; and, while they obeyed, they were happy in communion with God, and had dominion over God's creatures on earth.

VI. Of Providence

God upholds, directs and governs all things by his wise and holy providence, according to his own will and ordinances. In his ordinary providence, God works by means, but is able and free to work without and above them. The general providence of God extends to all creatures; but by a special providence he cares for his own people, and overrules all things for their good.

VII. Of the Fall of Man

Our first parents, yielding to the seductive temptation of Satan, sinned in eating the forbidden fruit, and thereby fell from their original holiness, and communion with God, and became dead in sin, and possessed of an evil nature; and the guilt of this sin was imputed, and this corrupt nature and death in sin conveyed, to all their posterity, by which every man, who naturally is engendered of the offspring of Adam, is very far from original righteousness, and possessed of an evil nature, prompting him to sin; yet, as in the body so in the soul, to some extent, the original parts, functions and powers were left.

VIII. Of Redemption

As through the disobedience of our first parents, condemnation rested on the whole human family, so through the obedience and righteousness of Jesus Christ, "who through the eternal Spirit offered himself without spot to God," redemption from the guilt and condemnation of original sin also passed upon the whole race of mankind; therefore those who die in their infancy and innocency are saved through the mediation of Christ, and the atonement made by him, and no one will be ultimately lost on account of that first transgression, but only because of his own sins, willingly committed.

IX. Of Free Will

Although man in his fallen and sinful condition is very far from his pristine state and purity, yet has he inherent inclination to worship, the power of his own free will to choose either good or evil, or to accept or reject the gospel of Christ, when it is addressed to his understanding; therefore every person is accountable to God, who, in righteousness, can judge every man according to his privileges, talents and works.

X. Of the Holy Scriptures

1. The light of nature to some extent manifests the wisdom, power and goodness of God, but does not afford that knowledge of God and his will which is necessary unto salvation; but God at sundry times and in divers manners revealed himself and his will unto his people; which revelation was committed unto writing, in a number of books and at different times, by several writers, and afterwards collected and arranged in one volume called the Holy Bible, containing the Old and New Testaments, and known also as the Word of God, the Holy Scriptures, &c.

2. The Old Testament Scriptures are useful to teach us a knowledge of God; to acquaint us with his manner of dealing with mankind, and especially, with his people; to lead us to Christ, and to confirm our faith in him; and they also contain a number of prophecies which are yet to be fulfilled.

3. The New Testament scriptures contain the knowledge of God, and of his will and purposes, as revealed by his Son our Savior; and therein we learn what God requires of us, under the gospel dispensation, that we may be saved by grace, and that we may be comforted by the Holy Spirit.

4. The Holy Scriptures contain the whole counsel of God—a revelation of the will of God in all things necessary for his own glory,

and man's faith, life and salvation; so that whatsoever is not found therein, nor may be proved thereby, is not to be required of any that it should be believed as an article of faith, or be thought necessary unto salvation.

XI. Of the Church

1. The universal church consists of all persons in every nation, who make profession of the Holy religion of Christ, and are submissive to his laws. As it is not possible for all these to meet together in one place to worship God and to observe his ordinances, it is right, and in harmony with the Scriptures, that they should be divided into local churches.

2. A local church consists of a number of persons, voluntarily associated together for divine worship, among whom the pure word of God is preached, the ordinances faithfully observed in the name of Jesus Christ, and discipline judiciously, lovingly and faithfully administered.

3. Before persons are received into the church, they must give satisfactory evidence of having a sound faith, and being truly converted,* and should express their willingness and resolution to be faithful members of the church; but no person shall be prevented from becoming a member, or be excluded from the church, because of his views concerning original sin, human depravity, election, eternal decrees, the intermediate state between death and the resurrection, the millennium and personal reign of Christ, and final restoration, as long as he does not reject any essential doctrine, neglect his religious duties, or his sacred privileges.

XII. Of the Sinner's Calling, or Conversion

God calls sinners by the Holy Spirit in connection with his word and providences, enlightening their minds, convincing them of the truth, convicting them of their sinfulness, showing them their need of a Savior, purifying their hearts by faith, by a godly sorrow leading them to repentance, which implies reformation of life, renewing their wills so that they come most freely to Christ as their only Savior, with an ardent desire to become faithful members of his church. Such an one is truly converted.

---

*For the difference between conversion and regeneration see Articles XII, & XIII.

XIII. Of Regeneration, Adoption, Pardon, and Justification

He who has been called of God, or converted, as set forth in article XII, renounces satan and sin, covenants with God, in Christ Jesus, to be faithful until death, and is immersed for the remission of sins, into the name of the Father, and of the Son, and adopted into the family of God; receives forgiveness of sins, being justified freely by God's grace, and accounted righteous before God for the merit of our Lord and Savior Jesus Christ, and not for his own works; and receives the gift of the Holy Spirit, according to God's promise.

XIV. Of Sanctification

No person should say that he has arrived at such a state of sanctification that he can no more sin in this life: but it is both the duty and privilege of Christians to grow in grace and in the knowledge of the truth, to die more and more unto sin, and to press forward toward the goal of holiness—the mark for the prize of our high calling of God in Christ Jesus. . . .

XXIV. Of Religious Ordinances

Ordinances are civil or religious, moral or positive, according to their origin and use, and the nature of the service or duty. A religious ordinance is a divine service or duty enjoined upon man by the authority of God. The ordinances enjoined by Christ are neither carnal nor merely eternal forms; but they are means of grace, and commemorative, symbolical or typical rites—the gospel in emblems; and hence arises the necessity of keeping the ordinances as they were delivered by the great Head of the church. The principal ordinances enjoined by Christ are Prayer, Fasting, Alms or Charity, Singing, Preaching the Gospel, Baptism, the Laying on of Hands, Feet-washing, the Lord's Supper, the Communion, the Holy Kiss, and the Anointing of the Sick.

XXV. Of Prayer

Prayer must be offered to God, in the name of Christ, and by the aid of the Holy Spirit. It must be fervent, pure, in harmony with God's will and accompanied with faith; and in our public prayers and family devotions, the Lord's prayer is to be used. Prayer, as used in this article, implies adoration, thanksgiving, confession and supplication.

1. Adoration is the ascription of honor and praise to God, being prompted by emotions of holy regard, and the utmost esteem, love and reverence.

2. Thanksgiving is the act of expressing gratitude to God for his manifold favors and mercies.

3. Confession consists in acknowledging to God our weakness, dependence, unworthiness, imperfection and sinfulness.

4. Supplication is the offering up of our desires to God, in behalf of ourselves, the church, and mankind in general.

XXVI. Of Fasting

Under the Gospel there is no day or time set apart for fasting; but it is both scriptural and rational, that, as the extraordinary dispensations of God's providence may direct, days of fasting, thanksgiving and prayer, should be observed by his people. During the fast there must be a total abstinence from both food and drink, and it should be observed with earnest meditation on whatever suggested it. By a proper fast our dependence upon God for all temporal and spiritual good is impressed on our hearts; we are made more grateful for his numberless blessings, and directed to a proper use and appropriation of his bounties; and it prepares us for all faithfulness to administer to the wants of the poor, and to send the bread and water of life to famishing souls.

XXVII. Of Alms or Charity

It is the duty of every Christian, as occasion may offer and he may be able, to give, gratuitously, money, food, or clothing, for the relief of the poor; and also to give, according as the Lord has prospered him, for the encouragement of charitable and benevolent enterprises, and, especially, for the support of the church and the spreading of the gospel of Christ. . . .

XXX. Of Baptism

Baptism is an ordinance enjoined by Jesus Christ, in the administration of which the believing candidate is immersed in water, for the remission of sins, "into the name of the Father and of the Son, and of the Holy Spirit," by which he is solemnly added to the number of the disciples and becomes a member of the church. Baptism is a sign of profession by which a person, having signified his purpose to serve

God, is visibly set over from the world into the church, thus symbolizing his adoption into the family of God. Baptism is a washing of the body in pure water by the word, called the washing of regeneration, symbolizing the cleansing of the soul from the guilt of sin, by the precious, atoning blood of Christ. Baptism declares him to be a member of a new society, signifying that he is a new creature in Christ Jesus. He is immersed into the name of the Father to declare his faith in the Father, to honor the Father, and to signify his new relation to the Father, in which he is owned as a child of God; he is immersed into the name of the Son to declare his faith in the Son, to honor the Son, and to signify his new relation to the Son of God, whom he accepts as his Redeemer and Savior, his Prophet, Priest and King, and as his advocate with the Father; and he is immersed into the name of the Holy Spirit to declare his faith in the Holy Spirit, to honor the Holy Spirit, and to signify his new relation to the Holy Spirit, in which he stands renewed by the Holy Spirit, and in which, also, as a newborn child of grace, he receives the Holy Spirit to sanctify and comfort him. And thus is the mystery of the Godhead and of godliness symbolized in holy baptism, when it is rightly observed.

XXXI. Of the Laying on of Hands

The Laying on of Hands, accompanied with prayer, is an ordinance to be observed on various occasions; first, when those who have been baptized are confirmed as members of the church; and, afterward, when brethren are consecrated or ordained in responsible offices to which they have been called, or when they are commissioned to important or weighty duties.* It is a solemn and impressive ceremony, significant of the conferring spiritual gifts and of power to use those gifts in the service of God, and of the responsibility imposed upon him on whom hands are laid. Acts 6: 6; 8: 17; 19: 6; 1 Tim. 4: 14; 5: 22; Heb. 6: 2. Also used in blessing of persons. Mark 10: 16.

XXXII. Of Feet-Washing

The washing of one another's feet is a religious ordinance instituted by Christ, before but in connection with the Lord's Supper. It commemorates Christ's condescension, humility, love and service,

*The Brethren observe the laying on of hands after baptism, and in ordaining bishops, and in anointing the sick.

and symbolizes the same graces in his disciples; and is emblematic of sanctification as baptism is of regeneration; and it is also a means of grace, in the use of which we become more humble, and willing by love to serve one another: and hence it has a tendency to make us more holy and happy. John 13: 1–17; 1 Tim. 5: 10.

XXXIII. Of the Lord's Supper

The Lord's Supper is a full evening meal which was observed and enjoined by Christ, as an ordinance, in the night of his betrayal. It is also called the communion, as it is an emblem of the communion of the saints, resulting from their feasting upon Christ; and it is also typical, pointing forward to the everlasting communion of all the good, which shall follow the marriage supper of the Lamb.

XXXIV. Of the Bread and Wine, or Communion

The ordinance of the bread and wine, emblems of the body and blood of the Lord, was enjoined by Christ to be observed by his disciples at the close, but in connection with, the supper. This ordinance is commemorative, and is to be observed in remembrance of Christ, and to show forth his death till he come. It is also called the communion, as it is an emblem of the communion of the saints, resulting from their feasting upon Christ; and it is also typical, pointing forward to the everlasting communion of all the good, which shall follow the marriage supper of the Lamb.

XXXV. Of the Holy Kiss

The Holy Kiss, also called the Kiss of Charity, is a religious ordinance by which the disciples of Christ manifest their love to one another, and mutually pledge themselves to be faithful, and to stand by each other under all their trials—to bear "one another's burdens, and so fulfil the law of Christ," and to press forward in the way of peace, love, and holiness. It should not be degraded to an ordinary greeting; and a distinction between the sexes must be observed.

XXXVI. Of Anointing

"Is any sick among you? let him call for the elders of the church; and let them pray over him, anointing him with oil in the name of the Lord: and the prayer of faith shall have the sick and if he have committed sins they shall be forgiven him."—James 5: 14, 15. . . .

XLI. Of the Resurrection and Judgment

"As in Adam all die, even so in Christ shall all be made alive. But every man in his own order; Christ the first fruits; afterward they that are Christ's at his coming." (1 Cor. 15: 22,23.) "For this we say unto you by the word of the Lord, that we who are alive and remain unto the coming of the Lord, shall not prevent them who are asleep. For the Lord himself shall descend from heaven with a shout, with the voice of an archangel and with the trump[et] of God, and the dead in Christ shall rise first. Then we who are alive and remain, shall be caught up together with them in the clouds, to meet the Lord in the air; and so shall we ever be with the Lord." (1 Thess. 5: 15–17.) "This is the first resurrection. Blessed and holy is he that hath part in the first resurrection: on such the second death hath no power, but they shall be priests of God and of Christ, and shall reign with him a thousand years." (Rev. 20: 5,6.) "For he must reign till he hath put all enemies under his feet. The last enemy to be destroyed is death." (1 Cor. 15: 25,26.) This destruction of death will be at the final resurrection, when the dead, small and great, shall come forth to stand before the Judgment seat of Christ, to be "judged according to their works." (See Rev. 20: 11–15.) "And when all things shall be subdued unto him, then shall the Son also himself be subject unto him that put all things under him, that God may be all in all." (1 Cor. 15: 28.) Hence we believe in the resurrection of the dead, both of the just and of the unjust; also in a righteous judgment, and just rewards.[1]

In contrast to J. W. Beer, whose ideas reflected the liberal or progressive wing of the Brethren, D. L. Miller was certainly in the mainstream of Brethren thought as the long-time member of the General Mission Board and of the ***Gospel Messenger*** *staff. About 1890 he wrote a twelve-page tract published by Brethren's Book and Tract Work in Dayton, Ohio, entitled* ***The Brethren or Dunkards, Incorporated (German Baptist Brethren Church).***

The Brethren are a large body of Christians, whose faith and practice are not generally known outside of their immediate localities. The errors in the books that attempt to describe the BRETHREN, as they call themselves, have been both numerous and lamentable. Starting with Buck's "Theological Works" and ending with the ponderous encyclopedias and standard dictionaries, error after error is found, and the faith and practice of the church have been greatly misrepresented. The statements that the Brethren are celibates, that they discourage marriage, that they do not marry outside of their own Fraternity, that they keep the seventh day Sabbath, that they live in communities, and other similar errors, set forth in the books, always have been without foundation. These misstatements, to be found in nearly all the standard works, show a lack of care, in obtaining correct information, that is far from commendable. . . .

FAITH AND PRACTICE

The Brethren hold the Bible to be the inspired and infallible Word of God, and accept the New Testament as their rule of faith and practice. In the subtleties of speculative theology the church takes but little interest. She is chiefly concerned in giving willing and cheerful obedience to the plain, simple commandments of Christ Jesus. The Brethren are, in every respect, evangelical in their faith. They believe in the Trinity, in the divinity of Christ and of the Holy Spirit, and in future rewards and punishments. Faith, repentance, and baptism are held to be conditions of salvation. These three constitute true evangelical conversion, and upon them rests the promise of the forgiveness of sins and the gift of the Holy Ghost.

BAPTISM

Baptism is administered by trine immersion. After being instructed in the principles of the Gospel, and having faithfully promised to observe the same, the applicant is taken down into the water, and, kneeling, reaffirms his faith in Christ and promises to live faithful until death. He is then baptized for the remission of his sins, into the name of the Father, and of the Son, and of the Holy Ghost; the administrator immersing the applicant face forward at the mention of each name in the Trinity. The administrator then lays his hands on the head of the kneeling candidate and offers a brief prayer in behalf of the one baptized, and he rises to be greeted as a brother, with the right hand of fellowship and the kiss of love, to walk in newness of life.

The Brethren follow closely the practice of the apostolic church, and admit none into fellowship until they have been baptized. In the language of Peter to the Penticostians they tell all believers to "repent, and be baptized in the name of Jesus Christ for the remission of sins, and ye shall receive the gift of the Holy Ghost." Acts 2: 38. Holding that baptism is only for believers, and those who have repented, they oppose infant baptism. Infants can neither believe nor repent, hence they are not proper subjects for baptism. Christ having sufficiently atoned for them, all children who die before coming to a knowledge of good and evil will be saved.

In defense of trine immersion they hold that the great commission, given by Christ, and recorded in Matt. 28: 19, Revised Version, "Baptizing them into the name of the Father, and of the Son, and of the Holy Ghost," teaches a threefold action. As there are three persons in the Trinity, each one of the Divine Three is honored in this form of baptism. As the three Persons constitute one God, and a belief in each of these one faith, so the three dippings constitute one baptism. In favor of their practice they have the testimony of all Greek scholars, who have examined the subject, the practice of the entire Greek church, and reliable history. These all show that trine immersion was the almost universal mode of baptism for centuries succeeding the apostolic age. Changes were gradually made from trine immersion to sprinkling, but the church that made the change, the Roman Catholic, still retains the three actions in applying water to the candidate. Nearly all the Protestant churches that practice sprinkling, retain the same form, thus testifying to the truth that the commission teaches a threefold action in baptism. Their baptism is accepted as valid by all religious denominations of any note whatever.

THE AGAPE, OR FEAST OF LOVE

The evening before his death, our Blessed Master, after having washed his disciples' feet, ate a supper with them and instituted, in connection with this sacred meal, the Communion,—the bread and cup. The apostles, led by the Holy Spirit, followed the example of their Great Leader and introduced the agape into the apostolic church. This feast of love, of which all the Christians partook, was a full meal, was eaten in the evening, and is called by the apostle Paul the Lord's Supper. The Communion of the bread and wine was given in connection with this meal. The love-feast was kept up in the primitive church for four centuries, but as the church grew in numbers and wealth, it lost its first love and spirit of fraternity, and the feasts of love were discontinued. The Brethren, in their reformatory movement in 1708 restored these love-feasts, and in this particular still follow the example of Christ and the practice of the apostles and primitive Christians, and keep the feast of love. A full meal is prepared and placed upon tables, used for that purpose, in the church, and all the members partake of the supper.

Before eating supper, the religious rite of washing feet is observed. Their authority for this practice is found in John 13: 1–17, "He riseth from supper, and laid aside his garments; and took a towel, and girded himself. After that he poureth water into a basin, and began to wash the disciples' feet, and to wipe them with the towel wherewith he was girded. . . . If I then, your Lord and Master, have washed your feet; ye also ought to wash one another's feet. For I have given you an example, that ye should do as I have done to you." The Brethren do not stand alone in the practice of this rite. The Greek church, with ninety million communicants, has adhered to feet-washing, as she claims, ever since the days of the apostles, and the patriarch of Jersusalem engages in feet-washing to-day near the spot where Jesus himself gave the example and the precept.

In their practice of the ordinance of feet-washing at love-feast occasions the Brethren follow very closely the example of the Master. Water is poured into a basin, a brother girds himself with a towel and washes and wipes his brother's bared feet, and in turn has his feet washed. The rite is in this way performed over the entire congregation. The sisters wash the sisters' feet and all the proprieties of the sexes are most rigidly observed. By this ordinance the Gospel principle of humility is set forth and by its observance all are placed on a common level. The rich and poor stand alike together in the great Brotherhood established by Christ.

After observing the ceremony of feet-washing, a blessing is asked upon the simple meal spread on the tables, and it is eaten with solemnity. It is held to be typical of the great supper at the end of the world, when Christ himself will be master of ceremonies. The important lesson is taught that we are all children of one common family, members of one common brotherhood, having one common purpose in view, and the bond of fraternity and loving fellowship is shown by eating together this sacred meal as did Christ and his disciples and as did the primitive Christians. At the conclusion of the meal thanks are returned and then, as the members are seated around the table, the right hand of fellowship and the kiss of charity are given. The salutation of the kiss of love in worship and in customary greetings, as enjoined by the apostles, is never observed between the sexes.

The Communion is then administered. This consists in partaking of the bread and wine in commemoration of the sufferings and death of our adorable Redeemer. In the Lord's Supper we are pointed forward to the evening of the world, to the great reunion of the saints. In the Communion we are pointed back to the cross. The emblems are passed from hand to hand by the brethren, while the officiating minister breaks the bread and passes the cup to the sisters. After this a season of earnest devotion follows, and then a hymn is sung and the services are closed for the evening. Love-feasts are held in each congregation usually once or twice each year, but as the members visit from congregation to congregation, during the love-feast season, they engage many times in this service during the year. . . .

They, in compliance with the instruction of the apostle, James, 5: 14, 15, anoint the sick with oil. This rite is administered only by the request of the sick. The elders are called and the sick member is raised to a sitting posture. The elder applies the oil to the head three times, saying, "Thou art anointed in the name of the Lord unto the strengthening of thy faith, unto the comforting of thy conscience, and unto a full assurance of the remission of thy sins." The elders then lay their hands on the head of the sick, and offer a prayer for the anointed one.[2]

BAPTISM

A satirical account, entitled "A Puzzled Dutchman," provides an introduction to the discussion of baptism. It was not written by a Brethren, but was printed as a tract by J. H. Moore and M. M. Eshelman, Lanark, Carroll Co., Ill., both prominent writers and publishers.

A Wisconsin paper contains the following good story:

One who does not believe in immersion for baptism was holding a protracted meeting, and one night preached on the subject of baptism.—In the course of his remarks he said, some believe it necessary to go down into the water, and come up out of it, to be baptized. But this he claimed to be a fallacy, for the preposition "into" of the Scriptures should be rendered differently, as it does not mean into at all times. "Moses," he said, "we are told, went up into a high mountain, etc. Now we do not suppose that either went into the mountain, but upon it. So with going into the water, it means simply going down close by or near to the water, and being baptized in the ordinary way by sprinkling.

He carried this idea out fully, and in due season and style closed his discourse, when an invitation was given to any one who felt disposed to rise and give his thoughts. Quite a number of the brethren arose and said that they were glad that they had been present on the occasion, that they were pleased with what they had just heard, and felt their souls greatly blessed. Finally a corpulent gentleman of Teutonic extraction, a stranger to all, arose and broke a silence that was most painful as follows:

"Mister Breacher, I ish so glat I vash here tonight, for I has had explained to my mind some things I never could beleif pefore. We read, Mister Breacher, that Taniel vas cast into the den of lions, and came out alife! Now I never could pelief dat, for de wilt peasts would shust eat him right off; put now it ish ferry clear to my mind, he was shust close py or near to, and did not get into de den at all. O, I vash so glad I vas here tonight!

Again we reat dat de Hebrew children vas cast into de firish furnace, and dat air always looked like a big story too, for they would have been purnt up; put it ish all plain to my mind now, for they were shust cast close py or near the firish furnace. O, I vash so glat I vas here tonight!

And den, Mister Breacher, it is said dat Jona vash cast into de sea and into de whalish pelly. Now I never could pelief dat. It seems like a peeg feesh story, put it is all plain to me now, he vash not taken into de whalish pelly at all, put shust shumped onto his pack and rode ashore. O, I vash so glat I vash here tonight!

And now, Mister Breacher, if you will shust exblain two more bassages of Scripture, I shall be O so habby, dat I vash here tonight! One of dem is vere it saish de vicked shall be cast into a lake dat burns mit fire and primshtone alvays. O, Mister Breacher, shall I be cast into that lake, if I am vicked, or shust close by, shust near enough to be comfortable? O, I hope you tell me, I shall be cast shust by a good vay off, and I vill pe so glat I vash here tonight.

The other bassage is that which saish, Blessed are dey who do these commandments, dat dey may have a right to the tree of life, and enter in through the gates into the city. O! tell me I shall get into the city and not shust close py, or near to, shust near enough to see what I have lost, and I shall be so glad I vas here tonight.[3]

This brief tract on baptism is similar to the multitude of materials Brethren were writing on this subject. Out of all of the material on the subject of baptism, one significant tract has been selected for inclu-

sion in this chapter. One reason for its selection was that it was delivered originally as a sermon, and printed nineteenth century Brethren sermons are rare. It was evidently taken down stenographically when it was delivered in the Elk Lick congregation in Somerset County, Pennsylvania, and prepared for publication by Howard Miller in 1877. Another reason for its inclusion was that it was delivered by S. H. Bashor, one of the leading Brethren preachers of the day. And a third reason was that it covered the subject quite excellently for its length.

PART FIRST

It is a conceded fact among all believers, that the only way to salvation is through Christ, and that he is the only author and finisher of the faith of Heaven's redeemed. By and through the knowledge from the revelation He has given us, we learn what is requisite to eternal life, and the only way we gain this eternal life is by complying, in full faith, with His requisitions.

It makes no difference what men believe, or what they preach, the truth will still stand for or against them. It is commonly said, that if we are honest, and our position be incorrect, our honesty makes it right. No so. Truth is not changed by our opinions. Anything that is right is right within itself, because God's word makes it right, and all our believing will not affect it. The combined powers of hell and earth will never change the laws of God or the truths of the Bible.

Jesus founded on earth a church, and gave in it certain ordinances that through their literal observance his people could gain the spiritual food, that will develop the soul into humbleness and meekness, and at last by conquering the flesh, can rise to a habitation above. These external ordinances are fully set forth in the Bible. And after Jesus had finished the work of redemption, he came unto his disciples, and said: "All power is given unto me in heaven and earth"; and in consideration, or by virtue, of the authority vested in him, he further said: "Go teach all nations, baptizing them in the name of the Father, and of the Son, and of the Holy Ghost." You will notice here that Jesus said, "go and baptize," and by the word "baptize," he aimed to convey an *idea,* and that idea implied a definite action that was so understood and practiced by those to whom it was addressed, and just what was meant and practiced as baptism of eighteen hundred years ago, is just what should be done to-day. Upon this we all agree. The question is not, whether it should be a water baptism or not, for upon this we all agree, but as to what this action is, is where we differ. There is a difference among us on this subject, and though this be so, this difference does not arise from a want of honesty on the part of any of us, but from the force of our educational surroundings, or a misconception of the Gospel upon the subject, or both.

I do not purpose to unchristianize any one, or to injure the feelings of one person. That is not my desire, but only to set forth the faith and practice of the German Baptist church on this subject. To use an expression more forcible than elegant, I am not intending a destruction of your spiritual dwelling-places, but if I can erect a better one by its side, will you not come and live with us? There are differences in our midst, and the only way by which we can arrive at a unanimity of sentiment, is to reason together. Some are so prejudiced that they will not reason upon this subject, and become angry, thereby leaving grave doubts as to the desire of such to obtain the truth. *Christians* never get angry on the subject of religion. And again, a man who will not reason reminds the thoughtful person of a tree with its limbs all on one side. Let us, in the spirit of love, reason together, and learn the safest and surest way to follow the full commands of Jesus. We differ on this subject, baptism, more than upon all others, and this difference was never made by the Master, for he prayed with his disciples that they should all be one, and so declare the Scriptures positively. God's people must all be of one mind, of one judgment, see eye to eye, and speak the same thing. Hence it is not likely that the true Son of God would institute in his church an ordinance that would create divisions among the people. Yet upon this subject we differ and contend, thereby doing more to the strengthening of sin and the cause of division, than to the glory of God. We, as a people, believe and practice differently from all other Protestants, the ordinance of baptism. And now, dear friends, if the position we take is correct, the Bible will sustain it. If the Bible will not sustain us, we are wrong. It does not make any difference what ministers say, or commentators write, or our people believe.

First, then, while others believe that by the word baptize Jesus meant to sprinkle, to pour, or to immerse, or all three, we believe that he meant to immerse, and that such observance alone was to be practiced in all ages until time is no more.

Our first argument in support of this position is drawn from the word itself. Jesus spoke in the Greek language, using the word "*baptizo,*" the primary meaning of which is admitted by all scholars of any note to be "to immerse, to plunge, to overwhelm." Those to whom this was addressed were illiterate, and they certainly would only get the primary meaning of the word, and in fact this is the only true meaning the word has out of a remote usage. Baptize is taken from *bapto,* the root, which has only three definitions, "to immerse, to overwhelm, or to dye by dipping," and it is a fact that the body of anything must be composed of the same substance as the root. Suppose we go through the forest and find a tree blown down. We examine the roots and find them to be walnut; what would we think on finding the stem covered by cherry bark surrounding hickory wood, bearing apple leaves and peach limbs? Would you not justly regard that a kind of botanical anomaly? But if you found walnut roots you are certain of finding walnut wood, bark and limbs. It is just the same when you go to language. If you find the root of a word to imply one thing, and the body or word itself to mean five or six other things, you have a philological curiosity. And in the absence of any knowledge of the Greek, the English alone would prove that immersion is a full baptism, for there are passages of Scripture where sprinkle or pour will not make good sense. Take for instance, Mark 1: 5, 6; "Then went out to him Jerusalem and all Judea, and all the region round about Jordan, and were baptized of him in Jordan." Now rendering the word sprinkle, it would read that all these people were "sprinkled of him in Jordan," which rendition is neither acceptable nor agreeable. That the ceremony consisting of pouring, of him in the Jordan, is equally unacceptable. Again, use the clause, "immersed of him in Jordan," and we have a construction at once agreeing with fact and sense. The point I wish to make is just this. You cannot sprinkle a man in Jordan, and that is the way it would read, were it "sprinkled of him in Jordan." That would have rather scattered things, would it not? "Well, but," says one, "we sprinkle clothes, and that conveys the same idea, and a correct one." Certainly it does, but it does convey the idea of sprinkling them in the river, or in other words, scattering them in the river, and not the one of sprinkling water. And if he poured them in Jordan, I suppose he must have got them in a vessel and poured them out. You see the point I wish to make. Now I suppose he could with propriety immerse them in Jordan, which he did.

They claim to pour, to sprinkle, to immerse and nine other definitions are given to this one verb baptizo expressing both action and effect, and I ask this intelligent audience who ever heard of a verb expressing both action and effect when used in one and the same construction? Verbs express action alone when used as such, and express a result or effect only when they are used as nouns, and then the difference is so apparent, that there is no danger of a misunderstanding. There are scholars here, and I leave you to ask them and their conscience, knowledge and the word of God to decide. Say, for instance, the word "walk" means to hop, to step, to jump, then a man could not walk until he could do all three. And if the word "talk" meant to laugh, to cry, and to halloo, it would be impossible for a man to have talked until he had done all three. Just so, if the word "baptize" means to sprinkle, to pour, and to immerse, as pedo-baptists say, a man is not baptized until he is immersed, sprinkled and poured. So much for this argument.

Our second argument is founded on the practice of the apostles proved from passages of Scripture, which we will consider in their proper connection. These men certainly understood what was meant by baptize, for along with the literal meaning of the word they had the Divine Spirit to lead them to truth. The first passage to which I will call your attention, to prove that immersion was the practice of the apostles, is the 21st verse of the 2nd chapter of 1st Peter. Turn over to the next chapter and by reading the 18th, 19th and 20th verses, you will find that Peter is speaking of the antedeluvians, and of being saved by water, "The like figure by which water doth now save us (not the putting away of the filth of the flesh) but the answer of a good conscience toward God." We learn by this that some had gained an incorrect idea of the rite of baptism. There were men, who, seeing the ordinance performed with the natural eye, and not understanding the spiritual import of it, gained the idea that it was for the cleansing of the flesh. Suppose pouring or sprinkling had been the mode practiced, then, would it have associated with its use such an idea? No, never: from the fact that in sprinkling but a few drops of water are placed on the head. The same is characteristic of pouring, and so little as only to wet the forehead, would never have conveyed to them such thoughts. But when they saw the apostles take the candidates for the administration of the rite down into the water, and dip them *beneath* the wave, they, as remarked, not understanding the spiritual import of it, but looking at it naturally, said it was to wash away the filth of the flesh, Peter says it is not true. Though we do wash the whole body in water, it is not to cleanse it, but for the gaining of, or the answer of a good conscience toward God. The Scriptures say, that in the mouth of two or three witnesses every word shall be established. We have one. Turn now for another, to Hebrews 10: 22, where Paul says, "Let us draw near with a true heart in full assurance of faith, having our hearts washed from an evil conscience, and our bodies sprinkled with pure water." My brother says I read wrong. I will try again. "Having our hearts *sprinkled* from an evil conscience, and our bodies *washed* with pure water." Now it is a fact that Paul is here speaking of baptism. I ask, would sprinkling or pouring suit Paul? It suits some of us very well now-a-days, but would it suit that old preacher back there, close to Jesus? Let us see. In pouring or sprinkling only a little water is placed on the head, as before stated. The head is not the body; hence nothing short of washing the whole body would suit Paul, and as sprinkling and pouring would not suit the man of God, and as they do not wash the whole body, then there remains only the ordinance as practiced by us. Will you go with Paul, friends, and believe and practice as he did? If that is your mind throw away your incorrect ideas, and have the body washed, figuratively speaking. Again we go to Rom. 6: 4, and find there that we are to be buried in baptism. "Hold! Mr. Bashor," some one says, "that means the spiritual baptism." How do you know? I ask. "Why," says the objector, "there is nothing said about water." Just as a man said to a minister some time ago: "You cannot find one drop of water here, and as you cannot, how can you prove water baptism?" "Well," said the minister, "it is said by Paul that Jesus died for us. Now how did he die?" Oh! that is easy enough proven," said the friend. "He was crucified." "That," said the minister, "is just how I know this is water baptism spoken of here. I go back and see where the act is recorded, and there find it to be water. So when it is referred to here, I learn by the history of its action what it is here."

Now to the point. In order to understand what the apostle means by the word "bury," it is necessary to know what the word meant at the time of its delivery to the people. Paul wrote to the Romans who burned their dead, and placed the ashes in an earthen vase beneath the ground; consequently to them the idea of a covering up, or burial, was conveyed, as a similar use would to any mind to-day. We say a man is buried. The idea conveyed is that he was placed in and beneath the earth. Yet people will be so inconsistent when it comes to being "buried with Christ," in baptism? If it takes enough earth to cover a man completely to form a burial, pray be consistent enough, to not use a less amount of water in a burial by baptism into Christ. Will you, or will you not? Now just be honest for once, and see where you stand.

I will, for once, refer to authors of note among the pedo-baptist denominations, to show that we are not alone in this view of the subject. Your own men contradict, in their writings, what they preach to make you believe and practice. I now call your attention to Dr. McKnight, a learned Doctor of Divinity. In his notes on this chapter he says, (Rom. 6: 4—"Buried in baptism"): "Christ's baptism was not the baptism of repentance, for he never committed sin. But he submitted to be baptized, that is, to be buried under the water by John, and to be raised out-again as an emblem of his future death and resurrection. In like manner the baptism of believers is emblematical of their death, burial and resurrection. Perhaps also it is a commemoration of Christ's baptism." Then in verse 5th, he says:—"planted together," etc.—"The burial of Christ and believers, from first in the waters of baptism, and afterwards in the earth, is fitly enough compared to the planting of seeds, because the effect in both cases is a reviviscence of a greater perfection." I quote this to show how a man, when expressing his own opinion gathered from his knowledge of primitive Christianity, the Bible and the design of the ordinance, will stand up in favor of immersion even though he, himself, does not practice it. Thus you see that learned pedo-baptist divines declare, when not in debate, that immersion is taught in this chapter. Also, John Wesley, the founder of the Methodist church, in his notes on this same Scripture says: "The allusion is to the ancient manner of baptism by immersion." So you see when Paul talked of being buried in baptism, he conveys the idea of an immersion, or a complete burial of the body in water in baptism.

"Well, but," says some one, "the Scripture says baptize *with* water, and of course, if we do that we must sprinkle or apply the water to the subject." The Scriptures say that the sacrifice was burned with fire. Have you any idea how that was done? I suppose, and so do you, that the sacrifice was placed in the fire. We say thresh wheat with a machine, but we place the wheat in the machine, and not the machine in the wheat. In dying a garment it is immersed, submerged, in the liquid, and not sprinkled or poured, but we say it is dyed with the liquid, which implies an immersion. So with cleansing clothing by a washing process. The statement that they are washed with water, means on the face of it, that the garments so cleansed were necessarily immersed in the water. Just so when John the Baptist baptized in Jordan. Of what was Jordan composed? Why, of water. Well, John took people in the Jordan, in the water, and baptized them *with* water, just in the sense of washing a garment, metaphorically speaking. Any child on reading the history of baptism in the Bible will infer that immersion is taught. Some years ago a learned pedo-baptist minister, on concluding a series of meetings, found seventy applicants for baptism, and they, on being interrogated, were willing to submit to sprinkling, but one, a very wealthy lady, said she wanted to be immersed as Jesus was. She, too, like her Master wanted to go down into the water. "Well," said the learned teacher, "this might have done years ago when people knew no better, and will do yet for vulgar persons, but decent people do not go *into* the water to-day." The lady, not withstanding his objections on the ground of decency, still persisted in her desire to be immersed. And as her wealth and influence were worth something to the church, he told her to come next day, and he would discourse on the subject, and if he failed to convince her, she should be immersed. At the appointed time he entered the pulpit, and began his sermon, taking for his text, the 8th chapter of Acts, on the conversion of the Eunuch, when he came to the 39th verse where it is said, "they both went down in to the water, both Philip and the Eunuch, and he baptized him," "What troubles me is, I don't know which was baptized, for it says, 'he baptized him.' Now we have a case of immersion here to-day, but according to the precedent I don't know if I am to baptize my sister or if she is to baptize me. If some one will explain this I will then know how to do the work." The lady listened with attention until he was through, then with a troubled expression on her face, went home. On her way she met old aunt Dinah, a colored woman of the Baptist persuasion, who came running to meet her, saying, "Don't you feel good now since you are baptized into Christ? Folks always do." "No," said the lady, "I was not baptized." "Why?" asked aunt Dinah. Then the lady related the preacher's discourse when he said he could not tell which was baptized, Philip or the Eunuch. "Well," replied the colored sister, "if you will show me that preacher, I will tell him who was baptized." "Who?" asked the lady. "Why," says old aunt Dinah, "the one who wanted to be." Here we have a case of immersion granted by a learned divine, and an old colored lady telling how it was done. I only relate this in answer to an argument offered by thousands of silly people, who do so in the absence of something better to bear them up in the practice of sprinkling.

Now one more thought and then I am done, and that is this: If Jesus Christ had intended to command sprinkling or pouring, could he not have used language plainer than the words used? Certainly. If he would have said pour or sprinkle we would have accepted it, and performed the ordinance in that manner. But if he meant to command immersion, could he have done it in language plainer than that used? Certainly not, as the only true definition of both the root and derivative *bapto* and *baptizo* mean to immerse; therefore Christ commanded immersion, and if Christ had introduced sprinkling, men would have not likely ever dreamed of immersion, as we are all the time seeking things easier than the way we have them. Jesus commanded immersion, but around the bed of an afflicted man, in the year A. D. 250, a council of bishops reduced it to pouring, believing that they had the power to change God's laws. This proves it of human invention. It never fell from the lips of Jesus Christ, nor was it practiced by the church. If it was, why did it have to receive the sanction of popes and bishops before it could be practiced by the church? Then after a while they went a little futher, and said that sprinkling would do, as the quantity of water had nothing to do with it; and now men have become so liberal as to get to heaven on dry land, or, in other words, without baptism at all.

Now, in conclusion, listen while I tell you that you stand on the shore and expose your ignorance and contempt for immersion while others are being baptized, yet, after the laugh is over, you will take us by the hand as children of God. You admit in your practice that we are Christians, too, and are God's elect; but your tongues condemn your practice. Then according to your practice we will ready the portal of heaven with you. And if we be right in our practice where will you appear? God help us all. When you laugh at us for immersing, you are laughing at Jesus Christ, at the apostles and even at your own fathers. Paul thought, when he was doing evil to the church, that it was only a few ignorant fisherman that he was persecuting, but the Lord came down in the majesty of his glory and proved that he, Jesus of Nazareth, King of heaven, was the recipient of all the afflictions of his people. Just so with your laughing at us, as you did today at the water. Not only at us, but at your own fathers and mothers, who are dead long ago and gone to rest, and at Jesus, and all the holy men of ages gone by, when amid storms and persecutions, and amid the rumble and roar of the waters of death they fought the battle, and came out victorious in the world above. It is not the amount of water that we want, but the complete obedience to God's word. Paul says, "One Lord, one faith, and one baptism." Now which will you take of the three? They cannot all be one. Sprinkling is not pouring, neither is pouring sprinkling, nor immersion either of them. They are three and must be three baptisms. Paul condemns two of them. Which will you drop? those instituted by man or the one introduced by Christ?

I will now close on baptism, asking you to give what I have said a serious thought, and if the Bible teaches differently, don't accept the baptism I teach, but if it is the word of the Lord, take it and practice it, and eternal life will be the result. To those out of Christ I say, come to Him and live. Paul in speaking to the Corinthians of certain ones sporting, out of the Lord, in the gayeties of life, says that they are dead while they live. Just think of the beautiful young bodies, loved and respected by all around them, having their minds in the channels of pride and vanity, all dead to God, dead to heaven, dead to all that is holy and good; and young men, who can do a vast amount of good, living and yet dead! Man was created in the image of God, but he lost that image through the fall, and he never can regain it only in Christ. Then, I say, come, dear friends, this morning and be planted in full faith in Christ and in the living quickening power of God. Grow up, and live. Dead out of Christ! Oh, what a thought! You say you injure no one; you are a moral man. If not injuring others you are ruining yourself. You are dead and out of Christ, and cannot regain what you lost only in Him. Come then and be planted in Him by faith, repentance and baptism, and grow up in grace, imitate him in all his ways, talk more like he talked, walk more like he walked, and weep like he wept, and heaven will be your eternal home. In the old church-yard sleep dear friends. You remember the time they grasped you by the hand in death, and whispered, "Meet me in heaven." You said you would, but you are out of Christ yet. Come and live with us the life they did and die in the Lord as he did, and over your grave will sound the same sweet voice of the Spirit: "Blessed are they that die in the Lord." Their labors are over and rest is found. I know you have good hearts, too good to give to the world, and Jesus loves you. Will you, will you, come with us this morning? "The Spirit and the bride say, Come, and whosoever will, let him come and partake of the waters of life freely." To the Father, Son and Holy Ghost be praise, now and forevermore. Amen.

PART SECOND

We now come in contact with another class, who, like ourselves, believe immersion alone to be baptism, yet differ in regard to how it is to be performed. They believe and practice single immersion as baptism, while we believe that not one, but three immersions constitute the baptism of the Bible. I used to go with my sister to see the Dunkards baptize people, and then I thought their way was wrong, for Paul in Eph. 4: 5, told me that there was only one Lord, one faith, and one baptism, and I thought if Paul was right the Dunkards were wrong; for he says one baptism, and they, I thought, had three, but after searching in lexicons and other books, I found that Paul did not say what I supposed he did. I thought he said one immersion, but he didn't say that; if he had brethren, our doctrine would easily be proven to be wrong. He, just like Jesus, spake in the Greek, and we must get the idea conveyed by him in the same way as if we lived in that age and understood the language as he did. He did not say one Lord, one faith, and one immersion, he did not use *bapto* or *baptizo.* If he had it would be one immersion, and we could not dispute it; that would be the way alone, and our baptism would be wrong, but when Paul spake he used a larger word than either *bapto* or *baptizo,* which as we stated would be one dip. He said one *baptisma,* one dipping. The difference is about this: if I say one strike, one motion of the hand will fill the word, but if, like Paul, I add the suffix ing, it would be one striking, and more than one motion of the hand would be not only allowable but would be fully expressed. Then the question arises: What gave rise to the Apostle's expression? Well turn with me, if you please, to Acts 19th chapter, and we find Paul at Ephesus among the same people to whom he is now writing. Here he finds certain disciples, says the word, and when he had found them, he asked the question: "Have you received the Holy Ghost since ye believed?" They said, "we haven't heard so much as to whether there be any Holy Ghost." "What? says Paul, "Then unto whose baptism were you baptized?" Paul did not ask them how they were baptized. Something else troubled him, and that was this, he knew that if they had been immersed by John they would have heard of the Holy Ghost, for he taught all his disciples that Christ when he comes would bring that with him. Matth. 3:11. Also he knew they were not baptized by Christ, for he taught his disciples that the Comforter would come not many days after, and Paul knew they could not have been baptized by either of these and be so ignorant concerning this matter. And more than this, he also knew that all who were immersed of the apostles, had received the Spirit, hence the query, "Unto what baptism were ye baptized." There was trouble somewhere and the preacher desired to find out where it was. Then they replied unto John's baptism. They did not say they were baptized by John, only said unto his baptism.

And now if you read the latter part of the eighteenth chapter you will find one Apollos, a mighty man in the Scriptures, but knowing only the way of John, was down here preaching, and when he was found by Aquilla and Priscilla, they took him and taught him more perfectly. They did not baptize him again, for he was baptized by John a proper administrator; they only instructed him or taught him the full revelation of God, which he knew but imperfectly. The idea I wish to introduce is just this, Apollo was baptized by John; afterward, being a man of enthusiasm, he, like many others, even to-day, went without any authority and began to teach others what he knew and to baptize them. Well, but says some one, could not John have authorized him? I say no, for John's mission was confined within himself, and he alone it was that was to prepare the way before Christ; and when Paul knew this baptism was administered by some one he rebaptized them and laid his hands on them and they received the Holy Ghost. The point is here, after a while those brethren at Ephesus talked this matter over, and the question arose, Why did Paul show this partiality? You were baptized by John, and we were baptized unto his baptism, only we by Apollos and you by John. That is all the difference. Why is this? We think Paul shows a difference. It is true, Paul could say, you are baptized alike, but Apollos being unauthorized invalidates your baptism, and the reason I rebaptized you is because we have only one Lord, one faith, and one baptism. If I had left you come in as you were, we would have two, one that was authorized and one that was not. Some have come to me and said, brother Bashor, I would join your church, but I can't be baptized over, just as if sprinkling or pouring was baptism. I ask them why? They say our preacher says we would commit an unpardonable sin if we let you baptize us. Well, Paul says in another place that by one spirit we are all baptized into one body even as ye are called in one hope of your calling, and I say we are the body of Christ, and if you ever get in with us you must be baptized with us, for we have but one baptism, performed but one way and by one class of men, and that is those who are authorized by the church. It takes a wonderful amount of ignorance I might say, to keep poor souls in a church by teaching them such doctrine as this, that they sin against the Holy Ghost in being baptized. I often wonder how men can stand up in the fact of this record of Acts 19th, and talk about sinning against the Holy Ghost! There is just one of two things about the matter. Either Paul was wrong, and he and these twelve disciples were lost, or our modern teachers are sinning by such teaching, or Paul was right. I always prefer to follow the safest men. Paul was working for Christ, and was moved by the Holy Spirit, and he did this to set us a plain example, and if it was right then it is now. I know he knew more of salvation than we do. Just one more thought and I am done with this. The Bible says, that which is not of faith is sin, and the person that lives in any other church and has no faith in their baptism, and has in ours, they will live in sin until they change.

It is certainly not wrong to do what is right, and if you see ours to be right, it is your duty to be baptized, let the preacher say what he pleases. I left the main issue, but trust I will be pardoned for the digression. We now offer another reason used by some, for Paul's expression in Eph. 4: 5. Divisions came up among the brethren, and some said I am of Paul and another of Apollos, and another of Christ, but the apostle says we must all be one; one Lord, one faith, one baptism for all, both jew and gentile, bond and free, and not as your action would indicate. He is not arguing about the mode, but is speaking of the ordinance, just as we say in common parlance, that we the Brethren have but one baptism. This conveys a perfect idea to the people, our single immersionist brethren, as well as others, yet no one would presume to suppose that by this we mean one dip in the act of baptism, but would only be understood as referring to the ordinance itself, as only being performed by us as believers one way, and so I understood Paul, and so he means one baptism or one dipping. Then when this matter was settled, I turned to 1 John 5: 7, 8. There I read, "There are three that bear record in heaven, the Father, the Word, and the Holy Spirit, and these three are one," and I also read in John 17: 21, and other places where Jesus said he and the Father were one, and I thought certainly if they are all one, what is the use of dipping a man three times to put him into this one God; but by a careful investigation I learned that they were one in a certain sense, and three in still a different sense. Then if we can find out in what sense they are one, and in what sense they are three, and then learn the true sense in which they are presented to us in the commission, we will know just how to baptize. First I must assert that they are not one person in office, but three. Now for the proof, for you know assertion is worth nothing unless it is proven. Go with me back eighteen hundred years and over, and we will follow the vast throng out to Jordan and standing by its waters we listen to the voice of the wonderful man of the wilderness declaring the way of the Lord, and while we listen his sweet voice is heard lisping the words of heavenly love. There is some one pushing his way through the congregation, a man called Jesus of Nazareth. There is something peculiarly attractive about the conversation as he approaches the prophet. He asks to be baptized. What do we hear? The prophet refuses, but the stranger persists, and they go down into the water, not *to* it, for they are already near it; *into* the water they go, and while all look on with a strange interest, the baptism is performed, and they come up out of the water. All is over we think, but hark! What is this! Look! yonder comes the spirit of God in the form of a dove, and like lightning it speeds downward and abides on the Master. Wonder of wonders. Nothing so strange ever transpired in Israel.

While we tremble at this wonderful manifestation, there is heard from the depths of his heavenly habitation, thrilling the soul, as it declares in thunder tones breaking the stillness of the wilderness, and silencing the ripple of Jordan, "this is Jesus the long looked for; this is the Redeemer; this is the Shilo of ancient promise; this is the crowned heir to immortal life." This is demonstrated today by John himself to be the peace maker of God and succorer of Jacob's posterity. Peace is to come and joy in him. But I forbear. Now then what do we have? Jesus on the banks of the Jordan, the Holy Spirit in the air, and the Father in heaven. Here they are set before us, not by men but by God himself, not as one but as three persons, in three distinct relations. This will appear as we proceed. Then Jesus said, "My father is greater than I," and over in that old garden of Gethsemane he knelt and prayed, saying to the Father, "Not my will but thine be done." This shows that while Jesus had a will of his own, independent of the Father's, he was subject to the will of the Father. Whose was the greater of the two? Now turn to John's gospel 15: 26, and Jesus says, "I will send unto you from the Father the spirit of truth." Also in Luke 24: 49 he says, "The power is to come from on high, which will be said by the Father and himself." So you see they are three in person and occupy three positions. The Father back in the garden of Eden devises a plan of redemption for man, when he was an alien. Then he sends the Son. The Son comes and tells us of the way to life, and dying on the cross redeems us. Then over the cross he hangs, a deep shudder, one terrible quiver, and the work is finished. Then when he leaves us he sends the Holy Spirit to bring to the remembrance of his people all the beautiful things he told for our instruction, consolation, salvation to comfort his people in all ages, and amid affliction's trials to give us the victory of life over death. Here are the three grand offices held by the divine personages, but one in creation, redemption, and preservation. We illustrate further; say for instance we get three apples from the same tree, the same twigs and limb, and bring them here and lay them on the table, one here, here, and here. Then I ask some of these little folks how many apples have we? They, all that can count, will say three. Well, but, says a brother, three apples you see, they are only one. How can that be say the little ones, why says he, they are three in distinction; they occupy three places on the table, and they grew on three different twigs, but they look alike, smell and taste alike, and in essence they are one; one in color, one in variety, one in size, one in flavor, but three in distinction. Just take the Father, Son and Holy Spirit. They are one in love, one in glory, one in mercy, one in justice, one in judgment, one in the welfare of man, but three in person and in office, relative to man's creation, redemption and justification. Take another illustration, for I want to make the subject clear. Say, for instance, that we the people of the United States are governed by one great power. But this one power is composed of three minor powers, the Legislative, the Judiciary and the Executive. The power of the Legislative is different from either the Judiciary or Executive, and they each differ from the other, but we all know they constitute one grand unit among the governments of nations. The three great powers of the Divine government are devising a plan of redemption and commanding it to be carried out, another doing his work, and the last keeping it in the minds of the people, preparing them for the soft death notes preparatory for victory.

Now I think I have clearly shown the distinction existing between the three, if we pursue the same course of thought previously referred to. The next point to find out is how this great trinity is presented to us in the commission, and then we will know how to baptize into this trinity correctly. We will, to do this, refer to our text, "Go ye therefore into the world, teach all nations, baptizing them in *(into* if rendered correctly) the name of the Father, the Son, and the Holy Ghost." Here the Master you see, instead of presenting three in the sense in which they are one, presents them in their distinct relations and offices, and this is certainly the sense in which they are three. Believers are to be baptized into the name of the Father, and of the Son, and of the Holy Ghost. Whatever men may desire and practice, I can but accept the literal rendition of the Divine commission. Three distinct persons are presented, and the command implies three distinct actions, one into each person. There is not one passage in the New

Testament that can be filled with one action, and here I take my stand, with this piece of logic in my mouth, that I will change my faith, practice and teaching, if it can be shown, and the man who will show it to me will get a nice reward in his labor. I might give you an analysis of the commission according to the rules of language, but then those of you who are not scholars would not understand it, and those who are scholars can do so for themselves, and if they can make anything less than three sentences, I would like to see it. And if these three sentences can be filled without three actions in baptism, I should like very much indeed to see the process by which it is accomplished, or at least understand the theory of it.

I want to show now by a practical illustration of the text, that it cannot be performed without the three actions talked of before. Say that a brother is holding a meeting close here and he comes to me and says, brother Bashor, I am in trouble. Well, what is the nature of your trouble? I ask. Then he tells me that he wants some advice. He has a convert that wants to be baptized, and says nothing short of trine immersion will satisfy him, and says he, I am not just so well satisfied in regard to that mode, and do not feel at liberty to administer baptism that way, now what must I do? I tell him that if he will do just as I say in baptizing this man, I will be responsible for all the sin committed in the act, but remember you are to follow my instructions in full, or I will not be responsible. Well, he says, I will do just as you say if you will be accountable to God for all the sins committed. Thus agreeing we start to the water. Finding the applicant, he proceeds to the proper depth in the water. Then when he is ready, I say baptize that man in the name of the Father. The man hesitates. I tell him to remember the agreement, you do just what I tell you. And if he does what I commanded, he will have to dip him once: no more, no less. That being accomplished, I say, and of the Son, and if he does as I tell him, he will repeat the action. That done, I say, and of the Holy Ghost, here he will repeat the action again. I now tell him, the man is baptized. Now then, I have the responsibility of this baptism resting on me. This man was baptized by trine immersion, because I gave the command, and the way I gave it, it could not be performed any other way, so I go to the commission and see how Christ commanded it. Here he tells me to baptize in the name of the Father, that is just what I told the man to do at the water. Jesus further says, "and of the Son," so I told the man no more and no less, than Jesus commands by saying, "and of the Holy Ghost." That is just the same way I talked to the man. Now I promised to be responsible for the act, and I now throw it all on the shoulders of Christ, as I only followed his instructions. So you see by this illustration just where we stand in the sight of Christ when we baptize by trine immersion. Well, but, says some one, I can't see what is the use of three dips in baptism after all your talk? it shows to me that the three being one, Father, Son and Holy Spirit, one immersion of the body will be sufficient. Suppose this to be the case with some man, and he goes home, and in the morning his wife says, I believe trine immersion is right, and I think I will be baptized that way. Yes, but says the husband, that preacher last night failed to prove it, and I can't see for the life of me how it will take three immersions to place a man in one God, especially when the three are one. The argument grows warmer here, and after awhile neither one being convinced, the husband being busy is compelled to go to work. So leaving his wife to study over the matter, he starts to the field. After working until twelve o'clock, a half an hour after the usual time for the bell to ring, he gets uneasy. Half past twelve, still no bell. One o'clock, two o'clock, and he unhitches, goes home, and what is his astonishment to find his wife cooly sitting at her work. Wife, he says, I want my dinner. Why she says, dear husband, you have eaten your dinner. Not to day, he says, for I am as hungry as I can be. I don't care how hungry you are, you have had your dinner, and to-day, too, at that. If I had please tell me when I partook of it, says he. His wife begins, don't you remember that you said this morning that because the Father, the Son, and the Holy Spirit were one, that one dip would baptize a person into all three. I soon saw the point you made, then I went to the Bible for proof, and while reading there I came to the place where Christ says, "A man shall leave father and mother and shall cleave unto his own wife, and they shall no more be *twain* but *one* flesh." And I thought as you were very hungry to-day I would eat for you, so I got dinner and sat down and partook of it, and that did for you too, because we are one. I do not want you to laugh, but think, for there is something here for you to think about. This shows conclusively that the system of logic that will prove single immersion upon the ground of the oneness in the godhead will prove that a lady can eat for one year, and if the husband never eats one particle of food he will be perfectly healthy, as he and his wife are "one flesh," and that is what food is to satisfy.

Some say, how can three immersions be one. I reply by asking him can three persons be one God. Is there not the same reason for both, especially when this trine immersion is to take a man into this triune God. There is the same harmony in this that there is in all of God's works and commands. In order to be a child of the triune God, we become one in each of the parts of the trine godhead. We must get into the Father; and how? By being baptized into him, not as the Son, but as our Father. And we must get into the Son; and how? We are to be baptized into him, not as the Father or Holy Spirit. We are to get into the Holy Spirit by being baptized into him, not as the Father or Son, but as the Holy Ghost, our comforter and protector. The difference is just this: The single immersionist takes a candidate into the water, and says, "I baptize you in the name of the Father," but does nothing futher; and says, "and of the Son," and still does nothing; then says, "and of the Holy Ghost," and when this is said immerses the candidate. He says he will baptize into the Father, but fails to do what he says; and when he says, and of the Son, he does not do what he says any more than if I say I will strike John, and Silas, and Jonas, and only strike Jonas. When I say I will strike John, I do nothing, and Silas, and still remain inactive. Then say, and Jonas, and then strike, I come just as near telling the truth in this case as the man who talks about immersing into the Father, Son, and the Holy Spirit, and only immerse once. There is one more thought I wish to present in this command, and that is this: If Christ had intended to command single immersion, could he not have commanded it in language expressing it plainer than that he used? Certainly he could. If he had said, baptize those you teach in the name of God, you would have it stated in terms so plain that none could contend for more than single immersion; or if he would have said in the name of the Father, or of the Son, or of the Holy Spirit, more than one action would not be implied. But if he intended to command trine immersion, how could he have commanded it plainer than he did in the commission? When we understand the force of language we must acknowledge that he could not have done so. Therefore Christ commanded trine immersion. Some contend that trine baptism will compel us to return to the shore after each act, yet such call our mode but one baptism while they reject the idea that it is necessary for three acts. Yet in trine immersion we have the baptism of Paul in his letter to the Ephesians.

So far from being alone in the mode of baptism, we have all the ancient churches on our side, and they all pronounce our form according to the divine command. The Greek church of seventy millions, practice immersion as we do, and the Greek church is the oldest in the world so far as organic succession. Alexander Campbell making reference to this church says, "they practice the ancient mode of immersion," yet after the evidence afforded by seventy millions, it is a pity that he did not practice his belief.

The greatest theologians fully agree with us in respect to trine immersion, though they practice differently. Martin Luther in reference to a Jewess convert said, baptize her by the ancient, or trine mode. Also Pingilly in his defense of immersion, a man of some note among the Baptists, to prove his position, cites authors who testify in favor of a three-fold immersion. And Chrystal, a minister of the Episcopal church, in his history of "The Modes of Baptism," declares that all other modes are purely the invention of man. He says we have the true or original baptism, but being an Episcopalian, objects to us upon the ground of organic succession, and the ordinary Baptist who comes up claiming organic succession and writing histories tracing their church back, goes only a few hundred years until they run into a muddle by claiming the identity with the Waldenses, who, as all know, that are acquainted with history, were trine immersionists. If they are posterity, spiritually, of this church, they have terribly demoralized themselves in this particular. Jesus says, "He is my disciple that loves me and keeps my commandments." He did not say anything about if you can trace yourself back to me organically, but if I do the will of my Father in heaven I shall enter there. Matth. 7: 21. And I prefer to live in a church where I can do the will of the Father without organic succession, rather than in one where I can claim that, and be deprived of doing as Jesus commanded. Our salvation is not insured on the grounds of organic succession, for in the Bible there is not one word said about it, or even intimated, but it is promised on the grounds of faith and obedience. And the man who boasts of organic or any otther succession, should be just as deeply interested in preserving the primitive simplicity and identity in point of obedience to the commandments of God, as the judgment will rest on this according to the language of the Lord himself. On one depends salvation and on the other the Bible is silent. I might quote many learned men, of all ages, and each will decide in our favor. Tertullian, Polycarp, Jerome, Luther, and many others of learning and ability, and then here comes in a cloud of witnesses innumerable, seventy millions of living Christians besides all that wrote on the subject and passed away, leaving as living monuments their testimony, establishing beyond controversy the tenableness of our position on this subject.

Now a few more thoughts and I am done. I have been baptized by trine immersion, and if I go to any Pedo Baptist church, I will be received into fellowship without questioning the validity of my baptism. Then I might go to any Baptist organization, and here I can come in, they tell me your baptism is safe, and will take me by the hand as a brother in the Lord, thereby acknowledging the correctness of my baptism. They bid me go on, and tell me I am safe and according to their practice and faith, I too, will be enabled so far as baptism is concerned, to say like Paul, "I have fought a good fight, and kept the faith, henceforth there is a crown awaiting me." But if ours be right, which all acknowledge, I ask, is yours infallibly safe, are you sure? Let us go back in the past in search of the old way. Three of us can travel together. We go back to Luther, Calvin, and others, hear them say trine immersion is right, but the other will do, we think. Yes, say they, though we know trine immersion was the ancient and established mode, we are the authority only, if man will try the others. We still go back through the eighth, ninth, and eighteenth centuries, here we see the difference in the practice of the Baptist church. And a Baptist brother says, why, my fathers from whom I came, have immersed thrice instead of once, as we do. He is astonished at the change they have made. And our Methodist brother, who has been pleased so often by his simile to see his astonishment, while my faith grows stronger. We still go on farther, after a while we come to the seventh century, and here in the river some are baptizing by single immersion. The Baptist's face grows brighter. He says, here are my brethren who say they belong to the mother church, old Rome itself. He is puzzled. Still on a few years, and at the fourth council of Toledo, amid Bishops and Popes, single immersion receives its sanction for the first time by any ecclesiastical body on earth. Here we stop. The fine theory gone. We leave him standing alone looking after the two men he has laughed at and boasted over so long. We go on peacefully in the ages about three hundred and thirty-five years and our Baptist brother overtakes us again. He says single immersion was practiced here. We ask by whom? He tells us by Eunomius. We make inquiry and learn that his story is correct, but we further learn the fact that he was a heretic, and so considered by his people in that day. Here then we bid him a final farewell, three hundred and thirty years this side of the cross. We are sorry to do so, for he has been a pleasant companion, but his path ends and he must stop, while we go on. After a few more years of trouble, we come to the bed side of an afflicted man, and find that a council of Bishops is being held, to see if it will be admissable to baptize this man by any other way than the established mode, trine immersion, because it is supposed by them that in this man's present state of health it will be injurious to immerse him. This finally carries, and the man is poured upon and called baptized. This proves that it was never practiced before. If it was, why did it take a council of Bishops to grant its introduction here? I am now left alone, my Methodist brother has landed at his journey's end. Stopped two hundred years this side of Christ. I travel alone still on within thirty years of Christ's time, and still the way is clear. I go on and on until I stand by the side of Jesus on Bethany's hill and hear him say, "Go ye my disciples teach all nations, baptizing them in the name of the Father, and of the Son, and of the Holy Ghost." Here then, as shown before, is the beginning of the gospel mode of baptism in command, as it falls from the lips of Jesus in terms so plain that any man not governed by prejudice, must admit a three fold action. Any way you take the subject we are on safe ground. No one immersed by this mode has ever died dissatisfied; they are said to be safe by all. They live and die satisfied, while those who have been sprinkled and poured upon, and baptized by single immersion, are continually (many of them) uneasy in regard to their baptism, when they hear anything upon the subject, and when reading the history of baptism or the account of its command, or see it practiced. Now in conclusion, I leave the matter with you and the Lord, and ask you to study the matter carefully and prayerfully, and if you find we are right come over with us, and together we will go down to the silver streamlet as it flows silently through the grove, and secure your peace with God in that form of baptism that was commanded by Christ and practiced by his church, until man, poor sinful man, perverted it and was led astray. I want to meet you all in heaven, where the associations so pleasantly began here, will be renewed, and amid the celestial shades of Paradise, on the margin of the River of Life, we can talk with the redeemed of all ages of redeeming love. Strive to enter in at the strait gate, the gate which will be opened by friends seated beneath the great white throne. Forsake all and follow Jesus, "For he that loves friends, wife, children, or even father or mother more than me," says Jesus, "is not worthy of me." Each has a soul to save, and it depends on our own practice to save it. The Lord help us this evening to say, I will serve the Lord for myself letting others do as they may. I must save my own soul, and I will forsake all and go to Jesus. Then yonder in the blessed home, where sin never enters, I'll live and sing forever. Trusting we part as friends, though differing, yet not quarreling, but searching for the truth. I trust we hope to meet above in the city of God, and be his children and he our dear Father, full of mercy, tender compassion and love, to him be glory forever and ever. Amen.[4]

The basic controversy over baptism, and the reason for so much preaching and writing about the subject, was between Brethren and non-Brethren. Actually the subject was not controversial among Brethren, as demonstrated by the fact that baptism was infrequently discussed on the floor of Annual Meeting. Most of the discussion centered around two issues. First, was a baptism in an indoor pool as valid as baptism in the outdoors? The leaders of the church were uneasy about this question. They preferred the outdoor arrangement but finally agreed to accept the indoor pool wherever it was the only alternative. The second subject related to the asking of questions concerning one's faith and repentance. When should the questions be asked? Before the baptism? During the baptism? After the baptism? In 1909 the Meeting decided to make no change about the decision of 1848 which had stated that the questions should be asked while the person being baptized was in the water. Such problems seemed important at the time but were hardly as important as the attempt by Brethren to convince non-Brethren that the distinctive Brethren form of trine immersion baptism was the most acceptable form in the Christian church.

LOVE FEAST

For Brethren the Love Feast included three major parts: the feetwashing, a common love meal, and the communion of the bread and the cup. Without question the most controversial part was the feetwashing. First, Brethren were one of the very few Christian groups which regularly practiced feetwashing; second, Brethren themselves did not agree on how it should be practiced. C. H. Balsbaugh, a well-educated minister, illustrated the controversy between Brethren and non-Brethren in a tract on feetwashing entitled ***Feetwashing. A Letter Addressed to the Lutheran Pastor of Hummelstown, Pa.***

SIR:—In replying to your diatribe on the desuetude of feetwashing, I will endeavor to keep in view the apostolic injunction, "be courteous," and not cauterize your feelings beyond what necessarily

Fig. 39. *R. H. Miller, late 19th century. (BHLA)*

Fig. 40. *Sarah Righter Major, first woman minister of the Brethren. (BHLA)*

Fig. 41. *Baptism in Stony Creek near the Stony Creek meetinghouse of the Flat Rock Church of the Brethren, VA, September 3, 1905. (BHLA)*

follows the application of truth to the fungus of error. Was Paul discourteous when he confronted a certain gainsayer, with the withering rebuke, "O full of all subtlety and all mischief, thou child of the devil, thou enemy of all righteousness?" Was he discourteous when he said to the Saints, "O foolish Galatians?" Was Stephen discourteous when he said to his perverse countrymen, "Ye stiffnecked, and uncircumcised in heart and ears, do ye always resist the Holy Ghost?" Was Christ discourteous when he said to the Scribes and Pharisees, "Ye fools and blind," or when he reproved his disciples for their stupidity and unbelief, saying, "O fools, and slow of heart to believe?"

However courteous our intercourse ought to be, however mild our deportment towards each other, however gentle and persuasive our efforts to elucidate the truth or combat error, we must yet beware of compromising the "Truth as it is in Jesus," and blunting the edge which the Spirit of God has given it. From no motive whatever should the Truth be suppressed when duty requires us to "contend for the faith once delivered to the Saints." The carnal fear of wounding our opponent's feelings, may only confirm him in his error, and bring death and self-reproach into our own souls.

When writing or speaking of those things which relate to our immortal souls and the endless future, I have an inveterate dislike to the employment of ambiguous language, unmeaning technicalities, and filigree phraseology. Nine tenths of all the discussional matter that issues from the press is either an insipid display of intellectual ability, or a vindictive outburst of wounded pride. I solemnly assure you that every word in this communication is penned in the spirit of prayer, under a deep, impressive sense that I will be strictly adjudged not only for every syllable in which my rejoinder is embodied, but for the motive which prompted this response. I beg you to bear in mind that if I severely criticise and call in question your character as a Christian, I do not arraign your character as a man.

Your recent attempt to show, in a series of pulpit discourses, the groundless and untenableness of the doctrine of Feet-washing, was a strange conglomeration of assumed premises, hasty, illogical conclusions, defunct dogmas, and dubious traditions. Like all attempts to rend asunder what God has joined together, your discourses were mostly irrelevant, and so extremely shallow, irregular and satirical, that an elaborate refutation of them would be a sheer waste of time and words.

Lengthy orations, great parade of theological lore, unsurpassed fluency and gracefulness of diction, and consummate skill in making hair-splitting distinctions, are no more evidence that such exhibitions are sustained by Divine Truth, than that the artificial fruit in the shop-windows is the product of the vital processes of nature. If persons are willing to accept assumptions for principles and assertions for facts, any thing may be seemingly proved or disproved.

You discoursed eloquently, but did not recognize the Bible as a standard in all matters of religion. You cast your old drag-net into the turbid streams of Tradition, which was encumbered with a vast heap of rubbish. To enter the pulpit with an armful of books—sectarian disquisitions—looks very much like "teaching for doctrine the commandments of men." Why not confine yourself to the Inspired Record. If the way of salvation is there unfolded so plainly that even a fool may not err, why did you find it necessary to rely on foreign evidence, and adduce human authority to substantiate your views? If you cannot show that Feet-washing is an immaterial and antiquated custom by exclusive reference to the Word of God, why attempt the proof at all? Whatever is Evangelical is also reasonable, and any doctrine that cannot be proven by express Scripture, or fair inferences deduced from established Biblical Truth, is unreasonable. Hence your brilliant but futile effort to demonstrate what does not admit of demonstration, was not only bad theology but bad philosophy.

But in endeavoring to make error appear like truth, you presented several facts, and referred to various passages of Scripture which, although perverted and misapplied, were so adroitly handled, so plausibly defended, and armed with such captivating logic, as to perplex the minds of some truth-seeking individuals, whose common sense enabled them readily to detect your grosser fallacies and the lameness of your general argument. To the consideration of these points I will devote a few pages, endeavoring to exhibit clearly the fallacy of your position, and enforce earnestly the absolute necessity of "hearkening unto God rather than unto men."

You said that Christ washed the feet of his disciples in conformity to the custom that prevailed in those times, and that beyond this it had no significance. Let us see. Peter was as well acquainted with the prevailing customs of his day as was Christ himself. He wore sandals (Acts 12: 8.) and could not have been mistaken with the object of Christ, had the ceremony instituted and practiced in that eventful night grown out of the fact the people wore sandals, had dusty feet therefrom, and consequently had their feet washed. When Jesus came to Peter for the purpose of performing one of the lowest offices in human estimation, the astounded disciple saith to him, "Lord, dost thou wash my feet?" Why did this apostle decline the proffered ministration of his Master? Why did he refuse to have his feet washed? For the very same reason that you will not have yours washed. He entertained the idea that Jesus had no other and no higher object in view than conformity to a custom the purpose and necessity of which he knew as well as he did the same reason in his reluctance to comply with his Lord's request as you are.

This is true in the sense above stated; but with regard to motive there is a vast difference—a difference like that of light and darkness—between the apostle Peter and yourself. That holy follower of Jesus said, "thou shalt never wash my feet," because he could not for a moment tolerate the thought that the great Miracle-worker, the "Wonderful, Counselor, The Mighty God, The Everlasting Father, The Prince of Peace," should stoop so low as to serve him in the capacity of a menial. You say, practically, "thou shalt never wash my feet," because you cannot brook the thought of stooping so low as to comply with an injunction so repugnant to the carnal mind. Peter was prompted by humility: You are prompted by the opposite motive. This is difference enough to show the want of spiritual relationship between you and Peter, and I may say between you and Peter's Master.

But mark the reply of Jesus to his wrong-minded disciple: "What I do thou KNOWEST NOT." Is not this incontrovertible proof that the ceremony had a different object and significance from that which attached to it as a social custom? If Peter had any knowledge of the custom practiced in his day and among his own people, why did Christ say, "What I do thou knowest not," if the act, as then performed, had no design apart from conformity to such custom? Will you pretend to say that Peter was ignorant of Feet-washing as practiced in his time? This supposition would be preposterous in the extreme, and yet this must have been the case, or else Christ uttered a blank falsehood, for he emphatically declared that Peter did not know the intent or signification of the solemn ordinance he was about to institute. If ever a Truth was written as with a beam of light from the eternal throne, it is this; that Jesus Christ instituted Feet-washing as a rite to be observed and kept inviolate by his followers until his Second Advent. The entire transaction as recorded in John 13, and the language employed by Christ on that memorable occasion, clearly and incontestibly evince the spiritual design and perpetual obligation of the ordinance.

But how ready was Peter to relinquish his preconception when Christ intimated the spiritual import of the act he was performing. As soon as the Savior announced the startling truth, "if I wash thee not thou hast no part with me," the convinced, subdued disciple meekly responded, "Lord, not my feet only, but also my hands and my head." Now that he saw that the act was typical of an inward washing, or was essential to his salvation, he was ready to be washed all over—feet, hands, and head—as an acknowledgement of his need of such purification internally.

But turn we now our special attention to the words of Christ. "Jesus saith unto him, he that is washed needeth not save to wash his feet." These remarkable and beautifully appropriate words illustrate two things. First, it proves that in baptism they were washed all over, and needed not to be so washed again, but were "clean every whit." Second, that Feet-washing is based on the same principle as Baptism, in its most prominent signification. Christ spoke of both in connection, and as resting on the same principle as far as the signification of the element used is concerned. He that is baptized—washed, feet, hands, and head—needeth not a repetition of such washing, because of the absence of that internal condition of which the outward layer is the symbol. But as long as we are pilgrims and sojourners, as long as we wander homeward through this wilderness of sin, we will have our feet soiled to some extent by the corruptions inseparable from the present state, and make Feet-washing a holy, solemn, positive requisition, by reason of our walking through a world that lieth in the "wicked one."

Now, if you admit the spiritual significance of Baptism, and yet insist on the necessity of its external observance—which I know you do—you cannot, with any semblance of consistency, make it appear that Feet-washing is not essential on the same ground. And if you hold, as you rightly do, that Baptism is necessary as expressing a purified, renovated moral and spiritual condition, you can in no wise show that Christians, through their earthly pilgrimage, are not so related to sin through their fallen nature as to render it necessary to wash each other's feet, thus illustrating, not the dominion, but the indwelling of sin, and the need of repeated applications of the blood of Jesus.

If you can truthfully affirm that you keep your garments unspotted from the world in an unqualified sense, and never commit sin, you have a valid plea against the necessity of Feet-washing in your own case; but if you must acknowledge the existence of sin in your life, thoughts or affections, be it ever so trifling, you bear witness against yourself. Out of thine own mouth thou shalt be judged. If the rejection of Baptism is a virtual denial of the pollution of our moral nature, and the necessity of regeneration, so also is the rejection of Feet-washing a denial of those sin-begotten infirmities that cleave to the best and holiest of God's children.

We living in sin renders it necessary to be born again and be baptized. Sin living in us renders it equally requisite for Christians to bemoan their indwelling corruptions, (the love of self in particular which stands in antagonism to the first commandment, and derogates from the honor of God,) and have their feet washed. Are you without sin? Do you not practically affirm that you are an exception to the great law which embraces within its range every child of God as long as we are in this body of sin—viz., "the love of sin which is in our members?" I doubt not you would be both afraid and ashamed to assert that you never do aught that is prompted by "sin dwelling in you;" and yet you declare boldly and openly the same thing by your non-observance of Feetwashing. In Baptism you admit the principle, and deny the divinely-prescribed form. In Feet-washing you deny both principle and form. In the first you are inconsistent. In the last you are skeptical. I use the term skeptical in its mildest sense—as indicating a spirit of indifference in relation to aught enjoined by Christ and his apostles. But allow me to ask, is not the rejection of the "Word" equivalent to a denial of its Author? If the denial of the entire Gospel is infidelity in its blackest type, is not the rejection of a part skepticism in a proportionate degree?

With reference to the Law it is said, "whosoever shall keep the whole law, and yet offend in one point, he is guilty of all." Is the Gospel less a rule of life and criterion of fealty than was the law? If "every transgression and disobedience received a just recompense of reward" in the Mosaic Economy, think you that God will wink at our peccadillos now, and suffer us to defy his authority and impeach his integrity with impunity? But I am anticipating what belongs to a point yet to be considered.

In one of your discourses you said that Christ washed his disciples' feet to teach them humility, but did not magnify the act into an ordinance for the observance of his followers. Let us test this principle. Regeneration is the work of the Holy Spirit, and is represented by Baptism. The participation of bread and wine in the Holy Sacrament represents the death of Christ and our personal appropriation of its benefits. Does Regeneration render Baptism a matter of indifference, or does incipient sanctification render the Communion obsolete? You reply in the negative in regard to both these institutions. On what ground would it be wrong to repudiate the authority of the divine behests, "repent and be baptized," and "this do in remembrance of me?" Plainly on the ground that God has as positively enjoined these symbolical ordinances as He has graciously wrought the spiritual changes and conditions which they represent. If then, Feet-washing is practical humility, or humility in a living, palpable form, with what show of reason can you plead for the grace of humility and at the same time reject its appropriate type, thus repudiating the very principle which is your only support in the vindication of all external rites, or typical acts, which rest on the same basis? If Feet-washing was practiced by Christ as a sign of humility, why not observe it for the same reason now? If Baptism and Communion are as appropriate representations of Regeneration and Sanctification now as when instituted, why should not Feet-washing be as fit an emblem of Humility, and as imperative a duty in this age of the Church as in the night of its institution? You hesitate not to say that Christ washed his disciples' feet as a token or sign of humility, thus unwittingly admitting that Feet-washing, when instituted, sustained the same relation to humility as Baptism does to Regeneration. When was this relation changed, on what ground, and by whom? Divine authority alone can make such a change valid, and can be effected consistently on no other ground than that humility must either be no longer possible, or no longer necessary. That this grace is as absolutely necessary now as ever is admitted by all, and this leads to the clear, self-evident conclusion that its relation to its primitive sign is unchanged.

You also urged the objection that Christ did not mean what he said, or that his language is not to be taken in a literal sense. When any one is guilty of such conduct—saying one thing and meaning something else—we denominate him a hypocrite. A very unenviable title, and when insinuated of the Son of God, it borders on blasphemy. You referred to Matt. 18: 3 to substantiate the preposterous and fatal tenet that Christ did not always mean what he said, as this supposition would prove that the language he used in reference to the conversion of adults would involve the necessity of grown persons becoming "little children'' in the stature of their bodies. This vagary will not for a moment bear the test of impartial criticism. Christ was unfolding to his disciples the nature of conversion, or rather the disposition of the converted, and the necessity of a mild, forgiving, conciliatory spirit, and by way of illustration alluded to ''little children,'' thus placing in a stronger and clearer light the truth he was elucidating. You know very well that what He wished to impress on the minds of his apostles was, not that they must shrink to the physical dimensions of ''little children,'' but they must exhibit the innocent, pacific, trusting, filial disposition of children. This is a point you will not dispute. In using the phrase ''little children,'' He had a figurative meaning, and he spoke figuratively. He meant precisely what He said. In the matter of Feet-washing it is the same. He had just been washing his disciples' feet, not figuratively but literally, and then addressed them in these significant and momentous words, ''If I then, your Lord and Master, have washed your feet''—''ye ought also to wash one another's feet. For I have given you an EXAMPLE, that ye should do as I have done to you.'' Your directory with reference to the injunction I now give you, is the very act you saw me perform this night; Ye shall do to each other ''as I have done to you.'' Can language be more plain, direct, and positive? He spoke not of a condition as in the case of ''little children,'' but of an act which he had then and there performed. He acted literally, (how could He do otherwise?) He spoke literally, and he meant literally. There is nothing figurative or metaphorical about it apart from the spiritual signification which attaches to all symbolic acts. That Feet-washing has a typical meaning does not obviate the necessity of its literal observance any more than the typical signification of Baptism exempts us from a literal compliance with the command to be ''buried with Christ'' in that ordinance. Christ literally broke the bread, and gave unto his disciples, saying, ''Take, eat, this is my body.'' So also the cup, saying, ''Drink ye all of it, for this is my blood.'' Is this sacrament to be observed literally, or does it consist only in participation of the spiritual benefits and advantages expressed thereby? You answer in favor of a literal, tangible sacrament. Is there not precisely the same reason for denying the necessity of partaking of the visible emblems of the Savior's sufferings on the ground that he used metaphorical language in speaking of conversion, as there is for rejecting Feet-washing on this ground? The bearing of Christ's words when alluding to ''little children,'' is just as strong and definite in one case as in the other. That Christ employed figurative language on some occasions, does not afford a shadow of evidence that he did not intend his words to be literally understood when speaking of Feet-washing. There are no two passages in the Scriptures that are less adapted to each other's illustration than Matt. 18: 3. and John 13: 14, 15. They have no connection whatever in parallelism of meaning, and yet Christ meant in both instances what he said. What! the Son of God guilty of ambiguity, or what is still worse, of hypocrisy? Christ not mean what he said? O wretched phantasy! O awful and malignant scheme of Satan to drown men's souls in perdition! It is this that introduced "sin into the world and all our woe." God has said, "Thou shalt surely die" if thou disregard my "Word," or violate my command. But the arch-fiend has positively declared, "Thou shalt not surely die," and succeeded in gaining the credence of the hapless pair. His great purpose was to bring enmity between man and his Maker, and thus augment the population of his own gloomy territory, and as soon as he had weakened man's confidence in the Divine Word, he had achieved his infernal purpose. It is to be deplored that the same malicious, "serpent," the same "lying spirit" is as busy and successful today in the diabolical work of persuading people that God does not mean what he says, as in the garden of Eden. What "damnable heresy" cannot be maintained on such a hypothesis? It is a daring impeachment of the Divine veracity, and strikes at the very root of Christianity. Christ has declared with solemn emphasis that if we have not our feet washed we have "no part with him." He meant what he said, and his imperative injunction will stand, despite all that can be said or done to invalidate it. "Heaven and earth shall pass away, but my words shall not pass away." No ingenuity of criticism, no evasion of sophistry, no effort of reasoning, no profoundness of erudition can make it other than what it is—the Word of Jehovah-Jesus, the "Judge of the quick and dead."

You said, moreover, that it is not wrong to wash feet, even as an apprehended religious duty, but that it is absurd and uncharitable to regard those as transgressors of the Gospel who do not view it in the light of a positive obligation. If it is not wrong it must be right. I admit there may be obligations of an individual character that are not binding on all alike: but there is no neutral ground to occupy in a matter of divine authority. On a point so self-demonstrative there is no possibility of evasion. If it is right for us to "keep the ordinances as the Lord delivered them to us" it must be wrong for you not to keep them. If we act in harmony with Truth, or if we do right in washing each other's feet, am I not justified in the assertion, (I shudder to think that the words fell from the lips of Jesus,) that you are liable to the realization of the fearful declaration contained in Rev. 22: 19. But if your course, your unqualified rejection of Feet-washing, is consonant with the Word of Eternal Truth, then it is equally plain that we are liable to be the unhappy objects of the appalling denunciation recorded in verse 18th. "If ye know these things, happy are ye if ye do them," which implies that if we do them not, this felicity will not be ours. "If I wash thee not thou hast no part with me." Awfully solemn words. They proceed from the mouth of Him who is "yea and amen," who says what He means, and means what He says.

In conclusion you remarked that if Christ's language requires a literal construction, and Feet-washing is a Divine Institution, then it follows that all those who do not keep the ordinance are lost. "If it is a Divine Institution." "IF." Between what heights of hope and depths of despair is this little monosyllable a fatal barrier. "IF." How often is this the weapon with which the carnal mind fights against the sword of the Spirit. "IF." This is the key that has locked the door of heaven against millions. "IF." Over these two letters countless multitudes have stumbled into hell. "IF." This robs God of his honor, plucks the crown from the brow of Emanuel, and places it on the head of the "Red Dragon." "IF." You might as well apply it to the Divine Existence as use it in this dubious sense in relation to Feet-washing. I think I have shown, clearly and incontestably, that the words of Christ in reference to Feet-washing, are to be taken in a literal sense, or that Christ meant what he said, and thus you stand a self-arraigned, self-judged, self-doomed man. I pray you not to be offended at the style in which this letter is written, (error always regards the pungent application of truth as austere,) but think only of the Sacred Truth it embodies, for the Truth, and the Truth alone, shall make you free.[5]

Balsbaugh's defense of feetwashing to the Lutheran pastor is a good illustration of Brethren controversy with other Christian groups regarding the continued practice of the feetwashing in the nineteenth century. A second type of controversy regarding feetwashing may be illustrated in the Minutes of the Annual Meetings. For some twenty years from the late 1860s to the late 1880s, the issue was discussed almost every year—at least a dozen times. The basic issue involved the "double mode" of feetwashing versus the "single mode" of feetwashing. The double mode was practiced by one person washing the feet of several persons assisted by another person who followed and wiped the feet of those washed; in other words two persons (double) were involved in the washing and the wiping of each person's feet. In the single mode, an individual washed and wiped the feet of one other person. In 1865 the double mode was the generally accepted practice in the church, as reflected in a decision of the Meeting in 1867.

Art. 27. Inasmuch as there are some members who are dissatisfied with the present manner of washing feet, and think that the one that washes should also wipe, can not the Annual Meeting grant a change, and bear with those that wish to practice as they understand it?

Answer: We consider it not advisable to make any change in the practice of feet-washing as heretofore practiced by the brethren.[6]

In 1868 the Meeting was again queried about feetwashing and agreed to appoint an investigating committee "to visit those churches in which to practice the ordinances of feet-washing differently to the general order of the brotherhood." Evidently two committees were appointed.

The first committee, which included such important Brethren as D. P. Sayler, H. D. Davy, James Quinter, B. F. Moomaw, and Moses Miller, visited the Philadelphia and Germantown congregations.

Whereas, the brethren of the Philadelphia and Germantown churches seem to feel assured that the practice of feet-washing in said churches has always been in the single mode, we find it necessary to bear with one another, and will do so, provided you restore the old order of the brethren, in having a full supper at communion meeting, the salutation of the kiss at the same time, and the practice of the two brethren praying at the commencement and close of our general meetings for worship, where there are two brethren present, concluding each prayer with the Lord's Prayer. If you will agree to this, we will report to the Annual Meeting accordingly. This was the last proposition submitted by the committee to said churches, and was accepted, with the qualification, as far as practicable. We are happy to believe its acceptance will be a step toward a more complete union between the churches we met in conference and the general brotherhood. The foregoing report is respectfully submitted to the Annual Meeting, with the hope that it will take such action upon the subject as will further the blessed cause of truth and righteousness.

This Annual Meeting accepts for the present, the foregoing report, with the clause, "as far as practicable," stricken out.[7]

This report from Philadelphia and Germantown suggested a possible explanation for the difference in the church in the practice of feetwashing. The original practice was probably the single mode, which was used in the oldest congregation in America in Germantown. However, as Brethren moved into the interior of Pennsylvania, new ideas and influences were introduced, perhaps from Ephrata, and the double mode of feetwashing became accepted. The Annual Meeting followed the primary movement of the Brethren westward across Pennsylvania, and across the Ohio River into Ohio and Indiana. In Illinois, this movement encountered the Far Western Brethren, who evidently were the descendants of the Germantown Brethren by way of the Carolinas and Kentucky.[8] *At any rate the Far Western Brethren practiced the single mode of feetwashing. The second committee appointed by the Annual Meeting of 1868 visited the Illinois Brethren and reported to the Meeting of 1869.*

Upon conferring with them and investigating the subject of difference in the practice of feet-washing, we found that in presenting their papers to the Annual Meeting in 1859, they reserved the right to themselves of practicing feet-washing as they did before, and thereby the Annual Meeting got a wrong impression; and, furthermore, what confirmed that impression was this: they agreed in the paper above alluded to, to give and take counsel, and did not state to the Annual Meeting their reservation in the practice of feet-washing. We found, in our conference with them, that they are still willing to abide by the compromise made in 1856, and fellowship the brethren as it was then agreed upon by the Annual Meeting. And we further got an expression from them, that they have adopted, and will adopt, the minutes of the Annual Meeting in full, except in the practice of feet-washing. And, as we learned by investigation, that there was a misunderstanding between parties, we laid down our power invested in us by the Annual Meeting to communicate, and return our report to the Annual Meeting, that it may act as it sees fit in the premises. And we further have to say, that we were kindly met and received by the brethren and sisters in Adams and Hancock counties, and found a Christian spirit manifested in them while we were with them, and only feel sorry that we could not effect a union in the practice of feet-washing. Signed by the committee: H. D. Davy, John Metzger, Samuel Lehman, Christian Long."

Whereas there has been a misunderstanding between the brethren in Illinois, visited by the committee, and the Annual Meeting; and, whereas, said brethren have accepted of the decisions of the Annual Meeting, and conformed to the order of the church in every respect except in the order of feet-washing; and, whereas, the different modes of washing feet have been much agitated among the brethren for some time past, neither to the edification of the brethren, nor to the promotion of holiness in the church; and, whereas, this Annual Meeting has given counsel, which it is hoped, will stop said agitation and let the subject rest; therefore, this Annual Meeting concludes to bear a little longer with said brethren, and see what the result will be. It also advises brethren, when organizing new churches, to organize them in the practice of the ordinances, according to the general order of the brethren.[9]

The questions regarding feetwashing evidently did not disturb the Annual Meeting for several years, but by 1871 the issue could no longer be quieted.

Whereas, this Annual Meeting finds, to its great regret, that the subject of feet washing, in its single and double mode, as the difference is called, has produced serious difficulties already among us, and threatens still greater difficulties in the future. Questions relating to this subject have come from different localities in the brotherhood, and it has assumed such a degree of importance as to commend it to the serious and prayerful attention of the brotherhood. Under these considerations, with prayerful reflection, the propriety has suggested itself to us of calling the elders of the brotherhood together to consider this matter, as the apostles and elders did to consider the case of circumcision. Acts 15:6. We have therefore concluded to request all the ordained elders of the brotherhood to meet in the fear of the Lord and under a sense of their responsibility in solemn assembly on Whit-Monday, 1872, at the place of our next Annual Meeting, to dispose of this subject as the peace and prosperity of the fraternity require.

In the meantime, no church should be organized under the single mode, neither should any church change from the double to the single mode. And in order to obtain all the information possible to present unto the council of elders above alluded to, we appoint the following brethren as a committee to ascertain, as far as possible, which was the first mode practiced by our brethren in America. D. P. Saylor, Jacob Reiner, and J. Quinter.[10]

In preparation for a special meeting of elders in 1872, D. P. Sayler prepared an exhaustive report based on all of the written and oral evidence which he could locate in trying to determine the origins of the two modes of feetwashing.

SAYLER'S REPORT TO THE ELDERS AT ANNUAL MEETING

Dear Brethren: In compliance with appointment by annual meeting of 1871, Art. 37, to ascertain, as far as possible, what was the first mode in the observance of the ordinance of feet-washing by the brethren in America, I, being governed or guided in the field of my research by this history: "The first appearing of these people in America was in the fall of the year 1719, when about twenty families landed in Philadelphia, and dispersed themselves, some to Germantown, some to Skippeck, some to Oley, some to Conestoga, and elsewhere. This dispersion incapacitated them to meet for public worship, and therefore they began to grow lukewarm in religion. But in the year 1722 Messrs. Baker, Gomery, Gantz, and Frantz visited these scattered brethren, which was attended with a great revival, insomuch that societies were formed wherever a number of families were in reach of one another."—Benedict's History of the Baptists, page 599. This, being from Morgan Edwards' "History of the Pennsylvania Baptists," is authoritative.

To visit these points, I started on a tour on the 27th of September, 1871, in my private conveyance, taking with me Elder Moses Miller, who kindly consented to go along. I was out 8 days, and traveled upward of 300 miles, traveling as many as 47 miles a day. And, passing from one point to another, we passed through territory not occupied by brethren, and, being strangers, we were obliged to lodge overnight and for dinner in public houses sometimes. Having learned that, although Oley had the second meeting-house built by the brethren in America, yet, by death, removal, and other causes, the church had gone down so that there had been no preaching there for forty years but of late years had been revived through the labors of Elder John Zug, so that it now numbers about sixty members, with David Eshelman elder, I could ascertain nothing, although Elder J. Zug is a living, walking encyclopedia on church matters. We did not visit this church, though we passed through its territory. We also learned that Skippeck was a point within the territory of the Indian Creek church. So we traveled east as far as to the old meeting-house in the Indian Creek church, which is in Montgomery County, and answers the historical Skippeck. We also visited all the oldest members named to us, in order to ascertain all the traditional information we could.

We did not find Samuel Harley, elder of the Indian Creek church, at home, neither A. H. Cassel, they having gone to a love-feast some distance away. This I regretted much, though Brother Cassel's son kindly showed us through his father's library, but, of course, we could ascertain nothing by a personal inspection of manuscript, etc., not knowing where to find them. In order to meet this deficiency I appointed Brother Abraham H. Price, who, in my stead, should have Brother Casssel to search all the written manuscripts in his library to obtain all the written information on the subject, and write the same to me. In compliance with this arrangement Brother Price writes: "November 18, 1871. I have done as you have requested me to do. I asked Brother Cassel whether he had a journal of the ancient church that would show or tell how the German Baptists practiced feet-washing. He said he had. Yes, a journal he has from the Germantown church wherein we can see many things to our satisfaction of the house-keeping of the old brethren in the church. But nothing of feet-washing, whether single or double, nothing in his library. But he has much to tell of what he heard of old Brother Fox and others. They tell him that single mode was the practice of the mother church in Germantown."

To give Brother Cassel an impartial hearing I insert the following letters from him. He writes voluntarily, October 19, 1865, as follows: "I have read your article on feet-washing (Gospel Visitor, Vol. 15, page 112) with a great deal of interest, and cheerfully endorse every word of it, excepting the assertion at the close, that the present order has been the order of the church since her organization in America, I can not endorse, because I know the contrary is the fact. But I am very well satisfied with the order as the church observes it. St. Paul's reasoning in I Cor. 12 satisfies my mind against any scruples on the subject. And, although it is an ancient order, as you have traced it eighty-one years back, and might be traced still further, it is, nevertheless, not the ancient, or first order, and can not be traced back to her organization in America. For that the brethren originally did wash and wipe is a fact that admits of no doubt, and therefore needs no argument to sustain it. But that many branches of the mother church did early deviate from it, is also a fact, and that some did never observe it that way at all, must be likewise admitted, among which is Indian Creek, one of its most early branches, and under the immediate patronage of the mother church at Germantown, did not observe it that way until many years after its organization, where, in compliance to the wishes of some of its members, the attempt was made for one to wash and wipe, but found it so inconvenient that we went back again to our former mode, and never attempted it since. This also proves the assertion of Brother Thurman in regard to Indian Creek having changed the order is entirely groundless."

"From all that I can learn, it appears as if the Brethren were at first somewhat indifferent about the mode, or, rather, as if they had left it optional, while some practiced it in this way, and some that way, even during the lifetime of its founders, and yet were all loving and sociable together as we are yet to this day with those that do still retain the ancient or first order.

"I said the brethren at first appeared somewhat indifferent about the mode of feet-washing. They did so, but justice requires me to say that they did not at all continue so, for A. Mack, Jr., was always inclined to observe it according to the pattern of Christ, and when upon his death-bed, in 1803, he was visited by several of his junior co-laborers, whom he admonished very feelingly to continue steadfast in the external forms of our religion, especially in that of feet-washing, for although he bore with the deviation, he for all grieved it on his death-bed. And to use his own words, he feared it was opening a bar in the inclosure for still greater deviations to creep in. They were faithful to his dying injunctions, and to this day observe the old mode of washing and wiping. But, oh, what deviations did they allow to creep in in other respects! I allude to the manners of holding love-feasts, and to their general intercourse with each other, etc. Yours in love, Abraham H. Cassel"

January 8, 1865, he writes again: "In the first place I would inform you yet of what I forgot to mention in the proper place in my former letter,—that for many years after the organization of our church the brethren had a deal of trouble concerning the time of washing feet, which occasioned two changes already. For, in the beginning of our fraternity, we washed feet after the supper and the breaking of bread was over. After observing it in this way for a while, we began to see a little more, and washed them between the supper and the bread, and that way we continued to do until I. H. Reitz' translation of the New Testament appeared. That and the arguments of a brother that understood the Greek language convinced us of our error. Since then we observe it as we still do, before supper. But concerning the mode, or order, of washing them, I can not find anything more explicit than what I have already stated, namely, that he who washed also wiped, and that A. Mack and the mother church at Germantown never did observe it otherwise, but, as already said, bore with the branches that deviated. Fraternally yours, A. H. Cassel."

In my charge to Brother A. H. Price I requested him to ascertain which were the next oldest churches to Germantown. To this he replies: "The first one was the Coventry church, in Chester County, and the next one was either the Indian Creek or Ephratah, we can not positively tell which. But this we do know, that feet-washing in these was always performed in the double mode." I, however, being guided in my research by the historical direction, and learning from that of the apparent simultaneous organization of churches at the four points named and that neither one is mother or the offspring of the other, but each being an independent organization by the same authority, and having ascertained all about Oley, Skippeck, and Germantown, I turned to Conestoga, which is in charge of Elder Christian Bomberger. Here I found a written record from the date of her organization, by Elder Peter Becker, of her first love-feast, the names of all her ministers, the names and dates of all her baptized. This record I was told is not in A. H. Cassel's library. I report as follows:—

The church at Conestoga was organized by Peter Becker, in 1722, and Conrad Beisel was baptized, and the first love-feast served by Becker, and, after the meeting, when Brother Becker was leaving the place, he told the brethren that he could not visit them regularly; he put the New Testament into the hand of Beisel, and told him he should do the best he could in church housekeeping. This way of authorizing Beisel to take charge of the church caused much dissatisfaction among the brethren, and to settle this he was elected to the ministry, in 1724, with John Hildebrand, deacon, to serve in the Conestoga church, under Peter Becker, bishop. Beisel, however, caused a schism in the church in reference to the Sabbath, which caused considerable trouble in the church, and, in 1732, it culminated in a separation, six brethren and five sisters adhering to Beisel, and twenty-seven remaining with Becker, all Conestoga members. This Beisel was baptized by Brother Becker, in the Conestoga church, and the same day communed, and was informally authorized to preach, and in 1724 was regularly elected to the ministry, and in December of the same year served his first communion.

Brother Becker was minister in Germantown and Conestoga churches till 1724. During his administration fifty-two were baptized in Conestoga church.

Brother Michael Frantz succeeded Becker. He was bishop thirteen years. He died in 1747. During his administration one hundred and nineteen were baptized.

Brother Michael Pfautz succeeded him, and was her bishop from 1747–1769, a period of twenty-two years. He died in the sixtieth year of his age. During his administration one hundred and sixteen were baptized.

Brother Christian Longana[c]ker succeeded him, and served three years, when the church was districted into three, namely, Conestoga, White Oak, and Swatara, Berks County. Jacob Stoll was ordained bishop for Conestoga, Christian Longanacker and Johannas Zug for White Oak, and Martin Gable for Swatara. Jacob Stoll was in charge of the Conestoga church from 1772 to 1822, a period of fifty years. He died in 1822, in the ninetieth year of his age. During his administration two hundred and sixty-three were baptized, and during the three years of Longana[c]ker seventy-nine were baptized. (This is the offspring a church must have to entitle her to the appellation of mother. Of these Germantown has none, and hence she is not the mother church.)

In 1815 (Stoll's administration) the Conestoga church elected Abraham Zug and Jacob Pfautz to the ministry at the same time, and in 1823 both were ordained together. Zug died in 1841, and Jacob Pfautz had charge of the church forty-one years, and died in 1864, in the eighty-eighth year of his life. During his administration three hundred and sixty-seven were baptized. In 1830 (Zug and Pfautz' administration) Christian Bomberger was elected to the ministry, and in 1864, the year Pfautz died, Conestoga church was again districted into three, namely, Conestoga, West Conestoga, and Ephratah. C. Bomberger was ordained for Conestoga, in whose charge the church now is, and up to the time of writing, October 3, 1871, of his administration, three hundred and ninety were baptized. In all this carefully-kept record there is not one word written on the mode of feet-washing, and as in Germantown and Indian Creek (the historical Skippeck) churches, we are dependent on tradition alone on the subject.

After having learned that Beisel was baptized by Becker in the Conestoga church, in 1722, and at the same time authorized to preach, and was duly elected to the ministry in 1724, and in December of the same year served the communion in the Conestoga church, thus identifying him with the early history in America, and keeping a written (now Printed) record of all that transpired in the church, whether good or bad, I turned my investigation in that direction, seeking written testimony. I made a special personal visit to the nunnery in Franklin County, Pennsylvania, but only learned that a David Landis (not a member, but one who communed with the church) had caused some little trouble among them in urging the single mode, and that in 1826 they had a meeting on the subject in Ephratah, and it was concluded to make no change, as the church had ever observed the double mode, and if that had not been the right way it certainly would have been revealed to the holy fathers and founders of the church. Elder John Zug having access to a copy of the Ephratah Chronica, I requested him to examine it and ascertain whether anything is written on the mode of feet-washing. He kindly consented to do so. He writes: "I have read the Chronica through, but find nothing by Beisel on the mode of washing feet; but it confirms the Conestoga record, that he, as a minister, served the community for the first time in the Conestoga church in 1724, etc. But on page 216 one George Adam Martin writes and says, 'Although I am separated in time and eternity from their (the Brethren) doctrine and teaching, excepting baptism, Lord's Supper, and feet washing, yet I have great respect before God towards them, especially towards Alexander Mack.' This G. A. Martin was baptized by the brethren in Martin Urner's Coventry church, in 1735. For what cause he afterwards went with Beisel I have not ascertained, but on pages 217, 218 it is written that this G. A. Martin and John Ham came to Ephratah on a visit, and stopped with Father Freedsome (Bissel), when the old father arose and said, 'Come, brethren, take a seat here, and I will wash your feet,' and Brother Nageley wiped them."

This, dear brethren, is the only written testimony I could find on the mode of feet-washing, in all the diligent investigation, and this you will observe was in the double mode, and this I think is conclusive testimony that the single mode was not practiced in the Churches when Beisel became a brother, for if it had been, in this act of hospitality the single mode certainly would have been in order.

Failing to obtain written testimony I made diligent search to ascertain all the traditional information I could. To this end the brethren pointed out the oldest living members, but I found none that ever heard tell of any other but the double mode being observed outside of Germantown. Elder John Zug remembers his grandfather well, who was baptized in the Conestoga church, in 1749, and was elder in the White Oak church, as was also his father, yet he never heard them mention the single mode outside of Germantown. My own great-grandfather was baptized in 1752, and migrated with my grandfather to Beaver Dam, Franklin County, Virginia, in 1772, and I communed with my grandfather several times, and had many conversations with him on church matters, and though he told me all about the changes in feet-washing, in reference to the time of washing, he never mentioned any but the double mode being observed.

The Antietam church, Franklin County, Pennsylvania, was formed and organized by emigrant brethren from Coventry, Indian Creek, and Conestoga churches, in the eighteenth century. I requested Elder J. F. Oller to ascertain all the information on the subject he could. He informs me that the brethren made diligent search, but have only traditional testimony. They have a sister ninety-two years old, whose mental faculties are unimpaired. She has a traditional knowledge from old members in her early age. She never knew or heard of any other than the double mode.

Thus, dear brethren, in all my diligent and personal research into the subject throughout different counties in eastern Pennsylvania, personally interviewing members who are far in their fourscore years, whose parents were members in the church, I failed to find even a trace of the single mode ever being observed in the churches outside of Germantown, excepting one time in the Indian Creek church.

Dear brethren, the result of my investigation may be summed up as follows:—

First. Peter Becker (and perhaps others) organized churches at Germantown, Skippeck (Indian Creek territory), Oley, and Conestoga, as near simultaneous as circumstances would admit, and while Germantown was the first, and had the first love-feast, she is, nevertheless, no more entitled to the appellation mother than any of the others. Mother implies offspring, and neither of the first-organized churches are her offspring, but all were organized by the same authority. And while the term is offensive, and belongs to the Papacy, let it be forever dropped.

Second. Tradition says the church at Germantown always observed feet-washing in the single mode; even so it says that all the other churches observed it in the double mode. And it is certain that none observed it in any other mode since the change as to time was made, excepting the one time in the Indian Creek church, which A. H.

Cassel says was done at the request of some of her members. But members who lived at that time, and are yet living, told me that it was done at the unceasing importunity of John Price, of Fitzwater, who preached at Germantown, and say but for him the members would never have thought of such a thing.

Third. Great stress is laid on the reported dying regrets and injunction of Brother Mack by the advocates of the single mode as given in A. H. Cassel's letter above, but as such regrets as reported are so unbecoming a great and good man, and a leader of a religious association, and are so clearly anti-apostolic, that, if true, I wish the mantle of charity had been thrown over his apparent weakness. St. Paul's dying words to Timothy were not, Don't do as I did. And I am very slow to believe what is reported as Brother Mack's dying regrets by his friends to sustain a doubtful favoritism. But if it is positively true that he had regrets, I think I see a different cause for it than bearing with the double mode. As seen above, Beisel caused a division in the church, and it was a long time before the brethren ceased to mix with them, and partake with them in their religious services. Brother Mack once left his charge, and dwelt with Beisel one year at Ephratah, and only left it when he became convinced that it would fall through. And Sister Saur time and again would leave her husband and home in Germantown, and seclude herself in Beisel's nunnery at Ephratah. So, if anything caused Brother Mack any regrets on his death-bed, I am much inclined to believe such a mixing in with a cut-off faction was the principal cause.

Fourth. Brethren from seventy to eighty years old told me they heard old brethren say that the church was the body of Christ, and that in her the ordinance of feet-washing must be observed by her members, where there is with God neither male nor female, bond nor free, but are all one in Christ, and while the church is the body of Christ and we members in the body, none dare to assume the position of Christ.

All is humbly submitted by

D. P. SAYLER[11]

The result of Sayler's investigation and of the meeting of "a large number of elders," who gathered on Monday before the 1872 Annual Meeting began on Tuesday to confer "with one another upon the subject they met to consider" was a terse decision inserted in the Minutes: "The following resolution contains the decision of the meeting upon the subject of feet-washing: Make no change whatever in the mode and practice of feet-washing, and stop the further agitation of the subject.[12]

Among the Brethren of the 1870s, however, it proved impossible to "stop the further agitation of the subject," and in 1876 the Meeting recognized that "several queries and requests relative to feet-washing" would have to be considered. It drew up an answer refusing to make any change "on the authority of the Annual Meeting," and then in an unusual response "deferred" the question.[13] *Such a response indicated the difficulty of formulating a response to the issue which would satisfy everybody.*

The Annual Meeting of 1877 again attempted to formulate an acceptable response:

As many brethren desire to wash feet by the single mode, will not this district meeting earnestly petition the Annual Meeting of 1877 to grant to any church of the brethren full liberty to wash by each member girding him or herself, and both wash and wipe the feet of another, when it can be done in peace and harmony? Answer: Inasmuch as the so-called double mode of feet-washing is the order of the general brotherhood, this Annual Meeting can not sanction the practice of different modes; but those churches which wish to observe the single mode we will bear with, when it can be done unanimously and without giving any trouble or offense in the church. And as there are different views on this matter among the brethren, we would caution both members and ministers in going from one church to another, that they shall not agitate and stir up the minds of the brethren on the subject.[14]

The decision of 1877 finally granted a degree of toleration to those congregations that wished to practice the single mode of feet-washing. But what about those situations where a change caused "trouble or offense"? The Annual Meeting of 1879 was asked about such a situation.

VI. We ask the Annual Meeting through the District Meeting to say what is to be done, as she says the double mode of Feet-washing is the general order of the Brotherhood, and that she cannot sanction the practice of different modes. Yet there are churches that know they are divided, and take a vote on Feet-washing and ascertain that the majority is in favor of the single mode, while a minority stands with the general order of the Brotherhood, and feels too conscientious to let it go. Now we plead with the Annual Meeting, through the District Meeting, to say what is to be done in such cases to avoid troubles.

Answer: We can see no better way to avoid such trouble than to follow the last decision of Annual Meeting which is to the effect that churches had better not change unless it can be done by unanimous consent. Where there is a small minority it is better to persuade it if it can be done, than to force that minority to yield.[15]

By the 1880s the Annual Meeting recognized that a change was taking place in many local congregations. The Meeting was asked once again to "establish one mode of feet-washing" in 1883, but responded:

Answer: We desire very much to see a uniform practice in the Church. But we see no way of accomplishing that object at the present time in the practice referred to in the query.[16]

In the Bridgewater, Virginia area it was reported that the deacons took a vote privately in each home with the following results: one against any change, thirteen favored no change but were willing to submit to a change, forty-one were neutral, and two hundred ninety-three favored a change to the single mode.[17] *Thus the change was made among many Brethren congregations, although in the division that took place in the early 1880s the Old German Baptist Brethren rejected any change in the practice of feetwashing.*

The Brethren were even more hesitant about making changes in the traditional practices regarding the second part of the Love Feast—the fellowship meal together. Occasionally the Meeting heard new ideas, but generally it treated them as it did in 1895:

4. The Neosho County church asks the Southeastern District of Kansas to ask Annual Meeting to give a decision on the right or wrong of the church changing, on Communion occasions, our time-honored custom of dipping in the dish, and substituting a saucer for each individual member.

Answer: We counsel our brethren to make no change in our time-honored custom in this respect.[18]

In the practice of the communion service of the bread and the wine Brethren were willing to consider changes. On one issue change seemed to come rather quickly and easily, but on a second issue the matter was prolonged and difficult. The first was the use of unfermented grape juice instead of wine. The Annual Meeting of 1875 placed the issue on a local option basis.

Art. 3. Is it considered according to the gospel for a church, at communion, to use the unfermented juice of grapes in place of wine?

Answer: We think it may be left optional to a church to do so, if the members are agreed.[19]

The Annual Meeting of 1876 was asked to reconsider this decision but refused. The question arose one final time more than fifteen years later in 1892.

Inasmuch as we look upon the use of unfermented wine at the time of our Communion services to be in harmony with our Gospel principles of temperance,

Therefore we, the Brethren of the Black River church, Mich., petition Annual Meeting through District Meeting that the Annual Meeting of 1892 recommend its use.

Answer: The District Meeting of Michigan concurs with the above and asks Annual Meeting to so recommend.

Answer by Annual Meeting: Inasmuch as we use unleavened bread in the Communion, we recommend our churches to use unfermented wine.[20]

Probably the impact on the Brethren of the nation-wide temperance movement, including such organizations as the Prohibition Party, the Women's Christian Temperance Union, and the Anti-Saloon League, eased the way for Brethren to make the change away from the use of fermented wine.

However, it was not so easy for Brethren to make another change which was being demanded; this change involved the more direct participation of the sisters of the church in the communion service. Evidently the traditional practice was for the presiding elder to break the bread to each sister individually and to pass the common cup to each sister individually. By contrast the brothers broke bread and passed the cup among themselves. In 1879 this practice was challenged in an Annual Meeting query.

VII. From 1 Cor. 10:16,17, and Gal. 3:28, would it not be more consistent with the Gospel for sisters to break the bread and pass the cup of communion as the Brethren do. If so we ask the District Meeting and Annual Meeting to grant the privilege. The District Meeting cannot unanimously agree to ask a change, and therefore submit it to Annual Meeting.

Answer: This Annual Meeting decides that it cannot make any change.[21]

Some of the more liberal sisters in the church were not willing to accept such a decision on a permanent basis. They proved very persistent, and in 1885 they raised the question again, only to have the Meeting "postpone it indefinitely." Six years later, in 1891, they called for a reconsideration of the decision of 1879; this time the Meeting decided to place the query "on the Minutes and deferred for one year."[22] *This action was sufficient to delay consideration of this issue for eight years, rather than one. Not until 1899 was action on the matter included in the Minutes. Because the Meeting agreed to appoint a committee to study the issue and the committee did report to the Meeting of 1900, the queries of 1899 were included in the report to the Meeting of 1900.*

3. (a) (Grundy County.) We, the sisters of the Grundy County church, seeing we have made the same covenant with God in Christ Jesus that the brethren have made, petition Annual Meeting through District Meeting to repeal former decisions against us and grant us the same privilege in the breaking of the bread and passing the cup that the brethren enjoy in fulfilling the Word of the Lord. See 1 Cor. 10: 16. (By authority of the Grundy County church.)

(b) We (the Lanark church) petition Annual Meeting through District Meeting to honor the sisters by allowing them to break bread, using like words of affirmation, and pass the cup as the brethren do, believing that a more sacred feeling would be felt among the sisters if they could share these privileges, and that such would be in harmony with the teachings of the New Testament.

(c) Inasmuch as Jesus broke the bread of Communion and gave it to his disciples (see Matt. 26: 26, 27; Mark 14: 22, 23; Luke 22: 19, 20), and Paul delivered the same practice to the church at Corinth (see 1 Cor. 11: 23, 24, 25), would it not be well for ministers who officiate at love feasts to break the bread for the brethren as well as for the sisters, and thus secure uniformity, and restore the order of Christ and the practice of the primitive church?

Answer: We recommend that a committee be appointed to investigate the Gospel grounds and the expediency of the change and report to Annual Meeting of 1900.

Answer: Decided that these papers be referred to a committee to report at next Annual Meeting. Committee: D. Hays, L. W. Teeter, I. B. Trout.

Report of the Committee:

We, the undersigned committee, ask to report the following, to wit: After a careful investigation of the question, our judgment is that Matt. 26: 26, 27; Mark 14: 23; Luke 22: 19, 20; 1 Cor. 11: 23, 24, 25, warrant us to administer the bread and cup of communion to the brethren, individually, in the same manner as the practice now is to administer them to the sisters.

We consider that this change would be in harmony with the teaching and example of Christ and also in harmony with the practice of the church during the apostolic period. Committee: D. Hays, L. W. Teeter, I. B. Trout.

Answer: Decided to spread on the Minutes and defer one year.[23]

So the Brethren were not yet prepared to grant equality to the sisters of the church. This time the delaying action lasted for six years, and in 1906 the same Grundy County sisters petitioned "Annual Meeting through district meeting, to grant us the same privilege in the breaking of bread and passing the cup that the brethren enjoy in fulfilling the Word of the Lord." The Meeting again appointed a five-man committee of E. B. Hoff, H. C. Early, A. G. Crosswhite, J. E. Miller, and D. C. Flory to study the issue.[24]

The committee now dragged its feet and reported to the Meetings of 1907 and of 1908 that it had not yet completed its investigation of the matter. In 1909 it provided a terse and rather ambiguous report:

The officiating minister, or ministers, shall break the bread and pass the cup of communion to both brethren and sisters.[25]

Evidently both brethren and sisters were to be equal, but on what basis? The Meeting was not satisfied with the answer, and consequently asked the committee to study the matter for another year. In 1910 the issue was finally settled after more than thirty years of discussion in an equally terse, but not ambiguous, decision.

We grant the sisters the same privilege of breaking the bread and passing the cup that the brethren enjoy.[26]

Thus an issue related to the practice of the Love Feast, which had undoubtedly caused much tension in the church, had finally been laid to rest.

DEFENSE OF BRETHREN BELIEFS

The Brethren during these years were constantly on the defensive in explaining their beliefs in relation to other religious groups. But on occasion they took the offensive in attacking other groups, especially if those groups had disputed Brethren beliefs. As a concluding section of this chapter, one pamphlet is included to illustrate the Brethren attack on other groups. Brethren had had various interactions with the Campbellites (Disciples of Christ) since the origins of that movement in the 1820s.

CAMPBELLISM WEIGHED IN THE BALANCE and FOUND WANTING

A WRITTEN SERMON IN REPLY TO ELDER C________

BY J. H. MOORE

(The following Tract is a written sermon, being a direct and pointed reply to some of the arguments and methods of reasoning frequently resorted to by the class of people whose doctrine is here fairly contrasted with the New Testament teachings. The term "Elder C________" is assumed in order to enable the author to reach points and explode arguments that otherwise could not be so successfully approached in so brief a form. "Whoso readeth let him understand.")

Respected Friends:—The gentleman having granted me permission to speak, I feel as though I ought to make a few remarks—the nature of the case seems to demand it. I am, however, no lover of debating, although I am of the opinion, that it may, when properly conducted, be promotive of much good.

I have no real desire to differ from my religious friends in regard to these important matters, but the love of truth rather constrains me to take some exceptions to a few statements, that have been made here. I will therefore intrude a little upon the time, and not detain you longer than seems necessary.

I, perhaps, could have chosen some other time and way to present my reply, but my remarks will be very personal. I do not care to talk of a man behind his back; whenever I have anything to say about a minister's sermon, I want him to hear it, and for these reasons I propose making my reply in the presence of Elder C________, that he may know just what I have to say about his discourse. I want him to hear it, and I would be much pleased if a few hundred of his ministers were present.

Much that he said is correct, and on many points I sanction his remarks, but shall take exception to those points on which we differ.

He stated that in the time of the apostles, there were plenty of *Christians,* but there were no *Dunkards,* which proves that *Christians* are one thing, while *Dunkards* are quite another. In reply, I remark, that while all agree that there were plenty of *Christians* in the time of the apostles, all must also admit that there were no *Campbellites* at that time, hence it follows that *Christians* are one thing, while *Campbellites* are quite another.

Elder C________ must not stand in his *glass* house and throw stones through my windows.

But he claims that *Campbellite* is not their *proper* name. I remark that neither is *Dunkard* our *proper* name. We call ourselves BRETHREN, now then, when he proves that there were no *Brethren* in the time of Christ and the apostles, I will give up the question.

He further remarked that the *Christian* church was in existence in the *first* century, but the *Dunkard* church did not exist until after the *seventeenth;* therefore the *Dunkard* church is not the *Christian* church. I reply by saying, that while it is a fact that the *Christian* church existed in the *first* century, it is also another fact that the *Campbellite* church did not exist till after the beginning of the *nineteenth;* therefore the *Campbellite* church is not the *Christian* church.

You see that Elder C________ has been making ropes, and now I am tying his hands with them, let him get loose if he can.

Elder C________ further stated, that one point of difference between the Christian church and the Dunkard church is this: The Christian church was founded by Jesus Christ, who sprang from the tribe of Judah, while the Dunkard Church was founded by Alex. Mack, who sprang from the tribe of Germany. I remark that it is a fact that the Christian church was founded by Jesus Christ, who sprang from the tribe of Judah, but on the other hand, the Campbellite church was founded by Alex. Campbell, who sprang from the tribe of Ireland, "of which tribe Moses spake nothing concerning the priesthood."

You notice Elder C_________ is good at digging ditches, but while I gently pass around he falls into them, and of course, he intended that they should hold me when he got me in, but the tide has turned, he is in and there is no place left to get out.

When it comes to taking the name *Christian* and then make a mere speculation of it in this kind of a way, I seriously object to it. I have no objections to them calling themselves Christians—we so the same—but then I don't want him to turn around and tell this people that I don't belong to the Christian church, simply because I refuse to believe and practice the doctrines and traditions of Alex. Campbell. He has endeavored to severely stigmatize me because I call them Campbellites, which he says is a term of ridicule. I cannot see where the ridicule comes in; when I use the term I do not mean anything bad—I don't mean that they are worse than Campbell, "the author and finisher of their faith." Webster also uses the term.

Elder C_________ says that Campbell never died for him, never bled for him, nor never arose from the dead for him. Well who said he did? Did Luther arise from the dead for those whom you call Lutherans? If you have a right to call a man a Lutheran, when Luther did not rise from the dead for him, have I not the same right to call you a Campbellite, when Campbell did not arise from the dead for you?

But he went still further and says, you may ask the most zealous Dunkard in "all the region round about," if a man can be saved without believing Dunkardism, and he will say yes, and then ask him if any one can be saved without believing Christianity and he will say no: this then proves that Dunkardism is not Christianity. I will answer this array of words by turning his own guns against him. You may ask Elder C_________ if a man can be saved without believing Campbellism, and he will say yes, then ask him if a man can be saved without believing Christianity, and he will tell you no; *ergo,* Campbellism is not Christianity.

The audience will notice that so far, I have been using Elder C_________'s own arguments against him. If his method is *untrue* then he has not proven one thing against us, and if *true* you can see at once just where *he* stands.

Having fully and fairly disposed of his arguments, in detail, I now proceed to advance facts, *which he dare not question.*

I. I call him a Campbellite because he believes and practices what Alex. Campbell believed and taught—in faith and practice they agree as much as any teacher and pupil in this civilized country. Campbell is the very "author and finisher of his faith"—he goes just as far as Campbell went, but no farther. If he believed and practiced what Luther taught, then I would call him a Lutheran. If he believed and practiced what Mahomet taught, then I would certainly call him a Mahometan; but as he believes and practices what Campbell taught, I certainly ought to have charity enough to call him just what he is—a Campbellite. Whenever he leaves off Campbellism and teaches Christianity, then, of course, he should be called after his teacher—a Christian.

There is no use holding Campbellism up to me and then call it Christianity—I lose confidence in the parties who do it.

In these statements, I do not mean to question the *honesty* of Elder C_________ any more than I would question the honesty of the four hundred and fifty prophets of Baal, or the sincerity of Paul prior to his conversion. I believe that they were all honest in their faith and practice—and so do I believe Elder C_________ to be perfectly sincere, yet honesty in any kind of work, does not prove the work to be right.

II. In many respects Campbell's system of religion is correct, while in others it is sadly deficient. The present remarks are not intended to reflect dishonor on the name of this remarkable reformer, but to stay the progress of his followers that they run not into the same excess of error. Among other good things taught by Campbell were faith, repentance, confession, and baptism for the remission of sins. These of course, he learned from the Bible, and in these points Elder C_________ is right when he follows him; but here comes in the trouble—Campbell practiced backward immersion, a method not as old as either sprinkling or pouring, never mentioned in the Bible, and Elder C_________ is following right in his footsteps. Christian baptism should be performed in the likeness of the death of Christ, who on the cross, bowed his head *forward* and gave up the Ghost, but Elder C_________ baptizes in the likeness of the death of Eli, who fell *backward* and broke his neck. Furthermore, this *backward* action in baptism is a modern invention, having been introduced since the commencement of the reformation. This feature, however, is not purely

Campbellism, but was adopted from the Baptists by Campbell, and handed down to his followers, who hold it up before the people under the name of Christian baptism, when it lacks more than 1000 years of being as old as Christian baptism.

I now offer a syllogism which Elder C________ may overthrow if he can: Christian baptism was practiced in the *first* century, but *backward* immersion was not practiced till the *sixteenth* century; therefore *backward* immersion is not Christian baptism.

III. In addition to this human tradition there is another trait about Elder C________'s method to show that he does not practice *Christian* baptism; and in this particular he imitates Campbell to the very letter. You have already observed that it is his failure to practice *single* immersion. This method should properly be called *Eunomian* baptism, in honor of its inventor, a heretic who lived in the fourth century. This is another feature that Campbell found in the Baptist church, and stamped it with his own signature, handing it down to his followers; they receive it in "an honest heart," and thousands of them are not aware of its human origin.

The following points of difference between *single* immersion and *Christian* baptism are worthy of a passing notice: Christian baptism was authorized by Christ, while on the other hand single immersion was introduced by Eunomius: Christian baptism was practiced by Christ and the apostles in the *first* century, but single immersion was not practiced till near the close of the *fourth* century; therefore single immersion is not christian baptism.

Campbell and his disciples practice Eunomian baptism, while on the other hand Christ and all his disciples practice *Christian* baptism.

IV. By referring to and carefully reading the 13th chapter of St. John, you will observe that Christ and his disciples practiced Feet-washing. But before they were through with the ordinance Peter turned Campbellite, and told his Lord that he should not *wash his* feet. Peter, like Elder C________, did not believe in feet-washing, but his Lord and Master was not long restoring him back to Christianity by just simply informing him, that if he washed him not, he should have no part with him. After they were through, then Jesus, "the author and finisher of their faith," told them the following facts and injunctions:

1. "Ye call me your Lord and Master."
2. "And I have washed your feet,"
3. "Ye also ought to wash one another's feet."

4. "For I have given *you* an *example,*"
6. "That *ye should* do as I have done to you."

The Lord gave them a command to observe, and predicated his right to do so upon the fact that he was their Lord and Master, according to their own statements. And as a master had a right to command his servants, so had he a right to command them. To show them their *duty* he simply told them that they *ought* to do it. To make the matter plain and easily understood, he set them an *example.* In order to show that it was binding, he simply told them that they SHOULD do as he had done, and to perpetuate the command, he afterwards told them to teach all nations to "*observe all* things whatsoever he had commanded them." If you examine Paul's letter to Timothy you will find feet-washing still continued in the Christian church, in the time of the apostles.

I simply desire to show you the vast difference between the Campbellite church and the Christian church. I do not propose to misrepresent them in the least, but tell the facts as they are, and then if you fail to take heed, it will not be my fault.

I have already intimated that Campbell is the "author and finisher" of Eld. C_________'s faith, and now repeat it, referring to the proof. Elder C. fails to practice feet-washing, and why? Not because it was not practiced and commanded by Jesus Christ, for he both practiced and taught it, not because the apostles failed to teach it, for Paul required it of the widow, but the reason, and the only reason, is that Campbell neither practiced nor taught it. Here is just where all the trouble comes in. That the Bible teaches feet-washing Elder C_________ dare not question, he *knows* this to be a fact, but Campbell fails to teach it, and as Elder C_________ is following Campbell instead of Christ, we in this way are able to account for his not practicing feet-washing. Campbell stopped before he came to feet-washing, or perhaps made a way of his own that does not contain feet-washing, now then I ask this intelligent congregation, where is Elder C_________? Is he in the way in which our Savior trod—where feet-washing is found, or is he over yonder where Campbell trod—where there is no feet-washing? No use talking about charity covering up a multitude of errors in this case, the facts are so plain that all the charity in the Universe can't cover them over so much but that you can plainly see that Campbellism is one thing, while Christianity is quite another.

V. The following argument will show as much difference between

Campbellism and Christianity as there is between *day* and *night.* I now refer to the *time* of taking the Communion. That it was instituted in the *night* by Christ himself will not be questioned by a single sane man in the religious world. This much then is a *fact.* Furthermore, Paul says "that the Lord Jesus, in the same *night* in which he was betrayed, took bread. We further find Paul at Troas taking it after *night:* this then is Christianity, but not so with Campbellism—their rituals require that it be taken in the *daytime,* generally about noon, and then they turn round and call it the Lord's *Supper,* as though people generally ate supper *before* dinner. That it was taken by the Christian church after night in the first century is a fact, and it is also another fact that it is now taken in the Campbellite church in the daytime. Now, then, if here is not as much difference between the two churches as there is between day and night, please tell me why!

Of our Savior, Luke says he took the cup *"after supper,"* which shows that they had a *supper*—a full evening meal. Paul calls it the *"Lord's Supper."* This practice they observed in the Christian church, but we find no such order in the Campbellite religion—they have nothing of the kind. Elder C________ will take a small bit of bread and a sip of wine—at noon too at that—then call it the Lord's Supper. He has about as much authority for calling a small bit of bread and a sip of wine, a *supper,* as the Pedo-baptists have for calling *sprinkling baptism.*

But then it is just as I told you near the beginning of my remarks, Campbell and not Christ is the "author and finisher of his faith." Campbell called it the Lord's Supper, and so must Elder C________. Campbell took it in the daytime, just about noon, so must his disciples; they must obey their Lord and Master, for he has given them an example that they should do as he has done.

VI. I will next allude to another important item and then briefly close my remarks. The New Testament in no less than five different places commands the Brethren to "salute one another with a holy kiss," or as it is sometimes termed, a "kiss of charity." Campbellism contains no such an injunction known to me. Paul has told us that if any man preach unto us any other gospel than that which we have received of him, let him be accursed. The gospel preached by Paul did contain the salutation of the holy kiss, no man who believes the Bible dare question this, but on the other hand the gospel preached by Campbell, and transmitted unto us by them that heard him, contains no such a command, it is simply another gospel, unlike that taught by the inspiration of the Holy Spirit by the mouth of the apostle Paul, one that does not contain the holy kiss, one that is from man and not of God.

But Elder C________ pays no attention to this teaching of the Spirit of God; he finds no trace of this law in the commands and traditions of Alex. Campbell, and for that reason, he is just what he is.

Had Campbell commanded the holy kiss, then it is more than likely that his disciples would practice it, but as they think it their duty to stop just where he did, they never come to this command, unless one of them is "converted from the error of his way," and walks steadfastly in the apostles' doctrine and fellowship.

If Paul *in disguise* were to come here, and say just what he has written on the holy kiss, Elder C________ and all his brethren would unite in calling him a *Dunkard* preacher.

I have now carefully examined all of Elder C________'s arguments, completely demolishing his entire building, and in addition to this, I have shown conclusively that he is a *Campbellite,* according to the proper acceptation of the term; he does just what Campbell has taught him, paying no regard whatever to the commands in the law of Christ, not contained in Campbellism. In addition to this array of facts, which he dare not question—I could present quite a number of others, but as I have already presented more than Elder C________ is able to gainsay, and as a "hint to the wise is sufficient," I think proper to close with the following conclusions.

VII. If we as a people "walk in all the commandments of the Lord blameless,"—a thing which we try with all our power to do—it will not hurt us any more to be called *Dunkards* than it hurt the disciples of Christ to be called *Nazarenes.*

We hold to the New Testament as the rule of our faith and practice, this we know is right whether other books are right or not. This contains the law and testimony of Jesus Christ, it is by this and not something else that we are to be judged in the last day. It is true that Campbellism contains some good things, but whatever they are they were taken from the Bible. I have shown you quite a number of items contained in the perfect law of liberty, that are not even so much as hinted at in the commandments of Campbell.

As before stated I do not question the sincerity of Elder C________, I only question the correctness of his doctrine, not because there are no good things in it, but because there are many good things that are not in it, that are commanded in the Testament.

I hope that while presenting these remarks, I have not failed to keep in view that degree of christian courtesy and forbearance, which the occasion justly demands, and have not affected the gentleman's feelings beyond what necessarily follows the proper application of truth in its full force.[27]

As Moore indicated in his closing paragraphs, the Brethren tried conscientiously to follow their understanding of the New Testament "as the rule of our faith and practice." Their practice of the ordinances of baptism and the love feast was based entirely on their understanding of the New Testament texts. Thus, Brethren claimed to have no other creed than the New Testament. In their discussions and debates with other Christian groups, they usually ended up turning to the New Testament. It was the basis of their doctrines and beliefs.

IX

DIVISIONS IN THE 1880s

The pressures of slavery and of the Civil War which divided the major denominations, such as the Baptists, Methodists, and Presbyterians, did not affect the Brethren in the same way. However, the changes that were taking place in the United States during the Civil War and the following period of Reconstruction did affect Brethren in a divisive way; and in the early 1880s the conflict came to a climax with the resulting division of the Brethren into three different groups. As might be expected, the division involved a conservative group, a liberal group, and a moderate, in-between group. In the terminology of the 1880s, the conservative group was called the Old Orders, or more correctly, the Old German Baptist Brethren. The liberal group was called the Progressives who subsequently took the name The Brethren Church. The in-between German Baptist group was called the Conservatives. This body officially took the name Church of the Brethren after 1908.

The Old Order Movement

The Old Order group explained their position in a lengthy document published early in 1883, entitled ***The Brethren's Reasons.*** *It provided an excellent summary of the decisions of the Annual Meeting which the Old Orders regarded as unsatisfactory. They had protested these decisions, but their protests were not accepted by the majority.*

——THE——

Brethren's Reasons

——FOR——

Producing and Adopting

——THE——

RESOLUTIONS OF AUGUST 24TH

CONSISTING OF A COLLECTION OF PETITIONS MADE TO THE ANNUAL MEETING FROM YEAR TO YEAR, BUT WITHOUT GRANT AND THE ACCOMPLISHMENT OF THE MUCH-DESIRED ENDS PRAYED FOR GREETINGS

To all the dear brethren and sisters in Christ, GREETING:

May the blessings of the Lord, with the communion of the Holy Spirit, rest and abide with His faithful Israel and all the true, devoted seekers after truth, which alone is able to save us and to make us conquerors through him that loved us, gave Himself for us, and redeemed us from all iniquity.

Fraternally,

SAMUEL MURRAY,
GEORGE V. SILER,
SAMUEL KINSEY

January, 1883.

THE OBJECT

The object and purpose of this pamphlet is to show how frequently the brethren did petition the Annual Meeting to put away the new and fast movements in the church, and to explain and set forth the REASONS and GROUNDS for producing and adopting the Resolutions of August 24, 1881; and to show the opposition that arose, the trying times that many at first had to pass through, and to leave upon record, for the benefit of our children and the rising generations, the work and earnest labors of the old faithful brethren, to maintain the order and hold to the "old landmarks" of the German

Baptist, or Dunkard Church, "which our fathers have set," and so hand it down to them "as we learned it."

The Brethren's Reasons, Petitions, Etc.

In these last days and "perilous times, some of the solemn predictions of the word of the Lord are being fulfilled, when iniquity abounds on every hand, and when evil men and seducers are waxing worse and worse, deceiving and being deceived;" when the right ways of the Lord are being more and more perverted, and when even the faith, the worship, and the practice of our own dear brotherhood had been altered and changed in many places by those who are "ever learning but never able to come to the knowledge of the truth," and by the sanction of the higher council, that many dear members, feeling they could not longer stand in fellowship with such grave departures from the faith, and with a clear and uncontaminated conscience appear before the Judge, did, by the Resolutions of August 24th, so resolve to sever their fellowship from such innovations and departures, lest they be partakers thereof, and endeavor, by the divine aid, to adhere more firmly to the once accepted and recognized faith and practice of the church, and thus regain and re-instate what in many parts of the brotherhood had been put away and lost sight of; and, the movement and resolution of the brethren having been much misrepresented, and very erroneous impressions having been made, together with reports of various sorts, causing much inquiry as to the real facts in the case, with the purpose and object of the part of the Brethren, or German Baptist Church, that it would be good to have printed, in pamphlet form, some of the petitions sent to the Annual Meeting from time to time, praying that body to adopt measures by which to do away with some things which were introduced into the church which caused trouble and threatened division. So, on the 28th day of November, 1882, after the forenoon services at a love-feast, held in the Wolf Creek Church, Montgomery County, Ohio, a number of elders and ministers convened at the house of Bro. John Kimmel, and there unanimously agreed that this be done, and where the brethren, whose names have already herein appeared, were appointed to collect and cause to be printed such petitions and other matter that will set forth the efforts that were made, and also show how such efforts were respected and treated, showing the reasons for the Brethren's movements in adopting the Resolutions.

We therefore, first, bring forward a petition sent to Annual Meeting in 1869, with its explanation and supplement, as follows:

EXPLANATION TO THE FOLLOWING PETITION

In order to correct reports and for the information of the brethren—those who may desire a copy of this petition—we deem it proper to make the following statement, or explanation:

After much serious reflections upon the present condition of the church, it came into the hearts of some of our oldest fathers in the church, that the time had fully arrived that a consultation upon this subject was highly necessary, and the 14th day of November, 1868, was selected to consider the matter. In the meanwhile, in order to know the minds of more brethren, a number of them met on the 13th of October previous, where about twenty brethren—mostly elders—expressed themselves as being much grieved at the present digression of the church, in many localities, from her ancient order and practice; and the sentiment generally seemed to be that something must be done, and accordingly it was agreed that our next Annual Meeting should, *in the first place*, be petitioned to fall back upon her ancient order in doing business, etc., and that in case it would refuse to do so, they were fearful that many churches would not be represented at the next Annual Meeting. And the 13th instead of the 14th day of November was named for futher consultation, where the following petition was produced and signed by many brethren. And now, inasmuch as many have requested a copy, and as copying so many by hand proved rather laborious, we have, by order of the brethren, printed a limited supply, which we will cheerfully forward, to *brethren only*, for which we make no charge, yet will accept any trifle that brethren may choose to give us, to cover cost of printing and postage. Address,

SAMUEL KINSEY, Box 44, Dayton, Ohio.

PETITION

We, the undersigned, elders, teachers, and visiting brethren from various districts of the church in the State of Ohio, being assembled in the fear of the Lord and prayer, upon the 13th day of November, 1868, for consultation upon matters with regard to the present condition of the church, do unanimously and *most earnestly* petition our next Annual Conference, to be held in the State of Virginia, in the spring of 1869, to change, at least in the following particulars, its present manner of conducting business, etc., etc., so that in the future our Annual Conference Meetings be conducted more in *simplicity* and after the manner of our first brethren.

1. From the elders present at the place of Annual Meeting let there be six or eight of the old experienced and established brethren selected, and these need not be selected like our representatives in Congress—a certain number from each state, as each state from its peculiar circumstances, condition, etc., has its peculiar laws adapted to its own wants, but not so with regard to the church. Her rules and understandings must be the same throughout all the states, and hence let those brethren be selected from either or all of the states, as prudence and the Holy Spirit may suggest; and let not their names appear on the minutes as "Standing Committee." After having withdrawn, let those brethren receive the queries, etc., from the different districts represented, and let them present the same in order before the meeting for consideration. A minute of the preceedings of the meeting to be kept by some brother present. Let those old selected brethren see that there be order, if necessity require, but let no brother be selected as (human) moderator; rather submit that office to the dictations of the Holy Spirit. Let all the business, we entreat be transacted in the great simplicity, and thus do away with those worldly-wise regulations, such as selecting a certain portion of the Standing Committee from each state, appointing a moderator, etc., and to have their names affixed upon the minutes.

These points we look upon as tending to elevation, through which also the business and power is gradually concentrating too much into the hands of a few. Let us all be members one of another, and above all, we say, *close the door* against that which has a tendency to elevate and exalt the mind, lest Paul would say of us, "But I fear lest as the serpent beguiled Eve through his subtlety, so your minds should be corrupted from the simplicity that is in Christ," (II Corinthians.)

We think it advisable that the minutes of conference be again read to all at the close of the meeting, and then let them be witnessed by several of the old elders, but avoid especially designating those who had been selected to receive the reports of the churches.

2. We petition conference to desist from sending committees to the various churches where difficulties exist. We advise that all churches who need assistance call upon the elders, etc., in adjoining districts to come to their help, for it is probable that in most cases these have a better knowledge of the case than those brethren sent to them from a distance. And let all cases where any of the ordinance or doctrinal points are involved be reported to conference, and let conference, after having considered the case, write accordingly to the

church where the difficulty exists. Let two brethren be chosen to carry and deliver the epistle to said church. This will be according to the practice of the apostles' days, for proof of which see the fifteenth chapter of Acts.

3. We further petition this meeting to counsel and advise Brethren Quinter, and Kurtz, and H. R. Holsinger, to publish nothing in their periodicals that disputes the practice of the precepts and ordinances of the gospel as handed down to us from Christ and the apostles, through and by the forefathers of the church; and let Brothers Nead, Kinsey, and all the brethren who write, be cautioned upon this head.

In conclusion we say, that if this Conference Meeting shall hear and grant this petition, well; but in case it shall refuse to do so, it is very probable that many churches will not be represented at our next Annual Conference, and hence the result will be a reorganization of our Conference Meetings by said churches in accordance with this petition.

SUPPLEMENT TO THE FOREGOING PETITION

To the Beloved Brethren and Sisters Wherever this may be Read, Greeting:

On Easter Monday, the 29th day of March, 1869, a number of the brethren and sisters of the "Miami Valley" churches in Ohio, assembled in the "Bear Creek" Meeting-house for the purpose of adopting measures consistent with the gospel whereby the church may be cleansed, if possible, from the doctrines and principles of the popular religion of the day, and to prevent the further introduction of said doctrines and principles into our fraternity.

Brethren, it is clearly seen that our church has varied much from her ancient principles of humility and self-denial. You who have been members of the church for many years, and have had experience, and can remember how our fathers and forefathers viewed and conducted matters in the church, can testify to the above truth; and for your sake it would be needless to particularize, but for the sake of those of our dear brethren who have not had the age and experience, and have perhaps never had the opportunity of becoming thoroughly acquainted with the fundamental principles of our church, we name a few items:

1. "*Protracted Meetings*." We are much in favor of an active and industrious ministry, and that, like our Savior, the apostles, and our old brethren before us, we "preach the word" wherever opportunities present themselves, and necessity seems to require; but we seriously object to the way in which those meetings are so frequently conducted. We have a reference here to the working upon the passions of the people, and without giving them sufficient time to reflect and consider the cost, hurry them into the church, and that without demanding of them a full compliance to the doctrine of self-denial, etc.; also, the "boasting" or loud spirit that so often will manifest itself upon such occasions, together with their tendency in general. That there is a "deceiving spirit" attending many of those meetings can easily be seen by observing the "Church News" department of some of our "periodicals." The spirit that was always manifested by Christ would instruct us that when the people are converted under the sound of our preaching, we "sound no trumpet," but that in the STILLNESS OF OUR SOULS we give God the praise. But this humiliating lesson which Christ taught is not much regarded now, for many of us do love to sound through our "papers," far and wide, the success that attends our preaching.

2. "*Sabbath-schools*." These schools in themselves present a very harmless and innocent appearance, and to many they may seem to be the means of much good, yet we must confess that their tendency, in short, is pride and self-praise. We find neither command nor example in the gospel for the establishment of such schools. The teaching of moral and religious lessons to our children is a Christian duty obligatory upon all parents, and should commence at home; hence the apostle admonishes us to "bring up our children in the nurture and admonition of the Lord." See to it, O parents, that you discharge your duty in giving to your children the proper instructions and in setting before them examples worthy of initiation.

3. "*Prayer Meetings*," "*Social Meetings*," and "*Bible Classes*." We find no scripture authority for so many varieties of meeting. Their tendency if closely observed, is a dangerous one, and by no means that of humility. Prayer, sociability, and the teaching of the scriptures, are among the principal features that should characterize ALL our meetings. These, with many other things that might be named, such as the way and manner in which our annual meeting are conducted, etc., etc., are of late years making VERY RAPID inroads into our church; and it is a fact which we have had to observe, that most generally

where the brethren have those new orders among them, fashionable dressing and pride (that abominable evil) are a natural consequence, and by some are even considered no harm.

These new things first originated among other denominations, and are in accordance with the general tenor and principles of their faith; but the tendency of these things does more or less conflict with the lessons of humility and self-denial, learned and ever held forth by the church of the brethren while in a state of simplicity, and were not introduced into her body while she strictly adhered to those lessons and continued in her humble state.

But, by and by, many of these new things were brought before our Annual Council Meeting, and that again and again, until finally the brethren gave way, and sanctioned them to a more or less extent. These things first presented themselves in a very harmless and plausible manner; but we tell you, brethren, all new things do scarcely, if ever, first appear in the form and habit of a lion. No; but like that of a lamb, and herein, dear brethren, lies the greater deception.

The most of denominations, when first set out, were a plain, self-denying people; but where are many of them now? So were our first brethren a plain and self-denying people; but where is our church now? Is she not rapidly following the same channel? Is not she too grasping and contending wonderfully for an *easy, pleasant*, and *popular* religion, in which there is less sacrifice and self-denial? Most assuredly so.

These, dear brethren are FACTS which can not be disputed, and they are facts of which many of you are aware. What say you, brethren? Shall we say, *Amen? Shall we quietly flow with the current and remain silent?* Or shall we EVEN LOOK ON and be content? Nay; verily, brethren, it will not do; we MUST sound the alarm; we MUST do our duty, if we would clear ourselves. While in the flesh we have a warfare, and if we would be *faithful* soldiers of Christ, *we must fight against wrong*, should it appear even in our very midst.

We, as God's "spiritual Israel," have become full of wounds, bruises, and putrefying sores that have not been closed; neither bound up; neither mollified with ointment. (See Isaiah I.6.)

Paul says to Timothy, "But *continue* thou in the things which thou *hast learned* and hast been assured of, knowing of *whom* thou hast learned them." (II Timothy III. 14.)

Hence we are opposed to these new movements and changes which are *continually* being introduced into our body; and we hereby request all our dear brethren everywhere, wherever this may come, that it and the petition attached be read at church meetings, and wherever an opportunity presents itself. Let all the brethren, and even sisters, too, who are favorably disposed, and who are yet firm in the order of the brethren as they had it in their *simplicity* many years ago, sign their names to the same. Let as many names, either private or in office, thus be added as can be had, after which let all be carried to the Annual Meeting, or if preferred, let it be forwarded in time to some of the brethren here, and they will carry it there. It would, however, be preferable to have all such petitions (after first passing through the church at home) go to the district meeting; but in case it is thought doubtful whether the district meeting would be favorable, it had better at once be forwarded to the Annual Meeting, or to the brethren here.

We believe there are yet many brethren in the churches who have not lost sight of the ancient order of our church, and we especially desire all to respond to this as soon as they can.

The brethren need not be alarmed, neither need they entertain the slightest fears in putting their names in this paper, and seeing we plead not for any *new thing* in which there may be danger, but "Thus saith the Lord, stand ye in the ways and see, and ask for the old paths where is the good way, and walk therein, and ye shall find rest for your souls." (See Jeremiah VI. 16.)

The object of our labors, in short, is, by the favor of God, to UNITE the brotherhood upon the ancient principles of our church, and thus save her from a corrupted Christendom; and in order to awaken us to our duties we would *sound the alarm*, and that LOUD AND EARNESTLY, and thus cause a *reformation* or COMING BACK to the ORIGINAL STANDARD of the brotherhood, and that there be as much accomplished as possible in this direction. The brethren in council on the 13th day of October, 1868, and again, the brethren in council on the 13th day of November, 1868 (whose names are attached to the petition), and we, the undersigned, again to-day do all most earnestly entreat our Annual Conference Meeting in 1869 to hear the accompanying petition, and to grant the requests therein stated, giving a definite reply, after which the steps necessary to be taken further will manifest themselves.

We, the undersigned, do hereby signify that we will be *firm* and *faithful* to that which is herein contained, and that we will be TRUE to each other "by evil report and good report."

After this supplement was read to the brethren and sisters at the above named meeting, one hundred and twenty-six of them signed their names to it thus signifying that they are yet willing to walk in the light while they have it, as Christ directs.

Paul says, "For though I be absent in the flesh, yet am I with you in the spirit, joying and beholding *your order*, and the *steadfastness* of your faith in Christ. As ye have therefore received Christ Jesus the Lord, so walk ye in him, rooted and built up in him, and established in the faith as ye have been taught, abounding therein with thanksgiving. Beware, lest any man spoil you through philosophy and vain deceit, after the tradition of men, after the rudiments of the world, and not after Christ." (Col. II. 5,8.)

It was agreed that this supplement should be printed for general circulation among the brethren, and all who desire copies of it can obtain them by addressing Brother

SAMUEL KINSEY, Box 44, Dayton, Ohio.

The following is the answer to the above, or COMPROMISE MADE BY THE ANNUAL MEETING:

Whereas, there have been certain petitions from Southern Ohio presented to this Annual Meeting, and which have been extensively circulated through the brotherhood, wherein the petitioners have set forth certain grievances, and desire some change or modification in holding the Annual Meeting, and also in certain practices among the brethren; and, whereas, this Annual Meeting desires to maintain all the practices and ordinances of Christianity in their simplicity and purity, and to promote the "unity of the spirit in the bonds of peace;" therefore, though it can not grant the changes and objects desired by the petitioners to the full extent petitioned for, it will make the following changes in the manner of holding the Annual Meeting, and endeavor to guard, with increased vigilance, against the abuse of the practices referred to in the supplement, by advising and urging the brethren to observe the cautions and directions in reference to said practices, as hereinafter stated:

1. In relation to the appointing of the Standing Committees we advise that the district meetings select old, experienced and established brethren; and that in signing the minutes we advise that a suitable number of elders sign them, but not as members of the Standing Committee, and the signers need not be confined to the committee.

We also advise that the minutes be read to all at the close of the meeting, provided there is time and it be found practicable to do so and that the term "moderator," as applied to the brother who keeps order, be dropped.

2. In relation to holding protracted meetings for worship we feel much impressed with the propriety of conducting said meetings in strict accordance with the gospel; that all disorder and improper excitement should be avoided; that care should be taken that the understanding be enlightened as well as the passions awakened; that on all occasions, when candidates for church membership are visisted and examined, they be dealt with as the gospel seems to require, and as the order of the brethren has sanctioned; that in noticing the success of preaching, we advise that the number of additions to the churches be omitted.

3. In relation to Sabbath-schools we feel the great necessity of guarding against the prevailing manner in which these schools are conducted; of cautioning the brethren who take any part in them against having festivals, or anything of the kind that does not comport with the spirit of Christianity, which such schools are designed to promote; that care be taken, lest pride be taught rather than humility, and that nothing be encouraged thereby that will conflict with the established order and character of the brethren, and that care should be taken that no offense be given to the brethren in these things.

4. In reference to the controversial articles published in our religious papers we counsel and advise our brethren Quinter & Kurtz, and H. R. Holsinger, to publish nothing in their periodicals that disputes the practice of the precepts and ordinances of the gospel, as handed down to us from Christ and the apostles through and by the forefathers of the church; and that brethren Nead, Kinsey, and all the brethren who write, be cautioned upon this head, and are hereby given to understand that a disregard to this counsel will subject a brother to the council of the church.

5. In reference to prayer meetings, social meetings, and Bible classes, we would say that we advise the brethren to be very careful in conducting such meetings when they have been introduced, and to conduct them not after the prevailing custom of the religious world, but in the order that the brethren conduct their meetings of worship; that brethren be cautioned against introducing such meetings where their introduction would cause confusion or trouble in the churches, and that elders always be consulted in introducing such meetings."

The meeting above referred to, on the 13th day of November, was held in the Stillwater Church, near Dayton, and the propriety of it first came into the minds of Elder Henry Kurtz and Elder Peter Nead, on a time when Brother Kurtz paid Brother Nead a visit; but, deeming it best to have a further consultation with the surrounding elders, the meeting of October 13th was appointed, which was held in the old brick house in the Wolf Creek Church.

It will be noticed that the first object of this petition was to reform the Annual Meeting from her worldly wise manner of doing business, her simplicity in Christ having even then well nigh departed.

In noticing the minutes of 1869, Article 1, as above given, it will be seen that there is some respect shown to this petition, but the request of the petition is not granted in full, and the objectionable things named in the supplement are still retained in the church. The petition did not come before the public meeting at all. The brethren, on presenting this petition to the Standing Committee, met with some opposition. But, although there was a spirit manifest to keep in check, to some little extent, those opposing elements; but not long, and the condition of things in all these respects became more grievous to the old-order-minded members than before.

In the year 1871 there was an effort made to more fully unite the church in the practice of feet washing (this subject having been agitated in the brotherhood to such an extent, that in various parts thereof serious troubles arose). We here give the subject as may be seen in Minutes of 1871, Article 37: [*The Minutes of 1871, Article 37, are quoted in the section on feetwashing in the chapter on Doctrines and Beliefs.*]

This subject being prayerfully considered as set forth in the aforesaid minutes, resolved itself into the decision and council of 1872. The following resolution contains the decision of the meeting upon the subject of feet-washing: "*Make no change whatever in the mode and practice of feet-washing, and stop the further agitation of the subject.*" (Article 17.)

From the above it is seen what is the recognized mode. This effort to unity on the subject of feet-washing had a good effect, causing some brethren who, previous to this, were inclined to some extent to favor the single mode to throw their entire influence in favor of the double mode. Although this effort did have a tendency to unity in the practice of feet-washing, there still remained in the church a spirit of insubordination. So in the year 1876 the subject was brought forward again. (See minutes, Article 25.) We here give it: "Several queries and requests relative to feet-washing being presented to the meeting, the following was prepared to meet the case: Whereas, the so-called double mode of feet-washing is the recognized mode of the general brotherhood; therefore, the Annual Meeting can not grant the liberty prayed for, and no church can change from the double to the single mode on the authority of the Annual Meeting." *Deferred.* By noticing the twenty-sixth Article of the same meeting (next query) a spirit of insubordination on the subject of feet-washing still existed.

In the year 1877 this subject is brought forward again, and the following disposition is made of it: [*Article 24 of the Annual Meeting of 1874 is included in the section on feetwashing in the chapter on Doctrines and Beliefs.*]

Here we notice that there was liberty granted by Annual Meeting to practice the single mode of feet-washing, and though a caution was given not to urge a change to the dissatisfaction of any of the members as set forth above, the caution was not regarded, as the door was now opened, and changes were forced upon churches, and that to the displeasure of many members. Because of this change being introduced and forced upon members much trouble was caused in some local churches, that it was needful for Annual Meeting to send committees to settle the troubles so brought about by this change of washing feet from the old recognized double to the single mode; but it became a noticeable fact that these committees sent to settle these troubles and to bring about a union again did not reach the much-desired end, and the troubles in some churches were getting worse. The minority very frequently had to yield to the single mode, being overpowered by a majority. But efforts were still made by the brethren to bring about and retain union by sending requests and queries to Annual Meeting again and again.

In 1879 a petition was sent to the Annual Meeting at Broadway, Virginia, with the request that she do away with those changes and new movements which were more and more introduced, and that she cease giving encouragement and latitude to the things that were evidently destroying the union of the brotherhood. The Standing Committee would not suffer the paper to have a hearing, but with a sort of threat returned it. Hereupon all the official brethren present from the Miami Valley, of Ohio, who were desirous to have the church fall back to her ancient order of things, assembled in the grove north of the meeting grounds for consultation relative to the matter, and when it was said that a *threatening* accompanied the return of the paper, the brethren discovered that their grievances would not be heard, and that any further efforts at the time would be useless, and they quietly submitted.

Now, the treatment that these queries and petitions received impressed the minds of many members with the view that it was useless to expect that the Annual Meeting would adopt any measures by which to rid the church of the things which caused the troubles.

It seemed that at this time, and even before this time, the elders living in the Miami Valley, of Ohio, were mostly looked upon from many parts of the brotherhood to make a move, and in some way or other to take a stand against those innovations which caused trouble, and in places threatened division. The elders feeling that there was a great responsibility resting on them, and feeling also the work to be of importance, the matter was taken into council from time to time; consequently, in the year 1879 five brethren were appointed to correspond with the leading elders and members of other states for the purpose of obtaining the views of the brethren from different parts of the brotherhood as to what course best to pursue. Many letters were received and forms of petitions desirous to be presented to the Annual Meeting of 1880. (Here let it be well remembered that the elders of the Miami Valley were much urged by members living in the valley, and from other parts of the brotherhood, to take a firm stand against the worldly movements of the church.) Some of our leading brethren did then say, and that in print, that the "church was shaking hands with the world." Others said, "We can not expect anything from Annual Meeting."

In November, perhaps on the twenty-fifth day, nearly all the elders of the valley met in council in the Salem Church to read and consider the letters and petitions which had now been sent in. This consultation of the elders, after reading many letters and several petitions, resolved itself into what is known as the "Miami Valley, Ohio, Petition of 1880," which we here insert.

A Petition from the Elders of the Miami Valley to the District Meeting of Southern Ohio, for the Annual Meeting of 1880:

DEAR BRETHREN:—We do hereby most earnestly petition the

Annual Meeting, through the district meeting, to consider the present condition of the church in her confused and divided state, and to make an effort by which may be removed the fast element from among us, which is the cause of the troubles and the divisions in the church.

Now, as all former efforts have failed, in sending query after query to the Annual Meeting, the exercising of patience and forbearance from time to time, all of which have accomplished but little, the so-called fast element gaining ground year after year, and one innovation after another being introduced among us, which if suffered to continue will lead the church off into pride and the popular customs of the world and the other denominations, we think we feel the propriety of a renewed effort on our part to accomplish the object of this petition.

We, in Southern Ohio, have of late years felt and observed the element more than ever, and in serious meditation have we felt the weight of Paul's language in I. Corinthians I. 10, and in I. Peter V. 12. We, as elders of the church, over which the Holy Ghost, we trust, has made us overseers, do feel that duty demands of us to make this effort, that we may have order, peace, and union again restored among us. We offer the following as the remedy, in our wisdom and judgment, whereby a union can be effected: namely, to hold to and maintain the ancient and apostolic order of the church in her humility, simplicity, and non-comformity to the world. And we feel that we can no longer suffer or tolerate those innovations in the church of Christ. The causes of the troubles must be removed before peace and union can be restored; and among some of these causes are the high schools among us, popular Sunday-schools with their conventions and celebrations, long protracted meetings, and the way they are generally conducted, by singing revival hymns and giving invitations to rise or come forward, a salaried ministry, and the single mode of feet-washing.

Now the things here named we do not regard as being in harmony with the spirit of the gospel, neither are they in harmony with the ancient and apostolic order of our church, and when we speak of the ancient order of our church we have reference also to non-conformity to the world, not only in dress, but in the building and fancy painting of our houses, barns, etc., after the custom of the world, the gaudy and costly finish put on them, and fine furniture, etc., to set off our rooms and parlors after the fashions of the world, together with fine and costly carriages, etc. In these things we confess that Southern Ohio has gone too far out of the way, and we hope will be willing to reform and make any sacrifice for Jesus' sake.

1. With regard to high schools among us, we fear they will greatly operate against the simplicity of the gospel of Christ, as well as create or cultivate the desire for an educated ministry, which is not in harmony with the teachings of Christ and the apostles, nor with the ancient views of the church. Paul says, "Knowledge puffeth up, but charity edifieth." (I. Corinthians VIII. 1.) "Mind not high things, but condescend to men of low estate." (I Corinthians I.) Again: "Be not wise in your own conceits." (Romans XII. 16.) The views of our old brethren were in perfect harmony with the gospel as regards this matter, as will be seen by reference to the following queries and decisions:

Annual Meeting of 1831, Article 1. "Whether it was considered advisable for a member to have his son educated in a college? Considered not advisable, inasmuch as experience has taught that such very seldom will come back afterward to the humble ways of the Lord."

Annual Meeting of 1853, Article 28. "Is it right for a brother to go to college, or teach the same? Considered that we would deem colleges a very unsafe place for a simple follower of Christ, inasmuch as they are calculated to lead us astray from the faith and obedience to the gospel." And in 1857, when the subject again came up, the answer of the Annual Meeting is definitely given thus: "*It is conforming to the world*. Knowledge puffeth up, but charity edifieth."

Thus we see that high schools were not permitted to come into the church for at least twenty-seven years after they were first urged.

2. Sabbath-schools we consider to be more of human origin than by command of Christ or his apostles, and hence are more of a worldly custom than of gospel principle and authority; are not in harmony with the apostolic order of the church, the principles of the gospel, and were never sanctioned by the Annual Meeting in the way many are and will be conducted. Paul says, "Fathers, provoke your children to wrath, but bring them up in the nurture and admonition of the lord." (Ephesians VI. 4.) This command is given to parents, and not to others.

3. Protracted or revival meetings, in the way they are generally conducted, are, we claim, not in harmony with the old order and the apostolic rules of the church. "And Paul, *as his manner was*, went in unto them, and three Sabbath-days reasoned with them out of the

Scriptures." (Acts XVII. 2.) Again: "And he reasoned in the synagogue *every Sabbath*," etc. Again: "And when the Jews were gone out of the synagogue, the gentiles besought that these words might be preached to them the *next Sabbath*." (Acts XIII. 42.) "And the *next Sabbath-day* came almost the whole city together to hear the word of God." (Verse 44.)

4. A salaried or paid ministry is also against the apostolic order. Hear Paul on this subject: "I have coveted no man's silver, or gold, or apparel; yea, ye yourselves know that these hands have ministered unto my necessities, and to them that were with me." (Acts 33: 34.) "What is my reward then? Verily, that when I preach the gospel I may make the gospel without charge, that I abuse not my power in the gospel." (I Corinthians IX. 18) Again: "Neither did we eat any man's bread for naught, but wrought with labor and travail night and day, that we might not be chargeable to any of you." (II Thessalonians III. 8.) And when Christ sent out his disciples, he forbade them the carrying or providing of gold or silver in their purses. These were to constitute *no part* of the considerations of the labors before them.

5. And with regard to the subject of feet-washing, what method had we best adopt to provide against the troubles growing out of having different modes of performing the ordinances among us? We hereby recommend and pray that the decision of 1872 be readopted by this meeting. The subject was brought before the elders of that Annual Meeting, a committee had been appointed, and a careful investigation made for a final decision to "*make no change whatever in the mode* and practice of feet-washing, and stop the futher agitation of the subject." And in 1876, when it again came up, it was decided that "no church can change from the double to the single mode on the authority of the Annual Meeting."

Now, the decision of 1872 should, we think, have forever settled the feet-washing question, and to this we desire to hold as the order of the church unless we can be convinced that the double mode is wrong, or that Christ will be pleased with different modes and practices of worship in his church. All do admit that the command is fulfilled by the ancient or general order, and why not abide by it? Why should we have such troubles in these last days with an ordinance that has so long stood under the blessings of God while the church prospered.

Dear brethren, in order to have permanent peace and union restored—which we hope all are praying for—we will have to deny ourselves of the recent inventions among us, and fall back and unite upon the principles of the gospel and the ancient principles and apostolic order of the church. Upon this we were all once united and satisfied until the innovations herein alluded to crept in among us, which are now disturbing our peace. Can we not, dear brethren, all acknowledge that we were not watchful and guarded enough in suffering those strange things to come into the church and repent for our want of faithfulness? Forbearance, we think, is the door by which these things came into church one after another, and now it seems there is no door to be found by which to get them out again.

Do not, dear brethren, find fault with us, and conclude we are taking too much upon us. We have, with sorrowful hearts, looked upon the very fast drift and movement of things in the church; and as all efforts to exterminate from the church the things which mar our peace have thus far failed, we saw no better course than the one presented. Our plain decisions have been disrespected and overruled, and if this state of things shall continue to exist, we will lose all our power in the controlling of the church. We, for the present, can see no better plan by which to restore brotherly harmony and peace than to direct our efforts at the causes from whence the disunion arises.

Now, we pray, dear brethren, that this may receive your prayerful and serious considerations, and our wish and desires are that it may pass the Annual Meeting without any compromise. Conrad Brumbaugh, Emanuel Hoover, Samuel Garber, Abraham Flory, Jacob Miller, David Murray, William Cassel, George V. Siler, Samuel Murray, Emanuel Miller.

The foregoing petition was agreed upon and signed by twelve elders at first and two more afterwards; one, however, of the first requested that his name be dropped, which was done. These elders being urged from various parts of the brotherhood, and especially by many members in the Miami Valley, to make this another effort by petitioning Annual Meeting of Southern Ohio. It was so done, and the district meeting agreed to send it to the Annual Meeting of 1880, however not with the entire approval.

At the Annual Meeting there was a *substitute* formed by the Standing Committee which, though it made a plausible appearance to restrict certain things, was destined to *retain* in the church about all the petition wished to have done away, and consequently the answer did not give satisfaction. The substitute and its resolutions read as follows:

"ARTICLE 23. Petition from Miami Valley, Ohio, was presented, and the following substitute was offered and accepted:

"WHEREAS, Our beloved fraternity has been considerably disturbed by the brethren holding extreme views, some being disposed to enforce more vigorously the order of the church in regard to non-conformity to the world, and the principle of non-conformity to the world in giving form to our costume, than has commonly been done by our ancient brethren; while some on the other extreme would abandon the principle of non-conformity so far as that principle has anything to do with giving form to our costume; and,

"WHEREAS, The principle of non-conformity in giving form to our costume, as well as in everything else, has been a peculiar characteristic of our fraternity, and is so stated in our written history, and has had its influence with our non-swearing, and non-combatant, and our general principles identifying our fraternity with the primitive and apostolic church in preserving us from the extravagant expenditures which both the religious and secular world have fallen into, and in obtaining for us as a body the characters of simple honesty, purity, and uprightness in the world; and,

"WHEREAS, It is thought by many, and even so declared, that as a body we are opposed to all improvement and progress; and,

"WHEREAS, Contention and strife in the church are great obstacles in the way of both its holiness and its usefulness; therefore,

"*Resolved*, First, that we will labor in the spririt of the gospel and in brotherly love to maintain the principle of non-conformity in giving form to our costume, and in every way that the recognized peculiarities of our fraternity require.

"*Resolved*, Secondly, that while we declare ourselves conservative, in maintaining unchanged what may justly be considered the principles and peculiarities of our fraternity, we also believe in the propriety and necessity of so adapting our labor and our principles to the religious world as will render our labor and principles most efficient in promoting the reformation of the world, the edification of the world, and the glory of God. Hence, while we are conservative we are also progressive.

"*Resolved*, Thirdly, that brethren teaching through the press or ministry, or in any way, sentiments conflicting with the recognized principles and peculiarities of our fraternity shall be considered offenders, and dealt with as such. And to specify more particularly the subject named in the petition, we offer the following as an answer:

"1. Inasmuch as there exists a widespread fear among us that the brethren's high schools are likely to operate against the simplicity of the gospel of Christ, as also to cultivate the desire for an exclusively educated ministry, to guard these schools, therefore, from producing these effects, we think the principals of these schools should meet and adopt rules that will prevent such tendency, and said rules be in harmony with the Annual Meeting.

"2. Sabbath-schools, when held in the spirit of the gospel, may be made the means of bringing up our children in the "nurture and admonition of the Lord;" but should have no picnics and celebrations, or any vain things of the popular Sunday-schools of the day connected with them.

"3. All meetings for worship should be held as our stated or regular meetings are held, and we be cautious not to use such means as are calculated to get persons into the church without gospel conversion—such as over persuasion or excitement, simply to get them into the church—but use the gospel means to get them to turn away from sin.

"4. In regard to a paid ministry, we believe it is not right in the sense for brethren to go and labor for churches in the hope of receiving money for services, and the offer of money as an inducement to brethren to preach, but to poor ministers who are faithful, both in the doctrine and practice of the church, we would encouarge giving toward their necessities, as also of defraying their expenses of traveling in attending to church interest.

"5. Inasmuch as our old fathers have always admitted the validity of both modes of feet washing, and as much as we desire a more perfect union in this matter, we cannot condemn either mode as being invalid. And inasmuch as former decisions have failed to settle this to the satisfaction of all, we advise more forbearance, and liberty to the conscience of our brethren in this matter, because both have been practiced among us, and the best way to stop the agitation of this question is to allow the same liberty of conscience for our brethren that we ask for ourselves. But this shall not be construed to annul the present decision and advice of Annual Meeting."

From this it will be seen that the Annual Meeting of 1880 did not read and act upon the petition itself, but the above "substitute" was made and presented to take its place. But the manner the petition is here disposed of, and the way in which the answers or resolutions coil around the high schools, Sunday schools, etc., so as still to retain these with the other grievances in the church, could not render satisfaction to the brethren, and, instead of putting these things *away*, it rather by these would-be restrictions, *recognizes* them as having a legal right in the church, which was thought was leaving things in a worse shape now than it was before.

And the terms the Annual Meeting here uses in defining her position, saying that, "While we are *conservative* we are *progressive*" (which though very true, for that was the exact position of the Annual Meeting at that time, is yet), was not satisfactory, for the brethren were praying to have the progressive movement *put away* and not retained.

And the terms which the Annual Meeting uses with regard to feet washing, saying that "our fathers always *admitted the validity* of both modes of feet washing," was not considered exactly correct nor consistent. The fathers bore with *or suffered* the single mode where it existed, as it lay comparatively quiet then, not causing much trouble, but both the fathers and the Annual Meeting until late years considered the double mode *the* mode and the only recognized mode, and hence the single mode was not considered strictly valid, or of equal propriety with the double mode.

And in concluding this matter the Annual Meeting says, "The best way to stop the agitation of this question is to allow the same liberty of conscience for our brethren that we ask for ourselves.

This, also, was very unsatisfactory to the brethren, for it was clearly seen tht every effort the brethren made to Annual Meeting to get these things out, she gave them but the more foothold. "Liberty of conscience." This was thought was only kindling the fire for futher disunion and contention—every one do as their conscience may choose to dictate! Conscience the guide! One of the most dangerous doctrines ever preached, and it came from the brethren's Annual Conference Meeting. The tendency, of the "conscience" may be a guide in one of the Lord's ordinancnes, it may be the same in another, and where, in such an order of things, can exist the Lord's people who are to be of "one mind" and "speak the same things?"

The brethren were by this time very nigh discouraged, and it was by many now declared as entirely useless and fruitless to go to Annual Meeting any more.

It was also discovered that the church was still more inclined to depart from her former established practices. We were informed by letter thus: (Speaking of a certain state district, composed of about eighteen or twenty local districts) "Here, as yet, all the churches practice the double mode; *but*," says the writer, "my impression is that in a year or two they will change solidly to the single mode. The drift of sentiment," says he, "is settling in strong in Indiana, Illinois, Iowa, Northern Missouri, Kansas, and in the East, toward the single mode."

Such a state of feeling existed in 1880, after the petition had been before Annual Meeting. It becoming manifest that the way it was disposed of did not, in the least, check this disturbing element. And not much wonder when it is said in the substitute in answer to the petition, "*While we are conservative, we are also progressive*."

About this time also other grave departures were not only thought of and advocated, but actually practiced. We will here cite to a few. First, the *reporting of sermons*. This was indulged in by some of our leading brethren taking their reporters and have them note their speeches as delivered to the audience, and afterwards published in their periodicals. This matter of making a public report even at our Annual Meeting was in former years not allowed, and brethren who are now at the head of the Annual Meeting take liberty, when they go to their regular meetings, to have their sermons noted. In the year 1870 a brother was severely censured and corrected for having brought a reporter, at his own expense, to the Annual Meeting of 1869, but now it is done every year, and the Annual Meeting says nothing against it. Their conscience allows them to do now what they would not allow H. R. Holsinger to do at first—in 1869.

Sunday-schools and Sunday-school conventions were at this time also more strongly advocated than ever, and it was clearly seen that the state of things were becoming more corrupt and determined continually.

Now, the way the aforesaid petition was disposed of, and the manner that things were moving in general, gave rise to a notice for a special council, as noted in the *Vindicator* of 1880, page 378. We give it here: "Having learned that many brethren in different localities and states think there should be a consultation of the brethren in order to learn the minds of one another, to know if all can be satisfied with the disposition that the Annual Meeting made of the Miami Valley petition, and if not, to learn what course would be thought best to be pursued for the good of the church, we have therefore agreed, after having had considerable correspondence with brethren in other states, and after having convened together in the fear of the Lord on the 9th day of November, 1880, to appoint a meeting for special consultation, to be held with the brethren in the Wolf Creek Church, Montgomery

County, Ohio, on the 8th day of December next, to which all our faithful and steadfast brethren—both in the ministry and at the visit—who are in favor of the *ancient and apostolic order of the church, as set forth in said petition*, are most heartily invited. Brethren coming by railroad will stop off at Brookville, in the Pittsburg, Cincinnati & St. Louis Railroad, about twelve miles west of Dayton. Brethren coming from other states beforehand are invited to stop and visit adjoining churches, if convenient. It will, of course, not be expected that any of those who have been expelled in any of the states will take part in the deliberations of the meeting. Signed by Abraham Flory, Samuel Murray, Emanuel Hoover. The brethren's papers will please copy."

We give this notice to show that the brethren in the Valley did not aim to take this into their own hands, but that a general consultation might be had. The meeting of the 8th of December was well attended by the leading brethren from different states, and after deliberating for nearly three days it was concluded that the Miami Valley petition again go to Annual Meeting. And it was moved by D. P. Saylor, that, with regard to feet-washing, the Annual Meeting shall be asked to fall back to her decision of 1872. It was decided that the petition shall go *direct* from this meeting to Annual Meeting. It was so agreed on and advised by the leading men of the Annual Meeting.

Minutes of the Miami Valley Council and the Petition.

At the special or great council meeting held with the brethren of the Wolf Creek Church, on the 8th, 9th, and 10th of December, 1880, brethren from the various states being assembled, the following resolution with regard to the subject of feet-washing, after the evils of the present manner of observing it were fully considered, was proposed and passed the meeting unanimously:

Resolved, That with regard to the mode of feet-washing, we ask the Annual Meeting of 1881 to re-adopt the decision of 1872, and repeal all decisions made since then that do in any wise favor or encourage the single mode. This resolution to be sent to the Annual Meeting of 1881 for confirmation.

The question was asked the meeting, Whether brethren had the right to petition the Annual Meeting and to sign the same. Answered that they had the right to do so and sign it, of course.

Question 2. Asked if the committee of last year authorized any brethren to go abroad, out of their own territory, to ordain two brethren. The brethren present of the last Standing Committee said they gave no such privilege.

Question 3. Is such a course legal? Answered that adjoining elders should be consulted in all such cases, and that if such work was done, it was illegal, and the elders are not bound to recognize it.

A decision of Southern Illinois was read on the same subject, which gives it as wrong to do so. It was, therefore, decided that,

WHEREAS, Offense has been given to churches by elders going from home and ordaining brethren without consulting the elders of the adjoining churches in which the ordination is made, and contrary to the general order of the brethren; therefore,

Resolved, That all elders be admonished not to do as above stated until next Annual Meeting, when the duties of elders in regard to this work will be more definitely defined.

A supplement to the Miami Valley petition was read, but it was concluded to consider the petition first.

Commencing at the petition the subject of high schools was first read. It was found that one great objection to these schools was, that some have assumed the authority to call them and advertise them as the "Brethren's School," when the Annual Meeting never gave them such authority.

Query 1. With regard to high schools among us, we fear they will operate greatly against the simplicity of the gospel of Christ, as well as create or cultivate the desire for an educated ministry, which is not in harmony with the teachings of Christ and the apostles, nor with the ancient views of the church. Paul says, "Knowledge puffeth up, but charity edifieth." (I Cor. VIII. 1.) "Mind not high things, but condescend to men of low estate." (I Cor. I.) Again, "Be not wise in your own conceits." (Rom XII.16) The views of our old brethren were in perfect harmony with the gospel as regards this matter, as will be seen by reference to the following queries and decisions:

Annual Meeting of 1831. Article 1. "Whether it was considered advisable for a member to have his sons educated in a college? Considered not advisable, inasmuch as experience has taught that such very seldom come back afterward to the humble ways of the Lord."

Annual Meeting of 1852. Article 12. "How is it considered by the brethren if brethren aid and assist in building great houses for high schools, and then send their children to the same? Considered, that brethren should be very cautious, and not mind high things, but condescend to men of low estate." (Rom. XII. 16.)

Annual Meeting of 1853. Article 28. "Is it right for a brother to go to college, or teach the same? Considered, that we would deem colleges a very unsafe place for a simple follower of Christ, inasmuch as they are calculated to lead us astray from the faith and obedience of the gospel." And in 1857, when the subject again came up, the answer of the Annual Meeting is definitely given thus: "*It is conforming to the world.* Knowledge puffeth up, but charity edifieth."

Thus we see that high schools were not permitted to come into the church for at least twenty-seven years after they were first urged; therefore,

Resolved, That this meeting petition the Annual Meeting of 1881 to re-adopt the answer to Query 28, of 1853, with the following amendment: "*It is conforming to the world*, and repeal all the decisions that have been made that favor high schools conducted amongst us by the brethren." The above passed the meeting almost unanimously.

Query 2. Sabbath-schools we consider to be more of human origin than by command of Christ or his apostles, and hence are more of a worldly custom than of gospel principle and authority: are not in harmony with the apostolic order of the church, the principles of the gospel, and were never sanctioned by the Annual Meeting in the way many are and will be conducted. Paul says, "Fathers, provoke not your children to wrath, but bring them up in the nurture and admonition of the Lord." (Eph. VI. 4.) This command is given to parents, and not to others; therefore,

Resolved, That we petition our next Annual Meeting to withdraw the right of holding Sunday-schools in the brotherhood.

Passed nearly unanimously.

Query 3. Protracted or revival meetings, in the way they are generally conducted, are, we claim, not in harmony with the old order and the apostolic rules of the church. "And Paul, as his manner was, went in unto them, and three Sabbath-days reasoned with them out of the Scriptures." (Acts XVII. 2.) Again, "And when the Jews were gone out of the synagogue, the gentiles besought that these words be preached to them the *next Sabbath*." (Acts XIII. 42.) "And the *next Sabbath-day* came almost the whole city together to hear the word of God." (Verse 44.)

Resolved, That this meeting petition Annual Meeting to revise the answer of Article 3 of the petition, so as to read, and we be not allowed to use, instead of the words "be cautious."

Passed unanimously.

The answer as revised will read thus: "All meetings for worship should be held as our stated or regular meetings are held, and be not allowed to use such means as are calculated to get persons into the church without gospel conversion—such as over-persuasion or excitement, simply to get them into the church, but use the gospel means to get them to turn away from sin."

Query 4. A salaried or paid ministry is also against the apostolic order. Hear Paul on this subject: "I have coveted no man's silver, or gold, or apparel; yea, ye yourselves know that these hands have ministered unto my necessities, and to them that were with me." (Acts 33:34) "What is my reward, then? Verily, that when I preach the gospel I may make the gospel without charge, that I abuse not my power in the gospel." (I Cor. IX. 18.) Again, "Neither did we eat any man's bread for nought, but wrought with labor and travail night and day, that we might not be chargeable to any of you." (II Thess. III. 8.) And when Christ sent out his disciples he forbade them the carrying or providing of gold or silver in their purses. These were to constitute no part of the considerations of the labors before them.

Resolved, That this meeting urge the elders of our fraternity to carry out the decision as given by the last Annual Meeting, which is as follows:

In regard to a paid ministry, we believe it is not right in the sense for brethren to go and labor for churches in the hope of receiving money for services, and the offer of money as an inducement to brethren to preach, but to poor ministers who are faithful both in the doctrine and practice of the church, we would encourage giving toward their necessities, as also of defraying their expenses of traveling in attending to church interests.

The above being disposed of the condition of many of the members in parts of the brotherhood was considered, and it was further

Resolved, That by the general voice of this meeting we advise our brotherhood to bear with all our brethren and sisters in the several localities who have been threatened by a majority who, perhaps, have limited their time—members who seem to want to abide by the general order and the petition, and against whom there is no individual charge existing. The united voice of this meeting is to bear with all such until the Annual Meeting shall consider the business of this meeting; and we further advise that all those who have been expelled for holding the sentiments in the Miami Valley petition shall be held as members of the church, and that they shall not be held to acknowledge simply for holding those views.

QUERY

With regards to the present missionary plan, with its "Board of Directors," etc., we are not in full harmony with, and do therefore offer the following:

That we ask the Annual Meeting of 1881 to recall said decisions of last year, in which we fear a paid ministry is encouraged, and urge it earnestly upon the brotherhood to be more actively engaged in spreading the truth amongst us, and to all as much as can be done, but in a more simple manner, after the pattern and advice of the church as given us heretofore.

Decided by this special council that this query shall be first presented to the district meeting.

The conduct of the brethren generally and the spirit of humility and Christian courtesy manifested during the time of this meeting was commendable, and had, we trust, its good effects. The special call for this meeting was by many thought to have been quite needful, and it is hoped that its salutary effects would be felt and appreciated by all.

By order of the Meeting.

SAMUEL KINSEY
Kinsey's Station, Montgomery Co., Ohio

Accordingly this petition was handed to the Standing Committee. But now these same Annual Meeting brethren who, on December 8th, helped and said it should go up begin to draw back, saying that it did not come there legal and would likely be objected to; so it was not permitted to come before the general council for consideration in the way it was agreed upon by these leading brethren, but was declared illegal. None of the leading brethren who helped to send the petition up again did defend it before the meeting save one; and not only was this petition thus rejected as illegal, but the following was passed against it at the same meeting:

"ARTICLE 22. *Resolved*, That the decision in regard to what is called the Miami Elders' Petition is as near right as any that can be reached upon the questions embodied in said petition, and prosperity of the brotherhood demands that said decision of Annual Meeting of 1880 remain unchanged."

In the spring of 1880 the brethren of the Dry Creek Church, Iowa, presented a petition similar in substance to the one from the Miami Valley, and passed it through the Middle District of Iowa to the Annual Meeting, but it got no further than to the Standing Committee.

In rejecting the Miami Valley petition, and then passing the foregoing resolution against it, and that by some of the leading brethren of the Annual Meeting who had agreed at the December 8th meeting that it should go up direct from there and have a hearing, did now fully settle and confirm the idea and lamentable fact that nothing could ever by expected from the Annual Meeting that would do away with the innovations which caused the trouble and threatened division. Here was laid the *cause* which was now *fully ripe* for a movement to afford relief. Here many of the fathers and members over great portions of the brotherhood, who felt to hold on to the former practice and usages of the church were not only disappointed, but much discouraged, and viewed it as useless and a waste of time and effort any more to go to Annual Meeting, and to quietly settle down with folded arms and see the church still more drift into a state of apostacy and general corruption they could not, and hence, inasmuch as the petition was rejected by Annual Meeting and did remain in the hands of the petitioners, notice was given through the *Vindicator* that a meeting would be held with the brethren in the Ludlow and Painter Creek Church, near Arcanum, Darke County, Ohio, on the 24th day of August, 1881. The object of that meeting was stated thus: "The meeting is intended for all the faithful part of the church in the various states and localities, that they may consult with regard to the necessary provisions for the preservation of a unanimity of sentiment in faith and practice, the purity of the church," etc. The day arrived and the meeting was well attended, brethren and sisters from various states being present. The meeting was opened by singing

"Come Holy Spirit heavenly Dove,
With all thy quickening power."

After an appropriate exhortation and prayer the seventeenth chapter of John was read. After a few brief exhortations on the chapter the object of the meeting was stated. The state and condition of the church was stated, and the efforts made by the brethren for years to bring about a better state of affairs, having failed at the Annual

Meeting—not the satisfaction rendered to meet the desired ends. It was stated, "This meeting has been called that a remedy may be arrived at by which to restore the desired object. A unanimity of sentiment is desired and should be had if possible."

Up to about the middle of day an interchange of views and the state and condition of the church in various parts of the brotherhood, together with what would be best to do, were the topics under consideration. About 1:00 P.M. the deliberations were resumed, and the following resolutions were proposed as a remedy:

Resolutions passed at the Special Conference, held with the brethren of the Ludlow and Painter Creek Church, near Arcanum, Ohio, August 24, 1881:

After a careful hearing of the present condition of the church from the brethren of Ohio, and from those that were present from other states, the following paper, with its resolutions, was considered and passed:

DEAR BRETHREN:—It is manifest that our church is in a confused condition, and that duty requires something to be done for the peace and union of our church. There is a spirit or element amongst us which is disturbing our peace. Our dear old brethren have borne it all patiently for about thirty years. Up to the year 1851 peace and union existed in the church. In the year 1851 the first paper was granted to be printed amongst us. In 1857 Sunday-schools were rather granted. In 1858 liberty was granted for long revival meetings and also high schools. These somewhat disturbed the peace of many brethren. Thus we clearly see that when the order of the church was once broken, one new innovation and deviation after another crept in amongst us to the sorrow of many brethren and sisters.

Two ways of observing the ordinances of the house of God also crept in amongst us, greatly disturbing the peace and union of the church. First—The supper was put on the table at the time of feet-washing. After a little some also wanted the bread and wine on the table at the same time. And now, also, two or three ways are suffered in practicing the ordinance of feet-washing. And the single mode is also strongly advocated, and was very nearly granted by the Annual Meeting of 1880. Money soliciting and begging is also granted, and what next the Lord only knows.

Dear Brethren, do we not clearly see that we are fast drifting into the popular customs of the world? Thus far our old brethren have suffered themselves to be led along until they feel to be led no farther in this current. So far they have borne all these things patiently, but have made many efforts by sending query after query to Annual Meeting, which accomplished but little in checking this fast element among us. A mild and friendly petition was sent to the Annual Meeting of 1880, praying that body to grant the request therein asked for. But instead of that they framed an unsatisfactory substitute and answer, many brethren considered it to be unscriptural with its answer, and we think it has been a cause of divisions in the church. Many brethren and sisters were, therefore, not satisfied with it, and so we sent it to the Annual Meeting again in 1881, when it was rejected and made out illegal with the council of December 8, 1880. Many tender feelings were wounded in looking over these proceedings, and hence are discouraged in making any further efforts or requests to this body, which, of late years, has been so much controlled by the fast element that it looks like as if the old brethren are but little regarded.

Now, dear brethren, you need not wonder or fault us, when we feel to be led no further in this popular current, and hence have made this another effort in calling a council to effect something for the peace and union of our church, to try and agree upon some rule or order for the Brethren's Church in the future. And we see no safer plan than to adhere more strictly to the ancient order of the church as practiced by the ancient fathers of our church, which we believe was in strict harmony with the spirit of the gospel, and in which a number of our churches were organized—in the same faith once delivered unto the saints, and hence about all believed in the universal practice of our ancient brethren, with a few exceptions.

Be it, therefore, *Resolved*, That we will more strictly adhere to the self-denying principles of the gospel, as practiced by our ancient brethren, and as set forth in our petition of 1880, to which we wish to hold. With this amendment as the petition mentions popular Sunday-schools, and revival meetings the way they are generally conducted, to be more clearly understood, we say that we feel to suffer none in the Brethren's Church, and then we will be sure to have no trouble with them. No Sunday-schools, no high schools, no revival meetings, no paid ministry, no missionary plans or mission boards, as now granted by Annual Meeting. No money soliciting or begging to carry out such plans. No single mode of feet washing, no musical instruments, as pianos, melodeons, and organs, etc. No unlawful interest to oppress the poor.

Resolved, Further, that we fully adhere to primitive Christianity as taught by Christ and his apostles in all his commandments and precepts, as practiced by our forefathers (the first above-named things we do not understand as belonging to primitive Christianity as taught by Christ and his apostles), and that we strictly adhere to a plain and decent uniformity of dress as soldiers of King Immanuel; that the brethren wear a plain, round-breasted coat with standing collar, hat, overcoat, and everything else to correspond. A plain way of wearing the hair and beard—no fashionable mustaches and no roached or shingled hair. The sisters also to wear a plain, modest dress and bonnet, also a plain white cap in time of worship or on going abroad; in short, that the brethren and sisters let their light shine as a light on a "candlestick," and not part or wholly under the "bushel," but to show to the world that we try to possess what we profess. And above all that brethren and sisters be more upon their guard and more reserved in their conversation, as that "unruly tongue is doing much mischief among us."

Now the above-named things we claim are in strict harmony with the spirit of the gospel, and thus we should strictly adhere to and fulfill our baptismal vow, which we made before God and many witnesses. Also, we look upon our many periodicals the way they are conducted as being very injurious to the cause of our Master.

We are by no means opposed to mission-work, if carried out in gospel order. Neither are we opposed to assist our poor ministers in such work; and when we speak of carrying out the ancient order of our church, we do not mean all little usages and customs that were amongst our people then, but to be more of "one mind" and speak and teach more the one and same thing as taught by the apostle. (Read Romans XII. 12, 16, 17; Galatians I. 6, 7, 8, and 9; II Thessalonians III. 6; I Timothy VI.5; II Timothy III. 5; Titus I. 10,11; Second Epistle of John X. 11; II Corinthians VI. (latter part of chapter); Revelations II. 14,15,20; Revelation XVIII. 4, etc.)

Now, after this resolution is accepted, we advise that all our members be counseled in every church in the valley, and in all other districts in our brotherhood that unite with us. Do the same to get the minds of the members. And we advise that two faithful and impartial elders be present at those councils, as we want nothing but honesty and fairness. But first, before any council is gone into, the members should be well instructed and enlightened in every point, showing no partiality nor forbidding brethren to give their opinion in love on both sides. After the members are well enlightened, let each member express his own mind, that a fair decision may be made, so we can learn how many will stand united to the ancient order of our church; and if some should ask time to consider, let it be granted them. To such the door of the church is open. But such as will express themselves not willing to stand united with the ancient order of our church, we could not help them, and if they would afterwards change their minds and wish to unite with us, they will then have to enter legally according to order, the door of the church to be open for them also; but such as will not stand united with us in the apostolic order of our church, would then have to be disfellowshiped from the old brethren's church.

Signed in behalf of the meeting by the following elders: Abraham Flory, Jacob Miller, David Murray, Emanuel Hoover, George V. Siler, Emanuel Miller, David Wise, Stephen Metzger, Samuel Garber, Nathan Haywood, Conrad Brumbaugh, William Cassel, Joseph Arnold, Jacob Metzger, Samuel Musselman.

However, before the foregoing resolutions were submitted for adoption considerable was said by a few brethren against the propriety of adopting them, although it was unanimously admitted that these resolutions were in harmony with the former usages of the brotherhood. It was also intimated, in answer to a question, that all those who would vote to stand by these resolutions would absent themselves from the then acknowledged Annual Meeting, which fact we think was well understood that such would be the case, unless the Annual Meeting party would come back and do away with the innovations as set forth in said resolutions. After considerable was said for and against the move of adopting the proposed resolutions by way of enlightening the members, a rising vote was taken, and a large number of members of both brethren and sisters rose up in favor of the resolutions being adopted, and it was so.[1]

The center of this movement was in the Miami River valley of southwest Ohio, as evinced in a number of actions taken in the meetinghouses of this area. The climax came in the Ludlow and Painter Creek meetinghouse in the adoption of the resolutions of August 24, 1881, which served as something of a declaration of independence for the Old Order group of Brethren. As was true of the Declaration of Independence of the United States of 1776, however, much conflict was to follow this action. The ***Brethren's Reasons*** *continued in outlining some of this conflict over the next year and a half.*

Fig. 42. *Prayer at Annual Meeting, 1881, the year of the Old Order division. (BHLA)*

Fig. 43. *H. D. Davy, Annual Meeting moderator 1865-1876. (BHLA) After joining the Old German Baptist Brethren he served as Annual Meeting moderator of that body 1886-1887 and 1890-1893.*

THE EFFECT

We will now proceed to give a brief sketch of how the adoption of the aforesaid resolutions affected the general brotherhood. But we will, in the first place, call the attention of the reader to consider well the *intention and purpose* of the resolutions.

First, it is seen that the intention was to rid the church of the innovations and movements as set forth in the various petitions and in the resolutions, and bring it back to former usages.

Second, and it is seen that no *compulsory* measures shall be resorted to; no coercive means to be used; nothing but fairness to be desired and practiced; and no member to be required to take their stand until a fair chance is given to be fully enlightened, if so need be, and then each choose for themselves. Time is to be given to each one to consider whether they wish to stand in fellowship with those who tolerate those innovations and deviations from the old order which caused this division, or whether they wish to stand with those who have now resolved to no longer go with that party who advocate and practice the departures from the ancient faith of the church. So each member could act from volition of mind, whether to stand identified with the new things as brought into the church, or from choice go with those who have now renounced them. Such a course, under these circumstances, was thought would be neighborly, brotherly, and Christian.

But instead of this course being pursued the same evening, perhaps after the resolutions were adopted, plans were already talked of by the opposers as to how they might defeat this work; and in a few days it was discovered that there was formed a party designated as the "conservative" Annual Meeting brethren. These at once and in haste commenced operations on rather rash and coercive principles. One-sided visits were ordered to members, and councils appointed without precedent or gospel authority. The work was carried on in this wise: Young brethren did hastily, without counseling their elders who had the oversight of them and the churches for years, and who had labored faithfully in building up the good cause, send visits and arraign thus their elders and others before councils, making them out as evil doers, obtaining judgment against them, casting them out that it might be fulfilled as the scripture saith, "Blessed are ye, when men shall hate you, and when they shall *separate you from their company,* and shall reproach you, and *cast out your name as evil.*" And no doubt some of those who were now so very busy in working behind their old brethren's backs in this of appointing councils and bringing those fathers and mothers into judgment for no other question than the part they took in petitioning Annual Meeting, and wishing to indorse and stand by the resolutions, did so, that they might quickly scare, crush, and kill out the work of August 24th; for some did afterwards, when closely questioned, confess to that effect.

But thank the Lord the brethren still live! The severer the treatment the firmer the brethren became. Every notch they made convinced the brethren but the more, and made them but the stronger. The Lord's ways are not man's ways. They first introduced changes and new orders into the church which caused the division, and now in their blind zeal they finish it. It seemed as though the Lord used them as instruments by which to accomplish the work of giving relief to his faithful few who were "groaning and paining to be delivered."

But there were exceptions. There were certain leaders who went from church to church, carrying on this sort of work, while there were hundreds who were and still are of a neutral inclination. Some did what they did do because they knew no better at the time, and have regretted it since. In some churches six or seven only stood for the old way at first, but soon increased to thirty or forty. In others sixty or seventy, but soon increased to double the number. Many stood back "for fear of the Jews," but in nearly all the states are they continually coming over to the old landmarks as fast as they can have the self-denial and fortitude so to do. It is however just here to say that these young brethren were encouraged to go on with this kind of work by certain rashly minded elders from other parts, who chanced to be in the valley at the time. On the 2d day of September (only nine days after the resolutions were passed) was a council meeting held in the same church where the resolutions were passed. Here the elder, two ministers, three visiting brethren, and a goodly number of members were already expelled for wishing to stand by the ancient usages of the church as set forth in the resolutions. Some were denied the privilege of giving their reasons in full why they preferred standing with the old order part of the church (it seemed as there were now two parts becoming manifest). Advantages were taken and unfairness was manifest in this council as well as in getting it up, for much was said to *intimidate* members; so much so that many felt afraid and did not act out their convictions of right immediately. This unfair and one-sided hasty work was carried on in most of the churches where there were any that dared to say they wished to stand with the old order part of the church. In some churches fifty and more were expelled at one time. Ministers and even old faithful elders, with all who wished to stand by the resolutions and could no longer fellowship the innovations, were forbidden the privilege to preach and worship in the church houses which their own hands had helped to build, offering them not a farthing of remuneration, nor any proposal of compromise; and instead of pointing to the gospel and "provide things honest in the sight of all men," they pointed to the supreme courts.

In places where the keys were held by the old brethren part new locks were put on by the Annual Meeting brethren, when at the same time the brethren proposed to open the house alternately or divide amicably; but all this did not satisfy them. This assumption of power of locking church houses was generally held and urged by the official part. The laity had very little or no say in the matter. This domineering power also assumed to say, even in public, that all those ministers they had expelled would subject themselves to a fine of five hundred dollars, if they did solemnize marriages, while the county judges who know the causes of separation said not so, but tell the brethren to go on as usual, we will recognize your work, which they did do.

Now, this public announcement that the old brethren could not legally solemnize marriages was no doubt purposely so said, that the prophetic language of Paul to Timothy might be fulfilled—"Now the Spirit speaketh expressly that in the latter times some shall depart from the faith . . . *forbidding to marry.*"

Many things were said at these expelling councils to intimidate and break down this reform work, and it was even intimated at several councils that it might come to pass that if those who were expelled were not careful they might be put into the ban. Loud predictions were made that this reform work of the brethren would soon come to naught—referring to factions who had been expelled and gone off years before for some of the very same new things that are now tolerated by this Annual Meeting party.

At some places the resolutions were read and pronounced very bad, and at some places they were pronounced good. Questions were so differently put to the members that many did not know how to answer. At one of those councils the reading of the resolutions was ruled out, so ordered by the elder in charge of said congregation, and yet the issue was to stand by the resolutions or remain with the general brotherhood and its Annual Meeting, the church not knowing as a body what was set forth in the resolutions.

This severing of the churches in this rash manner, and locking of church houses, and grasping all the church property, expelling of elders, minister, and some of the most faithful members, commenced in a few days after the meeting of August 24th, as already stated, and in about six or eight weeks twelve or fifteen church districts were visited in the Miami Valley, and all shared the same treatment. In the meantime the same kind of work had already been learned in Indiana, and was going on there. In this limit of time hundreds were expelled, and nearly all the church property taken, and the doors locked against them, the brethren making no resistance, but endeavored to bear it with patience. Much more could be said by way of setting forth the unfairness and harsh treatment manifested by this expelling party, but we forbear.

It is just to say that some who took an active part in this expelling of the old fathers and mothers in Israel, together with others that wished to stand to the former usages of the church, as set forth in the petitions and resolutions, did at first work with the brethren, signed the petitions, and urged the elders to come upon some plan to take a firm stand against those innovations, but afterwards changed their course, which, after helping and urging that a stand be taken, looked a little hard to see them turn as they did, and act a conspicuous part in putting down the very thing they at first helped to bring about. Others talked strong that something would have to be done for the church, but when it came to the point they turned back.

After this expelling and locking of church houses was principally done, it occurred to the minds of some that their work should be ratified by their Annual Meeting. Accordingly in the spring of 1882—perhaps five or six months after their work was done or rather well under way—a petition was presented to their Annual Meeting, which reads as follows:

WHEREAS, Certain elders and others became aggrieved at our Annual Meeting in her manner of doing business, and also at some of her decisions, and hence have framed certain resolutions in which are set forth the cause of their aggrievances; and on the 24th day of August, 1881, they met together from different states in the Ludlow and Painter Creek Church, Darke County, Ohio, where those resolutions were read, and some remarks made upon their merits, etc.; and after an explanation by their foreman, when he said 'that all who vote for these resolutions separate themselves from the general brotherhood and its Annual Meeting,' they then took a rising vote to ascertain who were willing to accept their resolutions, thereby causing a division in the brotherhood, and especially in southern Ohio, hence bringing about a necessity for the elders and officers of the church, who were still willing to stand by the general order and usages of our Annual Meeting, to bring the matter before their local churches, where all that have gone with the resolutions were excommunicated from the church; therefore

"*Resolved*, That we ask Annual Meeting, through district meeting, to endorse the action of the churches in southern Ohio and elsewhere in regard to those who have gone with the resolutions, and also to enter the same upon the minutes." Answer: "This Annual Meeting does endorse the action of the churches which expelled the members who accepted the resolutions referred to above." (Article 13.) This resolution passed their meeting without inquiry or explanation. (See their full report, page 58. One who gave such advice was the first to move to pass it.)

Inasmuch as we have already set forth with what kind of spirit this expelling was done, and how unchristianlike those who were expelled were treated, and as we also gave the causes, we will here only call to mind a few things on this action of Annual Meeting endorsing this work: First, it would have looked more intelligent upon the part of the meeting if this matter would have been brought to light before a vote was taken, it being a fact well known that but few, comparatively speaking, of that Annual Meeting understood the real issue of the causes of this expulsion, or how it was done. Second, it is just to state that this Annual Meeting did pass a decision in the early part of its deliberations, making its decisions *mandatory* (see Article 5), and then they ratify this expelling and house-locking without bringing before that body what was done, and how those who were expelled were treated. This shows advantage-taking and unfairness, and it *binds*, according to the mandatory clause, those who did not have a full knowledge of what was done, having no chance to know, because the question was not explained before it was passed.

But after all this expelling and closing of churches, denying of solemnizing marriages was done, it did not stop the work on the part of those who were thus ruthlessly dealt with. Church-houses of other denominations, private houses, barns, and school-houses were offered to the brethren, and in fields and groves congregations would meet to hear those preach who were thus formerly expelled, and so the good work went on, and in a short time hundreds came out from this "conservative" party, and united with those who had thus been set out. Some who had helped in the work of expelling afterwards saw their mistake, came and asked pardon, and also joined in with them.

On the 25th day of November, 1881, according to appointment previously made, a goodly number of the old order part of the church—as they were now called—met at the barn of Brother Abraham Landis in the Salem Church, Montgomery County, Ohio, for counsel, and there decided to use the word *old* in connection with *German Baptist Brethren*, setting forth their position and desires for the old church worship, and to designate them from the *new*, or those who introduced and admitted new measures into their body; also for the purpose of writing deeds and giving certificates of membership, for it was understood already for some years that those who contended for the old practices of the church were known as the "old brethren," or the "old order brethren." Here also were made arrangements for the Yearly Meeting, which was held at Brookville, Ohio, on Pentecost, of the year 1882. Arrangements were also here made to send brethren to other states, east and west, to help those who had been oppressed, and had made urgent appeals to the brethren of the valley for assistance. Suffice it here to say that many were found in the several states who had not enjoyed fellowship for several years, because of the innovations which could not be sanctioned by all, and which finally caused this division. It is but just to state here that in this arrangement—to visit such who had made appeals—a body of members were found in the East who had previous to the day of Pentecost, 1881, separated themselves from the innovations tolerated by the general brotherhood and its Annual Meeting, and who had convened in council in Frederick County, Maryland, on Pentecost, 1881; and it was seen from their minutes that they in council were a united body, and labored to bring about that unity which formerly existed in the Brethren Church. This body numbered nearly five hundred members. The visit to them was made at their urgent request, and was much appreciated and enjoyed by them, and they at once co-operated with the old brethren of the Miami Valley and the western states at the Yearly Meeting to fall back to the old order of the church.

The congregations of the old order brethren were soon in working order on the old platform, as set forth in the resolutions and petitions, and at the meeting on Pentecost, 1882, churches were represented from nine different states. Here, in order to place on record the very severe opposition that their opposers manifested, it may not be amiss to state that we were, by the legal authorities, informed that they sought their advice to know if the brethren could not be stopped from holding their Yearly Meeting; but the judge said to them, "No;" that the Constitution of the United States granted all believers the free right of worship. Equal to this it may also be proper to state that at one of their council meetings, where they were putting on new locks during the services, or about that time, to keep the brethren out, one of their elders arose and said he believed it to be their duty to do all they could to keep the old brethren from preaching. This language fully convinced one certain brother who heard it, and he left the meeting. Such was the bitterness and trying opposition the brethren had to contend against at this time; but it seemed they prospered but the more. The brethren's Yearly Meeting was well attended from the different parts of the brotherhood, and many members were in attendance. The business was done harmoniously, and in a way these meetings were held in days of yore.

At this time the brethren's congregations were increasing in some localities by members coming and identifying themselves with the old brethren, doubling and tripling the number that first came out, that it became needful to build meeting-houses again in some localities for the accommodations of the people, the brethren having no expectation of having access to the houses they helped build, having been locked out, and locks being changed, and this ratified by their Annual Meeting, as already set forth. The brethren were not willing to go to law with brother for their just rights, as this would have been a violation of one of the cardinal principles ever held sacred by the brethren church. Quite a number of church-houses were built in the Miami Valley and other parts of the brotherhood during the summer of 1882.

Here it may be just to say, in order to show the reader what continued opposition this reform work of the brethren met with by their opposers, that not only were former privileges and rights denied, but many things were said to operate against them, and some things were done as it seemed to stop the building of new houses. In the fall of 1882 a church building was commenced in the Grove Church in Miami County, Ohio, on a lot donated to the old brethren for the purpose of building on it a house for worship. This lot joined the lot on which stood the house which had been built in common. The lot now donated has on it a spring, and certain privileges to the water of this fountain had been granted by conveying it in pipes to the house that had been built in common. When this new building was commenced, it was set near the head of this spring for the purpose of also having the benefit of it, there being an abundance of water. After the building was well under way a suit of infringement was brought against them by their conservative brethren. The old brethren proposed a compromise, but wished to go on with their building. An injunction was served, the process of building stopped, and the old brethren were arraigned before the court on the 27th day of November, 1882. The following is the sheriff's notice to the brethren:

STATE OF OHIO,
Miami County, ss:

To the Sheriff of the County of Miami:

You are hereby commanded to notify John Filburn, Samuel Studabaker, Silas Arnold, James Brubaker, as trustees and deacons and pastors, Harrison Shull and Joseph Arnold, as pastors of the Old German Baptist Church in Bethel Township, Miami County, Ohio, James White and James Berringer, that they have been sued by Henry Gump, pastor, David Filburn, Jacob Hawver, Jacob Frantz, as the deacons, and Jacob Coppock and the trustees of the German Baptist Church in Bethel Township, Miami County, Ohio, in the Court of Common Pleas of Miami County, and that unless they answer by the 9th day of December, 1882, the petition of the said plaintiffs against them filed in the clerk's office of said court, such petition will be taken as true and judgment rendered accordingly. You will make due return of this summons on the 20th day of November, 1882.

Witness my hand and the seal of the said court at Troy this 6th day of November, 1882.

J. B. LATCHFORD.
Clerk of the Court of Common Pleas, Miami County, Ohio.

I hereby certify that the within summons and indorsements thereon is well and truly copied from the original summons.

J. M. CAMPBELL, Sheriff.

After the case was examined by the court it was declared no infringement, and the old brethren paid their own costs and can go on with their building. The notice served on the old order brethren by the sheriff distinctly declared that they were "sued." The bringing of this suit did not only hinder the process of building for the time being, but cold weather set in, and it could not be put up and enclosed so as to protect work already done.

Suits were also brought at other places against the old brethren by this Annual Meeting party. In Cedar County, Iowa, the conservatives sued the old brethren for the exclusive right to the church property, of which the following from the clerk will show:

In the District Court of Iowa in and for Cedar County:

This is to certify that a suit, wherein A. M. Zook, Noah Rudy and John Zuck trustees, etc., were plaintiffs, and Samuel Musselman and others were defendants, set forth in the foregoing copy of original notice, was commenced in said court by filing of petition by plaintiffs therein on the 11th day of April, A.D. 1882.

JESSE JAMES,
Clerk of District Court.

In an after note from Iowa we have the following: "As it was published in the May number of the *Vindicator* the church of the brethren of Cedar County, Iowa, were sued by the conservative party for the church property of said church. This is to state to all that said suit is now withdrawn by the plaintiffs, costs paid, and both parties occupy the house alternately." This was the decision of the court, if we understand it correctly, and is what the brethren had proposed to them before they had entered suit.

In the Falling Spring Church, Franklin County, Pennsylvania, it so happened that the old order part of the church had the charge of the several meeting-houses at the time of the division. Their opposers demanded the keys, the brethren refused to give them up, knowing if they did so they would be locked out; but they opened the houses for them also and offered to do so still. But this did not satisfy them, as it seemed they wanted the exclusive right, and so they entered suit in court against the old brethren for the keys, which suit is still pending, and up to the time of this writing, April 13, 1883, they have not withdrawn it that we have learned.

The following is a copy of the notice served on our brethren:

In the Court of Common Pleas of Franklin County. In Equity Between William Tolhelm and others, plaintiffs, and *David Bonebrake and others, Defendants.*

To D. Bronebrake and others, within named Defendants:

You, and each of you, are hereby notified and required, within fourteen days after service hereof on you, and each of you, exclusive of the day of such service, to cause an appearance to be entered for you, and each of you, in the Court of Common Pleas of Franklin County, Pennsylvania, to the within bill of complaint of the within-named William Tolhelm and others, complainants, and to observe what the said court shall direct.

Witness my hand, at Chambersburg, this 21st day of December, A.D., 1881.

J. McDOWELL SHARPE,
Solicitor for Plaintiffs.

NOTE:—If you fail to comply with the above directions, by entering an appearance in the Prothonotary's Office, within fourteen days, you will be liable to have the bill taken pro confesso, and a decree made against you, and each of you, in your absence.

J. McDOWELL SHARPE,
Solicitor for Plaintiffs.

Also on the 14th day of February, 1883, the conservatives of Darke County, Ohio, entered suit against the old order brethren for preaching and solemnizing marriages in the name of the Old German Baptist Church.

The following petition gives the names of the several parties and the particulars:

John Bollinger, Christian King, Adam Miller, John Crumrine, et al., vs. Emanuel Flory, Jacob Miller, George V. Siler, Emanuel Miller, Wiliam Cassel, Joseph Arnold, Jonathan Wenerick, *et al.*, Darke Common Pleas Court Petition.

The said plaintiffs complain of the said defendants for that they are members of and represent the whole membership of the German Baptist Church of Darke County, Ohio, a numerous body, and impracticable to bring this action in the name of all; and that the said defendants are also too numerous to bring before the court by name, dissenters from said German Baptist Church. Plaintiffs further aver that the said German Baptist Church was organized in the United States as early as 1719, and still maintains its organization; and that it has ever since its organization been styled and known as the German Baptist Church, been controlled in its church policy and ecclesiastical matter by a synod composed of members of said church from its different congregations, and designated as Annual Meetings. Plaintiffs further aver that for the purpose of settling conflicts and differences that might arise in the different congregations of said church the church was divided into districts composed of designated contiguous congregations, in which districts were held districts meetings, inferior to and subordinate to the said Annual Meeting; that said district meetings were composed of members or delegates from the different congregations within said district, and that all action of said district meetings were appealable to the Annual Meeting as the final arbiter in all matters pertaining to said church; that inferior to and subordinate to said district meetings, the said church is divided into local congregations. Plaintiffs further aver that at the different Annual Meetings from time to time since 1851 up to the year 1881 certain harmless innovations were made in the ancient dogmas of said church in regard to Sabbath-schools, revival meetings, high schools, the washing of feet, etc., in consequence of which innovations the said defendants felt aggrieved, whereupon a special district meeting was called by said defendants at the Ludlow and Painter Creek Church August 24, 1881, at which special district meeting certain resolutions were passed, repudiating the action and doings of the various Annual Meetings in regard to said innovations representing Sunday-schools, high schools, missionary work, feet-washing, etc., and before passing the said resolutions the said resolutions were remarked upon by the foreman of said meeting and explained, in which he said "that all who vote for these resolutions separate themselves from the general brotherhood and its Annual Meetings;" and that with this understanding, and being well informed of what they were doing, the said defendants voted for said resolutions and thereby withdrew from the general brotherhood and its Annual Meeting, and still withhold themselves from fellowship with said church. Plaintiffs further aver that in consequence of said action of defendants in withdrawing from the membership of said church the elders and officers of said church brought the matter before the local churches, when all of said defendants were excommunicated from said church, which action of the said local churches in excommunicating defendants as aforesaid was considered and affirmed by the Annual Meeting of said church, held at Arnold's, Kosciusko County, State of Indiana, in May and June, 1882. Plaintiffs aver that by the said action of said defendants at said district meeting at Ludlow and Painter Creek Church, Darke County, Ohio, and the action of said local churches and the action of said Annual Meeting held at Kosciusko County, Indiana, the defendants ceased to be members of the said German Baptist Church, or have any interest in or connection with said church. Yet plaintiffs aver that defendants, disregarding the rights of the said German Baptist Church and of plaintiffs, have organized new congregations under the title and name of the Old German Baptist Church, and by means of and by the use of said name, and falsely representing that they are the only true and genuine Baptist Church, thus are enabled to and are influencing members of said German Baptist Church to withdraw their connection with said church and unite themselves with said new organization, thereby disturbing the peace and harmony of said German Baptist Church, which they would not be able to do if it was not for the use of said name and such false representations; that by thus influencing the members of said church to withdraw they are producing contentions in the families of plaintiffs, and bickerings and strife between husband and wife and parent and child, members of said German Baptist Church, to the great damage of said plaintiffs and against the peace and good order of said church. Plaintiffs further aver that said excommunicated members of said church, defendants herein, are obtaining license to solemnize marriages as ministers in good standing in said church, while in truth and in fact they are not ministers in good standing in said church, or members of said church in any sense of the word; that by thus obtaining license and solemnizing marriages they are interfering with the rights and privileges of ministers in good standing in said church by appropriating the emoluments and benefits derived from solemnizing marriages to their members of said church, which would otherwise go to the benefit and support of regular ministers in said Baptist Church. Plaintiffs therefore pray that at the final hearing of this case they may, as against said defendants, by a decree of this court, be secured in the use of the name "German Baptist Church," and that defendants may be enjoined from appropriating the said name or calling themselves the "Old German Baptist Church," and that they may also be restrained from taking out license as ministers of the Old German Baptist Church, or of solemnizing marriages as ministers of the same.

JOHN BOLINGER,
By BODIE & SWISHER, Attorneys.

THE STATE OF OHIO,
Darke County, ss.:

Personally appeared before me John Bolinger, who, being duly affirmed, says the facts set forth in the foregoing petition are true, as he believes.

JOHN BOLINGER.

Affirmed to and subscribed before me by the said John Bolinger this 14th day of February, 1883.

EDWARD MARTIN, Deputy Clerk.

The brethren had a consultation on the 14th day of March, and decided to meet the case calmly and patiently as the Lord's people ever have when brought before governors and rulers to answer to the truth. "Yea, and all that will live godly in Christ Jesus shall suffer persecution."

The plaintiffs say they represent the whole membership of Darke County, Ohio. But the conservative church of Darke County manifested no disposition that we are aware of to withdraw the suit. But this suit was not entertained very long until it was met by a demur which was sustained by the court, and the court did cast out the case at the cost of those who brought suit. It would seem like a great piece of folly for these people to bring suit against the brethren in this way under the present provisions and blessings afforded by the Constitution of the United States.

It is presumable that these steps in these various suits were taken against this reform move on the part of those who did it because they thought it their duty; and perhaps it was needful, and the Lord suffered it so to be to show a line of distinction and to prove the kind of spirits that characterized the different elements and the soundness of their faith, for by these the observer is enabled the better to distinguish according to righteous judgment.

Many incidents could be given to show how this coercive spirit manifested itself even in individual cases before and during this general separation, but it is the design of this little work only to set forth for the benefit of all sincere, inquiring minds the general principle, with its after workings, which was the cause of the issues and separation of this once peaceful fraternity which made its appearance in America upwards of one hundred and fifty years ago. (See the writings of Alexander Mack.)

In conclusion we are happy and can thankfully say that the unity of practice and the oneness of mind as was once enjoyed by the church is again manifested in that part of the church which is now known and recorded as the OLD GERMAN BAPTIST CHURCH. Identity is already acknowledged, from Philadelphia to the West at least, at the time of this writing, as far as Kansas and Nebraska, and from North to South. Nearly one hundred churches are already established.

Now, in conclusion, a short admonition to our dear brethren and sisters. We wish to say to us who have come out from those innovations, and have passed through the trials which some have, let us see well to our doings, and that we in all things endeavor to adorn in gentle meekness our humble and holy profession. Many good brethren and sisters are at this time still looking on, and are not altogether satisfied with their standing in the conservative part of the brotherhood. Our motto and aim should ever be, "By good works we constrain others." (Jesus.) "If we have not the spirit of Christ we are none of his." (Paul.)

Dear members, let us try to learn to bear our trials and any mistreatment patiently, and though we write, publish, and make these things known for each other's benefit, information, and encouragement, let us not speak hard words against those who have taken from us our rights in church property. We read that some of the good people of old did take "joyfully the spoiling of their goods." No doubt they, too, at times, felt very sensibly that they were abused, but still they bore it all patiently.

We see that some of our old fathers and mothers in Israel who did much by way of building up the good cause, and brought it along until we could step in, are as illy treated as we, and they take it all patiently. Let us try and endeavor so to shape our walk and conduct in life that when we shall depart we may leave behind us worthy examples of true holiness and piety, which shall remain as living evidences of our sincerity in the cause of our Master. And above all may we by grace divine so struggle through life and battle for the Lord that we may preserve the purity of the church, and that in her sacred duties and holy obligations—famous for the preservation and keeping of all the ordinances of the Lord's house—we hand her *one faith* and *one order* of duties and services down to our children, as our fathers handed them down to us.[2]

The most difficult problem in the division was the settlement of claims regarding church property which had been built by the ancestors of both groups. Such problems were not settled easily. Another problem was the establishment of the identity of the Old

Orders. One solution was the publication of The ***Brethren's Reasons.*** *Another solution was the publication of a periodical, the* ***Vindicator,*** *and of tracts. Evidently, however, the Old Orders did not produce very many tracts. One interesting item, however, was published in 1884 by Henry Koehler. In sixteen pages he covered some forty different topics, beginning with basic beliefs about God and moving into more traditional Brethren beliefs about baptism and the love feast. The last half identified more specific Old Order beliefs. That section, together with the introduction and conclusion, is included here.*

—THE—
PRINCIPLES AND PRACTICE
—OF THE—
OLD GERMAN BAPTIST BRETHREN

COMPILED FOR THE USE OF ALL SOULS
WHO ARE SEEKING FOR THE
"OLD" AND THE PURE
WORD OF TRUTH.

PRICE EIGHT CENTS A COPY.

BY HENRY KOEHLER,
COVINGTON, OHIO.
1884
MIAMI UNION PRINT, TROY, O.

PREFACE TO THIS VOLUME

The writer of these pages was formerly a Minister of the United Lutheran and Reformed, or Evangelical Church. For more than twenty long years he preached doctrines which are contrary to the word of God.

He was a "blind leader of the blind." But the Lord gave him the true light, knowledge and grace to see his errors and through faith, repentance and Trine Immersion received the pardon of his sins, and was thus admitted a member of the only true church of our Lord Jesus Christ. By Prayer and a dilligent search of the Holy Scriptures, he found that the fraternity of the *Old German Baptist Brethren* are the Church founded by Christ himself, and is therefore the *old Apostolic Church.*

He found it his duty to unite with this church. His soul is made glad, and rejoices in the Lord, and His Salvation, because he was once a poor, erring, blind and lost sheep, in the desert of this world, and in the Babylon of Modern Christianity. But *now* he has found the pure and complete truth as it is in Christ Jesus, and is *now* a member of the body of Christ, *the* church which is built upon the Rock Jesus, against whom "the gates of Hell cannot prevail" or overpower.

The reader is kindly requested to prove, to examine the contents of these pages prayerfully, in the light of the New Testament; and he will, like the writer, find that the Old Brethren are the true Church of Christ.

Should he, of which there is not the least doubt, receive of the good Lord *light, knowledge and grace* to see and know his errors, then he will also receive from the same source the *necessary courage* to say adieu to the modern false christendom and give God in Christ Jesus, and the OLD TRUTH, all the honor.

Our blessed Lord and Saviour grant it. So to God in the highest *alone* be the glory!

H. KOEHLER.

Covington, Miami Co., Ohio, April 1st., 1884.

INTRODUCTION

DEAR READER:

"Grace be unto you, and peace, from God our Father, and from the Lord Jesus Christ."

We lay before you a short abstract of the principles and of the Fraternity of the Old German Baptist Brethren. We humbly and earnestly beseech you to read and examine the same with much care and attention. We are convinced that the same contains nothing else but what our blessed Saviour taught and enjoined upon all his followers; that is what the Apostles taught, the Primitive Christians and our forefathers believed and practiced.

We claim to be the only church which *has all, believes all, practices all;* as it is commanded in the New Testament. The modern Christendom (of to-day) is corrupt (in spirit) and has no right whatever to call itself any longer the church of Christ. It has forfeited all claim to do this. *We claim this prerogative.*

We deem it, therefore, our duty and in accordance with the spirit of the age, to call the attention of our friends and neighbors, in all love and humanity to the *primitive principles* of the New Testament, and if possible, to persuade all such to return to, or accept of the same, (by a loving faith). Dear reader, search, ask for the *good old way*. It is the *best* way; it is a sure way; it is "the narrow way" which "leadeth to life everlasting." It is the entire doctrine of the Lord, Christ Jesus, who says: "I am the way, the truth and the life;" "Search the Scriptures." Examine these pages in the light of the gospel and you will find that we have the truth, and try to believe, to teach and practice nothing but the *Truth*.

The New Testament alone can teach you and I correctly what we must do to be saved, and to bear *rightly* the name of a christian and to be a sincere and true follower of Christ Jesus. Listen not to the pratings of the learned and the wise of our age. They teach false doctrines, winning wisdom, strange things, and will lead you astray and bring you into error, unbelief and final destruction.

If they have the wool, they care nothing about the sheep. They are blind leaders of the blind, and whosoever follows them will most certainly fall into the ditch of unbelief, spiritual carelessness, and at last into the precipice of eternal woe! Therefore, build your salvation upon no other foundation, but on the Rock of Salvation, who is no one else but the Lord Jesus Christ. God will bless an honest seeker; he will surely succeed. The Lord our God bless all who may have a desire for the old, pure truth, as it is in Christ Jesus. Dear reader, we now pray you again to read, to examine and to prove the following truths and apply the same to your spiritual and temporal welfare, is our earnest prayer to God. . . .

XVI.

That the discipline of the church must be enforced according to Matt., 18, 10–17.

XVII.

That it is our duty to be subject unto the civil government, or authorities.—Rom. 13, 1, 2–3.

XVIII.

That war and retaliation are contrary to the spirit and self-denying principles of the religion of Jesus Christ. We therefore take no active part whatever in war or strife, and reward not evil for evil.

We are *defenseless*. Read:

Matth. 5, 21; Luke, 6, 31, 32, 33.

Luke, 9, 54–55; Matth. 5, 38–39, 43–44; Rom. 12, 14, 20–21; Luke 23, 34.

XIX.

That the swearing of oaths is contrary to the word of God. Read Matth. 5, 34–37; Jas. 5, 12.

XX.

That it is contrary to the principles of the gospel to go with our fellow men to law, or take advantage of the civil law in any case or manner. Read Matth. 5, 40–48.

XXI.

That a non-conformity to the world in dress customs, daily walk and conversation is essential to true holiness and christian piety.

"And be not conformed to this world, but be ye transformed by the renewing of your mind, that ye may prove what is *that* good, acceptable will of God."—Rom. 12, 2.

Read: 1st Cor. 10, 6; Eph. 4, 17; 1st John 4, 5.

3d John, 11 v.; John 17, 15–16; Matth. 10, 38.

Matth. 16. 24–26; Matth. 18, 8–9; Mark 6, 36;

Luke 14, 27; Rom. 8, 12–13; Gal. 5, 24; Col. 3, 5–7;

Titus 2, 12; Matth. 18, 1–5; Matth. 23, 12; James, 4, 6; Luke 18, 14; 2d Cor. 6, 16–17.

XXII.

That it is contrary to the word of God to wear costly apparel.

"But what went ye out to see? A man clothed in soft raiment? Behold. they that wear soft clothing are in kings' houses."—

Matth. 11, 8.

Read Tim. 2, 9–10; 1st Peter, 3, 3–4.

Isa. 3, 16–26.

XXIII.

That secret societies as Free Masons, Odd Fellows, Redmen, Temperance Societies, &c., are contrary to the Word of God, and that no follower of Christ should have fellowship with "the unfruitful works of darkness, but rather reprove them."

Eph. 5, 11–13; 2 Cor. 6, 14.

XXIV.

We maintain that the use of musical instruments, such as pianos, organs, melodeons etc., in Christian families and houses of worship are against the simplicity of the gospel, the self-denying principles of the New Testament, and contrary to our baptismal vow. Read:

James, 5, 12; Eph. 5, 19; Job 21, 1–14; Amos, 6, 5–6.

XXV.

That it is contrary to the principles of our fraternity, to take part in political affairs, to vote at the polls, and to seek or hold public offices, such as President, Governor, Judge, Sheriff, Constable, etc., etc.

These matters belong to the world. *We should leave such matters there.*

XXVI.

That the so called colleges and schools of learning and sciences belong to the world and that they are contrary to the sound doctrine of the New Testament. Read:

Rom. 12, 16; James 3, 13–17; 1st Cor. 3, 18–22.

We claim that the Public Schools are sufficient for the education of our sons and daughters.

We maintain further that for the so called modern Sunday Schools, with their methods, means of instruction, peculiar melodies (of which very many are anything but sacred), their music, libraries, teacher's conventions, picnics, concerts, children's meetings, missionaries, book concerns etc., are not biblical and apostolic foundation, and no necessity can be found, that they are void of all good fruit, and bring forth chaff instead of wheat. We reject the Sunday School as a worldly institution.

XXVII.

We maintain that it is contrary to the sound doctrine of the New Testament that ministers of the gospel should prepare themselves for their calling by a *classical* or collegiate education. It makes the sacred office worldly. It leads men to pride, envy, contention, to love disputing, perverting the word of God, and to a fleshly and worldly wisdom. If we look into the spiritual condition of the clergy of our age, we meet with the sad fact that among the same, unbelief, pride, a desire to pervert the scriptures, a grasping for money, titles, honors, offices, love of the world, a striving to please men, to rule, and vain glory and boasting are predominant.

There are also cases where these gentlemen live in open sin, immorality and crime; all in the most case, a result (there are of course exceptions) of their great learning and education. Read: Titus, 1, 10–16; 1st Tim. 6, 3, 4–5.

Paul in his letters to Timothy and Titus makes it clear to understand what the qualifications of a minister of the Gospel should be. Read:

1st Tim. 3, 1–7; Titus, 1, 5–11.

These qualifications, however, cannot be obtained by a course of study in a college, or theological school, but only by sitting humbly at the feet of Jesus and learn of him. We do not advocate an ignorant ministry. No! a minister should be able to *teach and expound* the scriptures. But we deny that their aptness to teach requires the attendance for a certain period at an institution of learning. But it requires a course of study, and a long one too—in the school of the Lord Jesus Christ—where the Holy spirit is the principal, and humility and prayer are his assistant tutors.

How many of the clergy of our age have been, or are educated in the school of Christ? Verily, not many! If the Church of Christ at any time needs learned men, HE, as the head of the church, will send them.

Remember Paul.

The history of the Church also proves this without a doubt.

Search dilligently the holy writ on this point and observe the teaching and conversation, of most of the clergy and you will find that we are right, viz: That a collegiate education is detrimental to the preaching of the word in its simplicity and purity.

XXVIII.

We maintain that it is contrary to the teaching of the New Testament to *pay* to the ministers of the gospel a *stated salary,* and hire him as a servant for a certian period. A salaried ministry degrades the sacred office, and is the cause of many sins on the part of preachers and congregations.

The church of Christ, adhering strictly to the apostolic rule, will love and honor her minister, whom she has chosen out of her own number, and provide for their family's necessities. There is no danger that the *true* church will neglect to see to it that their ministers are not wanting in food, raiment, shelter, money and comfort. This is a sacred duty of the church. Read:

Rom. 10, 14; 1st Cor. 9, 1–15; Rom. 10, 14–15.

Read the following passages and you will find that it is unscriptural to preach for the sake of money, and make the minister a mere hireling:

Matth. 10, 9–15; Mark, 6, 8–11; Luke, 9, 3–5;
Acts, 20, 33–34; 28, 30–31; 2d Cor. 11, 7–9; 12, 13–18.
1st Thes. 2, 9; 2nd Thes. 3, 7–9.

Now answer honestly this question:

Whether in our age, in most cases, the clergy are not mere worldly servants and mercenary hirelings, who use their office and follow their pretended calling as a trade?

XXIX.

We maintain that the "Mission Work" as it is carried on in our present time, is direct against the word of God and therefore ought to be rejected. We exhort our minisiters to be actively engaged in "mission work," in meeting the many calls for having the gospel preached and advise the churches also to encourage them to go, and that they show, thereby, a willingness to extend a helping hand in bearing the expenses of the ministry to go and assist those who ask for help in church work. We are, therefore, opposed to all missionary societies, mission funds, mission boards, mission officers, etc. We further maintain that it is the prerogative of the local church (and no one else) to have the exclusive oversight of the mission work, to meet every emergency alluring none to preach for the sake of money.

XXX.

We reject the *Protracted or Revival Meetings* and claim that they are a human invention and not in harmony with the apostolic rules of the church.

Read Acts 17, 2; 13, 42–43.

We encourage a diligent and active ministry and that our ministers preach the word after the example of Christ, the apostles, and our fore-fathers wherever an opportunity for it is found or necessity require. But if so-called churches and religious societies engage for a season in protracted meetings and thereby excite the people and create disorder, and force the people into the church without giving them sufficient time to prayerfully and earnestly search the scriptures; without giving them proper opportunity to examine themselves, and without demanding a complete obedience and self-denial, we claim that these meetings are not only against the teachings of the New Testament, but that they are dangerous, and hence are to be rejected. It is further to be considered, that in such meeting a *deceiving spirit* rules and that they lead to hypocrisy, spiritual pride and produce evil instead of good. The tree is known by its fruit.

We have nothing whatever to do with Protracted Meetings or Revivals with their mourners' bench, excitement, screamings, brayings, blating preacher, sermons, music, songs and melodies.

Churches, who have these innovation (P. M. [protracted meetings]) of late introduced and have not as yet so far progressed as to have the above-named things, as mourner's bench, etc., connected with the same, will soon enough introduce such fleshy and absurd things and will sound their trumpets (church papers) in praise thereof.

Preachers who engage in such nonsense please read 2 Tim. 3.

XXXI.

We reject the so-called modern Prayer Meetings, Social meetings and Bible Classes as void of all Gospel Authority. The New Testament is silent about such meetings and the tendency, design, purpose of the same, if closely observed, is dangerous and leads certainly not to humility. We can do no better, but to reject these things and hold fast to the words of Bro. Paul:

II. Tim. 3, 14—"But continue thou in the things which thou hast learned and hast been assured of, knowing of whom thou hast learned them."

XXXII.

We are against the display and ornaments in meeting houses. It is against the simplicity of the gospel and the self-denying principles of the true religion of Christ, to adorn meeting houses with steeples, bells, altars, pulpits, stands, carpets, organs, cushioned seats, etc. We also abstain from all display and ornamenting on or in our private houses.

Please read again Art. 21 [XXI, above].

XXXIII.

That it is *our* duty to care for the poor instead of giving them into the charge or care of poor-houses, orphans' homes, etc.

Read Mark 14, 7; Gal. 2, 10 Acts 11, 30; 12, 25; 24, 17.

XXXIV.

That it is our duty to help *all* poor sufferers, widows and orphans as far as it is in our power to do so.

Read Matt. 7, 12; 5, 42; 6, 1–4.
Luke 10, 29–37.

XXXV.

That it is against the Word of God to take unlawful interest. That it is contrary to the teaching of the New Testament to take interest from the poor.

Read Matt. 5, 42; 6, 19–24.

XXXVI.

That it is contrary to the teachings of the New Testament, and inconsistent for a Christian to take any part whatever in fire or life insurance, or excuse ourselves for doing so, by saying that they are benevolent enterprises, knowing at the same time that they never were or never will be the latter. These things belong to the world and it shows a want of trust and confidence in the fatherly care of God over his children, if they run after such enterprises and give them our time and our money, and burden our soul with worldly care.

Read Matt. 6, 25–34.

XXXVII.

That the marriage vow must be kept sacred.

Matt. 5, 31–32.

XXXVIII.

That it is *our* (not the Sunday-School's) duty to bring up our children in the nurture and admonition of the Lord, and to take care and provide for those of our own house.

Read Eph. 6, 4; I Tim. 5, 8; Gal. 6, 10.

XXXIX.

That it is our duty to be temperate in all things, and to do all, as far as is consistent, to stay the vice of intemperance. That it is inconsistent for a professed follower of Christ to frequent saloons, to drink, to gamble in any form and to sell his grain to brewers or distillers to fabricate therefrom beer and whiskey. Let us abstain from all, yea even from the least appearance of evil.

1 Thess. 2, 22.

XL.

That it is our duty to *pray* to *fast* and to *sing*.
Matt. 7, 8–9; I Tim. 2, 8; Matt. 14, 23; I Thes. 5, 11.
Matt. 26, 30; Acts 16, 25; Eph. 5, 19; James 5, 13.
Matt. 4, 2; II Cor. 6, 5; 11, 27; I Cor. 7, 5.

XLI.

That it is our duty and our privilege to believe all, to obey all and ENJOY all what the Holy Scriptures teach us, and that we thereby shall be happy in time and eternity.

I Cor. 3, 21–23.

CONCLUSION

Our Lord Jesus Christ, the fountain of all truth and the only infallible Head of his Church, bless this tract for the welfare of your own soul and body.

Dear reader, we admonish you once more, beware of false prophets and be not only readers and hearers but doers of the Word; build your house (your salvation) on a rock and not on sand. Hear what Christ says:

"Therefore whosoever heareth these sayings of mine and doeth them, I will liken him unto a wise man which build his house upon a rock. And the rain descended, and the floods came, and the wind blew, and beat upon the house and it fell *not;* for it was founded upon a rock. And every one that heareth these sayings of mine, and doeth them not shall be likened unto a foolish man which built his house upon sand. And the rain descended, and the floods came, and the winds blew and beat upon that house, and it fell; and great was the fall of it."—Matt. 7, 24–27.[3]

Koehler was apparently not a prominent leader among the Old Order Brethren, perhaps because he was a recent convert. However, he was probably better educated than most of the ministers in the group and thus better prepared to write such a tract.

PROGRESSIVE BRETHREN

In contrast to the Old Orders, who were not characterized by their outstanding leaders, to a large extent the Progressive Brethren movement was led by one man, Henry R. Holsinger. He had accumulated enough education to be fluent in both German and English and was a valuable assistant in Henry Kurtz's printing office in the 1850s. He proved to be more ambitious than Kurtz could handle—for example, he wanted to publish a weekly rather than a monthly journal for Brethren. Therefore Holsinger departed from the Kurtz establishment and eventually began a weekly called the **Christian Family Companion.** *It proved to be more progressive in nature than many Brethren appreciated, and within a few years concern over its content had reached Annual Meeting.*

Art. 2. Inasmuch as the Annual Meeting has frequently decided against the brethren voting, is it not inconsistent and even injurious to the brotherhood, for brethren to write, and editors to publish, any thing in opposition to those decisions?

Answer: We think that our brethren who write and print articles, should be very careful not to promote strife and divisions in the church, but peace, love, union, and holiness.[4]

Even this early, in 1866, the Meeting was talking about "strife and divisions," among the Brethren. What was being printed seemed to have a great influence. This type of influence was described vividly by Holsinger many years later when he was writing what might be considered his memoirs.

In fact, the church was in great need of reformation. One unfortunate feature in the state of the church at this time was that the congregations were in the care of incompetent bishops. By incompetence insufficiency is meant in literary attainmants, and all such shortcomings as may result from such condition. And no one suffered more personal humiliation from this state of affairs in the church than the writer. And we doubt whether any other person in the brotherhood had equal opportunity of knowing the facts as they existed, being the editor of the only weekly paper at that time. We had letters of a business character from almost every bishop, relating to some feature of church work, from every housekeeper, or some deputy into whose congregation the paper circulated. And those who did not take the paper could safely be set down as prejudiced or uninformed.

I can even now close my eyes and name a dozen churches with whose elders I was personally acquainted who could not read intelligently a chapter from the Bible or a hymn from a hymnbook, nor write an intelligent notice or announcement of a communion meeting for the paper. Some of them could deliver a pretty fair discourse in an extemporaneous way, more or less satisfactory to the people of the community in which they lived, but the more discreet of them could not attempt to preach at a strange place or in a town. Morally, they stood among the very best people in the community. They were honored of all men, independent of party, sect, or caste, for honesty, truthfulness, integrity, hospitality, and general benevolence. Had they been enabled to live the same Christian life in the private ranks, it would have been said of them, "Behold, a perfect and an upright man, one that feareth God and escheweth evil." Job I:8. But the very fact that he was a bishop, with all the virtues of a good man and none of the qualifications of his official standing, militated against him, and in many cases entirely destroyed his official influence. The office of a bishop carries with it more than piety and spirituality, even according to the sacred oracles. It bears with it a fitness to teach and a capability to use sound doctrine to exhort and to convince gainsayers. And even more so according to the usages of church and in religious literature. When a Methodist bishop comes into a community everybody is expectant, and nobody is disappointed, because no Methodist minister can become a bishop unless he can preach anywhere. This rule is inflexible, and so it ought to be, for the Word of God declares that a bishop "must be fit to preach." The Tunker people appear to have lost sight of the essential qualifications of this important official. It may, indeed, have been that men with the proficiencies under consideration were hard to find in most of the churches, but the fact remained that they were not sought for nor accepted when pointed out or nominated. There were other essentials, in the estimation of the board of examiners, which was always a council of elders, more readily found and more willingly accepted. It was called "the order of the church," particularly in dress. I have it from the lips of an elder of no mean repute, who served on the standing committee, and other important committees appointed by annual meeting, that if he were required to give the casting vote between two brethren with equal qualification as to spirituality and moral character, the one a man of learning and a preacher of eloquence, but who did not conform to the order in wearing his hair and clothing, and another who did conform to the order but could not preach, he would unhesitatingly accept the latter.

I remember one occasion, a love-feast in Somerset County, Pennsylvania, where fourteen bishops sat behind the table, and yet they pressed a second-degree minister who could not possibly have been ordained, to do the preaching. Similar incidents, varying only in number, were common in different parts of the brotherhood.

Such men as those just described composed the examining board for the candidate to the eldership in ninety-nine cases out of one hundred.

From this description the reader may form a pretty correct idea of the chances of promotion to an aspirant with short hair or store-bought garments and a worldly education with a godly life and holy conversation. From this grade of elders the standing committees of the general conference were elected, for none except ordained elders were eligible to the standing committees. From their ranks, also, were selected the members of the various committees sent to the churches by annual meeting. These, with the council of adjoining elders, constituted the consistory, and held the fiat of the Tunker power, from which there was no appeal.[5]

It should not come as a surprise that Holsinger was frequently in difficulty with the Annual Meeting. Perhaps the decision of the 1866 Meeting did not impress him greatly, for his recollection of his first encounter with the leaders of the Meeting was in 1867.

The first occasion which brought me prominently before the general conference was in 1867, in Carroll County, Maryland. The subject under discussion was that of ordaining deacons. The question had come up through the middle Pennsylvania district. When it was brought before the conference the delegate explained that no special opposition had been raised against sending it to the annual meeting, and that Brother H. R. Holsinger had championed it. Thereupon Elder H. D. Davey, moderator, called on me to open the discussion. This I proceeded to deliberately, by stating that I had used but little argument at the district conference; had simply stated that it appeared that the duties demanded of the deacons were strikingly similar to those required of the "seven" referred to in Acts 6:1–8; and that the seven had been set apart to their work by laying on of hands, and therefore I was favorable to installing our deacons and ministers in the same manner.

Immediately thereafter an old brother (if I am not mistaken, it was Abraham Flory, of Miami Valley) arose, and remarked that he was astonished that young brethren should advocate such ideas, since old Brother George Hoke, who is now dead, had so thoroughly explained the subject, and continued in the same irrelevant manner until the audience was thoroughly aroused. This had an exciting tendency, and quickly rising, I said that I could not understand why the old brethren did not kindly meet the arguments by Scripture quotations, or, in the absence of Scripture, produce the arguments which Brother Hoke had advanced, instead of giving shame for attempting to defend the plain reading of the Word of God.

Then my father, Elder Daniel M. Holsinger, arose and appealed to me to be careful or I would ruin my business. This remark greatly agitated me. I sprang to my feet, and, raising my hands aloft, exclaimed, "Thank God, I am not bound to truckle to the prejudice of any man or set men, for the sake of my business, as long as I have the use of these two hands wherewith to labor for the support of myself and family."

By this time the audience was excited to the highest pitch. I never before or since witnessed such intensity of feeling in an assemblage. The council was held in a dense grove, and men and women wept aloud, and several voices shrieked so as to waken the echo. A committee was appointed (I can not say how), who waited on me, and endeavored to persuade me to apologize, to which I finally consented, and attempted to do at the close of the day, but friends declared that the apology was more aggravation than the original offense. It was, however, accepted, and so the matter was permitted to rest, and the answer given to the query was: "Inasmuch as it does not appear plainly to all the brethren that it was always the practice of the apostles to lay hands on those appointed to any special duty, we therefore think it best to make no change at present in the order of installing speakers and deacons in their offices.[6]

Holsinger's actions and publications continued to disturb many of the Brethren, and he was censured by the Annual Meeting of 1870.

Art. 7. Whereas, S. Z. Sharp and H. R. Holsinger have drawn forth many expressions of censure, and have evidently greatly wounded the feelings of the members of the standing committee of last Annual Meeting, and also of very many members of the church, by the publication of certain reports that reflect very unfavorably upon the conduct of said committee; therefore, the brethren composing the western district of Maryland, in district-council assembled, do request the Annual Meeting to appoint a committee to investigate the facts of the case and determine what acknowledgments or satisfaction must be made to restore harmony and love again, and this to be attended to at the Annual Meeting of 1870. The foregoing request was granted, and Samuel Garber, D. B. Sturgis, Jacob Miller, Daniel Wolf, and John Crist, were appointed a committee of investigation. In due time the following report of the committee was submitted to the meeting and adopted: We, the committee appointed by this Annual Meeting to investigate the matter, decide as follows: First: Bro. H. R. Holsinger assumed an unprecedented and unjustifiable course in employing a reporter without authority from the church. Second: In not regarding the counsel of the last Annual Meeting (Art. 1, clause fourth), in publishing S. Z. Sharp's letter, casting severe reflections on the standing committee, which Bro. H. R. Holsinger knew, or ought to have known, was a misrepresentation of the facts in the case proved to us. Third: In answering the defense of the standing committee, his criticism and language were unbecoming a brother. (See "Christian Family Companion," Vol. V, No. 45, pp. 696, 697, 698.) And we also find that the committee did no more than duty required of them in rejecting the reporter. It is also clearly proved to us that the committee offered Bro. H. R. Holsinger all the privileges he formerly enjoyed, to make his own report.

In consideration of the above, we require, in order to restore peace and harmony, that Bro. H. R. Holsinger acknowledge that he did wrong, and that he asks the forgiveness of the church. S. Garber, D. B. Sturgis, J. Miller, D. Wolf, J. Crist. After the reading of the report, Bro. H. R. Holsinger made an acknowledgment satisfactory to the meeting.[7]

In 1870 the most conservative elements in the church—the Old Orders—began publication of The ***Vindicator.*** *Perhaps this was done in part as a reaction to some of Holsinger's activities. Let the periodical introduce itself.*

THE
VINDICATOR,

Of the ancient order, and self-denying principles of the church, as taught by the Savior and held forth by the early fathers of our Fraternity.

"Thus saith the Lord, stand ye in the ways and see, and ask for the OLD paths, where is the good way, and walk therein, and ye shall find rest for your souls."

Vol. 1. Dayton, O. March 1, 1870 No. 1.

The Vindicator,
at present, is published MONTHLY, at 35 cents from the first of March to the end of the year,
By SAMUEL KINSEY,
to be assisted by the advice and counsels of brethren Peter Nead, Daniel Miller, Abraham Flory, D. P. Sayler, Daniel Brower and others.

OUR PROSPECTUS

Dear Brethren: Please allow us to approach you with this little Paper which we thought proper to call VINDICATOR *of the ancient order, and self-denying principles of the Church, &c.*

We have, for several years, upon noticing the *state* and *drift* of our church, and the condition of affairs generally, had much thought with regard to the propriety and *necessity* of publishing a small paper for the use and benefit of the church; and we have at last, after consulting some of our old experienced fathers in the church, consented, by their assistance to attempt the work.

We feel, to a certain extent, our very unworthiness to do so; and it is with a degree of reluctance that we undertake the task; yet, prompted, as we trust, from a sense of duty, and the interest we feel in a "PURE AND UNDEFILED RELIGION," we have consented to engage in the work during the present year, at least. And, brethren, we would like for you to examine carefully and candidly what we may say and do; and should you, by the end of the year, conclude that good might result from our labors, we may continue longer—should we be spared; and issue more frequent, perhaps, than now.

It may, by some, be considered useless and uncalled for, to issue another Paper: seeing there are already several publications issued by the brethren. But, our object in this matter—to keep us in the "*wilderness,*" if you can gather the idea—see Rev. 12th chapter—will be approved of by the brethren, we think, when understood.

We believe that humility, simplicity and self-denial, are among the brightest graces that characterize our Fraternity: and for THESE we feel to contend (for we think we see the need of it) earnestly and faithfully. And in doing so, we feel willing to apply our little might and influence, as well as we can, in wielding the sword ingeniously and powerfully, yet *friendly* and *kindly,* against the popular inventions, as well as the modern improvements, continually attempted to be made upon the simple doctrine taught by the Savior. Our object is to labor against all such innovations.

To contend for the order of the brethren as it has been established.

To furnish the many scattered brethren and churches with all necessary information—as far as possible, and desired—with regard to church-government.

To labor against pride (that very prevalent and abominable evil) in all its various shapes and forms: together, with any matter of general interest, or of use and benefit to the churches.

In the church, is where we hope to labor considerably: yet while we would first try to "sweep at home," we must not forget our children, our neighbors, their children, and our brethren and sisters by nature every where. There is much room yet for the enlargement of the borders of our ZION.

No controversy between brethren admitted. The proper place to settle disputed points is, at our church, district and annual council meetings. There is *no good* resulting from it, but to the contrary, and we cannot allow the evil; our object being rather to UNITE upon the ancient principles of our body.

We hope we may not be *over strenuous,* or too *self-determined* in our ways, but in love humbly contend for that which may have a tendency to subdue, within us, a proud and exalted spirit.

We put the price of the *Vindicator* at 35 cents, from the 1st of March to the end of the year; and any brethren or sisters who will be so kind as to send us 8 or 10 names, will get a free copy. Write the names and addresses *plain,* so we make no mistakes.

We should be glad to hear from you all, and we hope you will pray for us that we may be wise and humble.

Yours, for the love and purity of Zion.

Address, SAMUEL KINSEY.
Dayton, Ohio.[8]

The introduction of The ***Vindicator*** *did not seem to daunt Henry R. Holsinger, and he continued to publish and say controversial things. In 1873, he was again in trouble with the Annual Meeting.*

Art. 8. Whereas, Bro. H. R. Holsinger has committed great offense to the brethren at our present Annual Meeting by pursuing the course he has. When complaints had been presented from various places or districts in the brotherhood of the language he used in his paper, and when a humble and meek explanation was expected by the brethren, he, before the whole congregation, made assertions and insinuations which grieved the brethren more than his previous offenses, and to the dishonor of the brotherhood. 1. The spirit that he, as a minister of the gospel, manifested, we consider altogether contrary to the gospel, and the profession and character of our brotherhood. 2. He declared that a brother, and the connection in which he made the remark showed that it was a brother of some eminence, would suppress the printing of the Bible. With no testimony before him warranting him to make such a declaration, we consider the charge a dishonor to the brotherhood. 3. In speaking against a brother, in warm and strong language, and in alluding to the business that had been done in the morning, which business pertained to a point which had given the brethren much trouble, but which was apparently settled quite as satisfactory as could have been expected, and when we felt pleasantly over it, he said, alluding especially to the elders, "They were asked to give the words of the Lord, and refused to do so." We consider this remark, in the connection in which it was used, injurious to the influence of the elders. 4. In saying that one of the brethren used sophistry in his speech, we consider a greater violation of Christian courtesy and brotherly love. 5. In declaring that he would never submit to a certain restraint that was under consideration, he plainly showed a spirit of disobedience and insubordination to the church. The offenses alluded to in the foregoing were by no means confined to the elders or standing committee, but they were very extensive in the congregation. The impropriety of the unchristian course pursued, grieved a large number of members, as their strong feelings, expressed after the meeting closed, plainly indicated. Now, in view of the foregoing considerations, we require a very humble acknowledgment of Bro. H. R. Holsinger, for his offenses, and an assurance that his course in the future shall be more respectful to the churches and elders, and more in accordance with the meekness and brotherly love inculcated in the gospel.

An acknowledgment made and the assurance given.[9]

For various personal reasons, including his difficulties with the Annual Meeting, Holsinger agreed to sell the **Christian Family Com-**

panion to James Quinter, who consolidated it with the *Gospel Visitor* with a combined title. Thus Holsinger no longer had a media to express his views or those of other progressive contributors. Since Quinter's editorial policy was much more cautious and acceptable to the Brethren, the tension concerning Holsinger at the Annual Meeting was significantly reduced in the next few years. However, Holsinger had too much journalistic blood in him to stay out of the business permanently, and in 1878 he was back again. Quoting him again:

In the fall of 1878, Elder Joseph W. Beer and myself commenced the publication of the "Progressive Christian," at Berlin, Pennsylvania, with the avowed purpose of advocating progressive measures and reforms. The publication did not meet with the patronage which was expected, partly for the reason that there were then six papers in the field. The paper was continued for about six months, when we became somewhat discouraged, and began to cast about for the cause of the failure. The annual meeting of 1879 had given the "Progressive Christian" a denunciation, of which the following is an account:—

Petitions had been sent up from northwestern Ohio, middle Pennsylvania, southern Ohio, first district of Virginia, and east Pennsylvania, demanding that "H. R. Holsinger shall make humble acknowledgments for past mistakes, and faithful promises for the future," and some demanding the peremptory suppression of the paper and severe censure of the publishers.

I can only give a few samples of the expressions used in the papers presented before the conference:—

"Whereas, Brother H. R. Holsinger, and certain contributors to the paper he is publishing, have committed great offense to many brethren, publishing slanderous articles against the general order of the brethren,—for instance, in No. 11 of the "Progressive Christian," in replying to D. P. Saylor on non-conformity to the world in dress, calling it 'Idolatrous Clothes Religion;' therefore, we ask annual meeting to stop such publications, as said publishers are sowing discord among their brethren, after the spirit of Korah, Detahn, and Abiram."

"Will not the annual meeting suppress the superfluous number of periodicals now being published in the brotherhood, and suppress the antiscriptural, from time to time."

"Whereas, Some of our periodicals make expressions unbecoming in refering to the government of the church and the transactions of annual meeting denouncing the system of sending delegates to annual meeting, or committees from the annual conference to settle difficulties in the churches, of which the paper called "The Deacon" has been guilty—and it is held by some brethren that the "Progressive Christian" is still worse—shall annual meeting suffer their conduct to continue, and thus open the door of mischief?" Answer, "No; and we call on annual meeting to bring them to order."

After discussing the subject pro and con, for several hours, the following answer was offered by the standing committee:—

"Whereas, Petitions were received from several districts, requesting the annual meeting to prohibit slanderous and schismatic articles from being published in the "Progressive Christian" and "Deacon;" therefore, it is required that the editors of the "Progressive Christian," and particularly H. R. Holsinger, make an humble acknowledgment to the annual meeting for publishing erroneous statements in regard to the church's principles, charging the church with idolatry, and stigmatizing some of its members with terms of reproach, ridiculing some of the practices of the church, and publishing inflammatory articles, some even from expelled members. 2. That the editors of the "Vindicator" and of the "Deacon" make satisfactory acknowledgment for writing and publishing similar articles as the "Progressive Christian." 3. That Elders John Harshey, James Ridenour, and Howard Miller be required to render satisfaction to the annual meeting for writing schismatic articles. 4. That the editors of all the periodicals be required hereafter not to admit into their papers any article that will assail the doctrines of the church, in regard to non-comformity to the world, the personal character of ministers, or the peculiar tenets or practices of the church. In order that this decision may be fully carried out, which we are anxious to have done, we appoint a committee to carry them out."

Several restrictions were also offered to the "Vindicator" and the "Deacon," as well as to a number of individual contributors, but the main object was the restraint of the "Progressive Christian."

In my defense before conference, I disclaimed any intended disparagement of the adopted practices and customs of the church, also declaring that what was said in regard to D. P. Sayler could not properly be applied to the church as a people, and further continued, "We are losing the proverbiality for integrity that the church once possessed, when a Tunker's word was as good as his note."

I claimed that by continually advocating externals to the neglect of the weightier matters of the law of God, the present state of affairs was produced; that the preachers are to be blamed for it. They do not advocate with sufficient force and emphasis and frequency the peculiar doctrines of the Bible. I also opposed all sinful extremes in dress, and assumed that there is a happy medium, which was the position occupied by the progressive portion of the church, and that the principles of our holy religion require meekness, cleanliness, plainness, and modesty, and that any garment which comes within these restrictions is sustained by the gospel and is acceptable to God, and may not be rejected. The ancient customs of the church should be respected, but ought not to be compared to the teachings of God's Word. . . .

After returning home from the annual meeting and discussing the works of conference, Brother Beer suggested that perhaps the paper was being conducted in too radical a spirit, while I thought it ought to be made radically progressive, inasmuch as there was no room for the expression of our views in any of the conservative papers; that the people were tired of policy, and required and desired more principle in their instructions, both from the pulpit and through the press.

This was the first occasion when we two men disputed on a course of procedure in our business relations of more than ten years, and this dispute was not upon the merits of the case, but as a matter of business policy. After talking over the matter, I proposed to sell my interest in the paper and rent the office to Beer, that he might test his policy proposition. The transfer was made accordingly, and the course of the paper was changed in accordance with the views of its new management. I continued to contribute to the paper in such articles as were deemed consistent.

Toward the close of the year Brother Beer discovered his mistake, and when subscriptions were being solicited for the following year, found himself hopelessly swamped, and discontinued its publication. It had been a verbal contract that if the paper were wrecked by the change of policy, I was to have the ruins. The paper lay dead until May, 1880, when it was resurrected by Howard Miller, and conducted in the name of Holsinger and Miller. Miller remained on the editorial staff only about two months, when I became editor, publisher, and proprietor. No other changes occurred in the management of the paper until after the committee had recommended the expulsion of its editor.

In the meantime I had been ordained to the office of bishop. About the same time the old Brothers' Valley church was subdivided into four separate congregations. They were called Berlin, Stony

Creek, Brothers' Valley, and Somerset churches. I was unanimously chosen elder of Berlin and Stony Creek, and by a large majority of the Somerset church. This elevation to position in the church created alarm in the ranks of the Tunker episcopacy, for, said they, "Now he is a bishop, and eligible to the standing committe, and if he should ever get on that committee, there would be no end of trouble" Accordingly, the elders set to work to avert this danger by writing personal letters to the leading men in their several localities, where it was thought it was mostly required.[10]

So Holsinger had finally been ordained a bishop, or elder, but he did not have the opportunity to serve on the Standing Committee. Since he was on one extreme in his views regarding the policies of the Brethren, it is interesting to note something of his attitude toward the other extreme, the Old Order group.

During the period 1880–81, the old-order element formulated rapidly toward separate organization, having had the advantage of several conferences, through which they had gained influence and passed laws which they were determined to enforce upon the progressive part of the brotherhood. In fact, the old-order element was intolerant, to the extreme of persecution, which they carried out as far as possible in a country of religious freedom. It was interesting to observe how they squirmed after the tables were turned and it was measured to them as they had measured to others. While in many things I was in sympathy with the old-order brethren because of their consistency, as a matter of fact they were the indirect source of all my trouble and persecutions. They furnished the ammunition, while the conservatives fired the guns, not intending to injure anybody. I grant them the credit of having been sincere in their motives, but sadly mistaken as to the matter itself.[11]

To return to Holsinger's interest in having a journalistic mouthpiece, he conveniently waited until May, 1880 to resurrect the ***Progressive Christian*** *from the ruins left by Beer, because he was certain that it would not be possible to consider anything about the paper at the Annual Meeting of 1880. Consequently, the paper had an entire year to operate without any pressure from the Annual Meeting. During the year, however, the opponents of the paper were springing into action and at least five different districts brought protests to the Annual Meeting of 1881. Holsinger remembered the Meeting well.*

The trouble was finally brought to a focus at the annual meeting of 1881, at Ashland, Ohio. At that conference no less than five district meetings presented strictures against the "Progressive Christian" or its editor. They originated in northern Illinois, southern Missouri, southern Ohio, and southern Indiana, all strong old-order territory. I quote the first entire to confirm the assertion made that the oppostion came from the old-order brethren:—

"Inasmuch as Brother H. R. Holsinger has been admonished by the annual meeting again and again, according to the minutes of annual meeting, to cease to publish articles conflicting with the general order of the old brethren and good feeling of the church, and still continues to do the same, we now request annual meeting to deal with him according to Matthew 18, and the decisions of annual meeting, either directly or by a committee, and if he does not hear the church, hold him as a heathen man and a publican."

The second stricture came from northern Illinois, which reads as follows:—

"Is it right for brethren to publish papers like the *Progressive Christian* and *Vindicator,* creating and fostering strife by publishing articles against the established order of the church? And if not right, what is to be done with brethren that publish such a paper or papers?"

"*Answer*—Not right for brethren to publish such a paper or papers, and any brother or brethren that publish such a paper or papers, shall make an humble acknowledgment for so doing, and promise not to publish such articles any more in the future, said acknowledgment and agreement to be published in their paper or papers."

In this query the *Vindicator* is included as a stroke of policy.

The third came from southern Missouri, another old-order stronghold. This query is equally strategic, but fraught with less policy. I quote only main parts of the queries and answers, as follows:—

"Is district meeting favorable to calling the attention of annual meeting to the character of the *Progressive Christian*, and require Brother Holsinger, its editor, to cease publishing articles of criticism on annual meeting and its decisions, and publishing his own articles advocating measures calculated to subvert the princples and rules of order of our brotherhood, in matters of plainness of dress, etc?" [. . . and against the exercise of the expelling power of refractory members, and if he refuse so to promise, should not Annual Meeting declare such publication contrary to the best interest of the Church of Christ, and provide accordingly?]

"*Answer*—This district meeting requests annual meeting to decide that the *Progressive Christian* and all like papers, purporting to be published by a member of the Brethren Church, do not reflect the spirit and principles of the church of Christ. [. . . The policy pursued by such papers is in direct opposition to the principles enunciated in Titus 3:1; 1 Peter 5:5; James 4:11 and 1 Peter 11:11. Editors and contributors who violate these principles of the Gospel, subject themselves to arraignment and trial before the congregation where they reside, or before Annual Meeting. We further request Annual Meeting to require our editors to conduct their respective papers according to Rom. 14:19, and Eph. 4:29, so that the body be edified, strengthened and unified in love and holiness].[12] We also look with sorrow upon the tendency to levity and jesting through the papers, and beseech writers and teachers to avoid the degrading habit, and to remember I Thess. 5:6,8; Eph. 5:4; 4:29; Titus 2:2; 12; I Peter 1:13; 4:7, and 5:8.

"And we further desire that annual meeting require Brother H. R. Holsinger to make confession for having violated the law of God in the manner in which he had conducted his paper."

The fourth query came from southern Ohio, and is as follows:—

"WHEREAS, H. R. Holsinger is publishing articles in his paper which have a tendency to bring about discord among the brethren, and have a bad influence outside of the brotherhood, we request, therefore, that a committe be appointed whose duty it shall be to take notice of that paper, and if articles still continue to appear contrary to the faith and practice of the church, that it shall be their duty to bring said Holsinger to an account as in their judgment they may deem proper and right."

"*Answer*—This meeting asks the annual meeting to grant and appoint the committee herein asked for, that it may carry out the decisions of 1879, Article 16."

The fifth originated in northern Illinois, of which I quote the following:—

"WHEREAS, H. R. Holsinger, editor of the *Progressive Christian,* is publishing [and circulating through his paper and by tracts,] unchristian and often untruthful reflections upon brethren, [made either by such who were subjected to their local church discipline, or by such who withstand and resist parts of our general and recognized church order;] and also publicly [through his paper charges brethren] with being untruthful, [in violation of the Gospel rule. Matt. 18:16.] And

WHEREAS, the tendency of such publications is to encouarge disorder and misrule among the churches, affecting the peace and prosperity of local churches, [and likewsie the harmony of our general Conference,] and,

WHEREAS, the churches of the south Missouri district unite their efforts with all the churches of our general brotherhood towards preserving the [principles and precepts of the Gospel as embodied in our] long-established [and general recognized rules and] order of church fellowship. Will therefore, district meeting consider [it advisable to declare] whether H. R. Holsinger, [or others,] can be [held and] recognized [by us] as a brother, conducting [a paper of the character of] the *Progressive Christian,* [now edited by H. R. Holsinger] and to declare whether [in its judgment] he can [of right and with propriety be accepted to][13] assist in general church work, or to serve on the Standing Committee.

"*Answer*—We view with fear the course pursued by H. R. Holsinger, in the manner of conducting his paper and of the principles he advocates, and we are unanimous in the conviction that it should be declared that we can not regard him as a brother, and that he should be excluded from all participation in general church work, and we place these our convictions in the hands of the standing committee, to act in the premises as to them appears to be necessary."

These several queries and answers were declared to be the property of conference. A motion was made by Elder Joseph Kauffman, seconded by P. J. Brown, that the meeting appoint a committee to take charge of the papers, and report to this meeting again.

. . . After some further discussion a motion prevailed that the papers be submitted to a committee of elders, and they report to the public council. The following persons were appointed on the committee: S. S. Mohler, Abraham Miller, Daniel Vaniman, Joel Neff, D. E. Price, C. Bucher, George W. Cripe, John Brillhart, and John Smith.

The committee laid its report before the conference at the afternoon session of the third day, which is as follows:—

"We the undersigned members of the committee appointed to consider charges against H. R. Holsinger and Samuel Kinsey, find that H. R. Holsinger is publishing a paper in which many articles have appeared criticising the work of annual meeting, and against the order of our government, as also against our order of observing the gospel principle of non-conformity to the world in wearing apparel, after having been again and again admonished by our annual meeting to be more and more guarded in his publications, and promised to do so, which promise he has not performed, but has continued his former course with increased effort. We therefore recommend that this meeting appoint a committee to wait on him in his church, and deal with him according to his transgressions.

"S. S. Mohler, Abraham Miller, Daniel Vaniman, Joel Neff, D. E. Price, C. Bucher, John Brillhart, G. W. Cripe."

[In reference to the complaint alleged against brother Samuel Kinsey, editor of the Vindicator, we find he has not used due caution against admitting articles into his paper having a schismatic tendency, and criticising the work of committees, etc., (See Vols. 11 and 12), and we recommend a committee to be appointed to wait on him in his church and deal with him as his case demands.

S. S. Mohler, C. Bucher, G. W. Cripe, John Smith, Daniel Vaniman, John Brillhart, D. E. Price, Abraham Miller, Joel Neff.][14]

The report of the committee was then put on its passage. In the discussion I made the following remarks:—

"I notice that these two papers end so differently, I would like to ask the reason for it. In my case you say, 'Deal with him according to his transgression,' and in Brother Kinsey's, 'as his case may demand.' There is a discrimination here that looks to me not exactly fair. You see Brother Kinsey confesses he is trying to maintain the old order and gets into trouble, and I am trying to maintain the gospel order, and get into trouble. . . . I am certain that I do not have a fair showing. There are some stray copies of my paper sent all over the brotherhood. Some articles are marked, calling the attention to their offensiveness as understood by the sender, while the reply to, or corrections of, said article never reaches the same party. The objections to my paper generally come from parties who are not regular readers, but only see an occasional copy sent to them for especial purpose. Hence, my strongest opposition comes from those who know the least about the "Progressive Christian." In conclusion, I plead for at least one man on my committee who was a regular reader of my paper, through whom I might expect an intelligent representation of my cause."

It was all to no effect, however, and the following committee was appointed, and which is known in Tunker history as "The Berlin Committee:" John Wise, Enoch Eby, David Long, Joseph Kauffman, and Christian Bucher.

I wish here to call the attention of the reader to several inconsistencies in the foregoing proceedings:—

First. One district complains that I had charged certain brethren with untruthfulness, and in the same sentence publicly charges me with having published "unchristian and untruthful reflections."

Second. To the lack of proof or evidence to establish the charges made against me. And so it was through my entire trial. It appears that the case was conducted on the presumption that, since I was in the minority, I must be in the wrong, and as they were in the majority and had the power over me, they must be right, without further evidence. I do not know what testimony was produced before the committee at Ashland, who had the complaint and formulated the charge against me, and I am certain nobody else can tell. It is evident that there was none brought before the conference by its absence. Not a copy of my paper was brought before conference nor a single article read before annual meeting in testimony of the accusations made against me. The same is true of the Berlin committee meeting, and at the Arnold's Grove annual meeting, when I was disowned. I do not mention these matters in the spirit of complaint, but as a remarkable fact in the history of an important case. It would certainly have made the case much stronger against me if the damaging articles alluded to in the complaint had been read before the council from my paper. That they existed is presumed, but presumption is not evidence, and if they existed, that they were available goes without saying.

The committee visited the Berlin church on the 9th day of August, 1881, and, after a sitting of two days, rendered the following verdict:—

REPORT OF BERLIN COMMITTEE.

"We, the undersigned committee, appointed by annual meeting to go to Berlin church, Somerset County, Pennsylvania, 'to wait on Elder H. R. Holsinger, and deal with him according to his transgressions,' do report as follows:—

"Met with the Berlin church on Tuesday, August 9, 1881, and were unanimously accepted by the church, H. R. Holsinger, included. And upon the question to H. R. Holsinger, whether he would concede to and accept of the general usages of the church in conducting this investigation, H. R. Holsinger declined, whereupon a lengthy discussion followed upon the following departure from the general usages of the church:—

"1. H. R. Holsinger employed a stenographer to take down and publish the proceedings of the council.

"2. The council to be held in the presence of persons not members of the church, which discussion closed by the Berlin church, saying that they had passed a resolution in absence of the committee, that they will have a full report of proceedings taken, and right on this passed, in presence of the committee, the following:—

"*Resolved,* That this council shall be held openly to all members, and persons not members of the Brethren Church will be considered present by courtesy only, and none but the members of the Berlin church and the committee are invited to participate in the business."

Wednesday, August 10, met at 9 A.M., according to adjournment. The chairman announced to the meeting that the committee feared the members did not understand the responsibilities they assumed yesterday, and proposed a reconsideration and rescinding of their decisions. After some investigation of the propriety of reconsideration, I gave liberty for any one to make a motion to that effect, but no motion was offered. After due time the committee retired and decided as follows:—

"In view of the above considerations, especially in view of the fact that Brother H. R. Holsinger refused to have his case investigated by the committee in harmony with the gospel as interpreted by our annual meeting, and consent of our general brotherhood, and inasmuch as Brother H. R. Holsinger and the Berlin church assumed all responsibility in the case, therefore we decided that Brother H. R. Holsinger can not be held in fellowship in the brotherhood, and all who depart with him shall be held responsible to the action of the next annual meeting.

"John Wise, Enoch Eby, C. Bucher, David Long, Joseph N. Kauffman."

Explanation by John Wise.—"Met with the Berlin church, on Tuesday, August 9, 1881, and were unanimously accepted by the church, H. R. Holsinger included. And upon the question to H. R. Holsinger whether he would concede to and accept the general usages of the church in conducting this investigation, H. R. Holsinger declined; whereupon a lengthy discussion followed. It may be a question in the minds of many. Why propound such a question? I answer, What gave rise to this was the following: Prior to our going to Berlin we saw in the *Progressive Christian* the announcement that Brother H. R. Holsinger had employed a stenographer, and that he proposed publishing in his paper a full report of the proceedings of that committee. We regard this as a departure from our established usage, as where a report is to be taken under such circumstances, all interested parties should have a part in the choice of the stenographer if it be agreed that one shall be employed. No member of that committee was interrogated in regard to this matter, and we regard the treatment towards us as unfair; and not only unfair in a business point of view and a departure from general usages, but contrary to the principles of our holy Christianity. We consider it not at all fraternal or brotherly that Brother Holsinger should have the matter of publication under his control. We are not misrepresenting Brother Holsinger, as I will read from the report, and as you will find in a pamphlet entitled 'The Stenographic Report of the Proceedings of the Committee for the Trial of Elder H. R. Holsinger, for Insubordination to the Traditions of the Elders.' In the progress of the consideration of the propriety of this departure we have the following: 'You have employed a stenographer to take a full report of the proceedings of the committee, to be published in your paper, which we think should not be done, as it is a departure from the usages of the general brotherhood.' "

While it is regarded as my privilege to comment upon the method pursued by the committee in the treatment of this case, I shall be confined as nearly as possible to the historical part of the case. The full report of the proceedings is upon record, and can be found in any first-class library in the fraternity, to which the reader who wishes more information than is herein contained is respectfully referred. There were present from a distance on the occasion the following: Elders James Quinter, I. J. Rosenberger, E. K. Buechley, C. G. Lint, J. B. Moser, and others.

The action of the committee is of unusual importance, from the fact that it became the entering wedge which divided a large denomination, one part of which became a new organization.

After the usual devotional services, in which Elder Quinter took some part, John Wise stated that they were present as a committee appointed by annual meeting to the Berlin church to investigate Brother Holsinger's case, and then said the first thing in order would be to know whether they are accepted by the Berlin congregation, and proposed to withdraw so as to enable the members of the church to express their opinion without any intimidation.

The committee then withdrew from the council room, and during their absence the church unanimously agreed to accept the committee.

The committee then objected to the house in which the council was being held as being too small. The church, however, decided in favor of the place. The committee would have preferred to go to the Grove church, about a mile out of town, but as that was outside of the Berlin church territory, the members could not consent to the removal. The afternoon session was held in the Methodist church. It was hard to understand why the committee should want larger apartments when they wished to exclude the audience.

The next objection was in regard to the reporter. John Wise stated that this was a departure from the usages of the general brotherhood, and that it was never so done to his knowledge on any former occasion, and therefore should not be done in this case. To which I replied that there never was a case exactly like this in the history of the Tunker Church; that I had employed the stenographer at my own expense; he was a member of the church, and was responsible and competent, and that for my own satisfaction and in justice to myself I had determined to have the report taken down in full, and that in this, my church uas unanimous in my favor, and consequently intimated that part was a settled matter; but in case of publishing the report I would be accountable to the church at large for any injury that might result.

After discussing the subject for some time, the committee retired again, and the church passed the following resolution:—

"*Resolved,* That we insist upon having a full report taken of the sayings and doings of this committee and council."

This ended the first half-day's business.

In the afternoon John Wise quoted the following passage of scripture, "But if he neglect to hear the church, let him be unto thee as a heathen and a publican," and then proceeded to argue, "You are to tell it to the church, not to a mixed assembly," and other arguments in favor of a private council. I then said: "It had been announced at our public meetings that this council would be a business meeting, and that none but members are invited; that others would take no interest in the business; that we were neither a military organization nor a secret society, therefore none were here by invitation, except members of the church. All who are present are perfectly welcome, so far as we are concerned, but no one will be expected to take part in the work of the council except members of the church. The general brotherhood is interested in the business of this council, and has a right to know what was done and how and why. This is no ordinary church meeting.

There is no similarity between this case and the passages of Scripture referred to. If I am guilty of any wrong-doing I am willing that the world shall know of it. Having been publicly accused, I am determined to be as publicly vindicated. If, however, the committee sees proper to exclude all except the Berlin church and themselves, I presume it is their privilege to do so, but *we* will not do it."

Elder Long asked, "Are you sure, Brother Henry, that your congregation will not do it?"

I replied that they could speak for themselves, that those in affirmative should rise and be counted, in response to which seventy-one members arose, and so that point was settled.

Elder Kauffman remarked: "We are here as a committee sent from annual meeting to do business. We dare not depart from the usages of the church. We must make our report to annual meeting, and dare not digress from our orders. We can not come here and sanction the idea of having this council meeting held open and public; neither can we sanction having the report of the proceedings published. And you should not ask us to digress from the usages of the church. If any such privilege be taken, we want the responsibility to rest right here with you.

To this I replied: "I can hardly see why the committee dare not digress from the usages. I know of no scripture that forbids them to make a new record of a new case. Can you not for once throw by the usages, and say that you will do 'as seemth good to us and the Holy Ghost'? Are you really bound by the usages of the fathers? I am sure this church has assumed the responsibility. The church has unanimously decided that we will have a full report and an open council. We have put ourselves upon record, deliberately making this statement in both German and English, and giving every member an opportunity to express his sentiments before taking the vote."

There was some further discussion between the committee and the church till late in the afternoon, when the following resolution was unanimously adopted: "That this council shall be held openly to all members, and persons not members of the Brethren Church will be considered present by courtesy only; and none but the members of the Berlin church and the committee are invited to participate in the business;" and so the first day's work closed with apparent hopeful feeling that in the morning the business of the committee would proceed. However, next morning the committee stated that they feared there was a misunderstanding, and that therefore they proposed to proceed to a careful explanation to the church; that they understood that the church presumed that the committee would go ahead with the trial; that yesterday they had demurred, and that they did so this morning; that they stood upon the authority of the gospel, and would submit to the usages of the general brotherhood; that they stood free from any further investigation in the matter. Said they: "We told you yesterday that we understood the usages of our brotherhood are based upon the Word of God. We are conscientious in the matter; and as a body of the brethren will not put ourselves on record, and then in less than twenty-four hours go directly against the record we made. We place ourselves on record, and we propose to stand upon the record we have made. You place yourselves upon record, and we fear you do not understand what you are doing. We will give you an opportunity to reconsider and rescind your action of yesterday."

The committee then paused for some time, waiting for an action for reconsideration, but no motion was made. I then endeavored to explain the situation to the congregation in German and English, so that there could be no possibility for misapprehension, after which a voice was heard, saying, "What I have written, I have written." I think the speaker was Brother Samuel Forney, one of the most venerable members of the congregation.

John Wise then said: "We consider the matter is fairly before the congregation, and if no action is taken we shall consider the matter as standing by the resolution. We have given time to hear from the congregation, but as there was no response, and as other business is being introduced, we now propose to withdraw and prepare our report.

At this point Elder Quinter remarked, "Then you don't give them the privilege of assuming the responsibility; I don't fully understand."

After some further speaking pro and con, hardly to the point, John Wise concluded: "Having been sent here by annual meeting, and as we were spending our time for the church, if you have any donations to make they will be gratefully received on the part of the committee. The amount of our expenses is $126. It is the general brotherhood I am addressing."

After several hours' retirement the committee returned, and rendered their verdict, which see above. Then they passed around to each individual member to obtain the assent to their decision, but all except one member answered no. This one was Elder John P. Cober,

M.D. He had voted with the church in favor of an open council and full report, but when it came to the final test he said, *"Ich gehe mitt den alte:"* I go with the old ones.

After the committee had finished its work and closed with prayers, the Berlin church met in council, and after some deliberations they unanimously passed the following resolution:—

"Inasmuch as Elder H. R. Holsinger has not violated any gospel order of the general brotherhood, and not having had a trial of the charges brought against him at the annual meeting of 1881, therefore the Berlin congregation, including the Meyersdale branch, will continue to work together with Brother Holsinger as our bishop, and we invite all who are willing to take the gospel of Christ as the man of their counsel, into church fellowship with us."

It will be seen that the whole issue hinged upon the open council and stenographer.

During the time intervening between the decision of the committee and the annual meeting of 1882, the question under discussion was whether I was in the church or outside of the church, and all the papers entered into investigation of the subject. S. H. Bashor wrote a tract entitled "Where Is Holsinger?" which was distributed by the thousands over the entire brotherhood, and was published in the *Progressive Christian.*[15]

WHERE IS HOLSINGER?

A Voice to the Lovers of Justice and Mercy:
and a Cry to the Household of Faith.

Read carefully and prayerfully.

With the issues of the past and the facts of the present a large number of our brethren are not familiar. For this there are several reasons, principally among which, is the fact that most of our church papers are controlled in the interests of what is familiarly called the conservative party, and upon all questions relating to our present difficulties, only one side is published, thus leaving the reader either biased or only partially informed. As this course has been pursued by them in relation to the charges brought against brother H. R. Holsinger, through Annual conference, and the work and the action of the committee sent to him, the brotherhood is, in the majority uninformed, and the public mind as a consequence, incapable of forming a just decision upon the merits of the case. This being true, it has been thought advisable by a large number of ministering brethren, including some prominent minds, that this present statement of the case should be made and circulated as much as possible among the brethren, that they may be able to form a just estimate of the case, and to work and decide accordingly, when the report of the committee is presented to next Annual Meeting for approval, and through consultation and general correspondence it was decided that I should look up the evidence and write the statement and print it ready for general circulation. As a matter of obedience to the wishes of my brethren, of duty to the general church, and justice to Brother Holsinger, I prepare and send this forth. I shall keep in view the facts of the case, and present only such evidence as is authentic, and can be sustained. If our church papers would have published a fair statement of the committee work and action this would not have been written, but since they failed to do this, and the brethren who know the facts and continue to fellowship Brother Holsinger, are censured by the uninformed, this is published. Read it carefully, and decide according to the evidence.

1st. No charge of immoral conduct has been brought, or was urged against Brother Holsinger. His character as a minister of the gospel stands unimpeached. In morals he is known as upright, honest truthful and just. All this is acknowledged by those most active in instigating the charges brought against him.

2nd. No charge of doctrinal heresy has been urged; and it is admitted that in all the doctrines of the gospel as held by the church, he is in union with all portions of the brotherhood and our general Annual Conference. We have no minister among us who preaches, and maintains the distinctive doctrines of the church more fully and strongly than he.

3rd. No specific charge of any character was urged against him by any of the Districts from which the general complaints came. The only charge presented was one of a general character, relating to the policy of the PROGRESSIVE CHRISTIAN. The declaration of brethren that their "feelings were hurt at the manner" in which the paper was conducted, formed the basis of this general charge against him, for allowing objectionable articles from brethren and disfellowshipped members to pass through his paper. None of these "objectionable" articles were specified by any district bringing an accusation. The general accusation was that he "published things contrary to the general usages of the church," and "wrote against" (not doctrines) "its order," rather customs. No specification was made and no formulated charge presented, showing what order was violated by Brother Holsinger. These general accusations were brought up and discussed before the general, or mixed audience of some three district conferences when brother Holsinger was not present to defend himself or his paper and patrons. They were then brought up before Annual conference and read twice and to some measure discussed, before the general public. The different papers (a report of which is in the minutes and report of annual conference for 1881) were then given into the hands of a committee to arrange and present to the conference, or for disposal. The committee examined the accusations and recommended that conference send a committee to Berlin, Pa. and wait upon Brother Holsinger, and give him a trial. Accusations of a like character, were also presented against Samuel Kinsey, editor of the *Vindicator*, and a committee was recommended also to be sent to his home and church.

Annual conference, or rather the standing committee, appointed a committee to visit Brother Holsinger, and give him a trial. Also sent one to the *Vindicator*. All this was done before public councils, in which were men of the world; and the general charge of disorderly work went out before the whole church and the world against these men and their papers. The authority given to these committees was that they should investigate the case, and make a decision according to the evidence brought in. None of the committee sent to Brother Holsinger were readers of his paper save one, and he only for a very short time, and all of them were known to hold sentiments of opposition to the element of the church he represented; one of them having actually assisted in framing one of the accusations against him. Of the committee sent to the *Vindicator,* one was a reader and contributer to its columns, and whose writings had been the most caustic and objectionable of any among its contributors. The other members of the committee were known to, in many respects, hold general feelings of sympathy and favor with the paper. We are willing to give the standing committee the benefit of charity in this partial showing for the two papers. Brother Holsinger consulted with a number of ministers (the writer being one) as to what course he should pursue in his trial. He was advised that as he had been publicly accused, and as he had been poisoned in the public mind by being thus publicly exposed, he should by all means seek a public trial, as no one doubted but he could easily obtain it. He was further advised to employ

Brother Albert Trent, a stenographic reporter, and give the report of his trial through the press. As he had been publicly accused he should be as publicly tried, and vindicated or condemned, was the general opinion. This the very spirit of fairness would dictate. This he was perfectly willing to do, as he said he was not conscious of having done any thing that men should not know.

The committee sent word as to the time of their coming, and every thing was in readiness to receive them, and all thought the trial would go on. Sister Holsinger entertained the committee and worked to make them comfortable. When they met at the church the question of accepting the committee was put and passed affirmatively. Brother John Wise, foreman of the committee said, in reply to a question: "In case the majority (of the church) should reject the committee, it becomes our duty to act with the minority, and make a report to next Annual meeting: If Annual meeting rejects our decision it will stop there," thus showing that the committee recognized the fact that they could only work with the majority of the church, and if the *majority refused* to accept their work, it could *only be legalized or enforced by next annual meeting.*

The committee then objected to the reporter, and also to the meeting being held with open doors. Brother Holsinger then took the vote of the church, and the united reply was, We want the council held openly, as you were openly accused, and *we as a church* will not close the doors against outside parties, and we also decide that brother Trent shall give a report of the trial, and you shall be as publicly vindicated as you were charged. This will be seen as the unanimous action of the church, and was all done publicly. The committee refused to hold an open trial, and brother Holsinger as the spokesman for the church, then told the committee if they, (the committee) wished to turn the people out and keep closed doors, they could do so, but this the committee persistently refused to do. They would not hold council with open doors, and would not close the doors on their own responsibility, but wanted the church to do so on their responsibility which they refused to do, as they thought the spirit of fairness demanded an open trial. The matter was discussed pro and con for a whole day before a public council, and in the evening the committee finally consented that if the church would assume the responsibility of an open trial, they could have it, though it was contrary to decisions of Annual meeting.

But next morning when the council opened, the committee had

reconsidered their action of the evening before, and would not proceed with the trial with open doors. The church again told them if they wished they supposed they could close the doors, but they must do it on their own responsibility as they (the church) would not close the doors.

The committee retired and brought in a decision, to the effect that H. R. Holsinger could no longer be fellowshipped by the Brotherhood as a member of the church, and all who hold with him should be held amenable to next Annual Meeting. When this decision was presented to the church for acceptance it was rejected by the whole church save one old brother. The committee when their decision was so fully rejected closed the meeting and left for home. Only one of them saying farewell to sister Holsinger, who had labored late every night to hospitably entertain them.

After the committee retired, the church remained in council unanimously decided to retain H. R. Holsinger as their minister and Bishop. The Stony Creek church also decided to retain him as their Bishop, as also did the Somerset congregation soon after.

Now, according to brother Wise's own statement, their report is of no force, as the majority—*the whole church* save one—refused to accept it "until next Annual meeting:" and if Annual meeting rejects the decision it will stop there.

Again; Article 1st of Annual meeting for 1872 reads:

"Has the church a right to pass decisions, or resolutions and enforce them to the expulsion of members from the body, without thus saith the positive law of the Lord? Ans. The church shall not expel any member without gospel authority."

The committee offered no *gospel authority* for their decision to expel brother Holsinger; more; they did not decide to expel him for what *he* had done, but because the *church* would not consent to a secret trial.

In 1876. Art 10, Annual Meeting minutes, read as follows:

A request that the Annual meeting limit the power of committees, so as not to allow them to expel a majority of the church unless their decisions be ratified by Annual meeting in open session. Answer, the request is granted."

If a committee can not expel a majority of the church without their decision being ratified by Annual Meeting in open council, certainly a committee cannot expel one member against the wishes of the whole church, or as brother Wise said, "until Annual meeting passes upon their report." It is held by a large portion of the Brotherhood of those acquainted with our usages and the above facts, that brother Holsinger is not expelled from the church, for the following reasons: He was not pronounced expelled, by the committee for violation of the gospel, or any written law of the church, including all the minutes of Annual meeting; but was pronounced expelled, because the *Berlin church,* refused by *unanimous vote,* to allow him to be tried in secret (or private council which is the same) after he had been publicly exposed. He was held responsible for the action of the Berlin church, and as before stated, the committee decided against him for what his church did and not for his own individual acts. It is contrary to the usages of our Brotherhood to expel one member for the action of a whole congregation, be he elder or otherwise. It stands without precedent of the past, decisions of A. M. nor gospel authority. And as a result according to decisions of Annual meeting, 1872 Art. 1st; and 1842 Article 12, the action of the committee is invalid, and stands of no force until ratified by Annual meeting in open council.

2nd. According to the gospel and our church usages, no member can be expelled against the wishes and protest of a large majority of the congregation in which he lives. Brother Holsinger's entire church council save one man, protested to the last against his expulsion, and holds him as a Bishop yet, because he had violated no gospel precept or principle.

3rd. According to the decision of Annual Meeting, Art. 10, 1876, a committee cannot expel a majority of a church unless their decision is ratified by Annual Meeting in open council. If this cannot be done by a committee, they certainly cannot perform the greater task of expelling one member with the sanction of only one other member against the vote and protest of the whole of the remainder of the council, at least not until their decision is ratified by Annual Meeting in open council.

4th. According to the Gospel and all the usages of the church, no member can be expelled without first investigating the charges against him and submitting to a trial. Brother Holsinger was not given a trial upon the charges against him, but was pronounced expelled because *his church* would not consent to anything short of a public investigation. Hence the action of the committee cannot be enforced until ratified by Annual Meeting in open council.

5. The committee pronounced him expelled because the church desired an open trial. After making this decision another committee

from Annual Meeting consisting of a part of this same committee, went to Bear Creek church, Ohio, and held an open council, in which another brother was tried. The following letter and testimonials prove this assertion beyond a doubt:

Ellerton, O., Oct. 4th, 1881.

We, the undersigned brethren, having been present at the *Bear Creek* council meeting of the 29th and 30th of August last, when the committee sent from Annual Meeting consisting of D. P. Saylor, C. G. Lint and David Long waited upon said church, do hereby certify that said council was held with open doors, and that there were a number of outsiders present. In short there was *no one* prohibited from being present who wished to be there.

James A. Ridenour,
John W. Fitsgerald,
John W. Watson,
John R. Denlinger,
J. P. Martin,
A. Beeghly,
A. Garvy,
J. M. Fouch,
M. C. Kimmel.

Also, according to a report of the committee sent to Beaver Dam church, Md., last year, as given by R. H. Miller in the *Primitive Christian,* the committee not only permitted a public council, but invited the "outsiders" to come in the grove and witness the committee's work concerning that church. I am informed by brethren in Rockingham Co., Va., that a committee sent there from Annual Meeting to adjust a difficulty, allowed an open council. And a committee to Ashland City church, last winter, conducted an open council. Now, whatever may be the decision of Annual Meeting in relation to open council, committee work has been done with impunity in open session, showing that according to the usages of committee work, a council can be held openly, and a public trial given, if the committee so wills it. If it was not a crime to hold an open trial at Bear Creek, Ohio, and Beaver Dam, Md., by some of the same committee who visited Berlin, the desire on the part of the Berlin church to have brother Holsinger publicly tried, did not form a sufficient excuse to decide to disfellowship Holsinger for what his church desired to do, and their decision is therefore invalid unless ratified by Annual Meeting in open council.

Another fact stands prominently before the mind. Holsinger was charged before Annual Meeting, which is an open council, and has a reporter. The reporter gave the charges against Holsinger to the public, and that report was printed by Quinter and Brumbaugh, and is now on sale to the public, the church and the world. The committee went to Berlin, and met before a public council, disputed for over one day with the church, before a public council, and finally brought in a decision to disfellowship brother Holsinger, (and submitted *it* to the church before a public council) because the church voted to not allow brother Holsinger tried in secret session, and decided to let the report of the proceedings go to the public before whom he was accused.

Now, for the above reasons the brethren still fellowship H. R. Holsinger, and will continue to do so until next Annual Meeting, holding that according to the gospel, the spirit of fairness, and the decisions of Annual Meeting, and the usages of committee work, and our general manner of expelling members, he is yet a member of the brotherhood and will remain such, and should be fellowshipped until Annual Meeting, when the committee's report must be accepted or rejected.

These reasons are also urged upon the attention of the brethren, that they may be able to act fairly and vote intelligently upon the matter at next Annual Meeting. We do not want a division in the church, and it is the universal desire of what is called the progressive party that union may be maintained, and we shall do all in our power to avert a separation and final trouble. But we hold that H. R. Holsinger has not had a trial, and has not been guilty of violating any gospel sufficient for his expulsion from the church, and we trust in the wisdom and Christian spirit of our brethren at large sufficiently to believe they will not ratify the decision of his committee. We do not censure the committee too strongly, as we believe they are only men, and under the strain of embarrassing circumstances made a mistake. It is said that Annual Meeting will always ratify the work of her committees, do what they may, but we know that Annual Meeting does not consist of a few men, but is a council of the whole church and will not sanction a mistake made by any committee. Where Henry Holsinger, or any other brother has done wrong, we do not wish to shield him; but we are not willing that he shall be cut off this way. It would be better, too, if our district meetings would effect as much of a change this coming year as possible, and not send radical men of either side as delegates to

Standing Committee, but send men who have not been actively engaged in this work, and thus allow our brethren to feel that a fair and impartial legislation will result. These agitations have more or less embittered those who have been actively brought forward in this matter, and they are only men, and may not be able to act as impartially as they should. We have confidence in our brethren, but the flesh is weak.

We want something done to avert the trouble that will result if this committee's work is ratified. We want union. We pray for union, and this is written that our brethren everywhere may know how and why brother Holsinger's committee decided as they did. If a division comes we do not want the sin laid to our charge. But we trust in the wisdom of God to guide events aright. We trust in God because He is good and we trust in the good sense of our people because we think the body of the church wants to do right. Those who are not readers of the PROGRESSIVE CHRISTIAN should take it, and read it, and they will see that it is not so schismatic after all. We plead for union on the Gospel, and all our efforts will be to maintain it by cultivating a love for each other, and justice to brother Holsinger in this matter, and all other Brethren involved. We believe; *we know,* that too much of the present opposition to him is personal feeling. He has been in the front ranks of the church so long that, as a natural consequence, much personal feeling exists against him; but no charge of immoral conduct or gospel violation can be sustained against him. We know that he, with others, has not pursued a course entirely free from objection, and in his mistakes we will not shield him, but we will fellowship him until next Annual Meeting because the decisions of Annual Meeting, usages of the church, and the terms of the gospel admit and demand it.

We would be pleased if our other church papers will copy this, as we think justice to brother Holsinger and the brotherhood demands it. At least we ask every brother to circulate it as widely among the brethren as possible that the church at large may have a fair statement of the matter.

In behalf of the whole progressive portion of the church, at the earnest solicitation of leading ministers and members this has been written, and in the fear of God is signed prayerfully and hopefully,

S. H. BASHOR.[16]

Bashor's tract prompted a critical response written by S. S. Mohler.

Fig. 44. *J. W. Beer, early Progressive leader. (BE)*

Fig. 45. *S. H. Bashor, early Progressive leader. (BE)*

Fig. 46. *Schoolhouse No. 7 at Arnold's Grove, near Milford, Elkhart Co., IN, where supporters of H. R. Holsinger gathered in 1882 to consider organizing a new church. (BE)*

PARTIAL REVIEW OF "WHERE IS HOLSINGER?"

Under Article 3rd, page 2 and 3, in the tract published by S. H. Bashor, reviewing the work done by the annual meeting committee, he exhibits considerable haste, in coming to the rescue of H. R. Holsinger, and in his haste he certainly presumes largely upon both the ACTION of the sub-committee appointed by the annual meeting to examine the papers which appeared at the A. M., of 1881, against Holsinger, as he also does upon the PREMISES which he assigned the Berlin committee, he rests his case, and condemns the work of the committee at Berlin. Now, as the writer of this was placed in a position that gave him, along with other members of the before-named sub-committee, an opportunity to know something of the facts preceding, and upon which the Berlin committee was appointed by annual meeting, we, (the writer), from a sense of duty to the brotherhood, and for the truth's sake, will notice some of Bro. Bashor's allegations contained in Article 3d of his tract. The points named by the writer of the above named tract in Article 1 and 2, on page 2, are embraced in the first two lines under Article 3d, which reads: "No SPECIFIC CHARGE OF ANY CHARACTER was urged against him by any of the districts from which the general complaints came." Charity would lead us to conclude that he did not read the contents of the papers presented against Holsinger at last A. M., but this is precluded by his own reference to those papers, on page 2, of his tract: where he says "a report of which is in the minutes and report of annual conference of 1881," showing that he did read them, knew their contents, and could have represented the facts in the case if such had been his purpose: and why he did not do so, he alone can tell. The statement with which he starts out under Article 3 of his tract, stands at variance with the facts embodied in those papers. The first paper on the minutes touching his case presents him, Holsinger, as "refusing to hear the church." The second, "of fostering strife." The third, for "advocating opposition to the principles and rules of our brotherhood" on points named. The fourth, substantially the same as the third. The fifth, for "publicly through his paper charging brethren with being untruthful," in disregard of the rule of Matth. 18th, to which he had subscribed and for publishing "unchristian and untruthful reflections." These several papers came forward to A. M. for the reason that he (Holsinger) had as early as the year 1870, promised A.

M. upon complaint against him to desist from pursuing the course which caused complaints at that time; and also made similar promises subsequently to 1870 upon similar complaints against him. The sequel thus shows that H. R. Holsinger made frequent promises and as often as he made them he violated them. The report of the sub-committee to the A. M. of 1881, embodies the history of the conflict inaugurated by H. R. Holsinger against the order of our brotherhood on points named in the frequent complaints against him, commencing as early as 1870, and ends with a recommendation that A. M. appoint a committee to "deal with him according to his transgressions." This presents the following facts: First, H. R. Holsinger stands before the brotherhood prominently as having made solemn promises to the general brotherhood through its highest council, but as paying no attention to the promises which he made. Second. His disregard of his promises thus made entailed the dissatisfaction that existed before he made those promises. Third. This resulted in bringing to the A. M. of 1881, five papers of complaints against Holsinger, representing a large part of the brotherhood. These papers were thrown together into one general charge by the subcommittee having charge of those papers, and in their report to the general conference they say that (Holsinger) "having been admonished again and again to be more guarded in his publications, and promised to do so, which promise he has not performed, but has continued his FORMER COURSE WITH INCREASED effort." Now upon what grounds Bro. Bashor bases his first and second articles of his tract is difficult to see. In the introduction of Article 3d, Bro. Bashor says: "No specific charge of any character was urged against him (Holsinger) by any of the Districts from which complaints came," which is equal to saying that owing to a confused notion about Holsinger, information is necessary: see page 1st of tract, and if the brotherhood was properly informed, then Holsinger would stand before the brotherhood as he (Bashor) declares him to be in art. 1 and 2 of his tract. The position which brother Bashor assumes is, that he, a young brother, places himself on record against five District meetings representing near if not altogether one hundred churches, embracing brethren of age and observation, with personal knowledge of Holsinger's proceedings long before he (Bashor) was even a member of our fraternity. The comparison between brother Bashor's statement and the facts in the case places him in a very awkward attitude towards our brotherhood, even when considered in a very charitable light.

Again we call attention to a further statement of brother Bashor on page 2 and 3 of his tract with comparison with the facts in the matter of Bashor's reference. Under art. 3 page 2, he says: "The committee examined the accusations and recommended that conference send a committee to Berlin, Pa., and wait upon Holsinger and give him a trial." On page 3 he repeats the words: "And give him a trial," second line top of page. On the 6th line he introduces the following statement, viz: "The authority given to these committees was that they should investigate the case and make a decision according to the evidence brought in." Brother Bashor overlooks the fact that the five papers against Holsinger before A. M. of 1881 appeared on the presumption that there existed evidence sufficient to establish all that those papers alleged against him. It then became the duty of the sub-committee appointed to take charge of those papers to examine on what evidence (if any) the matters alleged by those papers against Holsinger rested. This was done, copies of "The Progressive Christian" were called for, and the committee was furnished with a number. These were carefully examined and the charges contained in the five papers were found to be fully sustained. Upon which the sub-committee made out its report, and "recommended annual meeting to appoint a committee to wait on Holsinger and deal with him according to his transgressions," as the evidence before the sub-committee fully justify its recommendations. The Berlin, Pa., committee was then selected by the standing committee and approved by conference, and authorized to proceed to Berlin, Pa., and carry out the recommendations of the sub-committee. It will thus be seen that conference endorsed the finding of the sub-committee and made provision to carry into effect its recommendations. This left for the Berlin committee but one of two ways in which to proceed under the charge ordered by conference, viz., First, If the Berlin committee found H. R. Holsinger penitent for the wrong charged against him by the five papers presented before conference, and found him prepared to give satisfactory assurance that he will desist for the future from pursuing the course complained of by those papers, then, as in cases of penitence and promises, to delcare H. R. Holsinger absolved from any further discipline, and report a satisfactory adjustment of the complaints noted to conference. But, second—If on the other hand the committee found him unwilling to thus confess and promise, then to proceed as ordered by conference, "and deal with him according to his transgressions," on the ground of refusing to hear the church according to Math. 18th. The Berlin committee had NO OTHER CHOICE under its charge from conference. It was not sent to Berlin, Pa., to investigate, to hear evidence, to hold a trial. The investigation was held at ASHLAND by the sub-committee. It heard the evidence; Holsinger was before that sub-committee in the character, capacity and utterances of his own paper: by its pages he was fairly, clearly and fully represented, and by these he was on trial properly, and his character located. Had the Berlin committee proceeded to hold a trial at Berlin, hear evidence and reached a conclusion adverse to the finding of the sub-committee and its recommendations to conference, and endorsed by conference, this would have made it (the Berlin committee) superior to conference; or had it held such a trial, as claimed by Bro. Bashor, and reached the same conclusion as did the sub-committee under whose recommendations conference gave the charge to the Berlin committee, such a procedure would have been in violation of their charge, and subjected it to censure before conference. Conference, in accepting the report of the sub-committee endorsed its finding, as by competent authority, and hence there remained only one of the two ways above designated in disposing of Holsinger's case in order to answer to the matter contained in the five papers alluded to against Holsinger, which appeared before conference. The proceedings then in Holsinger's case, commencing with the origin of those five papers in the local church, endorsed by district meetings, approved by annual meeting, and by the Berlin committee are all in strict harmony with the principles of our church government and are legal, and Holsinger stands disfellowshipped—no longer a member of the Brethren Church.

It will be seen upon examination that the words INVESTIGATE, DECIDE TRIAL, as applied to the Berlin committee and indicating their charge from conference, are not in the report of the sub-committee to conference as Bro. Bashor would have the readers of his tract believe. Shall we believe that Bro. Bashor THOUGHT that these words were in the report of the sub-committee, as a reason why he predicated the action of the committee to Berlin as he did? It is to be feared that Bro. Bashor did not write up his tract for the purpose which he professes on page one, viz: "That brethren may form a just estimate of the case," but rather to divert the attention from the issue involved by Holsinger's efforts. The issue raised by Holsinger was: SHALL OUR CHURCH GOVERNMENT CONTINUE TO BE REPRESENTATIVE IN FORM, OR SHALL IT BE CONGREGATIONAL? Holsinger stood as the advocate of the congregational form against the representative, and his paper contained sentiments multiplied against conference work: its decisions, and recommendations of writers to "burn—destroy the minutes," and otherwise to create distrust among the members of our fraternity, and so serious had this become that no other process could reach the case, but the course adopted by conference in its charge to the Berlin committee, i.e., "to deal with him according to his transgressions," and pointed as is the fact, and yet true as Holsinger stood to his record, that issue i.e., of congregationalism confronted the Berlin committee at the threshold of its work at Berlin. Upon this issue Holsinger staked his interest in the Brethren Church. The work of the committee at Berlin would decide for one generation, at least, what should be our form of church government.

Holsinger, with his congregation, rose up and demanded of the "Berlin committee" to step out from the usages of our brotherhood, and proceed in their work as he and the Berlin congregation had mapped off. Thus the issue was drawn sharp to a focal point and the one or the other was the question which the Berlin committee was to recognize, and shape their work at Berlin accordingly: between the two there was no possible compromise. Holsinger resolutely persevered in the demand made by him and those in sympathy with him, that the "Berlin committee" surrender to them: to have done this, the "Berlin committee" would have surrendered the sovereignty of conference and recognized the local congregation its superior. This it refused to do, and by its refusal, maintained our representative form of church government, and as a consequence, Holsinger's excision from the Brethren Church followed, and the committee's report will doubtless show that it confined itself to the limitations of the charge given by conference and faithfully maintained the integrity of our brotherhood.[17]

Whatever the impact among the Brethren of Bashor's ***Where is Holsinger?*** *or Mohler's* ***Partial Review,*** *the 1882 Annual Meeting needed to deal with the report from the Berlin Committee. Here is H. R. Holsinger's account of what followed.*

FINAL DECISION OF CONFERENCE

The next chapter in the history of this case is the trial before the annual meeting of 1882, called the Arnold's Grove Conference, held near Milford, Indiana, May 30 to June 2.

The case was introduced by reading the report of Berlin committee, which has already been recorded elsewhere.

An explanation being called for, John Wise proceeded to explain. As the explanation is somewhat lengthy, I will quote only such parts as introduce new or foreign matter. On page ten of the report of annual meeting he says: "We have the decision of annual meeting that no member shall be expelled from the church without gospel authority, and the question has been propounded, Where is your gospel authority for declaring Brother H. R. Holsinger's connection with this body severed? I will endeavor to give some of them. I Cor. 5:11: 'Now I have written unto you not to keep company, if any man that is called a brother be a fornicator, or covetous, or an adulterer, or a railer, or a drunkard, or an extortioner, with such as one ye are not to eat.' I do not understand that a man must be guilty of all these crimes before the church has jurisdiction over him but if he be found guilty of any one of them the church has authority to deal with him. The next passage is 2 Thes. 3:6: 'Now we command you, brethren, in the name of the Lord Jesus Christ, that you withdraw yourselves from every brother that walketh disorderly and not after the tradition which ye received of us.' And the fourteenth verse, 'And if any man obey not our work by this epistle, note that man, and have no company with him, that he may be ashamed.' Also Rom. 16: 17, 18, which see. This is the gospel authority we claim which justified the action of the committee, and which we submit before this meeting."

Motion was then made and seconded to adopt the report of the committee. Pending the discussion, D. C. Moomaw "asked privilege to introduce a motion to delay action upon the question until next day, and for presenting some considerations as to the effect of this controversy upon the general brotherhood. We should have but one purpose before us,—the harmony of the church. The question occurs, Can this purpose be accomplished in a better way. I know you are willing to accede to every measure founded on the Bible and reason and justice to save Brother Holsinger. But that is not all that is at stake in this report. Not only is Brother Holsinger under the ban of the church, but all who sympathize with him. Why should we not exercise every measure to save him and those who are in sympathy with him?"

John Wise: "Why, we want that sympathy on our side."

Moomaw: "We should always exercise sympathy, but not at the sacrifice of a brother. We have an instrument to present to the meeting, which I will read: 'The olive-branch of peace is presented by

H. R. Holsinger to the annual meeting of 1882, as follows: I, H. R. Holsinger, do herein set forth the following declaration of purpose and conduct, which shall be my guide in my future relation with the church:—

"*First.* I humbly ask the pardon of the brethren for all my offenses, general and particular, committed through the "Progressive Christian" or otherwise.

"*Second.* I promise hereafter to administer the discipline of the church in harmony with its practices, and will cease to teach any system of government not in harmony with that prevailing in the church, as set forth by annual meeting.

"*Third.* I promise to cease to speak or write in antagonism to the general order of its practices as now prevailing in the church.

"*Fourth.* I promise to cease the publication in the "Progressive Christian," or any other paper, of anything, in fact, in opposition to annual meeting.

"*Fifth.* I promise to publish these declarations in the "Progressive Christian," and request that they be placed upon the minutes of this meeting.

"Now, I ask, in behalf of peace and of the salvation of a great number of brethren that they be allowed until to-morrow morning to settle this matter finally, happily, and peacefully."

Whitmore Arnold opposed any delay, and urged the passing of the report.

Landon West said: "We heard the charges against Brother Holsinger, and the decisions rendered, together with the reasons therefor. Now, we ought to allow him a defense, because if we do not we would throw him out without trial."

J. H. Moore, Addison Harper, D. N. Workman, R. H. Miller, and W. R. Deeter, favored deferring the question until to-morrow.

P. J. Brown asked, "If this report is acted upon, can Brother Moomaw's proposition for reconciliation be entertained afterwards, or will it be objected to as not coming regularly before the meeting?" To which the moderator replied: "Brother Holsinger can come to the door of the church, and be received any time the same as any expelled member. Brother Moomaw can have the privilege of presenting that paper after the decision of this meeting, but I think the meeting would rather that Brother Holsinger would present it himself and not through others."

Daniel P. Saylor did not consider the motion to defer action was in order. He said: "The committee are the servants of the annual meeting. They were appointed by it to go to Berlin and investigate certain matters. They did so, and then were rejected by the church there. The only alternate was to make a report of their doings to this meeting. This they have done, and now it is for this meeting to accept or reject that report. Their reputation must be maintained and vindicated. During the entire year the doings of that committee have been slandered and reviled. The work has been called infamous and I don't know what all. Tracts have been published and put out to injure the reputation of the committee. Now, unless this meeting gives an expression on their doings, their reputation is not vindicated. Vindicate their reputation at this meeting, then a motion to give way or submit to their overtures is in order, and I for one am ready to receive it the very minute after action has been taken on this report. Don't put it off until to-morrow morning. I am ready to receive it at any time. The reputation of the committee is at stake, and must be vindicated. If this kind of concession had been made to the committee, their report would have been very different from what it is, but no concession was made, and, consequently, on the testimony before them they made their report. It is now the duty of the annual meeting to accept that report and say they acted advisedly."

I then made the following statement: "I have lost my voice, and I am obliged to appear by proxy. My brethren have agreed to assist me and speak for me. That is the reason why the paper was presented by Brother Moomaw instead of by myself. I know its contents, and he was authorized to present the paper. I wish to say that if the motion now before the house will be passed, then this paper will not be offered. The concessions therein made were made in view to a reconciliation. A number of the brethren agreed that a better thing can be done than to adopt the report of the committee, which would expel me from the church, with all who are in sympathy with me."

Right here I will offer an explanation. It may not be clear to everybody why I would not present the paper offered by Brother Moomaw, after the passage of the motion before the house. My explanation is as follows: The passage of the motion to adopt the report of the Berlin committee would have expelled me from the church. There would then have been no recourse for me but to acknowledge the justice of the action of the committee, and make such other conciliations as they might demand of me, and thus be reinstated as an expelled member. That I could not then have done, can not now, and never will do. I should despise myself as a hypocrite and a coward of the worst class if I should consent to truckle to the whims of ignorance and superstition to such an extent as to recognize the righteousness of their cause. To have consented to the propositions of the olive branch of peace would have been simply to acknowledge myself a human being possessed of the common frailities of humanity, but to have then or now recognized the action of the Berlin committee as being a just disposition of my case, would have been to stifle judgment, conscience, and every sense of honor and manhood.

Robert H. Miller said: "This is a peculiar case of the trial of a brother, which occurred in a very peculiar manner. The report has come here condemning him. You have heard the report, and before the brother was ever heard at all, a motion was made to accept the report. We were asked to accept the report without hearing the brother at all. I have opposed that brother more than any one in the brotherhood. And though I have been against him often and contended with him long and much, yet to-day I am not ready to vote until that brother has had an opportunity to be heard. He has not been heard. Hence, I favor the motion to give all the time he asks for to make a full answer to the charges made against him. Then we will decide whether to accept this report or not."

I. D. Parker and P. S. Meyers favored the motion to defer, but John P. Ebersole said: "I am just like Brother Robert Miller; I have never been a friend of Henry's course, but I tell you when he comes up as he has done here, then I am in favor of deferring it. You are not only working for Brother Henry, but for hundreds of others. You will be expelling hundreds of others when you expel him. I am for mercy. Defer it until to-morrow, and give all the chance you can. If you do that you will show that you are willing to give him all that he can possibly ask for, and, mind you, it will be done for the benefit of the general brotherhood."

Daniel P. Saylor offered the following remarks: "There were charges brought against Brother Holsinger, and there was a committee appointed to go and investigate the matter, and deal with him according to his transgressions. The committee went there and investigated the matter, and gave him a trial, or offered to do so. He laid down the rules on which he would come to trial, but the committee would not accept, on the ground that it was not according to the Scriptures nor the usages of the brotherhood. He refused to accede to the requirements of the committee, and, as is the order and custom of the church, the committee has dealt with him, and their report is now before us. That report is what we have to act upon now. The brethren have spoken of mercy. I trust we are all on the side of mercy, but H. R. Holsinger never mentioned it in the arguments set forth by others to sustain him in defying that report. Nothing was said about mercy until it was mentioned here. I am opposed to deviations one moment. Would it be reasonable to send a committee to me and I reject that committee and not accept its rulings, and then come before the annual meeting with a compromise?—No. The matter is plain. Do not let our sympathies run away with our judgment."

Jacob Rife, Jesse Crosswhite, Lemuel Hillary, S. S. Mohler, Daniel Vaniman all favored immediate action upon the original motion. R. Z. Replogle remarked: "In the report of last annual meeting you will find that the committee was to wait on Brother Holsinger, and deal with him according to his transgressions. If you accept their report with the explanation of Brother Wise, they dealt with him according to what he did while they were present. Brother Holsinger thought that inasmuch as he was openly accused, first, through the various district meetings, and then the annual meeting, and lastly through the public report, he had a right to public vindication. He was expelled according to the report, as well as the explanation given, because he would not submit to a private trial."

Noticing that the time had drawn well into the afternoon, and witnessing evident indications of bitter feeling against me, and fearing that the question of deferring would consume the whole day, all to no advantage, I tired of the effort, and proposed that Brother Moomaw and his second should withdraw the motion.

The moderator then announced that the original motion was now under discussion, when S. S. Mohler said he thought it had been discussed fully, when I offered the following remarks:—

"I agree the one side has been argued, but the defense has not been heard from. One point presented by Brother Wise I wish to correct. He signified there were two charges brought against me: first, that of refusing to be tried according to the usages of the church, and having a stenographer; and second, for insisting upon an open council. In my view there is only one charge involved,—that of the stenographer. The open council was a matter entirely with the committee. The key of the church was tendered them, and they might have excluded the audience, and thus we threw the responsibility upon them. They could have held the council with closed doors if they had wished to, but we would not exclude any one from the council.

"This morning for the first time I heard the charge of raillery placed to my account. I certainly have not been tried for raillery. It was also stated by some of the speakers that I had a trial. All who have read the report know that is not a fact. I had no trial, and the report of the committee read this morning does not say so; neither does it charge me with any of the crimes referred to in the passages of Scripture. The report winds up as follows: 'In view of the above considerations, especially in view of the fact that Brother H. R. Holsinger refused to have his case investigated by the committee in harmony with the gospel, as interpreted by annual meeting, and the consent of our general brotherhood; and inasmuch as Brother Holsinger and the Berlin church assumed all responsibility in the case; therefore, we decide.'

"The report does not say that, because I was guilty of *raillery,* therefore, they came to this conclusion; but they simply acted upon previous usages. I have stated at different times that there never was a case exactly like mine in the history of the church, and that this being a new case the committee might have deviated from the usages, and acted according to common sense, and given me a fair hearing. When those passages of Scriptures were read this morning in confirmation of the decision of the committee, I thought Brother Wise should have done me the simple justice to except the one with which he wished to charge me. There were many strangers present who knew nothing of my case except what they learned here, and I demand of this meeting, whatever may be the result of the case, that you will clear me of any of the gross charges alluded to in the scripture read."

J. W. Beer said: "It has been stated, and repeated with emphasis, that the only question we had to decide upon was as to the legality of the decision. That is a mistake. The action may be legal, and yet should not be accepted. The apostle Paul says, 'All things are lawful, but all things are not expedient.' The action of the committee may be lawful, and yet the question of expediency might arise. I believe the action of expelling Brother Holsinger was too hasty. There was ample room for misunderstanding between him and the committee. There was a misunderstanding between the committee to whom the papers relating to Brother Holsinger were given at the annual meeting of 1881 and the annual meeting itself. Many present misunderstood the action of the committee. When the report was brought in it was advised that a committee be sent to H. R. Holsinger, to deal with him according to his transgressions. Brother Holsinger called attention to the difference of expression in regard to his case, and that of another. One of the committee on Holsinger's papers has since explained that it was not their intention to go to Berlin to investigate the case, for if the committee sent there had investigated the case, it would have presented its authority, and would have done the work which the annual meeting had sent it to do. Now, while that was the understanding on the part of the committee who recommended the committee to be sent to Berlin, many of us understood that the committee should investigate the case, and give him an honorable and a fair chance. I base my arguments on the expressions used by the Berlin committee when they came there. They stated that they came to investigate the case of H. R. Holsinger, and whenever the object of their visit was mentioned it was to investigate that case; and it was not until the report of that committee was brought in that the expression was used that they were sent to deal with him according to his transgressions. If the Berlin committee understood it was their duty to deal with Holsinger according to his transgressions, and not to investigate the case, why was it presented in this way? We have it in their own words that they felt it their duty to give him a trial. Hence, I feel the action was injudicious.

"Brother Holsinger was charged publicly at our last annual meeting. This meeting is not composed of brethren and sisters alone. There are present intelligent minds interested in the cause of religion not of our brotherhood. The charges were publicly made and publicly placed on record, in the report of annual meeting. He was also publicly charged in the minutes of our meeting. Under those circumstances it appeared to the Berlin church that they had a right to demand a public trial." . . .

The moderator then said, "The question has been called for, and I will have to put it before the house," when I asked for privilege of a final word, which was granted after some parleying. . . .

"But I am not able for this occasion. My voice is failing me, and I have a very severe headache. I will, therefore, submit all to you. I have always withstood all attempts to separate from the body of the church, but all has failed, and all that I can do now is to trust my case into your hands, and unto the guidance of the kind providence that overrules all."

The motion was then put before the house, and the report of the Berlin committee was adopted. So ended the second act in the drama.

I have not space to expatiate upon my feelings or the results of the decision. I walked out from under the council tent, thinking only of my congregation at Berlin. On entering the vast throng outside I was greeted by many of my friends and brethren and patrons, who offered words of encouragement and approbation. After consultations it was agreed to call a public meeting on Tuesday evening, May 30, at a schoolhouse a mile west of the place of conference, for the purpose of consulting upon the proper step to be taken. It seems prudent to state at this period that I was the least interested among all the aggrieved progressive brethren. I have, therefore, to thank my friends for my salvation in that dark hour of temptation. He who was merciful to the thief on the cross, caused the hearts of His own to have compassion on him who erstwhile would have been an outcast and wanderer.

FIRST MEETING AT SCHOOLHOUSE NO. 7

There was a good attendance at the schoolhouse for the short notice that had been given. Elder P. J. Brown was called to the chair, and, after devotional services, the object of the meeting was stated. The following motion then prevailed: "That we extend to Brother Holsinger our Christian sympathy, and until he is guilty of a violation of the gospel or well-defined moral principle, we will consider him as illegally expelled." A committee was appointed to draft a memorial to the standing committee, with a view of making one more effort to prevent a division of the church,—J. W. Beer, Dr. J. E. Roop, and David Bailey,—with instructions to report at next meeting.

The next meeting was held on Wednesday afternoon, May 31. The memorial committee reported the following:—

MEMORIAL

"ARNOLDS, Elkhart Co., Ind., May 31, 1882. *"To the standing committee—*

"DEAR BRETHREN IN ANNUAL MEETING ASSEMBLED, Greeting: We, your petitioners, would beg leave to say that we feel aggrieved at yesterday's action in the case of Elder H. R. Holsinger and his friends, and feeling that another division in the brotherhood is imminent, and deploring an event fraught with so much evil, we humbly petition for a joint committee, say of twelve brethren, half to be selected by progressive brethren and the other half by your body, and they prepare a plan for a general reconciliation between the annual meeting and all the brethren called progressive, and we hope you will hear us in this our earnest request, so that further division may be prevented.''

The report of the committee was adopted, and Dr. J. E. Roop and Elder J. W. Beer were appointed to carry the memorial to the standing committee and receive their reply, with request to ask for an early response.

The next session convened on Thursday forenoon, June 1. The committee appointed to carry the memorial to the standing committee reported having discharged their duty, and presented the following reply from the standing committee:—

REPORT OF STANDING COMMITTEE

''RESPECTED BRETHREN OF THE COMMITTEE: Inasmuch as the annual meeting of 1881 ruled out the Miami Petition upon the ground that it had not come through the district meeting, thus settling the question of her ruling, therefore the standing committee can not receive anything that does not come in regular order.

E. EBY, *Moderator.*

''JAMES QUINTER, *Clerk,*
''JOHN WISE, *Reading clerk.*
''*June 1, 1882.*''

The report of our committee was received, and the committee discharged with the thanks of the meeting.

It was now believed by all that every means had been exhausted from which any hope for compromise or reconciliation could be derived. The meeting had been standing still to ''see the salvation of the Lord,'' and now it was believed the time had come when the Lord said, ''Go forward!''

''The committee on resolutions then presented the following:—

REPORT OF COMMITTEE ON RESOLUTIONS

''Inasmuch as Christ gave His people a complete plan of salvation, containing neither too much nor too little; and inasmuch as no church during all the history of the past has successfully made additions to or subtractions from it through mandatory legislation without causing discord and troubles; and inasmuch as reformations have universally tended to reaffirm the primitive doctrine of Christ by divesting it of accumulated decrees, enactments, and laws made by church leaders, which have always tended toward abridging God-given liberty, and that church legislation has had a tendency in all ages to run into corruption and abuse of power, and the history of Christendom is full of examples of suffering and ostracism as its legitimate offspring; and,

"*Whereas,* We are already painfully reminded of the intolerant spirit it generates, and have witnessed it during the past in the expulsion of many of our dear brethren and sisters for no violation of the gospel or moral principle; and but yesterday were humiliated by what appears to us an act of great injustice; and,

"*Whereas,* Our annual conference is almost wholly taken up with legislation tending to abridge our liberties in the gospel, enforcing customs and usages and elevating them to an equality with the gospel, and defending them with even more rigor than the commands of God; and,

"*Whereas,* Through a conscientious opposition to this dangerous and unjust assumption of power and an honorable contention for the pure Word of God as our only rule of faith and practice has caused us to be styled 'troublers' and 'railers;' and,

"*Whereas,* Our avowed sympathy for the church in all her gospel principles has had no weight; our explanations have been misrepresented; our petitions have been slighted; our prayers have been unheeded; and all our efforts at reconciliation, which were honest and sincere, were frowned upon and rejected for most trivial reasons; therefore,

"*Resolved,* That we continue to sympathize with and fellowship all brethren and sisters who have been expelled without a violation of the gospel, and go on serving our Master by preaching the gospel and only the gospel, ever opposing every tendency toward religious oppression and intolerance, and corrupting of the church with the traditions and commandments of men.

"*Resolved,* That with Alexander Mack, we reaffirm the doctrine of the gospel being our only rule of faith and practice, and the doctrines of our church as it existed in its earlier and purer age, and before it was corrupted by the additions made by elders and their abuse of power.

"*Resolved,* That we recommend a convention of all those

favorable to restoring the church to its primitive purity, at which time it shall be decided what course shall be pursued for the future."

The resolutions were unanimously adopted, and a committee appointed and authorized to select a place and appoint a time, and give due notice of the convention contemplated.

The following resolution was adopted: "Resolved, That our motto shall be the Bible, and nothing but the Bible," and all who are in harmony with this sentiment are invited to meet in convention.

The committee on conventions reported as follows:—

CALL OF A CONVENTION

"In pursuance of a resolution passed at schoolhouse No. 7, Jackson Township, Elkhart County, Indiana, June 1, 1882, by progressive brethren, as follows:—

" 'Resolved, That we recommend a convention of all those favorable to restoring the church to its primitive purity, at which time it shall be decided what course shall be pursued for the time;'

"We, your committee, therefore have appointed said convention to be held at Ashland, Ohio, June 29, 1882.[18]

And thus after Holsinger's dismissal, Progressive Brethren began the steps of separation and division. They met as planned at Ashland at the end of June, 1882 and drew up a Declaration of Principles (Independence).

DECLARATION OF PRINCIPLES

"Declaration of Principles, adopted by the Progressive Convention, of the Tunker Church, held at Ashland, Ohio, June 29 and 30, A.D. 1882.

"When bodies, politic or religious, depart in intent or practice from the original purpose and principles of the founders of the government or church, and institute measures and policies which destroy the inalienable rights of the people, prohibit the exercise of individual opinions, and enact laws the enforcement of which is destructive of liberty and the higher interests of the governed; and when the welfare of the people is forgotten in the worship of forms and instruments, which are innovations upon the inherent principles of the law of nature and of God: and when character and reputation are considered matters the most trivial, are poisoned, polluted, and angered, without any possible show of just redress or the punishment of villifiers; when men are condemned without notice or trial; and when human charity and sympathy are trampled underfoot by those in authority, and the prejudices and jealousies of men rule in the domain of thought; when wisdom and discretion are dethroned, it becomes the imperative duty of the oppressed and misused to declare against such misrule and tyranny and in favor of good government and the exercise of individual and religious rights, the abolishment of all traditionary and unlawful measures, and a full return to the original spirit, intent, and application of the established law, which in this instance is the gospel. When continual efforts have failed to correct abuses, inaugurate general reformatory measures, and all systemized efforts, coupled with warnings, pleadings, and prayers, have been refused, and still more radical and unlawful systems adopted for the oppression of the people and the protection of illegitimate enactments and cruel rulers, it then becomes their unavoidable obligation to the law of God and the rights and welfare of man, to throw off the yoke of bondage, step out of the shadows of usurpation, upon the original platform of universal right, liberty, and truth, and declare their independence from all innovations or additions to the constitution of the law by which they are governed.

"When such final action is required, justice to themselves and 'a decent respect to the opinions of mankind required that they should declare the causes which compel them' to the declaration.

"We hold that in religion the gospel of Christ and the gospel alone, is a sufficient rule of faith and practice; that he who adds to the gospel takes from it, or in any way binds upon men anything different from the gospel, is an infidel to the Author of Christianity and a usurper of gospel rights.

"That the gospel recognizes the liberty of men and the church to establish expediences, instruments, and immunities, by which the education and spiritualization of the race may be successfully achieved in different generations and under various circumstances; but prohibits the elevation of these instruments or expediences to an equal plane of authority, with positive divine enactments, the penalty attached to the transgression of which is to be social ostracism or severance of church relation.

"That the only condition of approved membership in the kingdom of Christ is obedience to the precepts of the gospel upon the basis of a good moral character.

"That no man should be condemned or his liberties destroyed for any cause whatever without a fair and impartial trial upon the charges or complaints brought against him.

"That upon all questions of church government, the doctrines and commandments of men are paralyzing to the life and interests of the church. That in doctrine the church of Christ should universally harmonize, but on questions of government and customs may be congregational.

"That every possible means for the conversion of souls should be put forth at all times and under every circumstance.

"The history of the German Baptist Church leaders and conference, for years past, has been a history of continued departures from the primitive simplicity of the Christian faith in almost every essential feature of gospel liberty and church rule. That this may appear, let the following facts be investigated and carefully considered.

"When committee men have been objected to for lawful reasons, by persons on trial, the objections have been thrown aside by the committee, and the associate objected to allowed to serve, and such action subsequently ratified by conference.

"They have denied the administration of the ordinance of Christian baptism to penitent believers for reasons foreign to the teachings of the gospel; and in opposition to the express declarations of Christ. In disobedience to the teachings of the gospel they have made 'outward adornment and the wearing of apparel' a condition of full church relation.

"Women of the best standing in society and noble Christian character, have been ruthlessly expelled from the church for wearing a style of head-dress other than the bonnet and cap prescribed by church legislation.

"Ministers and others have been refused a hearing in annual, district, and local church conferences, and, in many instances, entirely ignored and forbidden communion privileges for wearing a different cut of clothing and hair than that prescribed by conference and church usage.

"The shape of particular garments, such as the head-dress and coat, have in various instances been legislated upon by annual conference and made conditions of church relation by supporters of conference rule.

"Brethren of good standing in their home congregations have, by private caucusing of jealous elders and ministers, without the knowledge or consent of the laity, been excluded from communion privileges, and these tyrannical and unchristian acts passed without notice or rebuke by conference.

"Minsters and papers 'Loyal' to annual meeting have slandered, abused, and misrepresented brethren of progressive views, so far as to attack character and defame reputation, when no possible opportunity of redress could be had, and these actions passed unrebuked by conference.

"Progressive brethren have petitioned for amicable adjustment of all difficulties, privately, publicly, and through conference, but these petitions have gone unheeded or were answered by suspension and expulsion.

"Practices have been admitted by members of conference in their home congregations, for which in other congregations they have expelled members of good character from the church.

"Ministers of good moral character have been suspended from the ministry or excluded from the church, without so much as a trial, against the almost unanimous vote, or without the knowledge of their home congregations, without gospel authority, for no other reason than pleading for union, opposing official corruption, and defending the perfection of the gospel as a rule of faith and practice.

"The rights of individual congregations have been trampled upon, their peace destroyed, and their final prosperity blighted by immoderate and unreasonable decisions of committees sent by conference.

"They have, contrary to the usages of the civilized world and the church in all ages, condemned individuals without the semblance of a trial.

"They have made the decisions of annual conference equal in authority to the Word of God, by declaring them mandatory.

"They preach for doctrines, the commandments of men, and make them tests of Christian fellowship, and neglect the weightier matters of the law, mercy, and faith.

"They have instituted mock trials to save men favorable to the tradition of the church, and give a show of fair dealing in the eyes of the uninformed and ignorant.

"Bishops, who have through dishonorable dealings for lording it over God's heritage, lost the respect and sympathy of their churches and communities, have been sent again and again on committees to settle important church matters away from home, and are to-day occupying high places at annual conference.

"They have made bishops separate and superior to the body and authority of the church, whereas the gospel declares them servants of the church.

"Throughout all these abuses and oppressions, the portion of the church known as Progressives have, in various ways, petitioned for justice, and a return to the primitive purity and simplicity of gospel church rule; nor have we been wanting in the spirit of fraternal feeling and Christian charity, which dictates forgiveness for injuries suffered and pleads forgiveness for offenses committed. We have used every means available to restore the church to its original position of 'the gospel, the whole gospel, and nothing but the gospel,' and having not only failed, but witnessed the farther departure of conference from this position by the mandatory act, we are now compelled to disavow equal and all responsibility in these departures and traditions, and submit to the necessity which demands declarations to the adherence of the gospel alone in faith and practice, upon the platform occupied by the apostles of Jesus Christ and our church fathers, independent of the abuses, traditions, and commandments of the annual conference of the German Baptist Church. We regret the necessity which compels it, but duty to the world, ourselves, our children, and to Almighty God, the Ruler of the universe, demands it; and that His name may be glorified, His cause advanced, and the usurpations of men denounced and opposed, we meekly bow to the dictations of justice, purity, and truth.

"We therefore reaffirm the primitive doctrines of the church, and disavow allegiance to all such derogatory and subversive ecclesiastical mandates, and declare our intention to administer the government of the church as in the days of the apostles and our faithful brotherhood.

"We thus renounce mandatory legislation, creeds, and everything that may be construed to holding anything as essential to salvation, except the gospel of Christ (Rom. 1:16), and thus declare ourselves as being the only true conservators and perpetuators of the brotherhood and its original doctrines and principles, and are, therefore, the original and true church.

"We also express our sincere regret and sorrow for the apostasy of our brethren in leaving the time-honored principles of the church by making additions to the gospel through mandatory legislation contrary to the Word of God, and we pray God to help them to see their error and return to the gospel of Christ—the platform of the brotherhood—from which they have departed by improper legislation; and until they return we will not regard any expulsions or suspensions which they may make, but will continue to fellowship all who have been or may hereafter be expelled without gospel authority or a just trial.

"We will continue to hold district and general conferences when necessity or circumstances demand and then only.

"The members in all our churches who accept the gospel of Christ as the only law in religion, shall be entitled to representation in our conferences, whenever held. And that this purpose may be appointed by this convention, whose duty it shall be to arrange for the holding of such meetings and for the setting in order of churches which may be left in a disordered condition by the late apostasy.

"In conclusion, we pray the blessings of God upon our efforts to adhere to and retain inviolate the original church government and doctrine of our fathers, and the church we so devoutly love."[19]

A much briefer statement, which was also quite important, attempted to clarify the relationship between these Brethren and the remainder of the Brethren. They wanted to make certain that nobody believed that they were departing from the "church founded by our fathers." In other words, if anybody had departed, it was the remainder of the Brethren.

"Resolved, That it is the sense of this [Ashland] convention that, as we are the true conservators of the doctrines of the Brethren Church, and have never strayed from the church founded by our fathers, nothing done in this meeting shall be construed as secession or departure from the original church organized in Germany, in 1708, or from the principles of the gospel as interpreted by our fathers, until the intervention of human traditions and the usurpation of authority by men in control of annual meeting. In every principle of nonconformity to the world and the practice of the gospel ordinances, we stand where we always have stood, and by the grace of God always will stand."[20]

One of the early actions of these Progressive Brethren, in addition to producing statements and resolutions setting forth their actions and beliefs, was to make "an effort . . . to consolidate with kindred denominations, and a committee [was] appointed to confer with similar committees, and recommended to make a special effort to ef-

fect a union with the people known as Congregational Brethren, Leedy Brethren, . . ." The committees met and at a later convention in Dayton, Ohio the following resolution was adopted:

"*Resolved,* That the brethren heretofore known as Progressive, those known as Congregational, and those known as Leedy Brethren are all one body in Christ, and that all sectarian titles that theretofore existed shall be forever dropped, and we will hereafter be known and know each other by the gospel name Brethren."[21]

Who were the Congregational Brethren and the Leedy Brethren? About 1880 a leader of the Congregational Brethren in Indiana, Jonathan H. Swihart, published in a one-page broadside a statement of the history and beliefs of that group.

A BRIEF SUMMARY
of the
FAITH and PRACTICE
OF THE
CONGREGATIONAL BRETHREN

in answer to the following questions

1st. When and by whom were the Congregational Brethren organized?
2nd. What do they believe and practice?

Questions like these are asked us almost daily, hence we will try, by means of pen and press, to answer many at once. Not necessarily to multiply words, we would say:

The Church of the Brethren has never, to our knowledge, been disorganized since its first establishment in Europe, under the leadership of Alexander Mack, in A.D. 1708; but at a later date some of the ordinances of God's house were practiced somewhat differently by the various congregations residing in different localities. But the Brethren did not allow those little differences to disturb their peace or prevent their worshiping and communing as one body until A. D. 1872, when the annual meeting had under consideration the different modes of feet-washing, then practiced in the different localities. While most congregations residing in the east and middle states practiced the "double mode," several of the churches in the west, viz: Illinois, Missouri, Iowa and California practiced the "single mode" which the Western Brethren (as they were then called) regarded as the only true gospel mode, as well as the first practiced in America. But the verdict of the annual meeting of 1872 denied the Western Brethren what they regarded as their gospel freedom in this matter. The latter, after they had duly considered the matter, set their resolutions to "obey God rather than man" and for that reason (no other) a number of Brethren were denounced by a committee sent by the A. M. as disobedient to the council of the annual meeting; but as they were not really disorganized, (as several Elders and deacons fell upon the side of the "single mode" with a number of lay members,) they carried their former resolution into effect and adopted the title "Congregational Brethren," as it was well adapted to their views of church government. Thus for over eight years the Congregational Brethren have worshiped God in peace, after the manner of their fathers, calling no man, nor body of men "father upon earth," "as one is our father who is in heaven." As regards the foregoing account, we know whereof we affirm, as we lived in the west. Six years ago last fall, (October 28, 1874), Brother Frank A. Hendricks of Jasper, Jasper Co., Mo., organized a small church in Elkhart county, Ind., by ordaining J. C. Cripe, and installing several deacons. Little Jake was, however, not quite long-winded enough to stand all the storms arrayed against him. So he went back to the old Brethren. Hope he may find shelter there.

WHAT WE TEACH AND PRACTICE

We teach that faith, repentance and baptism are conditions of pardon. We baptize only by trine immersion.

We hold to the principle of non-resistance, and do not swear with an uplifted hand. The Lord says: "Swear not at all." James says: "But above all things, my brethren, swear not."

We teach "modesty" in dress, but do not bind to cut or form.

We have no annual visits; only send visits to members when they violate the principles of the gospel. We hold that brother must not go to law with brother, and should be at peace with all men as much as in him lies.

We hold communion meetings frequently and in every locality where members live, though there be few living in such locality. At our "feasts of charity" we have a supper prepared, from which we rise and wash one another's feet (single mode) then sit down again and eat supper; not merely to gratify the appetite (if any man hungers let him eat at home,) but to honor the Lord. As soon as supper is eaten, without any further ceremony, we bless the communion bread, then break it, (in slices) after which it is broken by, and to, all around the table, male and female just alike, "for we being many are one bread and one body." After we have broken and eaten the bread we bless the cup (not cups) which is then passed from member to member until all have drank of it in remembrance of the great Head of the church; then we sing a hymn and all is done. We also salute the Brethren with a "holy kiss," but we endeavor not to make it a habit. Therefore do not salute as frequently as some do who practice the salutation. We also anoint the sick with oil—we first pray over them, then anoint them. See James v. 14.

We hold prayer and social meetings. All the members are at liberty to pray and prophesy, but all in order. "The house of God is a house of order."

When it comes to church business, of a financial character, the woman is to keep silent and not use authority over the man. We believe the gospel stands against secret societies, for the Savior says, "swear not," and "In secret have I said nothing;" again, "Let your light so shine that men may see your good works and glorify your Father in heaven."

We only recognize two grand grades of church officers, viz: Bishop and Deacons and such titles as Elder, Shepherd, Overseer, Bishop, &c, are synonymous terms, meaning officers of the same grades. A Deacon may be a Minister, but the title does not necessarily imply minister. With us Deacons are only elected or chosen by the congregation. They are then installed by prayer and the laying on of the hands of Elders. The primary object of such is to look after the financial wants of the church. Secondarily, they may preach and baptize, but do not lay hands on those whom they baptize: See Acts VI chapter, also Acts VIII, 15, 16, 17 and Acts XIX 6. None but Elders lay on hands in any case, as the gospel gives no authority to any other to do so. If our Deacons prove faithful and can make efficient ministers of themselves they are then ordained, having held the "mystery of the faith in a pure conscience."

OUR CHURCH GOVERNMENT

We believe that every church or congregation composed of members, Deacons and Elders, being thus fully organized, possesses within itself all the necessary elements of validity. Hence in all matters for which we have not a positive, "thus saith the Lord," we are independently congregational, each congregation transacting its own local business. Thus we avoid episcopacy and creed-making which are regarded as the most fruitful source of contentions and divisions among believers. We instruct our Brethren to observe carefully, Matthew XVIII 15, 16 and 17, and will not receive as a charge any matter between member and member, until the conditions referred to are strictly complied with. They must be told to the church (not the Elders) and the offending party then gets his "rebuke before all, that others may fear." We do not think the Lord meant by the expression, "tell it to the church" that we must tell it to the GENERAL church, but to that local church where such members live. Neither has a body of Elders any business to meddle with such matters any more than that the offended party is commanded to tell it to a body of representatives.

The Word says, "tell it to the church." It does not say, tell it to the Elders, or send for a committee. If the matter is either too great or too small to tell to the church, according to the DIRECT command of Christ, it is JUST RIGHT to keep still about it. If a matter is not worth telling openly to the congregation, we should keep our mouths shut about it and work for peace, exercising forbearance toward our Brethren, the dear purchase of our Savior's blood. If our Brethren commit gross evils, such as spoken of in Romans I, 29, 30 and 31; and Galatians V, 19, 20 and 21. We deal with them according to First Corinthians V. 13.

In conclusion, permit me to say, that the gospel of Christ is our only and self-sufficient rule of faith and practice. Our motto is "Unity in essentials, liberty and forebearance in nonessentials and all things charity." We have no objections to holding an occasional conference to keep up a good understanding among us, but a judicious thresher sets his machine when he has something to thresh, but it is not wisdom to run a machine while the harvest is growing. If a machine is kept in motion it must be fed or it will burst when the power gets high and it don't pay to poke in trash all the time merely to keep it from breaking to atoms. Let us stop the machine and go to cultivating the grain, so it will grow RANK and STRONG and choke out the tares, for it is not lawful to pluck them up.

J. H. S.

Bourbon, Ind.[22]

The so-called "Missouri Committee" of 1872, to which Swihart referred, was described in much greater detail by one of the participants, Franklin A. Hendricks, in a lengthy letter to The **Gospel Trumpet.** *Evidently, some members of the Spring River Valley church in Missouri had appealed for an Annual Meeting committee to come and consider ten grievances which were dividing the congregation. The list of grievances dealt with the method of feetwashing, plain dress, the church visit, preaching universal restoration, and the authority of elders and the Annual Meeting. The investigating committee decided that these charges were "admitted and proven," and that "there was either ignorant or willful guilt resting upon the ministry, and that they should confess it, and promise to do so no more, or they could no longer be continued as elders and teachers in the Brotherhood." To this the ministers answered decidedly that they "had no acknowledgement or promise to make." The result, of course, was that "they could no longer be continued as members in fellowship in the church." Franklin Hendricks concluded:*

Now, dear reader, let me say to you, that you now have the original charges as they first appeared. You have the committee's report, and you can see they give it a false coloring, and testify that all the Brethren elsewhere were cut off for the same things. These charges were against the Spring-River Valley church; and I know that the brethren in Newton County, Mo., were not cut off for these charges. They were cut off for refusing to wash feet in the Double mode. And for the same reason in Bates County, Mo.

Now I will give a short history of the proceedings of the committee in Jasper Co., Mo., where those charges were found to exist. Let me say to you, dear reader, after the trial had gone on for one whole day, one of the committee came to me and said, if we would adopt the Double mode of feetwashing, all the charges would be dropped; to which we would not agree. And when they asked an acknowledgement of us on all the charges but feet-washing, and we said we had none to make, they laid no penalty on us, but immediately asked us if we would organize new churches in the Single mode. And when we said we would, then John Harshey, as foreman of the committee, said our office was taken from us. And when we gave him to understand, that as we did not consider it in their power to take from us that which the church and the word of God granted to us, unless we transgressed God's law, and then that would cut us off. So they said we were cut off, and all that sided with us. Now this is a true statement of the case.

And now, dear reader and brother, let me say to you, there is a goodly number of us in the West, and we are living in peace and harmony ever since the separation. Since the division I have attended seven communions, where the ordinances of God's house were carried out to the letter, and in the spirit of our Master; where love was felt to flow from heart to heart, and we felt we were sitting together in heavenly places in Christ Jesus.

Our communion came off the third Saturday and Sunday in October, 1873. There were five ordained Elders present; and when the time had come, Eld. J [G]. W. McClintock, of Bates Co., rose, laid aside his garments, took a towel and girded himself, then poured water into a basin, and washed and wiped his brother's feet on his right, then delivered the towel to him, and he washed and wiped the feet of him on his right; and so on around, until all had washed and wiped. Then the Lord's supper was eat, and as some were eating, he took bread and blessed and brake it; and then the brethren and sisters brake it with one-another. After this he took the cup and blessed it; then it was divided among the brethren and sisters.

From here we went to Newton Co., and had a communion session with the brethren and sisters there, and had a good meeting, notwithstanding the weather was unpleasant on account of rain and wind, and rather cold for comfort.[23]

According to a letter probably written by Isham Gibson, and included as a part of A. H. Cassel's manuscript, "Some Account of the Origin and History of the Far Western and Congregational Brethren . . . ," Franklin A. Hendricks and his father Daniel Hendricks were two of those disfellowshipped by the Annual Meeting committee in 1872. Gibson had been a prominent leader of the Far Western Brethren in Illinois before he moved to Missouri.

Dear Bro. In Christ. [A. H. Cassel],

I lift my pen to let you know the condition we are in, here in, Missouri. You are aware no doubt from the Minutes of last A. M. that there was a Committee appointed to visit Cedar and Jasper Counties, and perhaps other Churches. Said Com. has done their work, and the following is the result. They have silenced Bro. Daniel Hendricks, and Bro. Franklin Hendricks, and disowned all who would not adopt the double mode of Feetwashing in Jasper County. And in Cedar County they silenced Bro. James Hendricks and disowned all in favor of the Single Mode. And in Barry County they did the same thing.

This information I got from the Committee themselves who arrived here in Bates County day before yesterday, and yesterday. We went in Council and the question was asked us in this way. "If Conference (A. M.) has or shall decide that the double mode of Feetwashing shall be the only mode will you submit, and adopt the double mode." Twelve out of the fifteen members present said they would not adopt the double mode except it was shown in the Word of the Lord. And for thus saying they were at once disowned. There was fourteen members not present, and out of that number, there is not more than three that will follow A. M. in preference to the word of God. So we stand now about six to Twenty three. So now Dear Brother you can see that the mode of Feetwashing is made a test of Fellowship. They had no charge against us except the one named above, to wit—the single mode.

Now dear Bro. you can have some idea of our Condition and perhaps also some idea of our feelings. Yet we are not discouraged—though we are cast down, yet not destroyed, for our Hope is in the Lord—our trust in his word. And this consolation is ours, that He will be with us untill the end. So we are weak, yet not forsaken, for his power is made Known through our weakness. Therefore we rejoice that we are counted worthy to suffer reproach for the cause of our Master.[24]

Thus several members of the Hendricks and Gibson families became leaders in the Congregational Brethren group, which in 1883 became a part of The Brethren Church.

In addition to the Congregational Brethren, the Leedy Brethren also became a part of the Progressive Brethren movement. H. R. Holsinger had learned to know personally some of the leaders of this group of Brethren and described their history in his ***History of the Tunkers*** (1901).

The Owl Creek congregation of the Tunker Church is one among the oldest in the state of Ohio. I am unable to give the exact date of its organization, but it is an established fact that a Tunker settlement existed in Knox County as early as 1811, and that the Leedys were among the first settlers. They removed from Morrison's Cove and other parts of Bedford County, Pennsylvania. They had either inherited the progressive idea, or developed it by diligent study of the Word of God, for as early as 1856 they began to agitate a reform movement in the church in favor of the single mode of feet-washing, and a few other points in which it appeared to them reformation was required.

In the autumn of 1858 a trouble began to take form, and was brought to a focus at a church business meeting, which had been called to prepare for the annual communion meeting. At this meeting the following question was submitted to the church: "Shall we continue the older order in the observance of the ordinance of feet-washing, or follow the example of Christ?" Only five members voted in favor of the order. However, through the influence of adjoining elders, the decision of the church was ignored, and the double mode continued. Those who had voted for the gospel mode were cited to appear before a committee of elders on September 14, 1858.

At this meeting the reform movement was advocated by Abraham Holsinger Leedy, Samuel A. Leedy, and Isaac Leedy; but we are not told who or how many championed the side of the old order. The decision rendered by the committee was to the effect that all those who had voted in favor of the single mode of feet-washing, could not be held in full communion with the church, and the expulsion direct of Samuel A. Leedy, and silencing of A. H. Leedy until he should recant. Brother A. H. Leedy weakened at the thought of expulsion, and soon after recanted, and was restored to his official capacity.

The matter was then referred to annual meeting, which sent the following committee to the Owl Creek church:—

Elias Dicky, Jacob Gerber, Peter Nead, Daniel Miller, John Metzger, and Henry D. Davy.

The committee convened on September 14, 1858. This solemn occasion had increased solemnity from the fact that during that day Elder John Multzbaugh, who had been one of the principal parties in bringing the charge against the members, had died.

The question presented to the membership was put in the following language: "Are you satisfied with the order of the brethren, and with the decision of the committee?" This question was put to each member in a private room, before the committee only, without a discussion of the subject, or the defendants having had the privilege of hearing the testimony of witnesses. This was in direct violation of one of their own rules, to which Elder Isaac Leedy called their attention, all to no effect, however. All who did not give an affirmative answer to the question were requested to withdraw. In their absence their case was decided. They were called in, and the verdict read, "You are disowned for refusing to hear the church." When they inquired when and where they had refused to hear the church, the committee was speechless, until Elder H. D. Davy whispered to the foreman, "The standing committee of annual meeting is the church."

Following is a list of those who were disonwed: Daniel Leedy, Abraham Leedy and wife, Samuel A. Leedy and wife, David Leedy and wife, Abraham Long and wife, David Garber and wife, Isaac Leedy and wife, Mrs. Samuel Whistler and daughter. Among the members were one minister, three deacons, and the treasurer, with the contents of the treasury. The church funds were appropriated to the relief of the famine-stricken people of Kansas.

In response to the report of the committee the annual meeting of 1859 replied: "We consider it best that the brethren, in meekness and patience, wait for the further manifestation of the will of God upon the matter." And it was recommended that the case be remembered by the brethren in general in prayer.

Samuel Whistler, a member of the River Brethren, united with them soon after, and was chosen to the ministry at the same time when Isaac Leedy was ordained to the eldership.

Owing to the fact that this church division was of a local character, the Leedy Brethren found it difficult to make much progress, although they were diligent in their duties. However, they had several small congregations at different places,—one in Hancock County, and one in Logan County, Ohio, and one in Whitley County, Indiana, as well as one or two organizations in Missouri. The ministers not named above were, Jacob A. Leedy, Simon B. Leedy, and Peter Deetrick. The Leedy Brethren were the stronger element at North Liberty and Ankenytown, and were fully organized when the consolidation was effected and a Brethren Church established. Circumstances, however, appeared to demand an entire reorganization. Accordingly, a joint council was held to investigate the difference between the two elements, on Wednesday, October 4, 1882. At this meeting the following paper was presented:—

"On opening the meeting for the business of the day, it was found that the Leedy Brethren differ from the Brethren in three points:—

"1. The Leedy Brethren omit the use of the Lord's prayer, holding that its use in all our meetings is not essential to Christian worship, that its use is not binding, neither is it objectional.

"2. That the Lord's Supper should be composed in part of lamb's flesh, to the prohibition of all other meats.

"3. That no questions should be asked of believers while kneeling in the baptismal waters. All questions should be asked before.

"On the first difference the Leedy Brethren consented to a more extended use of the Lord's prayer in worship. They had used it occasionally, and when worshipping with us would adopt its more general repetition. The brethren, too, think its use twice in every service not essential. They recommend its repetition once at each service, however.

"Of the second difference, the brethren do not make the use of lamb's flesh at the Lord's Supper a condition. They teach that the holding of the supper is more essential than the material of which it is composed. They have no objections to the use of lamb's flesh at the Lord's Supper, and could allow the Leedy Brethren the privilege of choice. They, on the other hand, are willing, when they visit other congregations, and other food than lamb's flesh is used, to forego their preference, and allow our practice.

"The last difference was considered that the only essential element involved in the question was that the faith of the believer be examined into. It could be done either in or out of the water."

Thereupon the consolidation was completed, and the Leedy Brethren and the Progressive Brethren ceased to exist, and the Brethren Church of North Liberty and Ankenytown was organized.[25]

Several conclusions about these Brethren divisions may be suggested. First, all three of the Brethren groups which emerged from the 1880s claimed to be the original Brethren of 1708, charging that the others had changed. The moderate, "in-between" group, officially after 1908 the Church of the Brethren, was by far the largest of the three in the 1880s and a century later in the 1980s. But its size did not necessarily assure that it was "correct" in its interpretation of Brethren beliefs and practices.

Second, the industrial revolution taking place in the United States made a major impact on Brethren in bringing about changes in the life of the church. Some Brethren fought the changes and some Brethren accepted the changes. The Old German Baptist Brethren (Old Orders) generally were opposed to the changes, as they made clear in The ***Brethren's Reasons.*** *The Progressive Brethren, or after 1883 The Brethren Church, were the most willing to accept the changes, such as the abandoning of plain garb. The Church of the Brethren group was somewhat less willing to accept change. Yet, by 1915 the Church of the Brethren was in some ways more "progressive" than The Brethren Church.*

Third, it may be suggested that the Old Order separation was based on a major controversy regarding some of the basic issues or practices of the church, such as Sunday schools and foreign missions (which they have continued to reject in the twentieth century). By contrast the Progressive separation was based to a large extent on a personality conflict between Henry R. Holsinger and some of the leaders of the Annual Meeting such as D. P. Saylor and John Wise. Issues were involved, of course, but the issues seemed to be more reconcilable in the case of the Progressives. They were not, however, reconciled in the 1880s.

CONCLUSION

In the five decades between 1865 and 1915 which have been covered in this book, the Brethren made greater changes than in any other five decades in their history—well, some Brethren did, that is. The "fast" element was making the changes, and the Old Brethren, or Old Orders, were refusing to accept the changes, as they explained in detail in *The Brethren's Reasons.* But they were a relatively small number of several thousand, and the large majority of the Brethren accepted change within the church. In fact, some of them wanted to move too rapidly and refused to accept the pace which the Annual Meeting was setting; they became the Progessive Brethren and also became a separate group, The Brethren Church, in the 1880s.

Among the many changes taking place, three developments in the last of these five decades may be set forth as symbolic of the whole era. The first was the change in the name of the largest of the three groups at the bicentennial Annual Conference in 1908 from German Baptist Brethren to Church of the Brethren. The simple fact of the matter was that by 1908 most Brethren could neither speak nor read German, and there were too many non-Germans in the church for the name to be correctly descriptive. For example, Christian Hope, the first Brethren foreign missionary, was not a German; probably, George Zollers, one of the first Brethren with whom Hope discussed Brethren ideas was not either. Both of them were recent converts. Zollers had earlier in life been a Civil War veteran and a crewman on a Pacific whaling expedition. Hope and Zollers and other non-German background leaders symbolize the thousands of Americans who were becoming Brethren during these years following the Civil War, a growth which contributed to the changes taking place in church life.

A second significant development was the Annual Conference decision in 1911 to accept the policy that distinctive Brethren dress, "the garb," would no longer be a test of membership. By that time, it was an accomplished fact that too many leaders and congregations were not following the decisions of the Annual Meeting with regard to the pattern of dress, which had been more effectively enforced in the years before and after the Civil War. Judging by the number of times the problem came before the Annual Meeting, variations in the pattern of appearance had been something of a problem for quite some time before 1911. Again, the large number of people seeking membership in the church but reluctant to accept the idea of a prescribed garb contributed to bringing about changes. To some progressive leaders at least, like Henry R. Holsinger, the mode of behavior and life seemed to be more important than the exact cut of the hair or coat. As Holsinger recognized on occasion, some leader with his ideas but with more tact and diplomacy might have succeeded in bringing about some of the changes he proposed sooner than actually happened. Probably, considering the way things had developed by the first decade of the twentieth century, the change in the policy regarding dress was inevitable.

The third event which symbolized the entire period was the election in 1915 of a prominent Brethren educator and leader, Martin G. Brumbaugh, as governor of Pennsylvania. Undoubtedly, he received some Brethren votes, which in itself was a significant change from the long-standing policy of non-participation in government activity. To campaign for office, as he had done, was an even greater change. In fact, the whole development seems incredible. But the Brethren were changing their ideas regarding the wider society in which they lived. They were clearly rejecting, whether they knew it or not, the idea of two distinct worlds—one for the Brethren, since they were but pilgrims temporarily in this world, and a second realm (with its standards) for everybody else. Or another, more sociological way to describe the change is to suggest that the Brethren were casting off their sectarian garments and putting on the vestments of a church group.

Finally, a word about the future. In the five years after this era ended in 1915, a turning point arrived, particularly in terms of the third major symbolic event just described. That turning point was the

First World War. In 1917 the United States entered the War and one of the first major developments was the Selective Service Act of 1917. This law severely tested the Brethren ideas of Biblical pacifism, for if it was now right to vote and campaign for office, was it also right to participate in military service? In many ways, the Brethren of the twentieth century are the direct products of these five decades from 1865 to 1915.

NOTES

CHAPTER I. GEOGRAPHICAL EXPANSION

1. Howard Miller, *The Record of the Faithful* (Lewisburg, Pennsylvania: J. R. Cornelius, printer, 1882 [Hereafter cited as Miller, *Record*]), pages 47–50, 66.
2. Miller, *Record,* pages 54–57, 66.
3. Miller, *Record,* page 66.
4. *Minutes of the Annual Meetings of the Church of the Brethren* (Elgin, Illinois: Brethren Publishing House, 1909 [Hereafter cited as *AMM*]), Minutes for 1895, page 619.
5. *Autobiography of Samuel Murray* (n.p. [1898]), unpaginated, in Brethren Historical Library and Archives, Elgin, Illinois. Hereafter cited as BHLA.
6. David Brower, *Brethren at Work,* January 30, 1879, as quoted in Gladdys Esther Muir, *Settlement of the Brethren on the Pacific Slope* (Elgin, Illinois: Brethren Publishing House, 1939 [Hereafter cited as Muir, *Pacific Slope*]), pages 65–66. For further information on the Brethren in the Northwest, especially Idaho, see Roger E. Sappington, *The Brethren Along the Snake River* (Elgin, Illinois: The Brethren Press, 1966).
7. Roy Thompson, "The First Dunker Colony of North Dakota," in State Historical Society of North Dakota, *Collections,* volume 4 (1913), pages 81–100.
8. BHLA, Emeline Hoff File.
9. *The Gospel Messenger,* January 14, 1890, page 24.
10. *AMM,* Reports, 1881, page 417.
11. Muir, *Pacific Slope,* pages 290–297, 345–356.
12. *AMM,* 1886, Article XVI, page 453.
13. *AMM,* Article 2, 1895, pages 614–615.
14. Roland L. Howe, *The History of a Church (Dunker) with Comments Featuring The First Church of the Brethren of Philadelphia, Pa. 1813–*

1943 (Philadelphia: privately printed, 1943 [Hereafter cited as Howe, *History of a Church*]), page 81.
15. Quoted in Howe, *History of a Church,* page 84.
16. Howe, *History of a Church,* page 85.
17. Howe, *History of a Church,* pages 86–87.
18. Howe, *History of a Church,* pages 88–89.
19. Floyd E. Mallott, *Studies in Brethren History* (Elgin, Illinois: Brethren Publishing House, 1954), page 278.
20. Quoted in Howe, *History of a Church,* pages 316–319.
21. Roger E. Sappington, *The Brethren in Virginia* (Harrisonburg, Virginia: Printed by Park View Press, 1973), page 286. See also D. H. Zigler, *History of the Brethren in Virginia* (Elgin, Illinois: Brethren Publishing House, 1914), pages 163–165.
22. *The Gospel Messenger,* December 2, 1890, page 744.
23. From council minutes quoted in Cathy Simmons Huffman, *The Hagerstown Brethren* (Hagerstown, Maryland: Printed by Hagerstown Bookbinding & Printing Co., Inc., 1983), page 6. I am very pleased to be able to use this book in this way, since Cathy was an honors student of mine at Bridgewater College.
24. *The Gospel Messenger,* April 22, 1890, page 248.
25. *The Gospel Messenger,* July 8, 1890, page 408.
26. *The Gospel Messenger,* August 5, 1890, page 476.
27. *The Gospel Messenger,* October 28, 1890, page 664.
28. *AMM,* Reports, 1895, page 619.
29. *AMM,* Reports, 1895, pages 620–621.
30. W. R. Miller, Galen B. Royer, Mrs. D. L. Miller, Millard R. Myers, Ralph W. Miller, *The Chicago Sunday School Extension* (Elgin, Illinois: Brethren Publishing House, 1904), pages iii–iv, 118–123.
31. *AMM,* Reports, 1894, page 602.
32. *AMM,* Reports, 1895, pages 618–619.

CHAPTER II. RELATION TO SOCIETY

1. *Minutes of the Annual Meetings of the Church of the Brethren* (Elgin, Illinois: Brethren Publishing House, 1909 [Hereafter cited as *AMM*]), Article 1, 1866, page 249.
2. *AMM,* Article 12, 1869, pages 280–281.
3. *AMM,* Article 38, 1866, page 256.
4. *AMM,* Article 45, 1866, page 257.
5. *AMM,* Article 22, 1872, page 305.
6. *AMM,* Article 9, 1875, page 324.
7. *AMM,* Article 3, 1876, page 335.
8. *AMM,* Article 22, 1891, page 541.
9. D. Warren Shock to Galen B. Royer; York, North Dakota, February 25, 1910, in Brethren Historical Library and Archives, Elgin, Illinois. Hereafter cited as BHLA.

10. Galen B. Royer to D. Warren Shock, Elgin, February 28, 1910, in BHLA.
11. *AMM,* Article 24, 1867, pages 264–265.
12. *AMM,* Article 7, 1869, page 280.
13. *AMM,* Article 21, 1871, page 296.
14. *AMM,* Article 23, 1891, page 541.
15. *AMM,* Article 2, 1874, page 315.
16. *AMM,* Article 13, 1875, page 325.
17. *AMM,* Article 10, 1888, page 481.
18. *AMM,* Article 22, 1890, page 521.
19. *AMM,* Article 9, 1909, page 898.
20. *Minutes of the Annual Meeting of the Church of the Brethren,* printed annually, Article 6, 1911, p. 7. Hereafter cited as *MAM.*
21. *MAM,* Reports, 1914, page 16.
22. *MAM,* Reports, 1915, pages 25–26.
23. J. W. Stein, *Christianity Utterly Incompatible with War and Retaliation* (Carthage, Missouri: The Press Book and Job Printing Establishment, 1876).
24. *AMM,* Article 21, 1874, page 320.
25. *AMM,* Article 27, 1875, pages 327–328.
26. See Roger E. Sappington, *The Brethren in the New Nation* (Elgin: The Brethren Press, 1976), pages 256–276.
27. *AMM,* Article 6, 1871, page 293.
28. Landon West, *Life of Elder Samuel Weir* (Tuskegee, Alabama: Normal School Steam Press, Fourth Edition, 1897), pages 10–11.
29. Landon West, "Our Appeal . . ." (Broadside, no date) in BHLA.
30. Galen B. Royer, *Thirty-Three Years of Missions in the Church of the Brethren* (Elgin: Brethren Publishing House, 1913 [Hereafter cited as Royer, *Missions*]), pages 202–203.
31. "Minutes of the General Missionary and Tract Committee," March13–14, 1903, in BHLA.
32. Royer, *Missions,* pages 203–204.
33. "Minutes of the General Missionary and Tract Committee," May 30–June 7, 1905, in BHLA.
34. J. H. B. Williams to Minta K. Fitz, Elgin, July 7, 1911, in BHLA.
35. Galen B. Royer to H. C. Early, Denver, Colorado, December 3, 1910, in BHLA.
36. "Minutes of the General Mission Board," December 21, 1910, in BHLA.
37. A. C. Daggett to Galen B. Royer, February 28, 1911, in BHLA.
38. "Minutes of the General Mission Board," April 6, 1911, in BHLA.
39. J. H. B. Williams to Minta K. Fitz, Elgin, July 7, 1911, in BHLA.
40. "Minutes of the General Mission Board," August 20–21, 1913; August 20, 1914, in BHLA.
41. "Minutes of the General Mission Board," November 25, 1913, in BHLA.
42. Galen B. Royer to Sallie G. Kline, Elgin, June 14, 1911, in BHLA.
43. *AMM,* Article 6, 1869, page 279.

44. *AMM,* Article 12, 1870, page 287.
45. *AMM,* Article 8, 1872, pages 302–303.
46. *AMM,* Article 13, 1895, page 617.
47. *AMM,* Article 24, 1871, page 297.
48. *AMM,* Article II, 1885, page 435.
49. *AMM,* Article 8, 1892, page 558.
50. *AMM,* Article 4, 1889, pages 496–497.
51. *AMM,* Article 5, 1905, page 813.
52. *AMM,* Article 20, 1870, page 289.
53. *AMM,* Article XI, 1886, page 452.
54. *AMM,* Article 10, 1889, pages 497–498.
55. *AMM,* Article 7, 1896, page 632.
56. *AMM,* Article 13, 1867, page 262.
57. *AMM,* Article VII, 1884, page 431.
58. *AMM,* Article 5, 1889, page 497.
59. *AMM,* Article 5, 1900, page 719.
60. *AMM,* Article 12, 1907, page 857.
61. *AMM,* Reports, 1908, pages 871–872.
62. *AMM,* Reports, 1909, page 902.
63. *MAM,* Reports, 1913, pages 8–9.
64. *MAM,* Reports, 1912, page 9.
65. *MAM,* Reports, 1914, pages 14–15.
66. *MAM,* Resolution, 1915, page 30.
67. *AMM,* Article 20, 1866, page 252.
68. *AMM,* Article X, 1878, pages 358–359.
69. *AMM,* Article 34, 1866, pages 255–256.
70. *AMM,* Article 23, 1870, pages 289–290.
71. *AMM,* Article 15, 1873, page 311.
72. *AMM,* Article XIV, 1877, page 349.
73. *AMM,* Article 5, 1894, pages 599–600.
74. *AMM,* Article 5, 1904, page 796.
75. *AMM,* Article 15, 1892, page 560.
76. *AMM,* Article 7, 1867, page 261.
77. *AMM,* Article 21, 1869, page 282.
78. *AMM,* Article 10, 1872, page 303.
79. *AMM,* Article 3, 1892, page 557.
80. *AMM,* Unfinished Business, Article 2, 1894, pages 597–598.
81. *AMM,* Article 11, 1895, page 619.
82. *AMM,* Unfinished Business, Article 4, 1904, pages 792–793.
83. *AMM,* Article 27 and Resolution, 1866, pages 254, 258.
84. *AMM,* Article 22, 1871, pages 296–297.
85. *AMM,* Article XVI, 1881, pages 398–399.
86. *AMM,* Article VI, 1886, page 450.
87. *AMM,* Article 2, 1889, page 496.
88. *AMM,* Article 19½, 1891, page 540.
89. *AMM,* Article 14, 1897, page 657.
90. Herbert Strietzel, *My Father and The First Dunker Colony in North Dakota* (LaVerne, California: privately printed, 1979), page 57.

91. *AMM,* Unfinished Business, Article 1, 1906, page 823.
92. *AMM,* Article 11, 1876, page 337.
93. *AMM,* Article IX, 1877, page 347.
94. *AMM,* Article 5, 1874, page 315.
95. *AMM,* Article 2, 1888, pages 478–479.
96. *AMM,* Article 3, 1888, page 479.
97. *AMM,* Queries, Article 4, 1893, page 580.
98. *AMM,* Article 21, 1876, page 339.
99. *AMM,* Article XVI, 1877, pages 349–350.
100. *AMM,* Article XIV, 1880, page 376.
101. *AMM,* Article XXI, 1881, pages 399–400.
102. *AMM,* Unfinished Business, Article 3, 1898, pages 669–670.
103. *AMM,* Article 5, 1909, pages 895–896.
104. Galen B. Royer to H. C. Early, Elgin, April 7, 1910, in BHLA.
105. *MAM,* Unfinished Business, Article 5, 1910, pages 5–6.
106. H. C. Early to Galen B. Royer, Penn Laird, Virginia, July 6, 1910, in BHLA.
107. Galen B. Royer to Frank Crumpacker, Elgin, April 8, 1911, in BHLA.
108. *MAM,* Unfinished Business, Article 4, 1911, pages 4–5.
109. Galen B. Royer to D. L. Mohler, Elgin, June 30, 1911, in BHLA.
110. *MAM,* Queries, Article 8, 1912, page 6.
111. H. C. Early to Galen B. Royer, Washington, D. C., June 8, 1912, in BHLA.
112. Galen B. Royer to H. C. Early, Elgin, June 12, 1912, in BHLA.
113. J. H. B. Williams to Otho Winger, Elgin, May 6, May 10, 1915, in BHLA.

CHAPTER III. FOREIGN MISSIONS

1. Quoted by Galen B. Royer from an article in *The Primitive Christian* (1880) in *Thirty-Three Years of Missions in the Church of the Brethren* (Elgin, Illinois: Brethren Publishing House, 1913 [Hereafter cited as Royer, *Missions*]), pages 76–77.
2. Elgin S. Moyer, *Missions in the Church of the Brethren* (Elgin, Illinois: Brethren Publishing House, 1931 [Hereafter cited as Moyer, *Missions*]), pages 107–108.
3. M. M. Eshelman, *The History of the Danish Mission* (Mt. Morris, Illinois: Western Book Exchange, 1881 [Hereafter cited as Eshelman, *Danish Mission*]), pages 5–6.
4. Eshelman, *Danish Mission,* page 10.
5. Eshelman, *Danish Mission,* pages 11–12, 14, 16–17.
6. Eshelman, *Danish Mission,* pages 42–44.
7. Eshelman, *Danish Mission,* pages 18–21, 26–27.
8. Eshelman, *Danish Mission,* pages 44–46, 62–64.
9. Eshelman, *Danish Mission,* page 28.
10. Eshelman, *Danish Mission,* pages 30–31.

11. *Minutes of the Annual Meetings of the Church of the Brethren* (Elgin, Illinois: Brethren Publishing House, 1909, [Hereafter cited as *AMM*]), Article VII, 1877, page 347.
12. Eshelman, *Danish Mission,* page 32.
13. Moyer, *Missions,* pages 126–128.
14. *The Progressive Christian,* January 3, 1879, page 2.
15. *AMM,* Article XVII, 1878, page 360.
16. *AMM,* Article III, 1879, page 365.
17. *The Progressive Christian,* June 13, 1879, page 2.
18. *AMM,* Article XVII, 1879, pages 368–369.
19. *The Vindicator,* 1880, page 228, quoted in Royer *Missions,* page 79.
20. *AMM,* Article III, 1880, pages 372–373.
21. *AMM,* Article XXIV, 1881, page 400.
22. Moyer, *Missions,* pages 158–160.
23. John S. Flory, *Builders of the Church of the Brethren* (Elgin, Illinois: The Elgin Press, 1925), pages 127–128.
24. J. E. Miller, *Wilbur B. Stover—Pioneer Missionary* (Elgin, Illinois: Brethren Publishing House, 1931), pages 63–67.
25. "Minutes of the General Missionary Committee," October 4, 1892, in the Brethren Historical Library and Archives, Elgin, Illinois. Hereafter cited as BHLA.
26. "Minutes of the General Missionary Committee," January 3, 1893, in BHLA.
27. "Minutes of the General Missionary Committee," February 27–28, 1893, in BHLA.
28. "Minutes of the General Missionary Committee," May 21–22, 1893, July 5, 1893, in BHLA.
29. *AMM,* Article 2, 1893, page 580.
30. "Minutes of the General Missionary Committee," October 3–4, 1893, in BHLA.
31. "Minutes of the General Missionary Committee," May 24, 1894, quoted in Royer, *Missions,* page 145.
32. Quoted in Royer, *Missions,* pages 146–147.
33. *AMM,* Reports, 1894, page 608.
34. *AMM,* Reports, 1896, pages 635–636.
35. Bess Royer Bates, *Life of D. L. Miller* (Elgin, Illinois: Brethren Publishing House, 1921), pages 192–194.
36. Moyer, *Missions,* pages 174–175.
37. *AMM,* Reports, 1899, 1900, 1901, pages 701, 722, 750.
38. Moyer, *Missions,* page 177.
39. Royer, *Missions,* pages 253–256.
40. Heckman's death is given as January 12, 1913, in Royer, *Missions,* page 258.
41. *A Brief History of the Church of the Brethren in China* (Elgin, Illinois: Brethren Publishing House, no date), pages 7–17.

CHAPTER IV. EDUCATION

1. *Minutes of the Annual Meetings of the Church of the Brethren* (Elgin, Illinois: Brethren Publishing House, 1909 [Hereafter cited as *AMM*]), Articles 3, 27, 1871, pages 292, 297–298.
2. *AMM,* Article 10, 1874, pages 317–318.
3. *AMM,* Article 14, 1890, page 518.
4. *AMM,* Article 2, 1893, pages 576–578.
5. *AMM,* Unfinished Business, Article 5, pages 846–849.
6. *AMM,* Unfinished Business, Article 1, 1908, pages 869–870.
7. Howard Miller, *The Record of the Faithful* (Lewisburg, Pennsylvania: J. R. Cornelius, printer, 1882 [Hereafter cited as Miller, *Record*]), pages 76–77.
8. Miller, *Record,* pages 79–80.
9. Miller, *Record,* pages 83–84.
10. S. Z. Sharp, *Educational History* (Elgin, Illinois: Brethren Publishing House, 1923 [Hereafter cited as Sharp, *Educational History*]), pages 108–109.
11. Miller, *Record,* pages 86–87.
12. Sharp, *Educational History,* pages 146–168.
13. Sharp, *Educational History,* pages 183–192.
14. Sharp, *Educational History,* pages 192–205.
15. Sharp, *Educational History,* pages 251–252.
16. Sharp, *Educational History,* page 256.
17. Sharp, *Educational History,* pages 274–302.

CHAPTER V. ECONOMIC ACTIVITIES

1. *Minutes of the Annual Meetings of the Church of the Brethren* (Elgin, Illinois: Brethren Publishing House, 1909 [Hereafter cited as *AMM*]), Article 16, 1876, page 338.
2. *AMM,* Article 10, 1899, page 699.
3. *AMM,* Queries, Article 8, 1907, page 856.
4. *AMM,* Articles 9, 19, 1871, pages 294, 296.
5. *AMM,* Articles 11, 21, 1872, pages 303, 305.
6. *AMM,* Article 9, 1873, page 310.
7. *AMM,* Article 6, 1874, pages 315–316.
8. Walter Carlock, Alvin Faust, E. Irene Miller, *The Studebaker Family in America* (Tipp City, Ohio: Studebaker Family National Association, 1976 [Hereafter cited as Carlock, *Studebaker Family*]), pages 81–82.
9. Carlock, *Studebaker Family,* page 83.
10. Carlock, *Studebaker Family,* pages 85–86.
11. Carlock, *Studebaker Family,* page 86.
12. Quoted in Carlock, *Studebaker Family,* page 86.

13. Quoted in Carlock, *Studebaker Family,* page 86.
14. Quoted in Carlock, *Studebaker Family,* page 88.
15. *AMM,* Article XXVIII, 1882, page 414.
16. *AMM,* Article 17, 1889, page 499.
17. *AMM,* Unfinished Business, Article 1, 1904, page 791.
18. *AMM,* Article 9, 1908, page 876.
19. *Minutes of the Annual Meeting of the Church of the Brethren,* printed annually, Article 8, 1911, pages 7–8. Hereafter cited as *MAM.*
20. *MAM,* Unfinished Business, 1912, pages 3–4.
21. *MAM,* Unfinished Business, 1915, page 7.
22. *AMM,* Article 1, 1873, page 307.
23. *AMM,* Article XXIX, 1882, page 414.
24. *AMM,* Article 8, 1883, page 421.
25. *AMM,* Article XVIII, 1886, page 454.
26. *AMM,* Article 10, 1896, pages 632-633.
27. *AMM,* Unfinished Business, Article 3, 1902, pages 763–764.
28. Galen B. Royer to D. H. Forney, Elgin, March 15, 1910, in the Brethren Historical Library and Archives, Elgin, Illinois. Hereafter cited as BHLA.
29. *AMM,* Article 10, 1849, page 106; Article 8, 1860, page 197; Article 9, 1873, page 310. In this section on the railroads, I am deeply indebted to one of my students, B. Kay Albaugh, who prepared an honors paper entitled, "The Impact of the Railroads on the Brethren—1865-1915."
30. *AMM,* Queries, Article 9, 1899, page 698.
31. *The Gospel Messenger,* September 5, 1896, page 576.
32. *AMM,* Queries, Article 2, 1897, page 654.
33. *The Progressive Christian,* January 3, 1879, page 3.
34. *AMM,* Article 28, 1858, pages 173–174.
35. *AMM,* Resolutions, 1870, page 291.
36. *AMM,* Committees, 1889, pages 510–511.
37. *The Christian Family Companion,* April 27, 1869, pages 254-255.
38. *The Primitive Christian,* May 1, 1883, page 273.
39. *The Gospel Messenger,* June 17, 1890, page 353.
40. *The Christian Family Companion and Gospel Visitor,* June 9, 1874, page 363.
41. *The Gospel Messenger,* November 25, 1890, p. 729.
42. *The Gospel Messenger,* May 6, 1890, page 281.
43. *The Progressive Christian,* April 30, 1880, page 2.
44. J. S. Mohler, *Railroad Sermon, Just the Thing for Travelers from Earth to Heaven* (Lanark, Illinois: [Moore & Eshelman?], no date), in BHLA.
45. *AMM,* Resolutions, 1903, page 789.

CHAPTER VI. POLITY AND ORGANIZATION

1. *Minutes of the Annual Meetings of the Church of the Brethren* (Elgin, Illinois: Brethren Publishing House, 1909 [Hereafter cited as *AMM*]), Article 14, 1868, page 271.
2. *AMM,* Article 25, 1870, page 290.

3. *AMM,* Article 17, 1871, pages 295–296.
4. *AMM,* Article 11, 1873, page 310.
5. *AMM,* Article IX, 1879, pages 366–367.
6. *AMM,* Article VIII, 1886, page 451.
7. *AMM,* Article XXII, 1882, pages 412–413.
8. *AMM,* Queries, Article 7, 1897, page 655.
9. *AMM,* Article 6, 1897, page 655.
10. *AMM,* Unfinished Business, Article 1, 1896, pages 629–630.
11. *AMM,* Article 6, 1895, page 616.
12. *The Gospel Messenger,* May 6, 1899, quoted in Roger E. Sappington, *The Brethren in Bridgewater* (Bridgewater, Virginia: Board of Administration, 1978 [Hereafter cited as Sappington, *Bridgewater*]), page 16.
13. *AMM,* Article 30, 1867, pages 265–266.
14. *AMM,* Article 7, 1871, page 293.
15. *AMM,* Article 17, 1874, page 316.
16. *AMM,* Article 4, 1887, page 466.
17. Sappington, *Bridgewater,* page 19.
18. *AMM,* Article 2, 1875, page 323.
19. *AMM,* Article XXX, 1877, page 353.
20. *AMM,* Article 2, 1867, page 260.
21. *AMM,* Article 19, 1887, page 469.
22. *AMM,* Queries, Article 8, 1905, pages 813–814.
23. *AMM,* Article 41, 1866, page 257.
24. *AMM,* Article XIX, 1882, page 411–412.
25. *AMM,* Queries, Article 1, 1894, pages 598–599.
26. *AMM,* Unfinished Business, Article 2, 1908, pages 870–871.
27. *AMM,* Article I, 1879, pages 363–365.
28. *Spirit of the Valley,* Harrisonburg, Virginia, May 31, 1879. From the collection of Agnes Kline, Bridgewater, Virginia.
29. *Annual Meeting Conference Bulletin,* 1879. From the collection of Agnes Kline, Bridgewater, Virginia.
30. *AMM,* Article XV, 1882, pages 409–410.
31. *AMM,* Article III, 1885, pages 436–437.
32. *AMM,* Articles 10, 12, 1897, page 656.
33. *AMM,* Unfinished Business, Article 1, 1903, pages 776–777.
34. *AMM,* Article VI, 1886, page 450.
35. *AMM,* Article 2, 1869, pages 277–278.
36. *AMM,* Article 27, 1876, pages 341–342.
37. *AMM,* Article 29, 1875, page 328.
38. *AMM,* Article VII, 1885, pages 437–438.
39. *AMM,* Reports, 1888, page 494.
40. *AMM,* Article II, 1884, pages 429–430.
41. *AMM,* Reports, 1893, pages 574–576.
42. *AMM,* Article 13, 1883, pages 424–425.
43. *AMM,* Reports, 1885, page 447.
44. *AMM,* Unfinished Business, Article 1, 1901, pages 738–740.
45. *AMM,* Article 12, 1875, pages 324–325.
46. *AMM,* Article 8, 1870, page 286.
47. *AMM,* Article 17, 1873, page 311.

48. *AMM,* Queries, Article 2, 1905, page 811.
49. Frank Fisher, "The Church's Care for the Aged and Orphan," in *Two Centuries of the Church of the Brethren* (Elgin, Illinois: Brethren Publishing House, 1909), page 370.
50. *AMM,* Queries, Article 12, 1908, page 877.
51. *Minutes of the Annual Meeting of the Church of the Brethren,* printed annually, Reports, 1910, page 4.

CHAPTER VII. PUBLICATIONS

1. Howard Miller, *The Record of the Faithful* (Lewisburg, Pennsylvania: J. R. Cornelius, printer, 1882), pages 89–92.
2. *Minutes of the Annual Meetings of the Church of the Brethren* (Elgin: Brethren Publishing House, 1909 [Hereafter cited as *AMM.*]), Article 7, 1873, pages 308–309.
3. *AMM,* Article 31, 1875, page 328.
4. *AMM,* Article XVI, 1879, page 368.
5. *The Progressive Christian,* August 8, 1879, page 2.
6. *AMM,* Article XXI, 1882, page 412.
7. *The Primitive Christian,* June 19, 1883, page 392.
8. *The Gospel Messenger,* July 3, 1883, pages 1, 9–10.
9. Quoted in Nevin W. Fisher, *The History of Brethren Hymnbooks* (Bridgewater, Virginia: The Beacon Publishers, 1950 [Hereafter cited as Fisher, *Hymnbooks*]), pages 56–57.
10. Fisher, *Hymnbooks,* page 53.
11. *AMM,* Article 20, 1873, page 312.
12. *AMM,* Article 18, 1872, pages 304–305.
13. Fisher, *Hymnbooks,* page 59.
14. Quoted in Fisher, *Hymnbooks,* pages 60–61.
15. *AMM,* Article 21, 1887, pages 469–470.
16. *AMM,* Article 7, 1888, pages 479–480.
17. *AMM,* Article 3, 1890, page 515.
18. *AMM,* Article 2, 1891, pages 532–534.
19. *AMM,* Unfinished Business, Report 3, 1893, page 579.
20. *AMM,* Article 11, 1898, page 676.
21. *AMM,* Article 2, 1899, pages 694–695.
22. *AMM,* Unfinished Business, Article 2, 1900, pages 714–715.
23. Fisher, *Hymnbooks,* pages 71–73.
24. Fisher, *Hymnbooks,* pages 71, 75–76.
25. Fisher, *Hynmbooks,* pages 85–86.

CHAPTER VIII. DOCTRINES AND BELIEFS

1. J. W. Beer, *A Summary of Religious Faith and Practice or Doctrines and Duties* (Berlin, Pennsylvania: H. R. Holsinger, 1878), in Brethren Historical Library and Archives, Elgin, Illinois. Hereafter cited as BHLA.

2. D. L. Miller, *The Brethren or Dunkards, Incorporated, (German Baptist Brethren Church* (Mt. Morris, Illinois: General Missionary and Tract Committee, no date), in BHLA.
3. *A Puzzled Dutchman* (Lanark, Carroll Co., Illinois: Moore, Bashor, & Eshelman, no date), in BHLA.
4. S. H. Bashor, *A Sermon on Baptism* ([Hungtingdon, Pennsylvania: Brethren's Publishing House] 1877), in BHLA.
5. C. H. Balsbaugh, *Feet-Washing. A Letter Addressed to the Lutheran Pastor of Hummelstown, Pa.* (Columbiana, Ohio: Office of the *Gospel Visitor,* no date), in BHLA.
6. *Minutes of the Annual Meetings of the Church of the Brethren* (Elgin: Brethren Publishing House, 1909 [Hereafter cited as *AMM*]), Article 27, 1867, page 265.
7. *AMM,* Reports, 1869, pages 277–278.
8. See Roger E. Sappington, *The Brethren in the New Nation* (Elgin: The Brethren Press, 1976) for further information on the Far Western Brethren.
9. *AMM,* Reports, 1869, pages 278–279.
10. *AMM,* Article 37, 1871, pages 299–300.
11. Quoted in Henry R. Holsinger, *History of the Tunkers and The Brethren Church* (Lathrop, California: Printed for the Author, 1901), pages 424–434.
12. *AMM,* Article 17, 1872, page 304.
13. *AMM,* Article 25, 1876, page 340.
14. *AMM,* Article XXIV, 1877, page 352.
15. *AMM,* Article VI, 1879, page 366.
16. *AMM,* Article 5, 1883, page 421.
17. Roger E. Sappington, *The Brethren in Bridgewater* (Bridgewater, Virginia: Board of Administration, 1978), page 21.
18. *AMM,* Queries, Article 4, 1895, page 615.
19. *AMM,* Article 3, 1875, page 323.
20. *AMM,* Article 6, 1892, pages 557–558.
21. *AMM,* Article VII, 1879, page 366.
22. *AMM,* Article IX, 1885, page 438; and Article 16, 1891, page 539.
23. *AMM,* Unfinished Business, Article 3, 1900, pages 714–715.
24. *AMM,* Queries, Article 5, 1906, page 829.
25. *AMM,* Reports, 1909, pages 893–894.
26. *Minutes of the Annual Meeting of the Church of the Brethren,* printed annually, Unfinished Business, Article 4, 1910, pages 4–5.
27. J. H. Moore, *Campbellism Weighed in the Balance and Found Wanting, A Written Sermon in Reply to Elder C--------* (Urbana, Champaign Co., Illinois: J. H. Moore, no date), in Special Collections, Library of Bethany and Northern Baptist Theological Seminaries, Oak Brook, Illinois.

CHAPTER IX. DIVISIONS IN THE 1880s

1. *The Brethren's Reasons,* bound as an Appendix in *Minutes of the Annual Meetings Of the Old German Baptist Brethren from 1778 to 1955* (Cov-

ington, Ohio: The Little Printing Co., 1956 [Hereafter cited as *Brethren's Reasons*]), pages 11-41.

2. *Brethren's Reasons,* pages 41-53.
3. Henry Koehler, *The Principles and Practice of the Old German Baptist Brethren* (Covington, Ohio: Miami Union Print, 1884), in Special Collections, Library of Bethany and Northern Baptist Theological Seminaries, Oak Brook, Illinois. Hereafter cited as BTS.
4. *Minutes of the Annual Meetings of the Church of the Brethren* (Elgin, Illinois: Brethren Publishing House, 1909 [Hereafter cited as *AMM*]), Article 2, 1866, page 249.
5. Henry R. Holsinger, *History of the Tunkers and The Brethren Church* (Lathrop, California: Printed for the Author, 1901 [Hereafter cited as Holsinger, *History*]), pages 473-475.
6. Holsinger, *History,* pages 476-478.
7. *AMM,* Article 7, 1870, pages 285-286.
8. *The Vindicator,* March 1, 1870, pages 1-2.
9. *AMM,* Article 8, 1873, page 309.
10. Holsinger, *History,* pages 484-486, 490-491.
11. Holsinger, *History,* pages 494-495.
12. Bracketed quotations are from *AMM,* Art. IV, 1881, page 392.
13. Bracketed quotation is from *AMM,* Art. IV, 1881, page 393.
14. Bracketed quotation is from *AMM,* Art. IV, 1881, page 394.
15. Holsinger, *History,* pages 495-508.
16. S. H. Bashor, *Where Is Holsinger?* (no publisher, no date), in BTS.
17. S. S. Mohler, *Partial Review of Where Is Holsinger?* (no publisher, no date), in Brethren Historical Library and Archives, Elgin, Illinois.
18. Holsinger, *History,* pages 514-529.
19. Quoted in Holsinger, *History,* pages 530-535.
20. Quoted in Holsinger, *History,* page 536.
21. Quoted in Holsinger, *History,* pages 536, 541.
22. J. H. S.[wihart], *A Brief Summary of the Faith and Practice of the Congregational Brethren in answer to the following questions* (Bourbon, Indiana: no publisher, no date), one page broadside, in Cassel Collection, Juniata College Library, Huntingdon, Pennsylvania.
23. F. A. Hendricks, "Editors, Gospel Trumpet," *The Gospel Trumpet,* December, 1873, pages 114-117.
24. A. H. Cassel, "Some Account of the Origin & History of the Far Western and Congregational Brethren . . . ," (manuscript, 1886) in Cassel Collection, Juniata College Library, Huntingdon, Pennsylvania.
25. Holsinger, *History,* pages 767-771.

INDEX

imes. Our young from

HARE CC.,
Elgin, Illinois.
when writing.

Preventer
ess!

Use Ten Years!

orn Preventer
vent the growth of horns
ranteed. It never fails if
than one cent per head.
on receipt of 75 cents.
big profit. Send for cir-

N, Mfg. Chemist,
Mount Morris, Ill.
when writing.

ero
IERY

ooler and refrigera-
d. An article that
house. WATER an-
l as ICE. Different
, durable, and guar-
n. Write for cata-
s,
CREAMERY Co.,
Peru, Ind.

OO LINE!"
ARMING
ands
E "SOO" RAILWAY
on EASY TERMS.
in Michigan and Wisconsin.
in Minnesota and North Dakota.
the CROP PAYMENT
ESTEADS
, Pierce, Benson, McLean
ounties in North Dakota.
"On the Soo Line,"
ns at from $2.00
per ton.
t opportunities for
uls,—"On the Soo
respectfully asked
horoughly investi-
the Soo Line," be-
new homes. Come
LAND PRIMERS
ailed free to any address
iable information.
or Homeseekers and
Settlers, and HALF
old Goods, Tools
tock,—"On the Soo

nd Industrial Agent,
INNEAPOLIS, Minnesota.
mmigration Agent,
DETROIT, Michigan
av. Immigration Agent,
MANCHESTER, Indiana

For further particulars apply to,
WM. H. MILLS,
Land Agent C. P. R. R.,
Fourth & Townsend Sts.
SAN FRANCISCO, CAL.

Your Home Furnished Complete For Cash Or Credit!

READ BELOW

...PEOPLE'S...
EASY PAYMENT STORE!

227 & 229 Chicago St.,
ELGIN, ILL.

oo

IRON BEDS, - - - - $1.75 and up
COUCHES, - - - - $4.98 and up
ALL-WOOL CARPETS, 49-75 cts per yard

oo

Come and See Us Before You

oo

GEO. E. DANI

Mention the INGLENOOK when writing.

1897
Brethren's Family Almanac

Our Almanac for 1897 has been greatly enlarged and well deserves a place in every family. Send *ten cents* for a copy, or, *better yet, send $1.50* for the GOSPEL MESSENGER from now to the end of 1897, and receive the Almanac

FREE.

☞ We also offer liberal inducements to agents who are prepared to push the sale of the Almanac. Write us!

BRETHREN'S PUBLISHING Co.,
Mount Morris, Ill.

Illinois Central R. R.
...TO...
FLORIDA
THROUGH SLEEPING CAR
...CHICAGO TO...
Nashville, Chattanooga,
Atlanta, Jacksonville.

New through Pullman buffet sleeping car service over the Illinois Central and connecting lines between Chicago and Jacksonville, Fla. This Chicago Jacksonville car is run over the well-known

DIXIE FLYER SCENIC ROUTE

via Lookout Mountain, and leaves Chicago daily at 6:10 P. M. on the Central's fast "Limited" vestibule train for the south, on which a dining car is carried serving supper out of Chicago. It will have connection at Mattoon with the Illinois Central's line from Peoria (by train to leave Peoria at 6:45 P. M.) and will arrive at Nashville the next morning, at Chattanooga the next afternoon, at Atlanta early the next evening and at Jacksonville the second morning after the departure from Chicago. Full particulars concerning the above can be had of agents of the Illinois Central and connecting lines.

A. H. HANSON,
General Passenger Agent, Chicago.
Or F. E. LAMBOLET, Agent, Coleman, Ill.

Mention the INGLENOOK when writing.

JOIN THE COLONY
...AT...
ERLING, COLORADO!

thousand members have written for infor-
about Sterling and South Platte Valley,
ado.
y have visited us. Several have invested:
D. L. Miller, I. B. Trout, L. E. Keltner,
B. Royer, Illinois; Eld. D. H. Neikirk, Dan-
abill, Pennsylvania; A. W. Ross, Indiana;
Eikenberry, Ohio; J. L. Kuns, Kansas; M.
r, Nebraska; G. L. McDonaugh, Union Pa-
R., and many others have purchased lands
own property. Many more have made se-
s.
vill pay you to write for our free advertising
. Then come and investigate personally.
Homeseekers' excursions from your town
a month. Buy your tickets to Sterling, Colo-
and return, via Union Pacific Railway.
will refund railroad fare to purchasers of
cres. Let us know soon as possible when
n come, how many in party, etc., so we can
ge to meet you. We will write you cheapest
best way to make the trip. Come before
advance.
show you the country free of charge.

olorado Colony Co., Sterling, Colo.
CE B. DAVIS, Pres't. W. E. KING, Sec'y.

100,000 ACRES GOVERNMENT LAND!
$1.25 per Acre.

In the Delta of the Colorado in San Diego County California. Semi-tropical climate. The land is adapted to the growth of Alfalfa, Stock, Citrus and Deciduous Fruits. For further information address, GILLETT & VAN HORN, Special Agents Imperial Land Co. Imperial, via Flowing Well, Cal. 5otf

Mention the INGLENOOK when writing.

CAP GOODS
LARGEST ASSORTMENT
BEST VALUES

Send Postal for Samples of Goods and Cut of Styles. We Make Caps to Order. Write To-Day.

Albaugh Bros., Dover & Co.,
Chicago, Ill.

DATE Clothing

If you want
RELIABLE GOODS, made up in a first-class manner and at reasonable prices we can satisfy you.

When you buy from us
you GET what you want. When you buy from your local dealer, as a rule, you TAKE what you can get.

We always guarantee Satisfaction
and refer to our many patrons, some of whom will be found in nearly any community where the Brethren reside. Samples of cloth from which we make our clothing, measuring blank, tape line and rules for ordering will be sent on application. Our rules for self-measurement are so simple, any-one can understand them.

We want to hear from you.

PHILLIPSON CLOTHING COMPANY
WARSAW, INDIANA.

LAUGHLIN
FOUNTAIN PEN
The Best at Any Price

Sent on approval to responsible people.

A Pocket Companion of never ending usefulness, a source of constant pleasure and comfort.

To test the merits of
THE INGLENOOK
as an advertising medium we offer your choice of these popular styles superior to the
$3.00
grades of other makes for only
$1.00

Unconditionally Guaranteed
Pre-eminently Satisfactory.

Try it a week, if not suited, we buy it back, and give you $1.10 for it (the additional ten cents to pay for your trouble in returning the pen). We are willing to take chances on you wanting to sell; we know pen values—you will when you have one of these.

Finest quality hard Para rubber reservoir holder, 14k. Diamond Point Gold Pen, any desired flexibility in fine, medium or stub, and the only perfect ink feed known to the science of fountain pen making.

Sent postpaid on receipt of $1.00
(Registration, 8c extra.)

This great Special Offer is good for just 30 days. One of our Safety Pocket Pen Holders **free of charge** with each pen.

Remember—There is No "just as good" as the **Laughlin**: insist on **it**; take no chances.

State whether Ladies' or Gentlemen's style is desired. Illustrations are full size of complete article. Address

LAUGHLIN MFG. CO.
335 GRISWOLD ST.,
DETROIT, MICH.

Mammoth New Catalogue Almanac
AND GUIDE TO POULTRY RAISERS
64 large pages, printed in colors. Description of all leading varieties of fowls, ... 30 fine Illustrations. Plans for Poultry houses. Remedies for all diseases. ... for Poultry Powders. The finest thing out—everybody wants one. Only 15c.
C. C. SHOEMAKER, Freeport, Ill., U. S. A.

ing order, every member of which is entirely satisfied with the location. They can not speak too highly of it, its climate and its possibilities. Enormous crops have been the rule for years back, and with the cattle business it is a sure thing. There is a large amount of excellent land for sale cheap, and on long time. If you are at all thinking of moving anywhere send for particulars. Information and personal attention cheerfully given. Write to

B. A. McALLASTER,
Land Commissioner U. P. Ry. OMAHA, NEBR.

Dr. Peter's Blood Vitalizer

is not a so-called patent medicine—not a cure-all—but a reliable household remedy, carefully compounded from medicinal herbs, leaves, roots, barks, etc., according to the prescription of a learned Swiss-German physician, which has been handed down from father to son for three successive generations.

Many a discovery in medicine has been hailed with delight, only to be thrown aside because it could not stand the test of time. Not so, however, with **Dr. Peter's Blood Vitalizer**, the old blood-cleansing remedy. It has been in constant use for over one hundred years and thousands have gladly testified to its curative properties.

Dr. Peter's Blood Vitalizer is an article of acknowledged merit. It is distinctly different from all other medicines. It may have its imitations, but it has no substitute. It not only expels the disease from the body, but it creates new, rich, red blood, and sound, solid, healthy flesh. It has won its way into popular favor without gaudy newspaper advertising, solely on its own merits.

It Purifies the Blood. It Promotes Digestion.
It Acts upon the Liver. It Regulates the Bowels.
It Acts upon the Kidneys. It Quiets the Nervous System.
It Nourishes, Strengthens and Invigorates.
It Opens the Pores of the Skin and Induces Healthy Perspiration.

In short, it is a family medicine in every sense of the word, and ought to be found in every household. It is pleasant to take and absolutely harmless. It is not sold by druggists, but only by local **Vitalizer** agents or the proprietor direct.

☞ Persons living in localities where there are no agents for the **Vitalizer**, and who have not previously ordered any, can obtain a trial box, containing twelve 35 cent bottles, at the special price of $2.00. Address at all times

DR. PETER FAHRNEY,
112-114 South Hoyne Ave. CHICAGO, ILL.

Eggs! Eggs!
Good Chance!

From solid Buff Cochins, $1.50 per 13; from best bred Barred Plymouth Rocks, good size, $2 per 13. Securely packed. Guaranteed.

11t13 H. S. ARNOLD, Lanark, Ill.

Mention the INGLENOOK when writing.

For Practical Training in
...Watchmaking, Engraving and Optics
...ATTEND THE...
Elgin Horological School
...Write for Catalogue to...
Elgin College of Horology, Elgin, Ill.

7t13 Mention the INGLENOOK when writing.

G. H. FINLEY,
...DEALER IN...
STAPLE AND FANCY GROCERIES

Cured Meats and Bakery Goods. Prompt Delivery to any part of the city. Will call and take your order. TELEPHONE No. 1571.

G. H. FINLEY,
130 Vine Street. ELGIN, ILL.

Mention the INGLENOOK when writing.

FREE SAMPLE
Send letter or postal for free SAMPLE HINDOO TOBACCO HABIT CURE
We cure you of chewing and smoking for 50c., or money back. Guaranteed perfectly harmless. Address Milford Drug Co., Milford, Indiana. We answer all letters.

Three Fine Book Presses

With an Aggregate Capacity of 40,000 Copies per Day, are now Installed in the Press Room of our Publishing House. Besides we have two steam jobbers. We Furnish anything,—from a Card to a large, well-bound Volume.

* * *

A N
A
t
BRETH

Agent
Ideal Wi
Good a
absolute
everybo
Write a
tory pro
JNO.

R
B
P
Ab
A cream of t
leavening streng
Food Report.
ROYAL BA

ONE
TRIAL T
That is what
Australian El
give all readers
who write soon.
the magical ef
Nervous
that all forms
tion, Kidn
ach trouble,
ness, Cata
all sympathetic
its wonderful
trial treatment
the MESSENGE
only $1.00. S
live agent in e
DR.

PURE-B
Ba
mo
St
in

I Sa
Are you not m
the horns
Brayton's C
will stop the growth
ural-born muley.
apply and sure to do
No more days of
Six years in actual
costs less than one c
of the United State
wanted everywhere.
A. W. Brayton, Ma
1otf

THE S